# Workers' Paradox

# Workers'

RUTH O'BRIEN

The University of North Carolina Press

# Paradox

*The Republican Origins of*
*New Deal Labor Policy,*
*1886–1935*

*Chapel Hill and London*

© 1998 The University of North Carolina Press
All rights reserved
Manufactured in the United States of America

The paper in this book meets the guidelines for permanence and durability of the
Committee on Production Guidelines for Book Longevity of the Council on Library
Resources.

Library of Congress Cataloging-in-Publication Data
O'Brien, Ruth Ann, 1960–
   Workers' paradox: the Republican origins of New Deal labor policy, 1886–1935 /
Ruth O'Brien.
      p.   cm.
   Includes bibliographical references and index.
   ISBN 0-8078-2430-5 (cloth: alk. paper).—ISBN 0-8078-4737-2 (pbk.: alk. paper)
      1. Labor policy—United States—History. 2. Industrial relations—United States—
History. 3. Trade-unions—United States—History. 4. Republican Party (U.S.: 1854– ).
5. United States. National Labor Relations Board—History. I. Title.
HD8072.027   1998
331'.0973—dc21                                                          97-48986
                                                                          CIP


02 01 00 99 98     5 4 3 2 1

Portions of Chapter 3 were previously published as "'Business Unionism' versus
'Responsible Unionism': Common Law Confusion, the American State, and the
Formation of Pre–New Deal Labor Policy," *Law and Social Inquiry* 18 (1993): 255–96.
Copyright © 1993 by the American Bar Foundation. All rights reserved. Used by
permission of the University of Chicago Press.

*For my mother, Virginia F. O'Brien*

# CONTENTS

# PREFACE

Few industrial relations experts would disagree with the statement that the present labor relations machinery—the NLRB—has been less than beneficial for the contemporary American labor movement. Noted industrial relations experts, such as Walter Galenson, have pushed for repealing the NLRA. Others have said that certification elections are a "blind alley" for organized labor.

Indeed, it is the present state of decline (and the recent possibility for resurgence) that has prompted many scholars to study the origins of American labor policy. The significance of this history is further underscored by the fact that the primary institutional apparatus, the NLRB, still stands. The National Labor Relations Act of 1935, erecting the NLRB, was amended only once in 1947 with the passage of the Taft-Hartley Labor-Management Relations Act.

The near consensus among industrial relations experts and labor historians that organized labor's present plight stems from the past is matched by their broad agreement about locating this past. Most have pinpointed the New Deal reform era of the 1930s. Some scholars recognize a pre–New Deal labor policy, though they argue that this policy was implemented by the state and federal courts and supposedly forestalled the growth of the American labor movement. For the most part, the pre–New Deal labor policy is used as a point of contrast to demonstrate that the New Deal labor policy was indeed a watershed. Hence, the origins of American industrial relations policy are generally said to lie in the 1930s.

There is no consensus, however, about what prompted the passage of the heart of this policy, the NLRA, or what is commonly called the Wagner Act. What motivated Franklin D. Roosevelt and the Democratic Congress to enact this particular policy? Were members of the Roosevelt administration, Senator Robert F. Wagner and the new urban progressive Democrats, union leaders in the AFL and CIO, the rank and file, reform-minded capitalists, or frustrated bureaucrats in the National Recovery Administration the principal actors responsible for the Wagner Act's design and passage?

Distinguishing between its intent and consequences, as some have done, makes the legislative history of the Wagner Act even more complex. Some labor historians suggest that the Democratic policymakers created a radical piece of labor legislation that was then deradicalized by conservative state and federal courts as well as the NLRB. Others argue that the Democratic policymakers purposefully created the NLRB to institutionalize industrial relations conflicts and limit organized labor's role in the economy. And still others suggest that, given the constraints of the political climate, organized labor and Senator Wagner, as well as his coterie of new progressive urban Democrats, built the most beneficial labor relations machinery possible for the American labor movement.

Implicit within these explanations about causal factors, principal actors, policy intentions, and policy consequences is one counterfactual assumption: without the 1929 crash of Wall Street and the ensuing Great Depression, the Wagner Act would not have materialized. As the narrative goes, the Wagner Act was part of the Democratic administration's response to a severe economic crisis. A crisis-reform sequence supposedly gave rise to the origins of American labor policy.

Further buried within this causal sequence is a cyclical conception of American liberalism. The most significant policies in American history have been the product of what are described as the "big bangs," the periods of massive political reform in the United States. The American liberal state, according to this view, is defined by a series of cyclical waves of reform. With each "bang," a new state emerges. As Eldon Eisenach describes, "American political thought endlessly reproduces inherent tensions between liberty and democracy."[1] American liberalism is therefore defined less by the course of history than by critical periods in this history. Moreover, this cyclical view also assumes that the liberal American state is regenerative and self-adjusting. New policies will be implemented and appropriate state apparatuses constructed to ensure that the United States recovers from severe economic crises.

This book suggests that American labor policy had, at once, a more mundane and a more profound beginning than described above. This policy was not the product of any one large crisis. Rather, it sprang from a series of relatively minor post–World War I political and economic crises. It argues that the New Deal Democrats cannot be credited with making the dramatic departure in labor rights and state capacity ascribed to them by many. Rather, key members of the Republican Party were responsible for developing the fundamental principles underlying modern labor policy. This book suggests that the emphasis on procedural, as opposed to substantive, rights for workers that these authors associate with the federal judiciary's interpretation of the NLRA emerged more than a decade earlier, when the Republicans formulated labor legislation in the 1920s.

Around 1900, progressive state and federal court judges first began establishing procedural labor rights of workers rather than the substantive rights of unions in a series of common-law decisions. They used procedural rights as a means of making organized labor responsible to the state. In the 1920s, the conservative majority and the progressive minority on the Supreme Court, led by William Howard Taft, elevated these decisions into a doctrine of "responsible unionism." At the same time, the Republicans in Congress and the White House transformed this judicial theory into legislative practice with the Transportation Act of 1920, the Railway Labor Act of 1926, and the Norris-LaGuardia Anti-Injunction Act of 1932. Three years later, when Senator Robert F. Wagner formulated the NLRA, he modeled this act on the Republicans' idea about "responsible unionism." That is, unions were confirmed as semipublic associations, open not only to the assistance but also to the scrutiny of the American state.

Overall, the Republican Party's contribution to labor policy underscores a paradox about the formation of labor policy and the development of liberalism in the United States ignored by the literature on "American exceptionalism." It suggests that the liberal state created a strict regulatory framework for labor-management relations after feeling threatened that the mainstream labor movement's capacity for collective power would undermine individualism and classlessness in American society. The very same individualism that accounts for the overall weakness of the American liberal state produced a statist labor policy. Slowly evolving over the 1920s and 1930s, this policy was founded upon a notion of "responsible unionism" that foreshadowed the type of unionism explicitly codified in 1947 with the restrictive Taft-Hartley amendments to the NLRA.

In their acceptance of the National Labor Relations Board during the New Deal, union leaders struck a Faustian bargain with the American state. The labor movement essentially abandoned its conception of voluntarism for "responsible unionism," and, given organized labor's plight today, we can see how this came at great cost.

There are many people to thank for their help and encouragement with this book. I am particularly indebted to Karen Orren, who could not have been a more demanding and challenging mentor. Not only is she an astute and clever critic, but she never failed to push me to push myself. Karen's own work on the role of the American liberal state and labor was also a great inspiration. At the same time, I appreciate the generosity of Sanford Jacoby, Eileen Lorenzi McDonagh, and David Brian Robertson, who read an early draft of the manuscript and provided me with constructive criticism.

I'm also indebted to colleagues and friends who gave comments on specific chapters and conference papers back when this project started as a dissertation. In particular, I thank the late Richard Ashcraft, Gerald Berk, Howard Gillman, Michael Goldfield, Victoria Hattam, John Laslett, Sidney Milkis, Jill Norgren, Susan Sterett, Christopher Tomlins, Michael Wallerstein, and Howard Wial for both their criticism and their inspiration. I appreciate permission from *Law and Social Inquiry* to draw from material in chapter 3 that this journal first published. Archivists at the Herbert Hoover Presidential Library, the Manuscript Division of the Library of Congress, the National Archives, and the State Historical Society of Wisconsin were consistently helpful. I want to acknowledge Mary Keyserling for giving me permission to leaf through Leon Keyserling's papers in his home office and for bringing the New Deal to life over lunch.

I extend my warmest appreciation to Claire Bowin, Martha Campbell, Nadine Cohen, Dubravka Knežić, Gary Remer, Charlie Roothaan, Naomi Reshotko, and Shona Kelly Wray, friends who were a constant source of understanding and good cheer. Cate DaPron deserves special mention for both her help in making this book readable and her camaraderie. Janice Bockmeyer, Jack Jacobs, and Dan Pinello were supportive colleagues, as were Greg Kvistaad and Spencer Wellhofer, who gave me the time and encouragement to turn my dissertation into a book. Mark Weisenfeld, who was generously assigned to me by John Jay College of Criminal Justice at the City University of New York, tracked down hard-to-locate sources, and Jocelyn Boryczka, from the Graduate Center at the City University of New York, helped compile final source notes. I also enjoyed working with Lewis Bateman, executive editor at the University of North Carolina Press.

Finally, I appreciate my family members, who never tired of hearing about this project. I'm grateful to my mother, who, by example, gave me the courage to pursue different thoughts and ideas. Kathleen I prize for her gift to help me restore my humor and gain a better perspective on how to get things done. Rudi Matthee I cherish for his unfailing generosity. Not only did he offer insightful comments about my work, but he did so in an atmosphere filled with love and support. I was also happy about Max Matthee-O'Brien's arrival. He unknowingly taught me how to enjoy early mornings again.

# ABBREVIATIONS

| | |
|---|---|
| AFL | American Federation of Labor |
| ARE | Association of Railway Executives |
| CIO | Congress of Industrial Organizations |
| CPPA | Conference for Progressive Political Action |
| GOP | Grand Old Party (Republican Party) |
| ICC | Interstate Commerce Commission |
| IWW | Industrial Workers of the World |
| NIRA | National Industrial Recovery Act |
| NLB | National Labor Board |
| NLRA | National Labor Relations Act |
| NLRB | National Labor Relations Board |
| NWLB | National War Labor Board |
| NRA | National Recovery Administration |
| RED | Railway Employees Department |
| UMW | United Mine Workers |

# Workers' Paradox

CHAPTER 1

# The Liberal Paradox
# and the Republicans' Interest
# in American Labor Policy

The liberal state, supposedly condemned to play the role of the night-watchman, was exactly as strong as it needed to be in order to fulfill its domestic and foreign political tasks.

—Franz L. Neumann, *Democratic and Authoritarian States*, 1957

The early American state is often described as "exceptional."[1] The federalist system of governance divided power between the nation and the individual states, promoting sectionalism and regionalism that prevailed far into the twentieth century and hindered the national state from monopolizing power and authority. Further, the United States was unlike European nation-states in that individualism, not class, was the dominant value in American political culture. Political scientists and historians also suggest that culture contributed to the state's exceptional nature by thwarting the emergence of working-class politics and a labor party.[2] As the story goes, the late codification of federal labor policy, among other social policies, helps to account for American exceptionalism.

It was not until the late nineteenth and early twentieth centuries that the federal government gained enough power and authority to be considered a full-fledged nation-state. According to students of state building, the government underwent this transformation during distinct periods of reform, most notably, the progressive and the New Deal eras. Although political scientists and historians have turned their attention to the construction of the nation-state, many of them are still mired in the debate over American exceptionalism. That is, they tend to focus on what preempted the emergence of a strong welfare state. The reform efforts of radicals, progressives, and New Dealers, these scholars show, fell short of their makers' dreams. While these studies of state building survey multiple facets of reform, their descriptions generally follow a single story line. Intentional or not, the progressive and New Deal reforms are said to have advanced an exceptionally weak American state.

This book tells a different story. Instead of emphasizing stumbling blocks, it focuses on the blocks that went into the construction of a crucial state-building policy—the modern American labor policy. It examines the contribution of the liberal state by contemplating more than the reformers' respective platforms. The book concentrates on the Republicans' involvement in the policy-making process. It argues that the policy started unfolding with the Republican Congress during reconstruction after the Great War and stretched over almost two decades—from the passage of the Transportation Act in 1920 to enactment of the National Labor Relations Act (NLRA) in 1935 by the Democratic Congress.

By underscoring the combined (though rarely the joint) efforts of the Democrats *and* the Republicans, this book highlights a fundamental paradox in American liberalism. That is, the very same individualism that accounts for the overall weakness of the liberal state produced a labor policy that demanded strong state involvement in labor-management relations. Instead of co-opting the American Federation of Labor (AFL) and the railroad brotherhoods, this policy brought the proverbial night watchman out of his booth to guarantee freedom of association for workers, not unions.

What is more, this paradox turns the concept of American exceptionalism on its head. Beginning with the creation of the Railroad Labor Board in 1920, American labor policy contained the notion of "responsible unionism," foreshadowing the explicit establishment of this form of unionism in 1947 with the restrictive Taft-Hartley Labor-Management Relations Act.[3] What would become the permanent federal labor policy was not responsive to the needs of unions but rather made unions responsible to the state. In other words, the American state was exceptional not because of its weakness but because its strength was derived from classical liberalism. Whereas some European nation-states built labor-management relations policies after World War I that could be described as corporatist, the American postwar policy was based on a traditional conception of liberalism. Precisely because of its disciplinary elements, American labor policy mirrored the paradox hidden within the classical conception of liberalism.[4]

Initially created to challenge the "divine right of kings," liberalism developed the notion of popular sovereignty to demonstrate why society should be endowed with the power and authority to direct the state. To John Locke, civil society and the liberal state could not exist without the consent of the people. The state of nature preceded Locke's conception of civil society; thus the liberal state governing such a society could only be perceived as its fabrication. Still, liberal philosophers like Locke gave the liberal state its own identity. This identity surfaced, however, during what could only be called an ontological moment in history. If civil society willingly surrendered its inalienable rights,

the normally societally driven liberal state had to respond by acting autonomously to protect these rights. As Locke explains, "Freedom from absolute,
arbitrary power, is so necessary to, and closely joined with, a man's preservation, that he cannot part with it, but by what forfeits his preservation and life
together."[5] Ideological self-preservation gave life to the liberal state.

In the 1920s and 1930s, Democrats and Republicans wielded the power and
authority of the liberal state when they developed American labor policy. In
so doing, these policymakers freed the liberal state from the constraints of
Lockean liberalism. In other words, members from both parties thought it either necessary or prudent to protect individualism, the foundation of American liberalism. To begin with, the Republicans in the postwar Congress experienced one of those Lockean ontological moments when it concocted a
restrictive labor policy for the railroads. This Congress could have rewarded
the AFL and the railroad brotherhoods for their cooperation during World War
I by enacting a corporatist labor policy. Recognizing unions as the collective
voice of labor or the functional representative of the public good would have
transformed the liberal state into a corporatist or a tripartite corporate liberal
state, sharing public power with capital and labor.[6] This type of cooperative relationship between labor, the state, and business would have made the individual rights of workers mutually inclusive with the collective rights of unions. As
it happened, however, union mobilization brought forth the paradox within
liberalism that strengthened the liberal state. Rather than remaking this state
into a corporate liberal state, the Republican policymakers thought the collective voice of organized labor posed a threat to individual rights, and they enacted a policy that safeguarded those rights.

This policymaking process was not confined to periods of Republican control. During the Democratic era in the 1930s, Robert F. Wagner and his legislative assistants developed the NLRA with the knowledge that the Supreme Court
had effectively overturned the American variant of a corporate liberal state that
had been instituted during the first New Deal.[7] In constructing the National
Labor Relations Board (NLRB), they ensured that unions received no direct
benefits or protection for fear that the Court would rule the revised labor policy unconstitutional. Following the Republican example of the 1920s, they
turned the focus of labor-management relations from the players involved—
individual workers, company unions, or regular unions—to the entire collective bargaining process.[8] Wagner and his legislative assistants strengthened the
power of the state by tightening the NLRB's enforcement mechanism to protect
the sanctity of this process.

Worker representation, combined with state involvement to ensure its implementation, became the backbone of American labor policy.[9] On one level,
this policy gave unions the ability to negotiate collective bargaining agreements

in which they represented the material interests of their members. By 1938, after the passage of the NLRA, union membership had more than doubled. On another level, American labor policy disengaged workers from unions, since certification and decertification elections forced unions to fight a never ending battle for their official position as collective bargaining agents.

Responsible unionism became the embodiment of liberalism when it was applied to organized labor. Tracing the deep strain of individualism buried within labor policy helps explain the labor movement's uneven march throughout modern American history. Labor policy affected the AFL and the railroad brotherhoods by protecting unionization at the same time that it preempted worker solidarity. Put simply, Republican and Democratic policymakers in Congress created contradictory regulatory structures that sparked unprecedented waves of unionization yet constrained organized labor. These policymakers cultivated a plan of action that generated a rift between workers and unions by placing unions under state control.

This type of control pleased neither the Democratic nor the Republican members of the state. What is more, no one constituency—trade unions, industrial unions, or the business community—had fashioned it for its own purposes. Hence, the liberal state's involvement in labor-management relations cannot be explained in terms of a simple dichotomy about state/societal relations, as some have argued. It influenced the identities and the strategies of political actors wherever they were situated in a public-private continuum, transcending this dichotomy. But how could the liberal ideology impose such a heavy obligation upon members of both the state and society?

### Formal Legal Constructs and a Policy Continuum

No one policymaker or administration inspired the vision of responsible unionism that underlies American labor policy. This policy evolved as the Republicans modeled their 1920 railroad labor policy on a relatively obscure state and federal court doctrine about organized labor's accountability during trade disputes. Between the late 1890s and the 1930s, some courts developed a fiduciary term, the "principles of agency," into a means of sustaining a *temporary* legal relationship between the union, or any voluntary association, and its members in order to promote collective bargaining.

The significance of these decisions was not that they created an important common-law precedent but rather that the legal reasoning underlying them showed that a meaningful debate was under way concerning organized labor's status under law. This debate, in other words, was qualitatively different from the negative exchanges between labor and the courts that William Forbath, among others, has described. Instead of examining "the significance of the courts' power to hobble labor legislation," the debate illustrates how state and federal courts' rendering progressive decisions formulated the legal reasoning that went into labor legislation.[10] Republicans in Congress, then, extended the same notion of agency to organized labor that they had supplied to unions, among other organizations, with the temporary authority to represent workers at the collective bargaining table when they developed a scheme for worker representation in 1920 and again in 1926. By 1932, Republican and Democratic progressive policymakers turned agency law on its head, using it to circumscribe the federal courts' use of the injunction. In 1935, Wagner drew on this legal relationship, stipulated both by the state and federal courts and in the Republican railroad labor policy (where it was manifested as the worker representation scheme), for inspiration.

At each legislative juncture, the respective policymakers faced a choice of competing ideological positions. And on each occasion, they extended the initial Republican labor-management relations ideology. Policy constraints did emerge and gain momentum, however. The initial Republican policymakers had a number of feasible policy paths available to them, ranging from instituting no policy to emulating President Woodrow Wilson's peacetime or wartime labor programs; by 1935, however, the choices before Wagner had narrowed. Wagner could model his policy on President Franklin D. Roosevelt's existing voluntaristic labor policies, under the jurisdiction of the National Recovery Administration (NRA), or on some compilation of the Republican labor policies developed in the 1920s. After several false starts, Wagner chose the latter, believing that it offered organized labor greater protection from unfair labor practices and deciding that it stood a greater chance of being upheld by the Republican-controlled Supreme Court.

By 1935, the question of Wagner's intent became secondary to his policy constraints. Wagner built the NLRA upon an ideology that had become self-sustaining.[11] It exhibited the signs of a formal system of law, although not under common law but under statute.[12] According to Max Weber, legal formalism was distinguished by reliance on general rules and abstract values rather than particular decisions and a concrete set of ethical values in support of capitalism or liberalism.[13] This statute-based system made a point of separating law and morality. It employed a procedural, rather than a substantive, form of justice that legal and legislative policymakers called "value-free." According to Weber, "formalism enables the legal system to operate like a technically rational machine. Thus it guarantees to individuals and groups within the system a relative maximum of freedom, and greatly increases for them the possibility of predicting the legal consequences of their actions."[14] Not being associated with values meant that a formal legal system became dominant and perpetuated its own ideology. As Weber explained, two types of domination exist: domination by "virtue of authority" and domination by the "constellation of interests."[15] Law was reflective of the former conception of domination. In other words, law becomes dominant not because it has the support of those who wrote it or those over whom it rules but because it is self-sustaining.[16]

Weber's conception of legal formalism helps explain the complexity of state action in the United States. Unlike traditional theories of the state that rely on questions of state capacity or that use the bureaucratic ideology of state managers to account for the origins of an institution, legal formalism shows how institutions develop lives of their own. According to Weber, ideology need not be bound up with the intent of one actor or constrained to one period. And unlike historians who concentrate on the dichotomy between the state and culture,[17] Weber claimed that the state's ideology derived institutional rules and regulations from the same components in political culture that it helped perpetuate.[18] He captured the reciprocity of relations between the state and society by focusing on the repressive *and* the liberating nature of the state.[19] Taking individual free will into account, Weber's notion of legal formalism demonstrated that the state alternately suppresses and emancipates a society and its culture.

In the case of American labor policy, a formal system of law, manifested in the application of agency law to labor unions as well as in a scheme for worker representation, opened new channels for union accountability that simultaneously (1) acknowledged organized labor's legality, (2) protected individual rights for all workers, and (3) reaffirmed the idea that individualism, not any form of collectivism, constituted the public good. Wagner and his legislative assistants, despite being great champions of labor, formulated particular provisions within federal labor policy that barely disturbed common-law constructs yet made great strides in changing public policy. The absence of their exclusive support for organized labor and their emphasis on individualism show that American labor policy mirrored an ongoing tension between classical legal orthodoxy and legal realism. In order to pass judicial scrutiny, these policymakers crafted the crucial provisions in the Wagner Act without raising the essential questions of state intent and motivation.[20]

What began as a minor trend in common law, with state and federal court judges using agency law to ensure that organized labor had the authority to represent workers during a collective bargaining process, was transformed first into a worker representation scheme under the Railroad Labor Board, then into the U.S. Mediation Board, and finally into the majority rule provision established by the NLRB. The danger in making such a "value-free" policy was that it would always be open to liberal *and* conservative interpretations. Legal formalism helps explain how organized labor's activities were provoked and then shaped by the state.[21] They were not the result of the state's reaction to them, as, for instance, the pluralists have long contended.

The scheme for worker representation was so successful because it made use of procedural rights already ingrained in American liberalism. Whether the scheme produced a friend of management or an enemy was not in question; labor law expressed no substantive or ethical value either embracing or rejecting unionization. It did declare, however, a need for greater state involvement, and thus the administrative agencies gained the prerogative to regulate the collective bargaining process. The emphases on both state involvement and the worker representation process made post–World War I labor policy different from wartime policy.

That there was a policy continuum between labor legislation in the 1920s and such legislation in the 1930s does not mean that the Republican Party supported the Wagner Act or that Wagner wanted to hinder unionization. Wagner has long been regarded as a champion of organized labor. Rather, the legal and legislative developments between the late 1890s and 1935 made labor policymaking a continuum. Labor relations machinery emerged that enacted a policy built on legal and legislative precedents—a policy that over the course of this period became self-sustaining. Both common-law precedents and Supreme Court rulings about class legislation and application of the principles of agency to labor law defined labor legislation in the 1920s and the 1930s. While Republican motivation determined the first stage of the labor policymaking process after World War I, the question of intent disappeared when Wagner directed the second policymaking stage during the New Deal period. The momentum behind the choice made by Wagner and his legislative assistants was not just the relative autonomy of the state but also that of the law.

This argument about the long-term creation of federal labor policy both in common law and in statute exposes the profound ways in which this policy contributed to the development of American liberalism. It reveals the limits of liberalism by gauging the level of tolerance the Republican and Democratic policymakers expressed about the most conservative unions—the AFL and the railroad brotherhoods—which themselves promoted the intolerance of the age by excluding new immigrants, women, and African Americans from their unions.

### Excluding Even the Exclusionary AFL

The irony of the AFL's position becomes particularly marked when its ideology of voluntarism is juxtaposed with the ideology of responsible unionism that lies behind the modern labor policy.[22] Well aware of the perils associated with class and collectivism, the AFL and the brotherhoods went to great lengths to avoid being identified with these concepts or with the more radical labor unions, such as the Industrial Workers of the World (IWW). In particular, Samuel Gompers, the president of the AFL, used liberty, equality of opportunity, and competition to illustrate how liberalism was a theory of social change and justice that could accommodate organized labor. Voluntary associations, such as trade unions, he declared, helped maintain liberalism. Developing these ideas into a theory of laissez-faire voluntarism, Gompers insisted that organized labor brought about change without violating the individual rights of either workers or employers. Unions could help restore the individual rights, equality of opportunity, and competition that industrialization had restricted.[23] By engaging in strikes and boycotts (actions that Gompers described as a freedom derived from their status as voluntary associations), unions compelled employers to bargain with their representatives and pay a "living wage" to their members.[24] Gompers developed a voluntaristic supposition that through self-definition and self-organization workers could force employers to give them a living wage and better working conditions.[25]

As long as unions were free from state protection or interference, Gompers proclaimed, they could compete within the capitalist marketplace and represent individual workers, who would otherwise have difficulty surviving in the newly industrialized society. Concretely, this meant that the AFL union leaders opposed protectionist reforms such as workers' compensation and unemployment insurance, whereas they backed legislation that provided anti-injunction relief, the right to organize unions, and exemptions from antitrust liability.[26] From the 1880s until the New Deal, organized labor fought hard to maintain its antistatist position in politics and thereby prevent the emergence of invasive labor–management relations policies.

Not all members of the AFL were equally committed to voluntarism, however. After World War I, the shopcrafts unions in the AFL and the brotherhoods temporarily abandoned this ideology and lobbied for state protection under the Plumb Plan, which proposed that the wartime federal control of the railroads be extended during peacetime.[27] These unions supported this plan because it had helped bolster their membership, particularly that of the AFL Railway Employees Department (RED).[28] Ideological positions farther afield from American liberalism, like the Plumb Plan, stood even less of a chance of being accepted by the American state than voluntarism.

The Republicans understood how the railroad unions had profited from federal control, and they categorically opposed extending this control for precisely that reason. Yet the Republicans did not stop there. After World War I, they made no distinction between the unions fighting for the nationalization of the railroads and the AFL's strategy of business unionism, which was informed by its ideology of voluntarism. During the union-busting campaign in 1919 and 1920, the Republicans cultivated the notion that all organized labor challenged liberty and equality of opportunity. Not surprisingly, the first labor policy, cast in the Transportation Act of 1920, deployed an administrative agency to regulate these threatening organizations. The policy that evolved, namely, the scheme for worker representation, while accepting unions as legitimate collective bargaining agents, made them surrender their organizational autonomy. Thereafter, administrative agencies gave unions a temporary privilege of collective bargaining. The Railroad Labor Board, the U.S. Mediation Board, and the NLRB protected the rights of individual workers but not organized labor.

American labor policy reflected few of the principles within voluntarism. Indeed, being grounded in responsible unionism, this policy did exactly what the AFL had fought against from the 1890s until the New Deal: it helped control labor's freedom of association. Labor relations boards established during the 1920s and 1930s, instructed to safeguard the public interest, could equally help unionization or thwart it. Hence, American labor policy gave organized labor only one certainty—that the state would always be in control.

## Standard Interpretations of the 1920s

The standard interpretation of the 1920s characterizes this decade as "devoid of political accomplishment" and "barren of public benefit."[29] Historians and political scientists provide evidence of this interpretation through accounts of the feeble Republican control of the White House and Congress. The presidencies of Warren G. Harding, Calvin Coolidge, and Herbert Hoover generally are described as failures.[30] In addition, after the postwar reconstruction in 1919 and 1920 Congress supposedly collapsed into a factionalized and fragmented body of governance, with neither the old guard nor the progressive faction of Republicans dominating.[31] Finally, historians and political scientists portray the Republican-controlled Supreme Court, led by Chief Justice William Howard Taft, as a powerful, albeit negative, political force.[32] Relying on old doctrines and precedents, the Court, many legal historians claim, expended most of its energy obstructing important pieces of state and national legislation. In particular, legal historians usually underscore how the progressive and conservative members of the Court rendered opinions on labor law, among other areas of law, that divided the Court.[33]

Outside the federal government as well, historians and political scientists show that only weak political movements and organizations existed in the 1920s. For instance, they question whether the progressive movement survived into this decade.[34] Labor historians argue that this decade constituted the "lean

years" within the American labor movement.[35] The notable exception to this
verdict is Robert Zieger's *Republicans and Labor*, the only study not to margin-
alize the period.[36] They use the fact that union strength struck its nadir to
demonstrate the significance of the New Deal labor legislation. Only business
is characterized as having any clout in the public policymaking process in the
1920s.[37] Finally, the two-party system supposedly went into decline.

To many scholars, the absence of strong state leadership or significant public policies comes as no surprise because the 1920s represent a period of clo-
sure: the end of the progressive movement, the collapse of the fourth-party
system, and the concluding chapter to the story of mass industrialization. To
others, this decade's position between the "big bang" New Freedom and New
Deal reform accounts for its relative unimportance.[38]

Four models further enrich these portrayals of the 1920s as an uneventful
era. First, the realignment model reinforces the argument that the 1920s mark
a period of party decline. A realignment occurs when a massive change in voting patterns results from a catalytic event such as an economic depression; the
electorate then demands that the government resolve the problems associated
with this event.[39] A realignment creates great interparty competition, after
which the ruling party pulls together and develops public policy programs that
entrench its power. Over time, however, the coalition of party elites can no
longer maintain the requisite party unity and two-party competition. Intraparty squabbling erupts and paralyzes the party in power, until another realignment occurs. Thus, the intraparty conflicts in the 1920s are seen as the
telltale signs of the collapse of the fourth-party system.[40] After Republicans
gained control of all three federal branches in 1896, the lack of two-party competition created intraparty strife in the Republican Party. By the 1920s, this
conflict forestalled the emergence of a regenerative Republican Party agenda.

Second, the American political development approach to political history
also perceives the 1920s as the end of an era.[41] This approach, along with
the organizational synthesis school, maintains that, for the most part, by 1920
the "search for order" had been fulfilled.[42] It makes politics dependent on the
larger scientific and economic transformations in society, and it shows how
these transformations produce new types of private and public organizations.[43]
As Martin Sklar has demonstrated, the federal government created different
forms of corporate liberalism to accommodate the reconstruction of corporate
capitalism.[44]

Third, theories of the state link economic changes and political reform.[45]
This model, however, regards the 1920s as an interim period, sandwiched between the progressive New Freedom and New Deal reform movements, rather
than a concluding period. The state-building approach suggests that the Ameri-

can state constructs a package of reform policies as a response to a war or an economic depression. Yet, unlike the organizational synthesis school, the state-building model contends that large macroeconomic *and* political events trigger state action. Still, because this model has not begun to study the state's reaction to micropolitical events, such as postwar worker militancy or intraparty squabbling, it has neglected the American state's policymaking powers in the 1920s.

Finally, the critical legal studies approach demonstrates how the New Deal policymakers were constrained by legal precedent.[46] Katherine Van Wezel Stone's groundbreaking article on industrial rights, for example, argues that Wagner, boxed in by legal constraints, based modern labor policy on procedural, rather than the stronger substantive, rights.[47] While Stone's work illustrates just how the NLRA's emphasis on procedural rights would help shape the course of the American labor movement, it does not tell the full story. Stone argues that these rights were the product of a legislative compromise made during the New Deal. By so doing, she misses the opportunity to show how the Republicans helped develop this emphasis on procedural labor rights before the New Deal.

### Revising New Deal History

Not all political scientists and historians believe that the 1920s warrant little attention. Most notably, Ellis Hawley offers an important revisionist study of what the "progressive" Herbert Hoover accomplished during his tenure as secretary of commerce and president, from 1920 until 1932.[48] Hawley suggests that voluntary associations, or "associational networks located in the private sector," composing what he describes as the associativist state, governed the political economy of the "New Era."[49]

In portraying the political economy of the 1920s, Hawley presents a new interpretation of corporate liberalism.[50] Public authorities granted voluntary associations and organizations a privileged position in the public policymaking process. Essentially, the federal government recognized these organizations as functional representatives of the public good. That is, they helped pass public policies that benefited their interests and the interests of the community at large simultaneously. The government shared its public power with these private associations.

Taking into account the fragile state of the progressive movement and organized labor, Hawley notes that not all voluntary associations attained this privileged policymaking position. During the New Era, progressives like Hoover thought that a technocratic business elite should help formulate public policy—

that only this elite group of business reformers had the expertise to advise the federal government on what type of public policy should govern society. Federal agencies were established, in fact, not to provide social protection but to "collaborate with and become attached to private orders."[51]

Further, some historians have used Hawley's conception of the associativist state to help explain the labor policy constructed in the 1920s.[52] In particular, Christopher Tomlins argues that the Supreme Court determined this policy, such as it was. In *The State and the Unions*, Tomlins characterizes the 1920s as a period of calm during which the Supreme Court and the federal and state courts directed labor relations, before Congress passed the storm of labor legislation in the New Deal reform period.[53] He contends that, in the period between World War I and the New Deal reform, the "courts had begun to show a tendency to allow that unions, like business corporations, enjoyed the status of legal persons."[54] Tomlins loosely associates union leaders and their members with the technocratic business elite who helped Hoover formulate the associativist state's policy program.

While offering a revisionist perspective of the 1920s that does recognize the singular importance of this decade, Hawley and Tomlins still do not show that the federal government or the court system played a positive role in public policy construction. Hawley argues that the associativist state's power was in the hands of the technocratic business elite; Tomlins suggests that the Court recognized the unions as part of this elite. This revisionist interpretation of the 1920s underscores the voluntarism, as opposed to the statism, inherent in the New Era. The associativist state undermines its own monopoly on power and authority by giving public power to voluntary associations and organizations.

### Traditional Liberalism and the American State

This book suggests that even these revisionist interpretations cannot explain the emergence of federal labor policy in the 1920s. First, neither Hoover's Commerce Department nor his administration formulated this policy. The technocratic business elite in the associational networks had no hand in its development. Nor did organized labor have the political strength to help shape what became the permanent American labor policy.[55] Both parties to this policy—the business community and organized labor—initially denounced it. Unless the federal government created a policy laden with antistrike provisions and compulsory arbitration, most members of the business community thought the labor injunction constituted enough of a labor policy. "Progressive" members of the business community, by contrast, suggested that privately implemented employee representation plans or company unions, not traditional unions, offered a solution to the "labor problem." Meanwhile, the AFL stuck to its theory of voluntarism that rejected state interference in labor-management relations.

The Supreme Court, the White House, and traditional progressives and old guard Republicans in Congress must be credited with the creation of American labor policy. They acted collectively as a "third agent," relatively independent of organized labor and the business community in formulating this policy.

Second, the Republican policy never embraced the values inherent in the policy package of the associativist state. The preeminent value of voluntarism, underlying this New Era state, was absent from the Republican labor policy. In the 1920s, in the name of the public interest, the Republican policymakers forced organized labor to sacrifice its organizational autonomy. They erected a "neutral" labor relations board to define the entire collective bargaining process; they did this to ensure that the private interests of the parties involved coincided with the public interest.

Recognizing administrative experts, creating neutral boards, and protecting the public interest meant that the Republican labor policy was not part of the associativist state. At the same time, this policy cannot be described as a holdover from either the pre–World War I progressive era or the wartime progressive period. American labor policy reflected the policymakers' atavistic attachment to the traditional ideas of liberalism and capitalism. Progressive and old guard Republicans, and later progressive Republicans and Democrats, developed a policy that accommodated organized labor by taking into account the judiciary's ideas of individual rights, liberty, and freedom to contract.

Further, the atavistic heritage of this policy was no accident. The Republican policymakers intentionally obstructed the AFL and the railroad brotherhoods so that they could not develop along the same lines as corporate liberalism and corporate capitalism. That is, liberalism and capitalism rested on the theory that the state should accommodate new social organizations, such as the corporation. Perceived as benefiting society as well as themselves, corporations were thus functional representatives of the public good. In contrast, the old guard and the progressive Republicans believed unions did not even potentially embody the public good. Legal realists battling against the classical legal orthodoxy of the conservative courts concurred. They fought repeatedly with the AFL about releasing unions from accountability, balking at its request for absolute freedom of association. Judges and jurists writing progressive decisions and articles recognized the liberating as well as the coercive effects of union activity that became part of responsible unionism. All of these policymakers, portraying unions as by nature self-interested and antagonistic, created a policy that represented an alternative to class conflict. These policymakers intertwined and interjected the normally antithetical ideals of the freedom to contract and the public interest with the theory of responsible unionism. In the 1930s, the Democratic policymakers learned that crafting federal labor policy along these preexisting lines was the most effective way to survive the scrutiny of a still conservative Supreme Court.

### Re-revising New Deal History and Democratic Party Control: Republican Involvement in Labor-Management Relations

In 1919, progressive and old guard Republicans within all three branches of the federal government made American labor policy part of the GOP's overall endeavor to build a "new order," in which the American state would concentrate its national power and authority on safeguarding the common good. So, instead of allowing market forces to dictate labor-management relations, as had been done before World War I, the Republicans insisted that the state regulate these relations for the railroad industry—which engaged in interstate commerce. As far as the Republicans were concerned, the federal government *should* interfere with the railroad employers' and workers' freedom to contract as a means of securing the public interest.

Chapter 2 of this book introduces the AFL and the progressive movement and reveals how each tried to influence the state and federal courts' construction of organized labor's liability in equity and under common law. Instead of focusing on the AFL's ongoing battles with the conservative courts, as most scholars have done, this chapter traces the ideological rift that would divide the AFL and the progressives. On the one hand, Gompers formulated voluntarism as a defense against the state, particularly manifested by the conservative courts, which the AFL had long argued should not interfere in labor-management relations. The AFL wanted organized labor to be free from liability under law. On the other hand, the progressive movement rebutted the AFL's notion of voluntarism by formulating its own ideology of responsible unionism. Progressives and legal realists thought the courts must hold unions partially responsible for their actions. Hence, they developed a limited means of holding organized labor liable. It was these ideological differences that kept the AFL and the progressives from forging an effective alliance against the conservative courts.

Chapter 3 explains how the progressives' fledgling ideology of responsible unionism, not the AFL's ideology of voluntarism, would have the greatest influence on labor law. It shows how the progressives' idea about limited union liability was employed by judges in the state and federal courts. Quite simply, they relied on this idea to resolve whether unions could be made liable for their actions as organizations. They determined what role organized labor played in the labor-management relations process. Progressives and legal realists developed a common-law doctrine that (1) recognized unions as voluntary, unincorporated associations lacking legal standing to negotiate binding trade agreements and (2) limited their accountability under common law.[56] At the same time, these courts issued a rash of injunctions thwarting union efforts to organize the workforce. With the AFL seeking absolute immunity from liability in equity, common law, and statute, the progressives, who acknowledged organized labor's limited liability, had more success influencing these courts. Judges whose decisions reflected progressive leanings and jurists who subscribed to sociological jurisprudence and legal realism together formulated an alternative theory of trade union legitimacy—responsible unionism—that gave unions accountability as just one group among many that were competent to represent workers before law.[57] They affected the formation of labor law by provoking a debate that led to the creation of American labor policy under statute. Combined, these judges and jurists developed the idea of responsible unions, manifesting in outline what would become the modern labor policy.

Chapter 4 shows how two factions in the Republican Congress used some of the same ideas about union liability as propounded by the progressive state and federal courts and so created a comprehensive labor policy for the railroads. After the congressional elections of 1918, the two dominant factions in the Republican Party—the old guard and the progressives—formed a temporary alliance in opposition to Woodrow Wilson's administration in order to construct a postwar Republican "new order." Searching for a railroad labor policy, the Republicans repudiated Wilson's wartime labor policy and constructed a policy amenable to both factions.

The Republican Party elite found the progressive state and federal courts' ideas about responsible unionism appealing. They reshaped the legal ideas of union accountability into a scheme for worker representation that recognized unions as one among many voluntary associations that could represent the railroad workers at the collective bargaining table. Providing these workers with representatives gave them a collective bargaining agent. Yet, because these worker representation provisions were kept temporary in nature, they did not endanger the traditional notions of contractualism and individualism inherent within the postwar Republican agenda.

Chapter 5 focuses on the implementation of the worker representation scheme. Over the objections of most railroad executives, the Railroad Labor Board cultivated a scheme for worker representation that helped organized labor. Although the board operated for less than five years, this scheme, which provided for greater state involvement in labor disputes, became entrenched in

American labor policy when the Supreme Court, led by Taft, upheld its constitutionality in *Pennsylvania Railroad Company v. United States Railroad Labor Board*.[58]

The unanimous Taft Court held that the Railroad Labor Board had the power and authority to implement the worker representation scheme because it had secured procedural rights for workers, not a substantive right that could conflict with employer rights. The Court's ruling disappointed the Pennsylvania railroad executives, who wanted this scheme to entitle them to form company unions. In particular, they wanted company unions to curb the unionization of the shopcrafts workers, who had organized because of governmental interference during World War I. To the surprise of most railroad executives, the Railroad Labor Board did not always further their interests.

Chapter 6 traces the reemergence of the Railroad Labor Board as the U.S. Mediation Board and explores the Republican coalition responsible for it. The Republican Congress, with the help of Calvin Coolidge's Republican administration, replaced the first, faulty Railroad Labor Board with the second, more successful U.S. Mediation Board. Essentially, it was the progressive and old guard Republicans who restored the ideological balance that would underlie the latter board. Again making the worker representation provisions the bedrock of Republican labor relations, they built the second board on the twin principles of the freedom to contract and the public interest.

Chapter 7 illustrates how the progressive Republicans extended the ideas inherent in the worker representation scheme and agency law to limit the labor injunction. After the Great Depression, the progressive Republicans temporarily abandoned their party and formed a bipartisan coalition with the progressive Democrats to challenge President Herbert Hoover's recovery policies. This coalition made the Republican labor-management relations principles part of its own agenda and passed the Norris-LaGuardia Anti-Injunction Act of 1932.

Reflecting responsible unionism, the act shifted the focus of anti-injunction legislation from the agent, or the union seeking immunity, to the activities associated with the collective bargaining process. Just as the Republican scheme for worker representation emphasized the collective bargaining process and not the agent, so the Norris-LaGuardia Anti-Injunction Act withdrew equitable relief for certain types of activities or conduct, and not for special classes or agents. The act assigned unions responsibility because of their activities: injunctions could not be issued against "certain defined conduct" that occurred during most labor disputes.

The labor relations policy developed by this new bipartisan progressive coalition then laid the foundation for the passage of the 1935 National Labor

Relations Act. Chapter 8 shows that the New Deal Democrats derived the centerpiece of their labor policy from the Republican notion of responsible unionism. Rejecting the New Freedom Democrats' legacy in labor law, Robert F. Wagner, a progressive Democrat, made the Republican duality of freedom to contract and the public interest the backbone of the NLRA. Joining the Republicans' quest for a new order, Wagner made organized labor and the business community dependent on the will and the whims of a quasi-judicial agency that was intended to safeguard the public interest. The National Labor Relations Board gave state managers, not organized labor or the business community, the discretion to determine labor-management relations. The Republican roots of the Wagner Act, therefore, *did* shape what became the permanent labor policy. What distinguished the Republican labor policy from the prewar and wartime Democratic policies were the penchants of the latter two for statism and for promoting the public interest. The Republicans built a labor policy, according to their interpretation of the necessary paradox within American liberalism, that made the public interest, not the private interests of the constituent parties, its centerpiece.

From the application of agency law under common law to the construction of the Railroad Labor Board, the U.S. Mediation Board, and the NLRB under statute, American labor policy constructed new channels for union accountability that simultaneously acknowledged organized labor's legality, protected individual rights for all workers, and reaffirmed the idea that individualism, not any form of collectivism, represented the public good. In so doing, labor policy began regulating and restraining organized labor instead of co-opting it, and this helped preserve the liberal state. By denouncing the collectivism that underlay the idea of worker solidarity, American liberalism removed the threat of being compelled to develop a tripartite corporate liberal state. Although Republican and Democratic policymakers occasionally cooperated with business, they never extended this same spirit of cooperation to organized labor. In the United States, the federal government and business, not labor, represent the public good.

The test of the self-sustaining nature of American labor policy came, however, only with a change in political climate. When unionization rates hit a historic high of 14 million after World War II (a sevenfold increase since 1932), a powerful coalition of Republicans and southern Democrats passed the repressive Taft-Hartley Labor-Management Relations Act of 1947, with large bipartisan majorities in both the House of Representatives and the Senate. Instead of repealing the Wagner Act, this conservative coalition used the same rhetoric Wagner and his legislative assistants had employed—of safeguarding the public interest and individual workers, not the private interests of unions and employers. Whereas Wagner had relied on this rhetoric to ensure that the conservative Supreme Court upheld his labor legislation, the Republicans and southern Democrats drafting the Taft–Hartley Act used it to undermine organized labor's strength in the economy and the polity.

Essentially, the conservative coalition took the idea of responsible unionism that had been implicit in the 1920s and 1930s and refashioned it into an explicit ideology. The Republicans and southern Democrats turned the main premise underlying this type of unionism—that neither business nor labor could be trusted—into a powerful policymaking tool, more powerful than any unreserved expressions of antiunionism. State regulation had been imperative under responsible unionism in the 1920s and 1930s to thwart the unfair labor practices conducted by antiunion businesses; now it curbed union activities and forestalled the unionization of new sectors of the economy.

Hence, despite the AFL's long-term efforts (from the turn of the century until the 1930s) to maintain freedom of association, the old guard Republicans, progressive Republicans and Democrats, and progressive judges and jurists left the door open to increased state scrutiny of organized labor's internal and external affairs. Responsible unionism, not voluntarism, defined American labor policy. "Whether its leaders admit it or not," wrote Louis Stark, a labor reporter, "the labor movement has developed into a quasi-public institution." In protest of the passage of the Taft–Hartley Act, he continued: "It is a mistake for the government to enact regulations for the internal government of unions. If it does it has to police them. Once embarked on this road, complete state control is inevitable."[59]

CHAPTER 2

# A Failed Alliance between
# the AFL and the Progressives

Injunctions of a flagrant, unjustifiable and outrageous character are
continually issued, and honest, law-abiding, and faithful citizen-
workmen are thrust into prison.

—Editorial from the *American Federationist*, 1902

When Samuel Gompers blasted "the flagrant abuse of the writ of
injunction by the courts" in the *American Federationist* from 1900 onward, he
never worried about losing progressive support.[1] Unlike regular court rulings,
the injunction was a judicial order that prohibited people from engaging in
specific activities like strikes or boycotts. Bull Moosers, midwestern insurgent Republicans, and urban-liberal Democrats, among others, all made anti-
injunction legislation part of their respective platforms for reform.[2] The progressive architects of legal realism also included the "labor injunction" on their
list of unfair and outmoded legal remedies employed by conservative courts.[3]
But when the discussion went beyond the imputation of "government by injunction," difficulties arose. The AFL and progressives cultivated distinctly different approaches to the reform of labor law.

For the mainstream American labor movement, labor law reform revolved
around one substantive issue—freedom of association. As long as the state,
manifested by the judiciary, left labor free to organize and bargain collectively,
Gompers thought organized labor could flourish in a relationship of "historic
compromise" with corporate capitalism. If labor law remained private, wage
earners could acquire their part of the American dream by organizing as an exclusive class along trade lines and compelling business corporations to join them
in collective bargaining agreements. Union autonomy, distinct class interests,
and antistatism were the enduring themes of what became known as the AFL's
ideology of voluntarism.[4]

But while the AFL sought labor legislation that would further this conception of voluntarism, some progressives repudiated the notion of class interests as antithetical to social efficiency, arguing instead for the creation of neutral, "expert" state regulatory apparatuses to promote the public interest by reconciling groups engaged in wasteful conflicts.[5] The AFL wanted immunity from prosecution under the Interstate Commerce Act of 1887 and the Sherman Antitrust Act of 1890, insisting that organized labor should be free from responsibility for engaging in interstate strikes and boycotts against businesses that refused to bargain. Progressive policymakers, on the other hand, demanded that unions be made collectively accountable for their actions and activities.

Progressive judges and jurists, critical of the very distinction between private and public law developed in classical legal orthodoxy, argued that private law already unfairly protected market relations.[6] Since business unionism espoused the very values underlying laissez-faire capitalism that they disparaged, these progressives did not further this type of unionism under common law. They renounced the ideal of a neutral, nonredistributive state fighting for a regulatory state of experts that accommodated groups in the new organizational society.[7] Unions should abide by specific legal rights *and* duties to help advance the public good. It was this idea about establishing limited union liability that would become the ideological cornerstone of responsible unionism.

Unlike voluntarism, responsible unionism was not developed and articulated by any one leader or a coherent movement. This progressive ideology took shape slowly from the early twentieth century until 1935, when some judges and jurists built the idea of limited union liability into law. This notion, however, should not be confused with the corporate veil of liability. Although the union and the corporation both represented large, unwieldy organizations struggling for legal recognition in the nineteenth century, they experienced vastly different legal histories. Beginning in the 1820s, corporations received charters of incorporation. When these charters became available to unions in the late 1880s, however, the American judiciary's hostility toward organized labor discouraged unions from using them. Few unions dared accept these charters: the benefit of gaining a legal identity as a competent collective bargaining agent, enabling the union as party plaintiff to sue its employer for the enforcement of such agreement, was offset by the potential cost of becoming a defendant in a damage suit. Without a legal identity, unions remained voluntary, unincorporated associations. Labor leaders could negotiate nonbinding collective bargaining agreements, enforceable only when they utilized extralegal measures, such as the strike. The AFL accepted this situation. Gompers thought collective bargaining should be regulated by the market, not the law. By contrast, many progressives, who also criticized capital for hiding behind the veil of corporate liability, thought collective bargaining should be enforced by law. Neither capital nor labor should escape accountability under law.

It was the progressive ideology of responsible unionism, not voluntarism, that would have the greatest impact on labor law. This ideological victory, however, cannot be attributed to the progressive movement alone. No matter how many concepts and ideas Gompers borrowed from laissez-faire capitalism in his campaign for voluntarism and business unionism, conservative judges and jurists spurned the idea that organized labor should be treated like capital. Business unionism threatened industrial capitalism. Conservative judges and jurists, along with old guard Republicans in the legislative and executive branches, reasoned that the interests of capital could be tantamount to the public interest, whereas organized labor's interests could not. For this reason, they had little difficulty accepting the progressive judges' and jurists' determination that organized labor should be made accountable for its actions.[8]

Progressive and conservative judges and jurists alike found responsible unionism appealing because it embraced the paradox within classical liberalism. Unlike voluntarism, this ideology provided that a traditionally weak state would increase its power and authority in labor-management relations. The progressive and conservative judges and jurists sanctioned state supervision in labor-management relations not for the promotion of organized labor's specific interests but to maintain the public interest.

### Whither the Community?: Voluntarism Defined

In the late 1880s, the AFL emerged and began to transform the mainstream American labor movement with its ideology of voluntarism.[9] Few labor leaders or journalists, when comparing voluntarism with the Knights of Labor's tradition of republican antimonopolism or the European labor movements' history of socialism or syndicalism, characterized it as visionary or romantic.[10] As an ideology that maintained a position of nonpartisanship, voluntarism offered American wage earners little sense of political community or citizenship. No inherent or learned understanding of republicanism such as the Knights propounded, or class consciousness as the European trade unionists advocated, united them. "The American worker . . . by reason of the larger opportunity for individual advancement in our economic system, does not think of himself and his children as being permanently fixed in a definite class," said John Spargo in a eulogy about Gompers, "and has therefore less of the sense of class solidarity and class consciousness."[11] Economic necessity brought wage earners together.

Casting aside lofty ideas like civic virtue, voluntarism embraced the laissez-faire principle in neoclassical economics that self-interest motivated most individuals. Unions, Gompers suggested, should be perceived as an extension of these individuals. In other words, the trade union had no special identity as a collect*ive*; it was merely a collec*tion* of individuals who preferred to promote their self-interest but lacked the power to do so. Voluntary associations afforded them that power. The AFL presented voluntarism to explain how they could bolster their competitive position in the economy. "If the workman neglects to protect his interests," Gompers asked, "who will do it for him?"[12]

Given voluntarism's pragmatic emphasis on economics, power, and competition, the basic theoretical tenets within this ideology and the strategies it employed became combined and confused. Gompers's conception of class interests, however, remained constant. Initially developed by Gompers as part of a reaction to the Knights of Labor's republicanism, voluntarism dismissed the idea that wage earners belonged in an alliance with small producers opposed to corporate monopolies.[13] First, Gompers challenged the notion that the structure of the economy should be altered. As John R. Commons wrote, "with Marx the individual was subordinated, in every respect and at all times, to a government of some kind that controls the economic foundations. With Gompers the individual was supreme but coerced, and was to acquire liberty by collectively imposing shop rules for control of the economic foundations."[14] Unlike the Knights, the AFL accepted and even embraced the new industrial age.[15]

Second, Gompers maintained that the American state should better accommodate organized labor, ensuring organized labor's freedom of association. Voluntarism eschewed the republican ideal that wage earners and small owners or producers formed a true bond. Gompers considered it a useless exercise for the wage earners to align themselves against the nonproducers who, for instance, owned or managed large corporations. An adversarial relationship between wage earners and all producers, large and small, shaped industrial conflicts. Wage earners should organize and unite as a class (one defined by experience rather than by birth), and they should use strikes and boycotts—the primary manifestations of labor's freedom as a voluntary association—to compel the employers to bargain with their representatives.[16] Only through such self-definition and self-organization, Gompers submitted, could workers force employers to give them a living wage and better working conditions.[17]

Third, voluntarism maintained a position of nonpartisanship and political independence. "What is wanted" Gompers said, "is the organization of the wage-workers, not on 'party' lines but on the lines of class interests." The AFL sent no wage earners to the polls with guidance about whether to vote for Republicans, Democrats, or third-party candidates. Gompers purged voluntarism of all references to republican citizenship and furthered a self-interested notion of worker solidarity. Wage earners derived only their economic identity from class awareness. Voluntarism contained a narrow conception of class interest: class had little to do with politics.

Yet Gompers's position on nonpartisanship did not preclude him from accepting self-serving legislation.[18] The state should guarantee labor's right to organize, since voluntarism restored individualism within American society. The AFL, he claimed, helped wage earners regain their individual sovereignty in the face of the newly emergent corporate economy that had made a mockery of their autonomy. "In our day it is idle for any one to entertain the belief that the workers can *individually* be successful in securing redress of wrongs," Gompers explained, "or the attainment of rights against the combinations of capital."[19] The organization of labor had been essential to create "actual" freedom of contract. "Resistance to encroachments of the combined power of capital is predicated," Gompers appealed, "upon the organization of labor."[20] The American state, he propounded, must respect organized labor's freedom of association and prerogative for privacy.[21]

Overall, voluntarism was based on fundamental American values. First, workers, like everybody else, behave in ways that reflect their self-interest. Second, these workers should be free to become a member of any association. The associations they join, moreover, should also be unhindered. According to Gompers, unions should be regarded as groups of like-minded people pursuing their self-interest. They had no special personality apart from their membership. Because people are self-interested by nature, it was potentially corrupt for any single person, authority, or organization to make a determination for another person. Extending the idea of freedom of association from the worker to the union, the AFL's strategy of business unionism, which manifested voluntarism, repudiated any type of state interference.

### Unincorporated Unions and
### the Difficulty of Being Nothing

While class interests were inherent in the ideology of voluntarism, antistatism evolved as part of Gompers's defensive strategy against the hostile judiciary. Before the passage of the Sherman Act of 1890, he thought that limited state involvement in labor-management relations could facilitate voluntarism. Indeed, Gompers lobbied for such involvement when he gave testimony in support of legislation permitting unions to obtain federal charters of incorporation.[22] At hearings before the Senate Committee on Education and Labor, he argued that incorporation better enabled unions to enforce contracts, discipline members, control strikes, and institute voluntary arbitration.[23] Responding to organized labor's lobbying efforts, in 1886 Congress passed an incorporation statute for unions.[24]

The legal status of incorporation, bestowed by Congress or a state legisla-

ture, allowed an association to act as a single entity.[25] This entity, first referred
to as a "fictitious person," received individual rights under law, namely, the
right to sue and be sued as a body.[26] Shifting the right and burden of accountability thus freed the members of an association from personal liability under
law.[27] In the United States, a business corporation formed the most common
example of an incorporated association. Beginning in the 1820s, state legislatures and Congress provided businesses with charters of incorporation that
permitted others to sue them yet limited their shareholders' liability.[28] As long
as corporations continued to be regarded as artificial persons granted existence
by the state, they remained formally limited in their legal capacities. They accepted these limitations in exchange for the special charters of incorporation
they had negotiated privately with state legislatures.[29]

In the late 1830s and 1840s, Jacksonian Democrats accused these state legislatures of giving corporations special treatment.[30] By 1850, a "free incorporation" movement arose to contest what became known as the "grant theory"
of corporate personality. This movement protested the special treatment that
corporations received. It had the unintended consequence, however, of sever-
ing the relationship between the corporation and state legislatures and leading
to a reconceptualization of corporate law. By the late 1880s and 1890s, a tendency to think of corporations as "natural entities" became evident in social
fact, replacing the grant theory of corporate personality and releasing corporations from the scrutiny of state governments that had extended charters to
them.[31]

Legal historians disagree about the exact date of the demise of grant theory.
Did the Supreme Court decision in *Santa Clara v. Southern Pacific Railroad*[32]
produce natural entity theory in 1886, or did it emerge in social fact a decade
later?[33] Whatever its origins, natural entity theory had a profound effect on
corporate development: it transferred a corporation's power and authority from
its shareholders to its directors and managers. Before the late 1880s, shareholders—who, after all, owned the corporation—directed all changes within
it. Under the new theory, directors and managers, who actually governed the
corporation, embodied it. But, not being actual property owners, these directors and managers faced no personal responsibility for corporate activities.
Moreover, the courts that employed this legal reasoning in the late nineteenth
century, the period of massive corporate growth, still recognized stockholders'
limited liability. Natural entity theory identified the corporation as an artificial
person, which meant that state legislatures lost their regulatory claims over this
new person; and it upheld limited liability. Meanwhile, an earlier development
in corporate law, the doctrine of substantive due process under Fourteenth
Amendment jurisprudence, protected the corporation from economic regula-

tion by bestowing upon it individual rights and privileges afforded because of incorporation.[34]

The demise of grant theory diminished the level of state control that corporations had to endure because of charters of incorporation; the rise of natural entity theory maintained the shareholders' veil of limited liability; and substantive due process protected the corporation from state interference, "squelching reform efforts that trenched on property or management prerogatives."[35] Recognizing the enormous privileges corporations enjoyed, the nascent AFL lobbied for its own charters of incorporation. The AFL's request for incorporation reflected both a wider search for its identity and the challenge that search posed for the wider polity.[36] Necessarily, in defining its legislative goals and needs to include privileges that had previously been withheld, such as incorporation, the AFL was questioning existing allocations of public resources. Gompers hoped that organized labor would gain the same rights and privileges that combinations of capital enjoyed, namely, the capacity to act as a collectivized single entity. He wanted an explicit recognition of the lawfulness of unions' existence. Charters of incorporation, Gompers thought, in the late 1880s, could put organized labor's bargaining relations with business corporations on secure footing.[37]

By the late 1890s, however, experience had taught Gompers that incorporation as such could never give unions security. The conservative state and federal judiciary dominating labor-management relations would interpret union incorporation no more sympathetically than it would other common-law doctrines and statutes applicable to organized labor.[38] For instance, it would have been unimaginable that the judiciary would apply natural entity theory to organized labor as it had to corporations. This theory would have given labor leaders the power and authority to govern a union without being held liable for its actions. Under natural entity theory directors and managers, who ran the corporation, were free from responsibility because they did not own it. Similarly, with labor, leaders could have escaped liability because the union derived its identity from the rank and file. Given the federal and state courts' hostility toward organized labor, labor leaders stood little chance of being treated like directors and managers of corporations.

The dangers of incorporating, Gompers decided, outweighed the benefits.[39] Incorporation would make the union, as a fictitious person, liable to be sued, risking loss of its accumulated membership funds.[40] "When courts so far transgress upon the rights of wage-earners, when they will invade the rights to which the toilers are entitled, you must excuse us," Gompers said, "if we decline your invitation to step into your parlor."[41] Or as several legal scholars wrote, "once a union assumes the dignity of an entity and is made responsible at law it might not be a difficult thing for an employer to show cause enough for enjoining the use of union funds that the union would be helpless in the pursuit of the strike."[42]

Gompers understood that the AFL's refusal to reconsider incorporation—incorporation thought by most legislators and lawyers, whether progressive or conservative, to constitute minimal state interference and hence to be quite reasonable—would be harmful to the acceptance and development of his strategy of business unionism and theory of voluntarism. Without a legal personality, unions were noncompetent bargaining agents: neither unions nor union members could appeal to the judiciary to enforce collective trade agreements. Here, Gompers's accompanying notion of the salience of worker militancy and his frank recognition of class interest (on both sides) surfaced. Ultimately, it was the market warfare of the bargaining process itself, and only that, that would teach unions and their employers the advantages of accountability under collective trade agreements.

Gompers's emphasis on the market, however, did not stop him from suggesting that the American state could protect the public from the necessarily disruptive consequences of the bargaining process, not by suppressing workers' concerted activities but by reinforcing the accommodations they arrived at. State and federal courts should recognize collective trade agreements as *sui generis* and therefore lend them support on this special basis alone.[43] Such agreements, he argued during a public debate with the "People's Lawyer," Louis D. Brandeis, could not be categorized as normal contracts, and neither disruptive worker militancy nor its equally disruptive repression would be necessary if courts simply respected these trade agreements. To be sure, neither trade unions nor their membership should be held legally accountable for the consequences of strikes and boycotts. As voluntary associations, unions should be out of the judiciary's reach. But, since trade agreements did *in fact* promote peaceful contractual relations, they should *in fact* be enforced. It was in the public interest for the state to furnish unions with certain noncompulsory rights and privileges.

Gompers perceived a relationship between his vision of organized labor's freedom of association and progressive jurisprudence or legal realism, and he suggested that labor law, like corporate law, drew "its lessons from history."[44] He rejected conservative or classical legal orthodoxy, which, ignoring the dramatic changes in the late-nineteenth-century economy, ruled on the idea that the common law resulted from formal logical patterns derived from natural rights rather than history.[45] The emergence of large enterprises undermined the wage earners' autonomy, he argued, and unions attempted to restore it.

Not all progressive jurists agreed with Gompers that organized labor had an absolute right to organize above all others.[46] They parted company with Gompers over his justification of organized labor's freedom of association. To them, Gompers provided a faulty, formalist definition of the union's categorical right to associate that substituted freedom for economic liberty independent of history.[47] Voluntarism emphasized the positive aspects of freedom of association, ignoring the coercive effects of such association.

Overall, Gompers did not spurn politics; he fought for anti-injunction relief, guarantees of the right to organize unions, and exemptions from antitrust liability.[48] But the fundamental goal was preventive: to maintain antistatism and to forestall the passage of invasive labor-management relations policies. Where the Knights of Labor and other earlier national labor organizations had been willing to align with Greenbackers and Populists in alliances propagating "state-related values," the AFL sought immunity from the state.[49] Unions, he thought, could better fend for themselves if unhindered by state regulation and unaided by state protection. When the Supreme Court made organized labor liable under the Sherman Act for restraints on interstate trade, in *Loewe v. Lawlor* (1908), it only strengthened Gompers's antistatist resolve.[50] He never wavered in his emphasis on class interests, but, between the late 1880s and 1900, his definition of appropriate state action changed.

### Without Hat in Hand:
### Progressivism and the Public Interest

Simultaneous with the AFL, the "progressive" movement emerged during the late 1880s. Few progressives, whether of the Bull Moose variety or from either of the major political parties, however, embraced the AFL's theory of voluntarism and its intertwined notions of class interest, antistatism, and pragmatic compromise. Most progressives supported organized labor, since unions empowered individual workers and gave them a modicum of the equality of bargaining power necessary to negotiate collective trade agreements with employers. But they never accepted what Gompers understood to be the ultimate necessity: that trials of strength be allowed to proceed unhindered. Rather, most progressives condemned strikes and the closed shop as inefficient and unnecessary, claiming that they disrupted the social order and undermined individual rights.[51]

Virtually all progressive organizers and spokesmen, however sympathetic to the labor movement, felt far more comfortable fighting for wage and hour legislation than for legislation advocating organized labor's right to strike. Their position on organized labor reflected the ambiguity of the movement itself.[52] Although the progressives led the battle to humanize capitalism through wage and hour legislation, for example, they never acknowledged that this economic system gave rise to social conflicts resulting from low wages. The progressives renounced special or class interests that had been created to humanize capitalism. Composed largely of highly educated middle-class professionals, the progressive movement purported that politics should not be defined by the crude struggle for power between capital and labor. As one progressive journalist wrote: "Labor cannot afford to jockey itself into the position of a special interest, insistently demanding what it concedes to be for its own good and reflecting general good. . . . Organized labor has political responsibilities as well as political rights."[53] Whether the progressive movement constituted a "status-revolution" of disaffected middle-class reformers or an extension of populism by agrarian insurgents, as historians have argued endlessly, it did not support self-interested groups locked in an ignoble politics of power.[54]

Not only did progressivism stand between labor and capital; it also embodied the crossroads between rural and urban America, laissez-faire and corporate capitalism, urban city machines and big national government.[55] The movement operated on many levels, with progressives channeling their faith in reform into science, social science, religion, and politics.[56] Some progressives sought only state and local political reform, whereas others focused on national reform. While some historians suggest that these many channels for reform call into question the very idea of a progressive movement, others argue that progressivism constituted a series of overlapping movements.[57] The manifestation of these many movements, moreover, underscored the depth of the progressives' ambiguity about reform and the malleability of their ideology.

At the center of the progressive ideology lay a belief in a morality that emphasized the public interest above class interests and placed civic virtue above self-interest. Whether they relied on science, social science, Christianity, or political campaigns against corruption, the progressives sought the restoration of morality in politics and society. What they characterized as "social uplift theory" mirrored the belief that moral structures shaped individual futures and "bettered" people.[58] Ambiguity remained, however, about what vehicle best altered this environment and furthered the public interest.

Indeed, what constituted the public interest depended on the particular leaders and their respective constituencies. For agrarian progressives from the Midwest, for instance, railroad regulation that promoted the shippers' interests over those of the railroad carriers was deemed in the public interest.[59] During the debate over the Transportation Act, the shippers' and the consumers' interests, not organized labor's interests, preoccupied Senators Robert M. LaFollette, a progressive Republican from Wisconsin, and George W. Norris, a progressive Republican from Nebraska, who had the strongest records in support of the AFL and the brotherhoods. Progressives from urban centers, on the other hand, argued that large corporate interests like Kelloggs, which relied on advertising and public relations to help them develop "welfare capitalism," fostered the greater good.[60]

Progressive Republicans and Democrats also bandied about the phrase "the public interest," making it into a measure of progressivism that coincided with their party principles. After Woodrow Wilson's election in 1912, progressive Republicans used their definition of the public interest to illustrate that only they, and not their Democratic progressive brethren, could be depicted as truly progressive.[61] The Democrats, they declared, failed the public interest test.[62] As Senator Norris argued, the Democrats could not call themselves progressives because they had long derived their strength from serving local groups like the Roman Catholic urban immigrants in the Northeast and agrarian populists below the Mason–Dixon Line.[63] In fact, the progressive Democrats hardly stood above the fray of special-interest politics. Their free-silver heritage, which they shared with the Greenbackers and the Populists, also made a Democratic claim to progressivism difficult to establish.[64] In response to the progressive Republicans' allegations, these Democrats chose not to deny their service to these immigrant groups but to deny that such service conflicted with the public interest.

Given the infighting and fragmentation, the most convincing accounts of progressivism depict it as a cluster of closely joined groups or movements whose members continually debated what made up the public interest.[65] Competing ideologies often directed reform programs. What made one progressive ideology more persuasive than another was often attributed to the effectiveness of the individual movement's rhetoric and strategy. The interplay of ideology, rhetoric, and strategy within progressivism as well as against the opposition accounted for the success or failure of a particular reform program.

It was within such a vortex of competing progressive ideologies, rhetoric, and strategies that the notion of responsible unionism unfolded. Initially, progressives articulated responsible unionism as a rhetorical response to the AFL's ideology of self-interest. Between 1890 and 1932, most progressive magazines and journals equated the mainstream labor movement—the AFL and the railroad brotherhoods—with special-interest politics.[66] As one progressive journalist explained, "So long as the unions stand hat in hand in the lobbies of the politicians, punctuating this servility with strikes and threats, they are a special interest and a poor one at that."[67] With its emphasis on organized labor's rights *and* duties and the public interest, the progressives' vision of responsible unionism was imbued with republican overtones.

Despite this common rhetoric, not all progressives agreed that organized labor compromised the public interest. Some progressives, notably Democrats and industrial pluralists from the John R. Commons school of labor-management relations, argued that labor, as a special interest, still fostered the public interest. President Wilson showed his support for trade unions by including an anti-injunction provision in the Clayton Act that, in part, freed unions from accountability under antitrust laws. After a great legislative battle, this progressive president also pressured Congress into giving the operating railroad unions, among other things, an eight-hour day. Meanwhile, labor economists like Commons and William Leiserson advocated that policy be made by organized groups that could negotiate among themselves, with the state acting as umpire.[68] Like the AFL, in its description of voluntarism, these labor economists professed that the interest of the individual should be identified with that of the group. Yet unlike voluntarism, industrial pluralism rejected the neoclassical assumption that individual desires shaped individual expectations.[69] Gompers's focus on individuals, Commons claimed, in no way sacrificed the greater good. "It was the individuality of the laborer that counted, and economic power for them meant power of the union to protect the individual in his job."[70] To him, institutions like unions could be regarded as "collective action in control of individual action."[71]

By contrast, progressive Republicans, who primarily represented the rural population as opposed to urban centers, and legal progressives,[72] who placed organized labor within a larger framework of state reform, wavered little from the notion that organized labor composed a special interest. Some progressive Republicans, for instance, criticized the Clayton Act for removing unions from statutory obligation under the Sherman Act. This legislation, they argued, constituted class legislation. Moreover, some progressive Republicans contended, this substantive legal reform offered a naive solution to a complex problem. As Senator Norris described, the labor relations provisions were a "makeshift, a delusion, a snare, and a fraud."[73]

Legal progressives, who developed this progressive jurisprudence in response to the classical orthodoxy of formalism, also disagreed with the industrial pluralists' emphasis on organized labor as a private, voluntary association. To law professors like Herman Oliphant, Wesley Sturges, Walter Nelles, Walter Wheeler Cook, and Felix Frankfurter, labor law reform belonged to a different family of institutional economics than the industrial pluralists described.[74] They followed Thorstein Veblen's idea that institutions evolved because of technological change and that these institutions created their own rules and regulations that positively shaped individual outcomes. Accordingly, the legal progressives advocated that the state play a greater role in regulating organized labor, a publicly constructed body.[75] As Cook explained, "We may find it necessary by statute to surround [unions] with legal regulations."[76]

## Responsible Unionism as Enlightened Self-Sacrifice

Responsible unionism matured slowly between 1890 and 1932, becoming an effective ideology in the 1920s as a result of a confluence of three factors. First, progressives writing in law journals began forming a consensus about organized labor and the question of limited liability in articles on group theory and legal personality.[77] Second, these law journal articles, as well as the ideas professed by Republican progressive legislators, accentuated the difference between the AFL's ideology of voluntarism and the progressives' notion about responsible unionism; particularly after the Supreme Court recognized the legal identity of an unincorporated union in the 1922 *Coronado* decision, the two ideas became more and more difficult to reconcile.[78] Third, the conservative courts made their constraints on labor under common law and equity more uniform, which in turn increased the possibility of labor law reform. The AFL thought its strategy worked better; the progressives insisted on theirs. Responsible unionism, progressive jurists and legislators argued with increasing conviction, served organized labor better than either voluntarism or the progressive Democrats' version of substantive labor law reform.[79] Procedural reform in equity, common law, and legislation, not substantive changes in statute, offered a more effective strategy for success against the conservative judiciary. These courts therefore helped polarize organized labor and the progressives.

The first practical manifestation of responsible unionism resulted in the incorporation debate. If unions incorporated, reasoned progressive intellectual leaders such as Brandeis,[80] the statutory rights and responsibilities thus provided would promote stability in contractual relations.[81] Employers and employees would have an obligation to uphold union-negotiated trade agreements.[82] Although objectively American unions represented "enlightened self-sacrifice," in practice they had "participated in . . . hasty and ill considered [activities], the result of emotion rather than of reason."[83] Expressing his views as a legal realist, Brandeis insisted that a union had no more right than any other association to "behave stupidly and immorally."[84] He favored incorporating unions, since thereafter they would be legally accountable for their actions, rather than in a position of "legal irresponsibility."[85]

Brandeis's insistence on public enforcement of responsibility upon unions reflected the raison d'être behind legal realism.[86] A strict private-public distinction in common law granted the state no role "beyond ensuring that the legal order was impartial and non-political," Brandeis and other legal progressives protested. And that reduced the state's capacity to address the ills "of an American society becoming ever more unequal in wealth and power."[87] The logic of the progressive position, giving the state directive regulatory authority to pursue the general social interest, applied as much to organized labor as to any other institution whose behavior touched the public's welfare.[88]

Unlike proponents of classical legal orthodoxy, Brandeis never championed creating a private system of law to govern labor-management relations. Brandeis's earlier exchanges with Gompers reflected the ideological rift that separated the progressive and labor movements. Refusing to endorse the AFL's pragmatic vision of voluntarism, which freely gave unions the power to perform their role, the progressives preferred their own conception of responsible unionism, which hedged these freedoms with legal controls. Both saw trade agreements as a good, but progressives saw them as a means to a greater public good—industrial peace—the goal of which made the interests of any one group or class incidental.[89] "The spirit which subordinates the interests of the individual to that of the class is the spirit of brotherhood—a near approach to altruism," Brandeis explained, "when it involves a sacrifice of present interests for the welfare of others in the distant future." The AFL, in contrast, saw as absolutely crucial the prior recognition of workers' vital class interests in securing and enforcing viable trade agreements. Public peace would be a valuable consequence of accommodations in the marketplace, but occasionally trials of strength would occur, and when they did, the results should not be rigged by the judiciary's hostile interventions against labor. Real peace came only from real compromises that resulted when contestants were not disabled from the vigorous initial pursuit of outcomes most favorable to themselves.

### God Save Labor from the Courts

After the public debate about incorporation between Brandeis and Gompers, representatives from the AFL and the progressives had few public exchanges about unionism. Instead, they asserted their respective ideologies in a battle against the conservative courts. After all, "it was in the courts," as Sidney Fine explains, "that the idea of laissez-faire won its greatest victory in the three and one-half decades after the Civil War."[90] The AFL's contest with these courts, in which it sought substantive legislative relief from the labor injunction, differed dramatically from the progressives' emphasis on procedural reform.

Proponents of laissez-faire constitutionalism and economic conservatism initially had the greatest success in the state courts.[91] Fighting legislative ex-

perimentation, conservative judges applied the doctrine of "implied limitations," which called upon the courts to intervene when the legislative branch
exceeded its authority. By 1885, however, when the New York Court of Appeals
delivered its judgment in *In re Jacobs*, laissez-faire constitutionalism and economic conservatism pervaded all levels of the American judiciary.[92] In 1895,
the Supreme Court extended the beginning of this type of conservativism to
its interpretation of a statute in *In re Debs*, upholding a lower federal court's injunction in the great Chicago railway strike. More than ten years later, the
Supreme Court found unions and their members liable for restraints in interstate trade under the Sherman Antitrust Act.[93] Thereafter, state and federal
courts regularly provided employers with equitable protection from organized
labor's activities.[94]

Equity law had evolved with common law. Under the Anglo-Saxon tradition of law, a separate court system—the equity courts—represented the
"conscience" of the medieval English state by dictating legal policy.[95] In the
United States, no separate court system emerged for equity law on the federal
level; instead, common law predominated. Conservatives, who in the late 1890s
until 1937 controlled the federal judiciary and developed legal formalism,
thought equity law subverted the legal reasoning underlying common law.
They saw equitable relief as a partial tool used by the state, particularly for the
protection of private property.[96] Common law needed no "conscience," the
conservatives contended, since it decided cases without reference to policy.[97]
Distinctive legal remedies—damages and injunctions—largely accounted for
the difference between common law and equity. The judiciary issued equitable
protection only if no adequate common-law remedy existed because it was so
much more powerful than the latter. Unlike a court ruling in either criminal or
civil law, the injunction prevented someone from conducting an activity. An
injunction prevented a "crime" before it was committed. For instance, the labor injunction prohibited workers from participating in a strike or a boycott if
it could destroy an employer's property.

According to the conservative members of the bar and bench, the labor injunction represented just such an exception: it offered employers a remedy
necessary to protect the destruction of private property. By 1895, labor injunctions replaced the criminal conspiracy trials in civil courts, becoming the
dominant form of legal redress.[98] "The extraordinary remedy of injunction has
become the ordinary remedy," wrote Felix Frankfurter and Nathan Greene,
legal progressives.[99] Because injunctions did not require a trial by jury, employers found them a fast, formidable weapon given the increase in industrial
conflicts at this time. State and federal courts issued omnibus injunctions,
which enjoined thousands of employees involved in any one strike, or they

rendered ex parte injunctions from evidence of affidavits that gave unions or employees little time to respond. From 1890 until 1928, trade unions or their members defended themselves in eighty-three cases, or 18 percent of all the Sherman Act cases.[100] Over the single decade of the 1920s, injunctions curbed 25 percent of all recorded strikes.[101] The state courts issued more injunctions against labor than the federal courts. But as Frankfurter and Greene suggested, "though [the federal injunctions] were not binding [they] exert[ed] weighty influence upon state courts."[102]

Injunctions allowed the courts to continue regulating industrial conflict without facing legislative reform.[103] Edward Berman, a progressive social scientist, hypothesized that the development of new legal doctrines could not account for this increase. Like the conservative Waite, Fuller, and White Courts before it, the Taft Court applied to labor law the doctrine of substantive due process, freedom to contract, and restraint of trade.[104] Judicial activism provoked by the Court's interpretation of anti-injunction legislation, Berman claimed, explained why organized labor faced more injunctions during the 1920s than ever before.[105]

### An Industrial Magna Carta or a Fraud?

From 1894 onward, the AFL led the battle for legislation that exempted unions from liability under the Sherman Antitrust Act. In 1914, when the Democratic Congress passed the Clayton Antitrust Act amending the Sherman Act, organized labor thought it had won this long-sought-after legislative goal.[106] Gompers said the labor relations provisions in this act represented "the Industrial Magna Carta upon which the working people will rear their structure of individual freedom."[107] Yet progressive Republicans, like Senator Porter J. McCumber of North Dakota, called these labor relations provisions a "piece of deception, a fraud."[108] The Republican senators John J. Blaine of Wisconsin, who served on the Judiciary Committee, and William E. Borah of Idaho also characterized these provisions as inadequate and misleading.[109] The progressive legal expert Edwin E. Witte, who often worked for Norris and LaFollette, said that the labor relations provisions drafted by Congressman Edwin Y. Webb, a Democrat, intended "to please labor and yet make no change in the law."[110]

Although the Clayton Act embodied an essential part of President Wilson's New Freedom legislative program and the progressive Republicans supported many planks in this program, the labor relations provisions reflected a difference in reform strategy between the progressive Democrats and progressive Republicans that remained unresolved until the policymaking process that yielded the Norris-LaGuardia Anti-Injunction Act of 1932.[111] The president's reliance on the Democratic caucus in Congress helps account for this difference. Bipartisan progressive cooperation did not produce the Clayton Act.[112] As the Democratic congressman Charles C. Carlin of Virginia described, "The Democratic Party is now about to fulfill its promise made to the great labor organizations and the farm organizations of this country."[113]

Nonetheless, it was the AFL, not the Democrats or Republicans, that initiated the formulation of these provisions.[114] The first draft of the Clayton Act contained no labor relations provisions. Presumably, organized labor would be liable for interrupting interstate commerce as it was under the Sherman Act. Hoping to rectify this oversight, Gompers and the AFL protested to the president. Wilson responded by extending labor relations provisions that gave defendants jury trials in contempt cases, limited the federal courts' authority to issue injunctions, and declared unions and groups of farmers free from being considered illegal combinations in restraint of trade. To the AFL's chagrin, however, the president granted organized labor and the farmers only partial immunity in interstate trade cases.[115]

Organized labor's success in securing these concessions made the progressive Democrats vulnerable to the accusation that they pandered to labor like a special interest. Supposedly, Wilson and the Democrats passed this legislation knowing that the Supreme Court would strike it down. According to Norris and other progressive Republicans, Attorney General Thomas Gregory informed Wilson that the breadth of the labor clauses in the Clayton Act would cause them to be misinterpreted or useless.[116] George Wickersham, who served as attorney general during Taft's administration, also argued that the labor relations provisions, particularly section 20, were class legislation that the Supreme Court would strike down as unconstitutional.[117]

At best, the most optimistic progressive legal reformers explained, the labor relations provisions in the Clayton Act might be seen as unclear. Understanding that the ambiguity of these provisions left room for interpretation before the Supreme Court ruled on the constitutionality of the Clayton Act, Gompers initiated a public debate. He led a campaign to persuade the federal courts that unions should now be exempt from prosecution in restraint of interstate trade.[118] Taft, a leader of the old guard Republicans, also used the ambiguity of the labor relations provisions—for his own purposes. First, he accused the Democratic Party of pandering crudely to the labor vote. "It will be legislation establishing a privilege for a class that is supposed to be powerful in votes," Taft said, "without any real reason for the distinction."[119]

Second, he insisted that the simple declaration that human labor could not be classified as an interstate commodity had no bearing on organized labor's accountability.[120] The AFL was mistaken to assume that because the Sherman Act made it illegal to impose restraints of trade in articles of commerce, the declaration that human labor could not be considered a commodity was tantamount to making unions immune from enjoinment.[121] Unions had been held liable for damages in earlier decisions, Taft explained, not because union members refused to sell their labor but because their actions interfered with interstate commerce. For instance, in *Loewe v. Lawlor* (commonly referred to as the Danbury Hatters case), the Court ruled that a secondary boycott by an AFL-affiliated union violated antitrust laws.[122] Organized labor had been accountable not because its members were interstate commodities but because each member had intended to restrain, and succeeded in restraining, interstate trade.[123] The very humanness of union members made organized labor more susceptible than business corporations to these charges. While charters of incorporation allowed shareholders to circumvent antitrust laws because corporations had the capacity to act as fictitious persons, union members and their officials could be held accountable for combining and conspiring to restrain interstate trade.[124]

In 1921, the Supreme Court first began interpreting the constitutionality of the labor relations provisions in the Clayton Act. Taft himself joined the Court as chief justice in 1921. In a number of cases, the Supreme Court rendered these labor relations provisions, as well as a state anti-injunction law, useless.[125] Neither unions nor union members were exempt from prosecution, whether in restraint of trade or as a protected class under legislation. The Court refused to limit the federal courts' power to enjoin organized labor. Supposedly, unions deserved no special treatment or exemptions under equity law. In fact, the Court's interpretation of the labor relations provisions in the Clayton Act made the federal courts more likely than ever before to issue injunctions against unions and union members. As the progressive Republican senator George Norris said, "I can not get away from the impression in studying these injunction cases and the statutes intended to limit injunctions, that the courts immediately instead of limiting them enlarged them."[126]

Throughout the 1920s, the injunction represented the most formidable weapon against organized labor. Employers hostile to organized labor found it an effective way to quash union-organizing campaigns. The AFL, by contrast, had a limited arsenal of effective weapons. Most courts recognized the strike, the boycott, and the picket only for "good" cause.[127] As Frankfurter and Greene explained, "The damage inflicted by combative measures of a union—the strike, the boycott, the picket—must win immunity by its purpose."[128] "When the objectives of concerted action are higher wages, shorter hours and improved working conditions," they elaborated, "all measures in themselves not tortious may be employed."[129] But if the purpose of a strike, for instance, was "one degree more remote," as was the case with strikes over union recognition, courts questioned the legality of the means as well as of the ends.

While Gompers continued lobbying for freedom of association, progressives like Frankfurter and Greene, among others, underscored this imbalance of legal remedies by suggesting that precedents in labor law reflected poor legal policy. Karl Llewellyn, a legal realist, wrote, "Law takes on the aspect of engineering." [130] The progressives' quest for labor law reform reflected their position against the rhetoric in support of laissez-faire capitalism. The progressives shared the notion that law and economics had a reciprocal relationship and that acknowledging this relationship could help them determine appropriate policy. For this reason, they advocated changes in legal procedures, not substantive changes in law, believing that such changes would lead to better labor policy. It was on the issues of economics, policy, and procedure that progressives parted company with both the AFL and the conservative courts.

Although progressive legislators, judges, and jurists alike condemned the labor injunction, they argued that providing unions with immunity was not "good" policy. Aside from the Clayton Act's failure to protect organized labor, progressive Republicans and legal progressives thought unions should have no special privileges, such as exemptions from prosecution under equity law. As Walter Wheeler Cook, a legal realist, explained, "It seems clear that we cannot permit the unions to acquire a substantial monopoly of furnishing labor in a given line without at the same time providing by legal regulation of some kind that the union is open on fair terms to all alike." [131]

### Conclusion

The AFL and the progressives had fundamentally different visions of state–labor relations. What ultimately separated these two groups was their disagreement about human motivation. For Gompers, people were motivated by their self-interest. Laborers organized, not because of economic injustices, but because they thought a union would fulfill their economic self-interest. Gompers's short-lived suggestion that unions be incorporated was no departure from this worldview.

Unlike some proponents of incorporation, Gompers never argued that organized labor was entitled to this legal status on theoretical grounds. He did not believe that a union had a special identity, separate from its membership. Rather, the AFL witnessed the great rights and privileges that the courts awarded incorporated corporations, making Gompers think that organized labor should seek the same rights and privileges. To Gompers, incorporation represented a good legal strategy, not a theory of organizations.

When Gompers realized that the dangers of incorporation were potentially greater than the benefits, he not only abandoned this strategy but also argued that organized labor must be unfettered by all legal constraints. Although the labor injunction was clearly the most damaging constraint, Gompers made no distinction between equity law and other types of law. Gompers launched a sweeping campaign. He declared that organized labor should be liberated from all forms of legal restraints, including any imposed on the collective bargaining process.

The progressives agreed with the AFL that the conservative courts had unfairly restricted organized labor when they gave employers injunctions. But the progressives began their campaign for labor law reform from an entirely different vantage point than the AFL. Unlike Gompers, they thought people could rise above their self-interest. To them, workers help achieve the public interest by organizing into unions. In theory, they professed, an organization, like a trade union, could both enlighten and discipline its membership. Yet, in practice, they conceded that organized labor often engaged in self-interested practices like strikes that undermined the public interest. A number of key progressives like Brandeis and Frankfurter favored the incorporation of labor unions because they thought it could advance collective bargaining *and* promote the public interest. The progressive ideal of labor law reform fell between a repudiation of the injunction and a repudiation of immunity.

For the progressives, incorporation represented a procedural, not a substantive, reform like immunity from the labor injunction. Procedural reforms, they argued, represented the best strategy against the conservative courts. In other words, the application of an equitable remedy like the labor injunction was unfair, not the remedy itself. Progressives like Senator Norris went so far as to conclude that the AFL's campaign for immunity was both absurd and infeasible. First, it was absurd because no group or organization could ever be considered above the law—whether it be common law, statutory law, or equity law. And second, the AFL's campaign was infeasible because the conservative courts would use this naive conclusion to strike down all reform efforts.

To many progressives, the AFL's practice of business unionism meant that it had foolishly misplaced its faith in the marketplace. They thought that the law should regulate the economy. To them, reforming procedures in equity, common law, and statutory law could help regularize the collective bargaining process. It was on the issues of economics, policy, and procedure that progressives disagreed with the AFL and advanced responsible unionism.

## CHAPTER 3

# Responsible Unionism

## *The Progressive Conception of Union Liability*

Labor cannot afford to jockey itself into the position of a special interest, insistently demanding what it concedes to be for its own good and reflecting general good. . . . Organized labor has political responsibilities as well as political rights.

—*New Republic*, 1919

In 1922, the U.S. Supreme Court upheld the "enormous verdict of $600,000" against the United Mine Workers of America. This ruling, the *United Mine Workers of America v. Coronado Coal Company*, caused a public uproar.[1] Some journalists speculated that it would "arouse [the workers] as the *Dred Scott* decision fired the liberty-loving men and women of America and as the infamous *Taff-Vale* decision in 1901 spurred the British toilers to action."[2] Others feared that "at last capitalism ha[d] found a way to kill the labor-union movement."[3] Meanwhile, members of the business community hostile toward labor rejoiced. A reporter for the *Los Angeles Times*, a newspaper that never hid its antagonism toward labor, wrote: "This decision, stripping away the special privileges heretofore extended the unions through political cowardice, places upon them full responsibility for their deeds."[4]

Neither organized labor's fears nor industry's hopes about damage suits ever materialized. Ironically, what made the *Coronado* decision important was not that unions could be sued for damages but that it helped establish a legal relationship between the unincorporated union and its membership that would later regularize the collective bargaining process. This decision justifiably outraged the mainstream labor movement by undermining voluntarism and thwarting the practice of business unionism, or the idea that collective bargaining should be market-driven, but instead of undermining unionism, as Gompers predicted, it helped institute what is identified here as the precursor of "responsible unionism."[5] It did so because organized labor's new identity would give the state an active role in the collective bargaining process. The state—embodied by either state and federal courts or administrative agencies—determined whether a union had the authority to represent its membership on a case-by-case basis.

This idea about organized labor's identity in the *Coronado* decision was reached not by the conservative justices on the Supreme Court but as a result of a consensus with their progressive brethren. It was on the urging of the progressive justice Louis D. Brandeis that the Supreme Court, led by the conservative chief justice William Howard Taft, decided unanimously that unions could be sued for damages in civil suits.[6] For Brandeis, the issue of personality should not be questioned by the Taft Court. He had long contested the AFL's fears about incorporation, arguing that accepting partial liability for its membership was the union's best defense against the labor injunction. As Felix Frankfurter, a legal realist, explained, "The real problem . . . is not to deny that a trade union *is*, but to work out the legal scope of its activities."[7]

Brandeis, an early espouser of responsible unionism, had little trouble persuading Taft, who wrote the *Coronado* decision, that unincorporated unions could be held accountable for their actions. Reluctant to ascribe to unincorporated associations a distinct personality, Taft made unions liable by employing the principles of agency. Unlike incorporation, these principles held unions accountable without assigning the status of agent specifically to the union. This type of law provided unions with legal standing as agents and principals, because of relationships they entered into both with and on behalf of their members. Under these principles of agency, the labor union, or indeed any voluntary association, sustained a *temporary* legal relationship with its members. Labor leaders or individual union members had standing to sue an employer under common law or seek an injunction in a court of equity.

The Taft Court's use of agency reflected the evolution of a progressive ideal in legal history, not legal precedent. That is, the consensus that the progressive and conservative justices reached was found in the decisions of some judges who built a progressive idea of limited union liability into law. Like Brandeis and Taft, these state and federal court judges relied on agency theory as a means of circumventing the incorporation dilemma. When union members sued employers for a breach in a collective bargaining agreement, these judges ignored the issue of personality and used agency law to establish the union as a competent contracting party. Instead of granting unions fictitious corporate personalities, they depended on agency law to hold unions accountable without assigning the status of agent specifically to the union.

Unlike the *Coronado* decision, however, these state and federal court cases established the union as the party plaintiff, not the defendant. A small number of state and federal judges quietly cultivated a progressive conception of union liability from the established common-law category of agency. On the one hand, the legal theory of agency provided unions with the authority to contract collective bargaining agreements for their members. Either the union or its members could hold an employer responsible for violating such an agreement. On the other hand, agency law made unions (as well as their members) liable as defendants for damages incurred during labor disputes. To regularize organized labor's position under law, certain members of the judiciary promoted the ideas underlying responsible unionism.[8]

As some state and federal court judges experimented with union liability, only occasionally finding middle ground with some judges who followed classical legal orthodoxy, the AFL stood firmly behind its position of voluntarism. Gompers encouraged neither the union as an entity nor its members singly to enter a courtroom.[9] Yet competition with the judges who rendered these progressive decisions alone did not obstruct the AFL's voluntarist avenue of reform and give birth to responsible unionism. These decisions, particularly the first *Coronado* decision, raised important issues that sparked a heated public debate. The conservative courts, most notably the Supreme Court, compounded the issues in this debate by condemning the AFL's efforts to obtain absolute freedom of association. During the 1920s, by arguing that unions must be accountable for their activities in interstate commerce, the Court rendered decisions that undermined the labor provisions in the Clayton Antitrust Act, the primary legislation protecting organized labor. The AFL's problem with the conservative courts bolstered the progressives' determination that unions accept a limited conception of liability not in common law but in statute.

To the progressives, law revolved around questions of explicit and implicit state policy, whereas, in Oliver Wendell Holmes's words, "judges are shy of reasoning from such grounds."[10] Common law emerged from formal logical patterns derived from natural rights. For this reason, these progressives thought that an emphasis on the functionalism of common-law concepts like agency and personality, not a change in substantive public policy, would help them break through the orthodoxy of the conservative courts in their attempt to set the agenda for statutory reform in labor law.[11] They took advantage of a "space for formation"[12] outside both organized labor's and the state and federal courts' interpretations of labor law to develop their own theory of trade union legitimacy.[13] Yet the progressives' use of established legal categories was not the only irony in the development of responsible unionism. Their effort to make the private law of market relations more equitable in a long struggle between "progressive" and "classical" legal thought helped create a theory of trade union legitimacy that, when cast in public terms, proved highly intrusive on organized labor's sense of its own legitimacy and, ultimately, confining.

## Political Responsibilities as Well as Political Rights

From 1900 until 1935, progressive state and federal court judges developed a subtle reform of labor law that fell somewhere between repudiation of the labor injunction and immunity for organized labor. They exchanged one form of legal restraint—the injunction—for another—the enforceability of collective bargaining agreements. While the progressives knew better than to expect antiunion employers to consider this an even exchange and abandon the labor injunction, they nonetheless hoped to regularize or legitimize the collective bargaining process. Organized labor, some judges and jurists decided, would profit from being credited with a functional description of its accountability. As it was, the AFL was being attacked for its attempts to be acknowledged as a special class deserving of immunity under law.[14]

Building a progressive policy about labor law, these judges and justices on state and federal courts acknowledged that unions had the legal authority to negotiate collective bargaining agreements. In other words, they bypassed the formal condition that as unincorporated associations the unions had no authority to negotiate these agreements. Some courts refused to enforce collective trade agreements, reasoning that the unions' original composition as bodies of people lacking any concurrence of wills gave them no competency to contract.[15] Others ruled that the agreement itself could not be enforced since it lacked mutuality of obligation and remedy.[16] Progressive jurists like Wesley Sturges underscored the state and federal courts' "remarkable lack of uniformity" about organized labor's legal standing. "There is no reason," he argued, "[for the judiciary to hold] that an unincorporated association is not a legal entity."[17] The conservative courts did so as a "method of statement" justifying their decision under common law but, more important, indicating their predisposition not to accommodate organized labor. According to John Dewey, the courts manipulated the issue of legal personality, or the lack of it, to further their own political purposes.[18]

By contrast, some judges and justices did not allow the issue of organized labor's personality to stop them from recognizing organized labor's contractual authority. Although they never settled who would act as agent and who represented the principal, these judges tried to regularize collective bargaining by emphasizing organized labor's capacity during the collective bargaining process. To do so, some judges and justices grounded this authority in agency law, describing the relationship as one of an agent who agrees to act for, and under the direction of, a principal in order to enforce agreements.

Once introduced, agency offered the courts a new direction in labor law. If a court established that individual workers had ratified a collective trade agreement or had given a union prior authority to represent them in a process of negotiation, an unincorporated union could be perceived as a competent agent. The court confirmed the union's liability for injury by evaluating its collective bargaining activities. As long as the court was satisfied that the union truly represented its membership, the union needed no fictitious personality to negotiate collective trade agreements. The issue of liability stemming from the union's personality as an incorporated association could be ignored.

Slowly and quietly, a progressive approach to labor law reform matured, and agency principles emerged as a general legal mechanism through which courts could ensure union accountability. This established a new, and malleable, linkage between unions and labor dispute activity. Judges serving on state and federal courts counted on the principles of agency to demonstrate how the unincorporated union, as a party plaintiff, could be regarded as a competent bargaining agent. Feeling that they would thus have the power of the state behind an agreement gave workers incentive to join a union. The courts regularized collective bargaining by enforcing these agreements either for unions or for their individual members. In some cases, these courts issued injunctions against employers who broke such agreements. In others, they made the employer compensate an individual worker for damages.

### The Theory of Usage and Custom

The theory of usage and custom formed the first doctrinal alternative to conventional contract theory to be employed by some progressive state and federal courts in labor relations matters.[19] In 1907, the Alabama state supreme court decided, in *Byrd v. Beall*, to enforce a collective trade agreement that had been negotiated by an unincorporated labor union.[20] This court categorized as a usage or custom some trade agreements that established work conditions for a collective of workers. Usage or custom, as the Alabama state court defined it, created a "method of dealing, adopted in a particular place, or by those engaged in a particular vocation or trade, which acquires legal force, because people make contracts in reference to it."[21] In *West v. Baltimore* (1927), in the West Virginia Court of Appeals, Judge William N. Miller ruled that a railroad carman could not sue the Baltimore & Ohio Railroad Company and the Brotherhood of Railway Carmen for being furloughed unless he had been party to the trade agreement between these two.

In practice, the categories of usage and custom supplemented rather than replaced individual employment contracts. Thus, in *Hudson v. Cincinnati, N. O. & T. R. Co.* (1913), the Kentucky Court of Appeals ruled that a usage supplemented an individual employment contract by, for example, providing guidelines for disciplining and discharging employees or establishing work conditions, hours, or wages. The individual employment contract remained the sign of employment. In *West v. Baltimore*, Judge Miller held that a usage or a custom must be incorporated into an individual employment contract before it could be considered binding.[22] The worker, therefore, received no protection from the union-negotiated contract per se. "There is here no evidence that the plaintiff had voted for the contract under which he claims seniority rights." Miller explained that "the arrangement as to seniority was between the brotherhood and the railroad company, not between plaintiff and the company."[23] There were other limitations. Because the courts regarded it as part of an *individual's* employment contract, the usage or custom lent no contractual character to the relationship between the union and its members. A worker who questioned the union's seniority rules, for instance, could not be held responsible for violating a trade agreement negotiated by his or her union. Thus, in *Hudson*, the Kentucky Court of Appeals ruled that the trade agreement negotiated by a brotherhood imposed no rights or duties upon its union members.[24] Each railway worker had to incorporate the trade agreement negotiated by the union into his individual employment contract before it would be upheld by law.[25]

Indeed, whether workers recognized and ratified their union's trade agreement became the controlling issue in most state and federal court cases that invoked usage or custom theory. In 1904, the Missouri Supreme Court had heard *Burnetta v. Marceline Coal Co.*, in which the defendant, the employer, tried to prove that a usage bound the plaintiff, a workman, to abide by a union-negotiated trade agreement. Evidence showed that the defendant asked the plaintiff whether he knew "the rules of the employment contract." But the Missouri state court held that the mere statement "I understand the rules" was not "to be construed as an agreement to labor under these certain rules. A contract [to work] under the rules of an organization is not to be inferred from a simple fact that he is a member of the organization."[26] Citing this case, the Kentucky Court of Appeals ruled in *Hudson*, and again in *Piercy v. Louisville & Nashville Railway* (1923), that without positive evidence of a worker's ratification, individual employment rules took priority.[27]

The more conservative federal courts and the majority of the state courts applied the category of usage or custom rarely, the U.S. Supreme Court never. Nor did the state courts that enforced trade agreements ever take the category's doctrinal development very far, for its limitations were too obvious. Usage or custom provided no means of closing the circle of accountability around an employer, union members, *and* a union. Under the category of usage or custom, the union could be recognized as neither principal nor agent. The enforceability of the agreement depended wholly on the membership's unanimous support for it. If one worker challenged the agreement, it would not be enforced.

### Third-Party Beneficiary Theory

Third-party beneficiary theory became a second progressive means by which some state and federal court judges enforced collective trade agreements.[28] This route was first taken in 1914, when a progressive New York Supreme Court justice ruled, in *Gulla v. Barton*, that a trade agreement had legal weight because it constituted a "contract made by [the employee's] representative for his benefit." In this case, Joseph Gulla, a member of the United Brewery Workmen of America, recovered damages for the violation of his individual rights under a collective trade agreement. The New York Supreme Court awarded Gulla the difference between the wages he received and those that had been negotiated by the union. Gulla knew nothing of the trade agreement that gave the brewery employees higher wages than his individual employment contract did. The New York court held, "We have, therefore, a situation where the plaintiff received from week to week the wages contemplated by the contract of employment between him and the defendant, and his union unbeknown to him had made a contract for his benefit, based upon a separate consideration passing from the union, that he as a member thereof should receive a greater compensation."[29]

Like the state courts that enforced trade agreements by categorizing them as a usage or custom, the New York Supreme Court demanded evidence that the brewery union acted on the worker's behalf.[30] Unlike usage or custom theory, however, third-party beneficiary theory imposed no obligation upon the party (i.e., the union member) who benefited from the agreement: union members were passive third parties; unions were both principal *and* agent. In *Gulla v. Barton*, the New York Supreme Court awarded a union member damages when an "employer" violated the trade agreement.[31]

Only workers profited from their union's negotiation of a collective bargaining agreement. Third-party beneficiary theory held employers liable for their own breaches of agreements but allowed them no remedy against individual workers' breaches. The employer could sue the negotiating union only for a violation of the agreement.[32] Just as when applied to corporate law, third-party beneficiary theory offered the individual players—in this case the workers covered by the agreement—great protection without personal liability.

Given these implications, only a few state tribunals, most notably New York and Ohio, used third-party beneficiary theory to enforce trade agreements. Like usage or custom, though in a different way and with different consequences, the doctrine failed to close the accountability circle around all three relevant parties. In particular, third-party beneficiary theory underscored the union's unincorporated status. As a legal jurist wrote, "There is no indication that any consideration was given to the question of how an association, presumably incompetent to contract on its own behalf, could enter into a contract on behalf of third parties."[33]

### Agency Theory

Agency theory was the third and final means employed by state and federal court judges to enforce collective trade agreements.[34] Like usage or custom, agency theory did not recognize the union as a party to a contract. The union itself asserted no rights under a trade agreement; only its members gained these rights. The union's role was confined to negotiation and administration of the contract *for* its members. The court recognized the union as the negotiating agent for workers in a particular firm or factory and clarified the lines of accountability.

The application of agency theory to labor law was first explained in 1909, in the Sixth Circuit Court of Appeals' decision in *Barnes v. Berry*. In this decision, the court refused to enjoin members of the International Printing Pressman Union for breaching a trade agreement, because they had not ratified this agreement.[35] District judge Andrew M. J. Cochran, the appointee of a progressive Republican governor, John Crepps W. Beckham, wrote that "the [International Union] board was not empowered to bind the [local branch of the International Printing Pressman] Union, but had to report what took place between them and the Typothetae committee to the next convention of the Union for its consideration and ratification; and immediately after the contract in question was entered into both of those Unions protested against it on the ground that the Union board had exceeded its authority."[36] The terms of the collective trade agreement, the Sixth Circuit Court ruled, applied to only those union members who sanctioned their union's agreement.[37]

Agency theory rested on proving the union's authority as the workers' agent to enter into agreements on their behalf. In *Schlesinger v. Quinto* (1922), for example, the progressive Appellate Division of the New York Supreme Court first established that the union in question—the International Ladies Garment

Workers' Union—had indeed been chosen to represent the workers' interests, and then it confirmed a lower court decision enjoining an employers' association from violating the trade agreement that it had negotiated with the union.[38] The court, which included Robert F. Wagner, who later sponsored the National Labor Relations Act of 1935, acted on the grounds that the union had the authority to negotiate a binding trade agreement with "the consent of the members." Individual workers had "authorized officials chosen by them through more or less democratic machinery" to represent their interests.[39]

To summarize: three progressive routes to enforcement of collective trade agreements had been attempted selectively by a few state and federal court judges. No composite of the three doctrines could be pasted together, since the judges writing their decisions prescribed different, irreconcilable roles for the union to play in the negotiating process. Usage or custom doctrine ignored the union's role as an official contracting agent and made the trade agreement dependent on the individual worker's continued approval. Third-party beneficiary theory neglected the worker and treated the union as both principal and agent. Agency theory seemed the most promising, in that it recognized the workers as principals and the union as their agent; but the courts demanded ratification before they would recognize a trade agreement as binding, and no standard practice of ratification or authorization was available. Whether the local or the international union represented the worker added to the potential for confusion under agency theory.

### The Liability of Corporations and Unions

The significance of the application of agency law to organized labor becomes most apparent when placed in context with the legal progressives' thoughts about its application to the corporation. In their critique of classical legal orthodoxy from the early twentieth century onward, legal progressives noted how agency law accommodated the corporation, another unwieldy organization, as it negotiated contracts. Walter Wheeler Cook, for instance, traced a development within agency law that undermined the individualism inherent within the will theory of contract.[40] Stockholders, for example, did not necessarily control the activities of their directors. In turn, directors could not monitor their managers' everyday operations. Agency law, Cook argued, had been adapted to recognize the long chain of corporate command. As will theory had heretofore claimed, corporations did not make contracts on the basis of a true concurrence of wills or assent. Contracts could "arise," as Cook explained, "where there has been no mutual assent."[41]

Arthur Corbin, another proponent of legal realism, also highlighted these developments in agency law to show that modern contract law subverted will theory, or the idea that corporations made contracts with the actual consent of controlling parties. As evidence of the changes in agency law, he cited the doctrine of third-party beneficiary to demonstrate that "contractual relations between the offeror and the acceptor may also operate to create rights in a third person." [42] A corporation, for example, could be liable for its workers' actions even if the shareholders had not conferred actual authority or given their consent to a specific contract as will theory demanded. "By being assigned," Corbin explained, "a debtor could become bound to pay a perfect stranger." [43]

With will theory and agency law combined to undermine contract law, Cook and Corbin argued that the courts established a doctrine of "apparent" rather than "actual" authority. In other words, stockholders and directors who owned and controlled corporations failed, in fact, to govern them. Given the complexity of the corporation, Cook and Corbin maintained, patterns of actual authority between contracting parties rarely surfaced in which the stockholders and directors ratified each and every decision made by their managers and employees. Instead, state and federal courts accepted the doctrine of apparent authority that made it more difficult to hold corporations accountable for their activities. Having found evidence to support this theory, Cook and Corbin advocated that the doctrine of apparent authority should increase corporate liability under tort and contract law.

For both Cook and Corbin, the legal justification for the use of apparent authority could be found in the argument that contract law had long been based on the "manifested intentions," as opposed to the particular intentions, of any one player in a corporation. This rendered the source of corporate obligation immaterial. Corbin equated the doctrine of apparent or ostensible authority with the preindustrial age, in which masters had answered for their servants when the latter had been negligent. Similarly, Cook and Corbin thought corporations should rise above the question of fault and be accountable collectively for their stockholders, directors, managers, and employees. The relationship that this enterprise fostered, after all, brought it great benefits or profits. Thus, it could afford to bear a greater degree of responsibility. Legal progressives like Cook and Corbin, among others, developed this "audacious view" into what they called "enterprise liability" in accordance their conception of social justice. [44] As Cook explained, with the reform of labor law legal progressives stipulated what policy they thought should underlie the reform of corporate law.

Although the idea of enterprise liability did inspire the construction of workers' compensation legislation, it failed to widen corporate responsibility under tort and contract law as Corbin and Cook had pictured. Instead, the erosion of the will theory of contract exposed by agency law worked to the corporation's advantage. "On one hand, the corporation made agency law more significant than ever, since the corporation necessarily pursued business through agents," one legal historian describes. "On the other hand, the corporation subverted fundamentally individualistic assumptions behind the law of agency."[45] To hold corporations accountable, judges made legal concepts with the doctrine of apparent authority objective. That is, they utilized the idea of a "reasonable person" instead of identifying the individual actually in command. The doctrine of apparent agency meant that these courts relied on "reasonable, average, or customary practices," rather than actual intent. But instead of holding corporations more accountable for unreasonable practices, in social fact the doctrine of apparent agency gave them more room to maneuver because of the concurrent changes in the theory of corporate personality.

As explained in chapter 2, corporations started receiving charters of incorporation from state legislatures in the 1820s. These charters, issued under the grant theory, recognized the corporation as an artificial creation of the state and therefore directly under the state's jurisdiction. But it had become increasingly difficult to hold corporations accountable. By the 1890s, with the emergence of natural entity theory, agency law, and the so-called corporate veil of liability, if a corporation no longer owed its existence to a state legislature, then it could be released from special duties. Agency law changed the face of the corporate personality, making it into a "supra-individualistic" being that no longer had to take responsibility for its actual intent.[46] At the same time, the corporation's fictitious personality protected it from economic regulation; equal protection under the law and the doctrine of substantive due process thwarted such regulation.

Applying the principles of agency to labor law appealed to the progressives for the same reason as applying them to corporate law: they explained the activities of a large, unwieldy organization. Unlike the development of enterprise liability, the application of agency law to organized labor never subverted will theory.[47] Individualism remained constant because the progressive and conservative courts assessed consent and obligation of the individual worker in determining the enforceability of a collective bargaining agreement. The question of intent was only partially abandoned. The category of usage or custom raised the question of control or fault because the courts demanded proof that the collective bargaining agreement had been ratified by a particular employee. Under this category, the courts saw collective bargaining agreements as complementary to individual employment contracts. Third-party beneficiary theory embraced the doctrine of apparent authority but then provided unions with no exclusive jurisdiction. Like a usage or custom, this theory made individual contracts binding. Finally, agency theory relied on actual authority. Trade union leaders had to demonstrate that their membership had appointed them and had ratified collective bargaining agreements. Individualism remained vital to agency law because neither progressive nor conservative courts settled on a policy similar to enterprise liability.

Neither legal progressives nor other progressives distinguished between control or fault and benefits or profits in the legal relationship between the union and its members, because they could not agree on what type of social duty to assign to organized labor. First, for instance, most progressives denied organized labor the *absolute* freedom of association and the right to strike that the AFL hoped to gain by statute. Rather, they saw industrial disputes as a zero-sum game between labor, business, and consumers.[48] "Immunity" or a "legal exemption" was never the progressives' or legal progressives' policy motto. Large corporations, by contrast, had conservative judges, jurists, and Republican Party leaders intertwining corporate well-being with that of the economy.

Second, whereas progressives and conservatives alike recognized that directors, managers, and stockholders united in a corporation for profit, neither group credited organized labor with fostering the same type of mutually inclusive environment. Progressives who backed organized labor thought individual workers should organize to gain better work conditions, but they opposed sacrificing the worker's autonomy. They rejected the closed shop, for instance, because it violated individual rights of nonunion members. To them, the ratification and authorization of collective bargaining agreements had particular importance.

Third, some state and federal courts used the principles of agency to help them resolve the issue of providing the union, a collective body, with enough authority to formulate enforceable trade agreements. They identified unions as neither a special class under statute nor a fictitious person under common law. Ignoring the question of what rights an unincorporated association possessed in the abstract, they adapted available doctrines—a theory of usage or custom, the third-party beneficiary theory, agency theory—to address the concrete issue of making trade agreements enforceable.[49] The law of agency could be only roughly substituted for personality.

Finally, when the U.S. Supreme Court declared in the 1922 *Coronado* decision that an unincorporated union had enough personality to be held liable for damages, it used the doctrine of actual, not apparent, agency. At first glance, the Supreme Court appears to have used agency law as a procedural tool to determine the liability of these unions. But after the legal reasoning behind the *Coronado* decision is explored, the import of this tool in labor-management relation becomes evident. "The issues are not purely legalistic," wrote several jurists, "but are shot through and through with economic considerations. Moreover, in deciding that a union is suable a court inevitably raises a whole series of questions as to what should be the public policy." [50] Whereas the progressive state and federal courts used agency law with the union member or union as party plaintiff, the Supreme Court relied on it with the union as defendant. [51]

In both the state and the federal courts the doctrine of actual agency was dominant. It accentuated the individualistic notion of intent underlying the union's action. Unions stood little chance of becoming supraindividualistic beings, as corporations had, under this doctrine of agency. This meant that when conservatives, like Chief Justice Taft, joined with progressives to apply the principles of agency to labor law, they gave organized labor no concrete position before common law. "The determinative inquiry," one law student wrote, "must concern itself with the question of authorization." [52] Hence, a court or some administrative body must always be on hand to determine whether the union is authorized to act for its members.

### A Rare Reversal: Coal and Union Culpability in the *Coronado* Decisions

In *United Mine Workers of America v. Coronado Coal Company* (1922) and *Coronado Coal Company v. United Mine Workers of America* (1925),[53] the U.S. Supreme Court, led by William Howard Taft, ruled that unions had fictitious personalities and could therefore be liable as entities in a damage suit under the Sherman Act.[54] Instead of using agency law to supply unions with enough authority to negotiate collective trade agreements, the Court used the law of personality to proclaim that the International United Mine Workers of America (UMW) and local District No. 21 were liable for damages under civil law and the doctrine of "actual" agency to prove their liability. While the Court held neither union accountable in the first *Coronado* decision, a second decision, which brought new evidence to bear, made the local union answerable and caused it to settle with the Coronado Company.[55]

The first *Coronado* case created a heated public debate about organized labor's role in American society. "No case which has recently come down from the United States Supreme Court, with the possible exception of the child labor cases," several commentators from the Chicago bar said, "has been the subject of more general comment, both lay and professional, than the so-called *Coronado* case." [56] Proponents and opponents of unionization immediately made dire predictions about how the *Coronado* decision would affect organized labor.[57] Gompers expressed outrage at the Taft Court, because the *Coronado* decision made unincorporated unions party to civil suits, establishing a precedent that damaged the "very foundation of the organized labor movement of America." [58]

Some supporters of organized labor, namely, the progressives, did not share the AFL's outrage.[59] Frankfurter challenged the idea that unions should be immune from prosecution. By establishing the UMW's liability, the first *Coronado* decision, he thought, represented "a source of gain to labor." This decision pleased Frankfurter because it reflected the influence of Brandeis, an early espouser of responsible unionism, as well as Taft.[60] Wesley Sturges, another legal realist, argued that the *Coronado* decision supplied organized labor with a much needed notion of "association responsibility."[61]

Throughout the 1920s, the Taft Court had an almost permanent minority of three liberal and progressive justices and majority of six conservative justices.[62] But with the *Coronado* decisions, both the progressives and the conservatives agreed that unions could be sued and then used agency principles to determine the extent of the union's liability in a labor dispute.[63] The progressives hoped that it would instill organized labor with a strong sense of social responsibility. They also thought that acceptance of this responsibility, combined with a higher standard of evidence than that employed by the labor injunctions awarded in equity law, would help legitimize organized labor. The conservative justices, meanwhile, always maintained that unions were liable for damages incurred upon business.[64] Taft, moreover, led the conservatives on the Court in concocting a precise equation for labor union activity. When Taft wrote *American Steel Foundries v. Tri-City Council*, about peaceful picketing, Willard Atkins and Reed Kitchen, progressive jurists, explained that "even though it be true that peaceful picketing in practice means that labor is allowed an exceedingly limited range of activities, it is one thing to say, 'Go ahead as far as you go ahead peacefully'; it is another thing to say, 'You cannot use picketing at all.'"[65] To explain why the Court offered this picketing formula, these progressives wrote that "coercion or the appearance of it is a thing to be conserved and used only to the extent it is necessary."[66]

Despite the AFL's fear that the *Coronado* case would deplete strike funds and destroy the labor movement, few courts followed the federal precedent establishing organized labor's limited liability. First, state courts, like the North Carolina court, ignored the *federal* precedent, suggesting that "the holding is controlled by the provisions of paragraphs 7 and 8 of the antitrust law."[67] Federalism limited the import of the *Coronado* decision.[68]

Second, the question of organized labor's legal standing had been motivated by policy or politics and not by common-law precedent. Wesley Sturges, for instance, explained that "the union's position as an unincorporated association gave it no immunity at law." Enabling statutes existed in many states, moreover, giving employers the opportunity to sue a union as an organization. "If any court has decided that the association cannot sue or be sued," Sturges argued, "there is no reason, no justification for the court having made such decision. . . . *The only answer in such case is: because it has.*"[69]

Third, most antiunion employers rarely brought unions before civil courts. They preferred the labor injunction because it provided swift relief, forestalling unionization more effectively than damage suits could. Damage suits were unwieldy, and these antiunion employers might not be able to collect the damages awarded by a court. After all, the use of criminal conspiracy had been abandoned, in part, because it proved too clumsy.[70]

The significance of the *Coronado* decision rested not on the Taft Court's new interpretation of the union's common-law standing or in the precedent this decision found. Rather, the decision represented a watershed in labor history because of the tremendous debate it stimulated about labor law reform. In particular, it brought the latent debate between the AFL and some progressives to the foreground. The AFL, progressive judges and jurists, and progressive legislators fought over the union member's legal status. While the AFL saw the *Coronado* decision as a defeat, legal progressives and progressive legislators thought it provided organized labor with the opportunity to become a legitimate, *public* player.

Because they understood the Taft Court's opposition to class legislation and its position on freedom of contract, which stopped the Court from recognizing unions as beyond the reach of labor law, the progressives thought the *Coronado* decision gave organized labor an effective means of pursuing labor law reform. Sturges, for example, articulated how agency law in the *Coronado* decision embodied the notion of union representation. "Representatives are deemed to represent the association," he said, "that is, all the associates, and the decree or judgment which determines their rights, concludes all as respects the common interest."[71] Noting the same connection between common law and statute, a law student wrote that the question of union liability and agency law revolved around the issues of authorization and ratification, which less than ten years later gave progressive legislators the blueprint for the Norris-LaGuardia Anti-Injunction Act.[72]

When the first *Coronado* case came to the Supreme Court in 1921, the justices concentrated primarily on two questions: First, could the Coronado Coal Company sue an unincorporated union (the UMW), and second, had the International UMW or local District No. 21 restrained interstate commerce?[73] In its decision, the Taft Court unanimously recognized the Coronado Coal Company's right to sue both the International UMW and the local UMW but then found them free from liability in this particular dispute.[74] Brandeis, who often led the progressive minority on the Court, was instrumental in gaining the chief justice's concurrence on the second point.[75]

To justify the Court's position that the UMW could be sued, Taft opined that Congress, presumably, had no intention of allowing large, unincorporated associations to commit illegal actions with impunity.[76] In a dictum, he explained that "undoubtedly at common law, an unincorporated association of persons was not recognized as having any other character than a partnership in whatever was done, and it could only sue or be sued in the names of its members, and their liability had to be enforced against each member. But the growth and necessities of these great labor organizations have brought affirmative legal recognition of their existence. . . . We think that such organizations are suable in the federal courts for their acts, and that funds accumulated to be expended in conducting strikes are subject to execution in suits for torts committed by such unions in strikes."[77] Taft mentioned few common-law precedents, relying instead on the argument that unions had been tacitly recognized as legal entities in the Clayton Act of 1914 and the Transportation Act of 1920, among other pieces of national legislation.[78] He derived their personality from what one contemporary commentator described as the legislative and executive regulation of labor "after referring to acts of Congress, recognizing trade unions, authorizing incorporation of trade unions, admitting representatives of organized labor to a commission on labor relations and providing for action by the Railroad Labor Board."[79] Taft also referred to the *Taff Vale Railway Co. v. Amalgamated Society of Railway Service* decision in England that rendered unions per se accountable in civil suits.[80]

After some trepidation, the Court's progressive minority joined its conservative majority in recognizing union liability.[81] Brandeis, who had called for the incorporation of unions since 1902, persuaded them. Extending charters of incorporation would have made organized labor responsible for its activities, and this type of responsibility reflected the progressive jurisprudence he and Oliver Wendell Holmes, among others, helped construct between the 1890s and the 1930s. They thought private interests, such as individual or collective contracts sought after by business and labor, should always be open to legal scrutiny. Trade unions, Brandeis said, "need something to protect them from their own arbitrariness."[82]

Brandeis realized, however, that a conservative judiciary might seize on incorporation as a way to hold unions liable in damage suits indiscriminately, and this realization convinced him to be more cautious. In 1920, upon first hearing that then Chief Justice Edward D. White planned to uphold the lower courts' decisions, he prepared a dissent. Any expansion of federal court jurisdiction under the Sherman Act against organized labor, he thought, would be disastrous.[83] But in 1922, when Taft declared that the union could be brought before the court as an entity and that both the International UMW and District No. 21 had violated the Sherman Act, Brandeis reversed his position. According to Dean Acheson, Brandeis's law clerk, the justice now joined Taft's majority in an attempt to limit union culpability.[84]

Before voting with the majority, Brandeis convinced Taft to change his mind about the UMW's responsibility for property damages during the *Coronado* dispute. First, on a substantive level, he persuaded Taft that District No. 21 had participated in a local strike and therefore could not be held accountable for restraint of interstate commerce.[85] In his earlier dissent, Brandeis wrote that "the wrongdoers conspired to prevent the operation of the plaintiffs' mines and in large part destroyed them. But their conspiracy was not to restrain interstate commerce."[86] Although he had opposed the distinction between manufacturing and mining in *Hammer v. Dagenhart*, a child labor case, Brandeis applied it here to organized labor's advantage. Brandeis distinguished the *Coronado* case from *Loewe v. Lawlor*, in which the Court found that the AFL had conducted an illegal boycott that restrained interstate commerce.[87] If the Court held the UMW, District No. 21, or any locals liable under the Sherman Act, unions would be liable, in effect, for all damages incurred during such disputes.

Second, in terms of the procedural law of agency, Brandeis persuaded Taft that the International UMW could not be held liable for the local union's activities unless it expressed intent to restrain interstate commerce. Brandeis tempered his conception of union culpability with the doctrine of "actual" as opposed to "apparent agency." The international would have had to direct District No. 21 and its locals. "The protection of the first *Coronado* decision remained available to unions whose leaders either had no falling-out among themselves," as Alexander Bickel explained, "or kept their mouths shut."[88] With the International UMW doing just that, "there was no evidence from which the jury could infer 'actual agency' by the District No. 21," Frankfurter argued, "and without such 'actual agency' by the district in carrying out the authority of the International the latter is not chargeable for the autonomous action of the district."[89]

In the end, the Court's interpretation of substantive *and* procedural law determined the outcome in the *Coronado* decision. It was the combination of the Court's ruling on the inapplicability of the Sherman Act, the suability of the union per se, *and* the doctrine of actual agency that distinguished this decision. Aware of the import of agency, Frankfurter wrote in the *New Republic* that "the great gain to labor of this ruling can be best measured by contemplating the consequences of the reverse."[90] When the two lower courts handed down their respective decisions, he explained, they had ignored actual agency. Instead, they had based their rulings on a broad definition of restraints in interstate commerce under the Sherman Act on procedural provisions included in the common law of personality, and on the doctrine of apparent agency. These courts had made the International UMW and District No. 21 responsible because of the former's "power of discipline, secured to it under the union's constitution," as well as its "nation-wide aims."[91] Organized labor's intent could be discerned from the particular union's constitution, which defined its personality or legal identity.

In offering what Frankfurter described as a "rare" unanimous reversal of two lower courts, the Taft Court gave "large freedom of action to local unions."[92] The International UMW and District No. 21 operated independent of each other. "If the decisions of the lower Court had been allowed by the Supreme Court to stand," Frankfurter elaborated, "every local strike conducted by workers affiliated with a national or international union, and in furtherance of a common purpose, would subject the International to liability for money damages or—still worse—to injunction."[93]

Concurrent developments in corporate law also underscored the significance of the Court's use of the doctrine of actual agency. By contrast, most state and federal courts no longer applied this doctrine to determine corporate responsibility. The activity of the corporation in question could be brought properly before a court only if its personality had been established. The law of agency, understood as actual agency, was subordinated to the law of personality because of the doctrine of apparent agency. Corporations accepted responsibility for the activities of their members, including stockholders, directors, managers, and employees. These developments indicated, moreover, that under common law, the corporation had acquired a relatively stable relationship with its directors, shareholders, and managers. Stockholders, directors, and employees became involved in a corporation with an understanding of this relationship. Stockholders who acted as principals profited from limited liability, since the public policy undergirding corporate law openly protected them to ensure continued investments, which, after all, promoted the public good of a healthy economy.

Organized labor, on the other hand, profited from no such fixed relationship under statute or in common law. First, the question of whether the international or the local could be the individual union member's agency muddled the relationship. Second, union leaders lacked knowledge of their relationship to their members; they could not anticipate the Supreme Court's reaction to collective action. These leaders also had no bargaining power over employers in anticipation of due process under common law. Unlike the law of personality and agency for corporations, in which the doctrine of apparent authority was used to determine corporate liability, the Court traced the international union's accountability through its "actual," or expressed, authority. In other words, the International UMW could not be held responsible for damages during a strike unless its leaders had specifically told the leaders at District No. 21, who then informed their members, to incur these damages. "There is no need normally to decide this question," a law student wrote in *Columbia Law Review*, "on the basis of equivocal manifestations of 'approval.'" As he illustrated, "the following facts were held to be insufficient to show that the International union had approved of the local union's conduct: (1) an officer of the International union had knowledge of the wrongful acts and did nothing; (2) statements approving the behavior in question had appeared in the official journal of the International union; (3) no disciplinary action was taken against the local; (4) the conduct of the local had benefitted from the International body."[94] The actions of the international or the local action, not the "manifested intentions" declared in the UMW's constitution, determined whether either union paid damages.

Whereas the law governing corporations used the procedural categories of personality *and* agency, the *Coronado* decisions made them more distinct. As stated above, the doctrine of actual authority, which had been all but discarded in corporate law, determined the UMW's liability. On the one hand, this doctrine demanded a greater standard of proof. To be liable, the international must have directed and ratified the local's actions during the strike. On the other hand, it meant that the Court formulated no notion of limited liability. The international and the local unions' directives would be assessed in each case at bar. Each union had only a temporary line of authority and therefore a corresponding amount of liability. Whereas under corporate law shareholders and directors had been assigned specific relationships in the corporation, the different layers in unions, the international and the local, made the notion of agency all the more unstable and fluid.

### No Veils for Labor

The temporary nature of organized labor's authority became apparent just three years later, when the Coronado Coal Company brought new evidence before the Supreme Court. In the second *Coronado* case, the Taft Court ruled, again unanimously, that District No. 21, but not the International UMW, harbored the intent to restrain interstate trade. The Coronado Coal Company prevailed because it had obtained information from a disgruntled union officer who indicated that without a doubt the local union had directed the violence against the mines.

After sifting through the evidence with great caution, the Court responded negatively about the international's involvement. "Evidence of participation by [the UMW's] president was insufficient," Taft wrote, "to show participation by the organization itself or to bind it on principle of agency."[95] Unlike a corporation, the union was not bound by its officers' actions *as such*: evidence was required that the union's actions had been ratified or endorsed in each particular instance before liability could be demonstrated.[96] As Taft put it, in a unanimous decision, "In our previous opinion we held that a trade-union, organized as effectively as this United Mine Workers' organization was, might be held liable, and all its funds raised for the purpose of strikes might be levied to pay damages suffered through illegal methods in carrying them on; but certainly it must be clearly shown in order to impose such a liability on an association of 450,000 men that what was done was done by their agents in accordance with their fundamental agreement of association."[97] The UMW president, according to Taft, never authorized strike activity on behalf of the international; thus the union itself was not accountable for its members actions.[98] The plaintiff, he explained, had the burden to prove that the union had planned and calculated a strike as part of its "official" business:

> A corporation is responsible for the wrongs committed by its agents in the course of its business, and this principle is enforced against the contention that torts are *ultra vires* of the corporation. But it must be shown that it is in the business of the corporation. Surely no stricter rule can be enforced against an unincorporated organization like this. Here it is not a question of contract or of holding out an appearance of authority on which some third person acts. It is a mere question of actual agency which the constitutions of the two bodies settle conclusively.

Well aware of the problems involved with expressing intent, the UMW had carefully planned the Coronado strike in private. And in the absence of records or proceedings about this strike, the Taft Court had found that it could not be characterized as "official" business. "Actual agency" had not been demonstrated, and union members naturally did not endorse this strike publicly after the fact, particularly since it involved the murder of two nonunion men and the torching and dynamiting of mines—among other acts of destruction by the mine workers themselves. Taft declared that "where wrongful acts have been neither expressly nor impliedly authorized or ratified, the union funds should not be held liable, nor should non-participating members of the union be held responsible."[99]

Even though organized labor's obligation to pay for damages depended on concrete evidence, unions secured only a temporary reprieve from liability. Actual agency provided unions with short-term authority and liability. In the first *Coronado* decision, the UMW hoped that the Court would not recognize its authority to have issued the strike and to have encouraged the workers to wreak havoc on company property. But in the second decision, when new evidence implicated the local union, the Court still would not release either individual union leaders or members from accountability. The Taft Court had "proof of intent of the leaders of District No. 21 to prevent shipments to neighboring states."[100]

Temporary liability meant, in turn, that organized labor had no corporate veil.[101] If a court held a union member liable for damages in an illegal strike, it considered this liability, a personal one. Taft stated that "as a matter of substantive law, all the members of the union engaged in a combination doing unlawful injury are liable to suit and recovery."[102] Limited liability, one of the most beneficial aspects of incorporation, never reached organized labor once the Court recognized unions as suable enterprises.[103] Instead, organized labor and its members remained accountable.

To compensate for organized labor's potentially double liability (which the AFL had well noted) the Court agreed in its first *Coronado* decision that the test to determine this liability was to be conducted not arbitrarily but according to strict rules of evidence. A corporation paid for its members' improper activities, but the courts found no fault or blame for its loss of control. A union, by contrast, could be blamed with the discovery of liability based on intent. In practice, organized labor would rarely be held responsible for damages, but in theory this decision set a dangerous precedent. It also made the public perception of organized labor as reckless and irresponsible seem like the reality, leaving unions vulnerable to state supervision.

### Interweaving Old and New Labor Law

From the outset, the AFL had been far less sanguine than judicial progressives about the course of their jurisprudence, underscoring the dangers lurking in the precedents that the Taft Court had established in the *Coronado* decisions. "The important point of the [first] decision," a perceptive staff member of the AFL wrote, "is that *while it becomes a possibility to sue the union directly, the individual liability of the members apparently may continue in the eye of the court, precisely as theretofore.*"[104] In other words, organized labor was saddled with all of the detriments but none of the advantages of incorporation.[105] Unions as such could be sued for damages incurred during labor disputes. Yet holding the union responsible, as an organization, released none of its individual members from responsibility, since the Court recognized no veil of limited liability covering them. As the AFL staff member elaborated, "the union becomes a corporation so far as service of process is concerned, but its members yet remain a partnership in fact, so far as the liability of each for the acts of the other is involved."[106]

The AFL equated the *Coronado* decision with the *Taff Vale* decision that made unions liable for civil suits in England. According to Gompers, "The

Court has laid down the principle that a voluntary corporation is liable to be held for damages by any act committed by one or a group of its members, no matter how far unrelated they may be in distance or supervision."[107] When this happened in England, however, "within a year Parliament passed the Trade Disputes Act, in which the decision was rectified." Parliament made unions free from civil liability and criminal conspiracy.[108] In the United States, neither Congress nor individual state legislatures had had much success battling equity or specific common-law doctrines.[109] Since the turn of the century, union leaders had called repeatedly for the state and federal courts categorically to abandon the use of all equitable remedies in labor law.[110] "The Clayton Act," Gompers said, "was supposed to have given the wage earners of this country the same protection that the Trade Disputes Act gives the English workers."[111] Throughout the 1920s, when "the federal judges either ignored its provisions or would declare certain portions of it unconstitutional," the AFL continued to issue a blanket denunciation of the labor injunction.[112] Union leaders would settle for nothing less than freeing unions, the ultimate voluntary association, from responsibility under equity.[113] Hence, Gompers condemned Taft for relying on "a precedent in ancient and out-lawed British law findings, ignoring the modern British law, upon which all modern British court decisions have been founded."[114]

Nonetheless, Gompers disagreed with the progressives' idea that unions should be held partially liable.[115] As the *Chicago Tribune* reported, "The contention of the unionists has been that the trade union is an unincorporated association, like a partnership, and could not be held responsible for the acts of its members. Funds owned by the union, under such a doctrine, would be immune, and the individual injured would be held to sue individual members of the union."[116] With the *Coronado* decision, Gompers maintained that "it [was] inconceivable how the Supreme Court [could] rule trade unions" to be liable after the Clayton Act "specifically exempted" them.[117]

Aware of the Supreme Court's actions, most progressives and legal progressives thought the AFL should stop following this path of reform. They thought organized labor must concede established legal doctrines and then circumvent them with a combination of procedural and substantive reforms. Frankfurter warned that "complete immunity for all conduct is too dangerous an immunity to confer upon any group. Psychologically, such a victory would have wreaked its vengeance upon the union and its leaders."[118]

First, all but the AFL thought unions stood little chance of being recognized as beyond the reach of statute, equity, or common law. The U.S. Supreme Court considered attempts to gain immunity not germane—or unconstitutional as class legislation. A reporter for the *Chicago Tribune* wrote that "in contending for immunity from a collective responsibility imposed on other as-

sociations [unions] have raised an issue of class legislation to which no individual could be wisely indifferent."[119] As Frankfurter said, "there is no technical procedural reason why a trade union, like any other association, should
not sue or be sued."

Second, legal progressives like Frankfurter thought the AFL should appreciate the progressive influence in the *Coronado* decision. Brandeis's narrow
construction of the interstate commerce clause, arguing that manufacturing
but not mining fell within its jurisdiction, freed the International UMW from
liability for every strike and boycott instigated by local unions or their members. The difficulty associated with establishing union liability rested not with
the procedural issue of personality but with the use of agency; if the doctrine
of apparent agency had been combined with personality, organized labor would
have been crushed. "If legally responsible," Atkins and Kitchen explained,
"every union would be likely to have its funds enjoined by a bonafide or a
'planted' member."[120]

The Court's reliance on personality *and* agency law meant that it furnished
unions with a test rather than a new status before the common law. With the
doctrine of actual agency the Court implicitly recognized the fluidity of the
collective bargaining process. It determined "if in fact they act as local unions
in a predominantly local controversy and not as the immediate instruments of
their central organization."[121] Only if evidence demonstrated that a union had
requested its membership to participate in certain economic activities *and*, in
turn, if members asked their union to negotiate a trade agreement could legal
accountability be shown. As the Court put it, "liability [would be] sustained
with substantial evidence of the members' participation in or ratification of
torts committed."[122]

The *Coronado* decisions put organized labor on difficult terrain. But, as
Frankfurter correctly anticipated, these decisions gave employers no ready
means of holding unions accountable for damages. Although employers could
pursue three overlapping parties to action—the union, individual labor leaders, and individual members—few did so because they had little hope of re-
covering damages, and the labor injunction proved an effective tool without
the same constraints. The Taft Court's rulings could not be judged in terms of
monetary damages against organized labor but rather in the debate they opened
that constrained its independence.

### Conclusion

The progressive judicial theory of responsible unionism, with
agency law finding the employer and the union accountable, helped shape the
development of the Republican labor policy. After World War I, refashioning

the principles of agency common to all three alternative doctrines for enforcing trade agreements, the Republican Congress developed its own labor policies in the 1920s along the lines of responsible unionism. In the 1920s, this Congress redrafted the principles of agency into a legislative form with the worker representation scheme in both the Transportation Act and the Railway Labor Act of 1926. During World War I, worker representation had prevailed, but it had been voluntary in nature, and the state had played a minimal role. By contrast, the worker representation scheme in the Transportation Act demanded state participation.

Progressives had initiated the application of the principles of agency to labor law to serve as a means of finding a determinate legal relationship between an association and its members. Yet the manner of agency's application created no long-lasting legal relationship. The relationship had to be verified and reverified with each activity in question, reopening the issue of authority and liability. The responsibilities of the International UMW and its district locals could be defined only by the activities of their leaders and members. Room for verification and reverification not only left unions vulnerable to legal action, but it also meant that the American state played an active role in the labor-management relations process.

This state, however, can only be characterized as a liberal, not a corporatist or a corporate-liberal, state. It still championed individual rights inherent in classical liberalism before the rights of any group or association. Unlike state-labor relations in corporatism or corporate liberalism, the individual worker, not the union, was the primary focus of American state-labor relations. Deriving organized labor's identity from the principles of agency meant that the state gave the union only a temporary grant of authority to represent its membership. In other words, the American liberal state emphasized the procedural rights of individual workers. It never gave the union a permanent identity or substantive rights associated with this identity. State involvement in labor-management relations increased the power and authority of the state as it scrutinized organized labor's activities to ensure that unions did not trample on the rights of their members.

CHAPTER 4

# Congress Is as King

## *The Republican Roots of*
## *Railroad Labor Policy*

Facing the opportunities of reconstruction, the United States begins
with politics.
— Norman Hapgood, *New Republic*, 1918

American participation in World War I placed liberalism at a crossroads. The strong state that had been erected to operate the wartime machinery—and the spirit of cooperation this emergency inspired—brought the
state, the business community, and organized labor closer together. A "new
era" began with the coming of reconstruction, however. The congressional
elections of 1918 contributed to the breakdown of wartime cooperation as
Republicans and Democrats struggled over who defined this era. With more at
stake than "politics as usual," members of both parties realized that their success at recasting, reformulating, or restoring American liberalism would determine reconstruction policy.[1] The Republicans won the majority in Congress
with the promise of a "return to normalcy."

Despite the Republicans' campaign for normalcy, reconstruction was not
to return the nation to its prewar position. The railroad labor-management
relations policy established by the Transportation Act of 1920 demonstrated
that while the Republicans rejected redefining liberalism by extending wartime
programs like the Railroad Administration, they reformulated, rather than restored, American liberalism in accordance with their ideology. Faced with the
same constraints about class legislation as the state and federal courts, which
had first articulated responsible unionism, the Republicans furnished the state
with a comprehensive role in labor-management relations. Whereas the judiciary transformed the principles of agency into a general means of holding
unincorporated unions accountable for their actions, Congress recast these
principles so that railroad unions had collective bargaining authority, and also
liability, under a scheme for worker representation. It was this scheme, not the

particular institutional configuration of the Railroad Labor Board as a quasi-judicial agency, that became entrenched in U.S. labor policy.

What made this scheme for worker representation different from others was that, like the doctrine of actual agency, it required state supervision.[2] Organized labor felt the power of the state during the union recognition process as well as during the resolution of labor disputes. Although the Railroad Labor Board used arbitration—a known tool for settling disputes—rather than designing new, innovative machinery, it inaugurated modern labor law by circumscribing organized labor's access to the collective bargaining table. Whether the particular labor policy arbitrated, mediated, or adjudicated labor disputes, organized labor depended on the worker representation scheme for recognition. The Republicans developed a procedure for worker representation that embraced the same notion of temporary authority as the principles of agency sanctioned by the state and federal courts.

But why would the Republicans, striving to return to normalcy, develop such an ambitious labor policy?[3] Divided since 1910, the two dominant factions within the Republican Party, the old guard and the progressives, reunited and began devising this railroad policy in 1919. First, the old guard, which had little sympathy for organized labor, accepted the scheme for worker representation with the hope that it would diminish the strength of the railroad unions, particularly the newly organized shopcrafts workers. Not granting these unions exclusive authority to negotiate collective bargaining agreements, they thought, left room for the formation of company unions. Although they never shed their hostility toward organized labor, the old guard's position marked a significant change. Heretofore, the old guard had relied on equity and common-law remedies (most notably the labor injunction), not legislative solutions, to resolve industrial disputes.

Second, the progressives sanctioned the worker representation scheme because it provided a legislative solution, albeit a second-best one, for addressing the "labor problem." Some progressives thought the postwar policy should overtly recognize the brotherhoods operating the railroads, whereas this scheme lent the operating *and* nonoperating unions, as well as other worker representatives, legitimacy as collective bargaining agents. Organized labor received no exclusive right to represent the railroad workers. These workers, on the other hand, did receive rights, namely, the right to select their own representatives.

Third, the special circumstances surrounding the 1918 election and Woodrow Wilson's wartime presidency insulated the Republicans from normal electoral forces and gave them the opportunity to model the railroad labor policy on their own belief structure. The institutionalization of the House of Representatives and the Senate also made the GOP elite more autonomous within

Congress than ever before. Organized labor and the railroad executives, the constituents of this policy, had little lobbying strength after World War I.

After all the compromises from the legislative battle had been negotiated and settled, the Railroad Labor Board reflected the old guard and progressive Republicans' preference for strong state scrutiny in labor-management relations. Its formulation also exhibited how the Republican Party operated as part of the state.[4] Neither public opinion nor the private lobbying efforts of organized labor or of the railroad industry effectively influenced these policymakers. The party elite, like bureaucratic state managers, embodied the "third agent" promoting such change, independent of interest groups and classes.[5] Just as the Republican Party leadership was not an instrument of the capitalist class, it also was not a tool of the electorate. Yet, unlike bureaucratic state managers, these Republican state agents based their labor-management relations policy on a political ideology, not an ideology of bureaucratic institutionalism or organizational development.[6] That is, the Republicans made the worker representation scheme, which became the backbone of American labor-management relations policy, an expression of their traditional liberal values.

Supposedly, the collective voice of organized labor posed a threat to individual rights. This necessitated the creation of a policy that safeguarded those rights. Accordingly, the Republicans guaranteed freedom of association for workers, not unions. Their new emphasis embodied the paradox within American liberalism. While the liberal state normally derived its identity from society, the Republicans justified expanding the state's power and authority to ensure that workers, who were important members of society, would not surrender their inalienable right to freedom of association. Whereas most studies associate state expansion with a corporate liberal state, this chapter shows that the Republicans increased the power and authority of the traditional liberal state.

Being grounded on a political ideology of traditional liberalism rather than an ideology of organizational development explains the Republicans' broad influence on the development of modern labor-management relations. If the Republicans had built a new bureaucratic apparatus that did not become part of the American ideology as the Democrats' wartime labor relations machinery had during World War I, undoubtedly it would have been dismantled by the Democrats once they came into office during the New Deal. As it was, the Republicans created a labor-management relations policy that depended on liberal values that were the intellectual property of neither the Republicans nor the Democrats. When the Democrats developed their own labor-management relations policy, they decided that it was politically expedient to retain these values.

## Roads Not Taken

The traditional liberal underpinnings of the Republican railroad labor-management relations policy were not a foregone conclusion. Aside from the labor policy the Republicans formulated themselves, two other policy options, each reflecting a distinct ideology, stood before them. First, these Republicans could have re-created the pre–World War I Democratic policy that roughly resembled the trade union policy in Britain, constructed on a theory of voluntarism.[7] In both the United States and the United Kingdom, union leaders initially wanted voluntarism to prevail because it gave them, not the state, the leverage necessary to pressure employers to sit at a collective bargaining table.

Second, the Republicans might have proclaimed that Wilson's wartime industrial relations policies had been a successful corporatist experiment and extended them during peacetime, as the Netherlands and Germany had done with their own corporatist wartime programs.[8] During World War I, Wilson co-opted the AFL and the railroad brotherhoods, among other members of the mainstream American labor movement, and made them functional representatives of the public good. That is, he invited them to offer their expertise and to advise the government about labor, both organized and unorganized.[9] Wilson needed organized labor's support to pull the country out of its isolationist position; in turn, labor leaders wanted him to institute policies that protected organized labor's right to bargain collectively without violating its organizational autonomy. Both Wilson and union leaders profited from their new relationship.

Dissatisfied with these policy choices, and the ideologies behind them, the Republicans constructed a different policy for the railroad industry that reflected responsible unionism, the judiciary's new vision of organized labor and labor law. On the one hand, the old guard and progressive Republicans thought the public interest demanded that unions in the railroad industry be regulated, not released from responsibility or co-opted. To them, the public interest should not be perceived as an abstract ideal. They built their conception of American liberalism on the premise that individual rights should not be sacrificed to promote the rights of any one class. In the context of labor-management relations, this meant that the public interest left freedom to contract unimpeded.

On the other hand, the Republicans balked at equating organized labor's interests with the public interest.[10] They chose not to develop a corporatist industrial relations policy, like the wartime industrial relations policies in the United States, the Netherlands, or Germany. According to the Republicans, organized labor lacked the will and the capacity to represent the public interest. Both the old guard and the progressives had little regard for self-interested classes—be it a class of workers, organized into unions, or a class of employers—and often made distinctions between self-interested classes and public interest organizations. The corporation, for example, was thought to embody the public interest, and for this reason, the American state recognized it, albeit informally, as a functional representative of the public good. The AFL and the railroad brotherhoods, by contrast, never received such an acknowledgment from the Republicans, who considered organized labor inherently self-interested and unable to represent the greater good. To the Republicans, the public interest stood for more than the sum total of private contractual interests. Employers, workers, and unions should sacrifice their self-interests for the greater good. A state regulatory apparatus should be on hand to ensure that organized labor behaved "responsibly" and did not undermine the public interest.

### Factionalism, Reunification, and the Postwar Republican Ideology

Beginning in 1917, the progressives reestablished their ties with the old guard in the hope of bringing the Republican Party to power in Congress, carrying the next presidential election, and drafting reconstruction policy.[11] Above all, the progressives and the old guard knew they must reunify the GOP to restore its hegemony in national politics.[12] Because neither faction had gained support since the 1912 election, the progressives found the old guard's patronage necessary to the party; likewise, the old guard needed the progressives' backing in the polls to regain the majority in Congress and the White House.[13] After extensive negotiations in late 1917, these two factions reunited and recaptured Congress.[14]

To underscore the new spirit of reconciliation, former president William Howard Taft, the leader of the old guard, met with former president Theodore Roosevelt, who had challenged him during the 1912 Republican convention.[15] The old guard also solicited the progressives' support in electing a national party chairman. But after a dispute staged by Roosevelt, George Perkins, Harold Ickes, and Senator William E. Borah, the progressives' candidate, William Hays, a moderate Republican, prevailed against John T. Adams, the old guard's favorite son.[16] The old guard tempered the progressives' victory, however, by diminishing Hays's formal power as national party chairman.[17]

Immediately after Hays's election, the progressives and the old guard began their congressional campaign. Despite some lingering animosity, in 1918 these two factions rediscovered parts of their Republican heritage. Both factions desired a strong national party organization. Senator Henry Cabot Lodge, the old guard congressional leader, sought such strict party loyalty from the rank and file, for example, that he convinced three progressive candidates to with-draw from primaries.[18] In exchange, the old guard supported the campaigns of some progressive senators from the Midwest and the Far West. Incumbent progressives Borah, George W. Norris, Knute Nelson, and William E. Kenyon and four new Republican progressives won seats in the Senate.[19]

The demand for party loyalty was not unique to the 1918 congressional election, however. Both factions had fought long to maintain a strong, central-ized national party organization. To them, a party should direct rather than re-spond to the public. They harbored elitist views of political representation. "If there is a weakness in representative bodies today," Charles Nagel, an impor-tant old guard member, described, "it is their too ready response to superficial popular demand."[20] Nagel and other old guard members recommended that a group of highly moral men rule the country. A real statesman would not change his public policies in order to meet "each shifting breeze of opinion or puff of passion," Nicholas Murray Butler, an old guard ideologue, opined.[21]

The progressive Republican reformers also held elitist views about political representation. One of the cornerstones of progressivism, the idea of an ad-ministrative state run by experts, contained a deep strain of elitism.[22] Like the old guard, the progressives prided themselves on establishing a national party elite that could direct the public good.[23] Between 1905 and 1913, they fought for antiparty reforms such as the referendum, voter recall, and direct primaries, in an attempt to clean up state and local party politics. Corrupt "bossism," the progressive reformers argued, sacrificed the public interest for groups and classes of constituents.[24] As the progressive Republican senator Robert M. LaFollette Jr. explained, instead of recognizing class or special interests, the "American citizen [should be viewed] as a unit."[25]

The Republican progressives shared more with the old guard, however, than a desire for a centralized national party organization, an elitist conception of political representation, and statism. On the brink of a new era, they hoped to reassociate the Republican Party with industrial change.[26] Initially, the GOP had emerged as a dominant national political party in 1894 and 1896, when both the new industrialists and the wage earners believed that this party had reacted better than the Democrats to the profound industrial changes that swept the country.[27] During these realigning elections, they pushed a nation-alist policy agenda that used federal powers to further economic expansion and industrial capitalism; with it they defeated the Democrats associated with the agrarian populists and the urban immigrant party machines.[28]

The GOP's elitist and nationalist perspective also explained why the pro-gressive Republicans never abandoned their party's economic platform.[29] Un-like the progressive Democrats, the progressive Republicans cultivated a vision of large-scale corporations and "good trusts," regulated by expert administrators, that promoted the public good. The New Freedom coalition of Democratic progressives and William Jennings Bryan's agrarian radicals, in contrast, had insisted that all monopolies were "bad monopolies."[30] Some agrarian radicals attacked capitalism itself, whereas most progressive Republicans hoped to humanize the face of capitalism.[31] As Nicholas Butler described, "The new development is cooperation and cooperation as a substitute for unlimited, unrestricted, individual competition has come to stay as an economic fact."[32] The progressive, regular, and old guard Republicans developed federal economic regulation, for instance, to protect free competition from being crushed by monopolies and to help wage earners collect compensation for accidents at the workplace.[33]

### The Administration Adrift:
### Decentralization and the Democratic Defeat

In the early part of the century, the Democrats shared a desire for a decentralized party organization and limited government; thus from 1896 until 1912, a string of local party organizations constituted the national Democratic Party.[34] In fact, this sectionalism and provincialism paralyzed the party.[35] So it was the progressives' bolt from the Republican Party in 1910, not the political unification of the Jeffersonian populists and the urban immigrant machines, that accounted for President Wilson's election two years later.

Once in office, Wilson faced the daunting task of trying to build a Democratic coalition. The new president put forth a legislative agenda—the New Freedom policy of reform—that attempted to please both the Jeffersonian populists and the urban immigrant machines. But despite his best efforts, Wilson could not unite all the Democratic factions.[36] His coalition collapsed under the pressure of war. First, the midwestern progressive Republicans and the socialists, adopting noninterventionist positions during World War I, abandoned the Democratic coalition. Second, the sectionalism that had weakened the Democratic Party from 1894 until 1912 reemerged when Wilson stopped catering to the special interests of all the sectional party elites.[37] While southern party elites still championed Wilson, party elites from the crucial midwestern states refused to back him.[38]

Thus, in the elections of 1918, the Republican Party profited significantly from the sectionalism dividing the Democrats.[39] In the House of Representatives, the old guard Republicans dominated the Northeast, taking 88 of 119 seats.[40] Similarly, the Republicans took 90 of 105 and 43 of 53 seats in the Midwest and the West, respectively.[41] The Democrats' losses in the West rep-

resented the biggest blow to the party since six years earlier, when they had
held only 15 of the 34 seats. Only the southern vote remained solidly Democratic after the congressional elections.[42]

Aside from sectionalism, the lowest level of two-party competition in American history and a record low voter turnout befell this election. One-party elections prevailed in 30 percent, or 128 districts, of the country.[43] While little two-
party competition had existed in the South since before the Civil War, the
number of one-party elections, with progressive Republicans as the victors
of these districts, increased dramatically in 1918.[44] Almost 25 percent of the
successful candidates won with more than 60 percent of the popular vote.[45]
In addition, 21 percent fewer Democrats participated in the election, with
3,148,000 voting, than in the 1914 and 1916 elections, which had 3,962,000
voting.[46]

After the 1918 elections, the Republicans had 237 of their members in the
House, the Democrats held 193 seats, and minor political parties filled 5 seats.[47]
In the Senate, the Republicans secured a slim majority of 48 to 47. All combined, sectionalism, the lack of two-party competition, unsafe seats, and low
voter turnout helped insulate the Republicans in Congress.[48] "The President had all the strength which comes to a man in that position in time of
war," gloated Senator Lodge, "which was used ruthlessly for the benefit of the
Democratic Party . . . and yet they were beaten."[49] Their huge success in the
election made the Republicans somewhat independent of public opinion, em-
powering them with the capacity to act as state agents and develop a reconstruction policy.[50]

## Congress Is as King

Once in office, the progressive and old guard Republicans tried to
maintain party unity.[51] "[My] one desire," Lodge declared, "[is] to give the
Republican party control in the Senate and maintain its unity on the great issues."[52] To do so, he realized, the old guard must negotiate with the progressives. Twelve senators called themselves progressives; given the slim majority
of two between the majority and minority party, they commanded great institutional leverage. As Lodge said, "[If the GOP] as an organization fails us, there
is nothing else." Similarly, the majority of 237 to 191 in the House, with as
many as 40 progressives, empowered these Republicans.[53] Committed like their
old guard brethren to making the GOP the national party of reconstruction, the
progressive Republicans wielded their power as a swing bloc within the party.[54]
Competition between these two factions helped them shape reconstruction
policy agenda, upstaging the Democratic administration.[55]

Since the progressives might regard his advances with suspicion, to ensure party loyalty Senator Lodge sought help from Hays, who had led both factions through the congressional elections of 1918.[56] These two party leaders understood that Congress had undergone a significant institutional transformation when the Republicans lost their majority in 1910. Although the Democratic caucus that governed Congress while Wilson implemented his New Freedom policy program had permitted the Republicans to delay any resolution, by 1919, the old guard realized that they must now answer the progressive Republicans' call for reform.[57]

First and most important to such reform, the party leadership took seniority into account when they determined committee assignments.[58] The so-called seniority rule professionalized and institutionalized Congress as it loosened the majority party leadership's grip on the rank and file, giving individual members more autonomy.[59] Committee chairmen, not merely party leadership, became the ruling party elite.[60] Until 1925, the Steering Committee rather than the Speaker of the House governed the House of Representatives as the "overlord of all standing committees."[61] Similarly, a conference composed of the majority party elite tempered the Senate leadership's actions.[62]

Second, given the new party leadership structure in the House, Lodge and Hays focused exclusively on recapturing the loyalty of the progressive Republicans in the Senate.[63] In the hope of putting the progressives on the defensive, Hays and Lodge portrayed the conflict that tore apart the GOP as a personal disagreement between Taft and Roosevelt. They put the progressives on the defensive on policy issues, like the tariff or railroad regulation; this minority faction had to explain why it threatened to disobey the "official" party line.[64] Third, the old guard neutralized the progressives by providing their faction with more bargaining power in Congress—they made trusted old guardsmen the chairmen on the most important committees.[65] Fourth, directing the reorganization caucus, Hays and Lodge gave the moderate progressives, who had pledged their loyalty exclusively to the Republican Party in 1918, chairs on the remaining important committees.[66] Finally, after accommodating the moderate progressives in the Senate, the old guard isolated the strident progressive Republicans, namely, Senators Johnson, Norris, Borah, and LaFollette, who threatened their control of the congressional party apparatus.[67]

## Repudiating Democratic Wartime Policies

After reconstituting Congress, the progressives and the old guard stood united in their opposition to Wilson and the Democrats' attempts at reconstruction. World War I ended just one week after the congressional elections, and the GOP forestalled reconstruction in the interim period before the presidential election of 1920.[68] At the same time, the progressives and the old guard party elites blamed the Democratic administration for "unpreparedness for peace" resulting from the absence of a reconstruction policy.[69] As examples of Wilson's unpreparedness for peace, the Republicans pointed to a wave of race riots in the South during the summer of 1919, the high crime rate in urban centers, and inflation that had led to price increases of almost 100 percent since 1914 while wages declined by 10 percent during the same time period.[70] They also exhorted that Wilson's wartime policies contributed greatly to the postwar political and economic turmoil. Wilson's labor policies, the Republicans insisted, recklessly instilled unions with a sense of "arrogance" that, in turn, created industrial chaos.[71]

During the war, Wilson had permitted organized labor a voice in the decision-making apparatus and promoted a policy protecting labor's right to organize and bargain.[72] Even before American intervention in the war, he sought organized labor's backing to help pull the country out of isolationism.[73] With radical unions, like the Industrial Workers of the World (IWW), in opposition to the war, Wilson co-opted members of the mainstream American labor movement only.[74] Once the United States entered the war, Wilson built an administrative agency that endorsed the right to organize and bargain collectively in return for a "no-strike" pledge from the AFL.[75]

Wilson established the War Labor Conference Board to recommend labor policies, and eventually he created the National War Labor Board (NWLB) to follow the principles established by this first board.[76] The NWLB prohibited business and industry from dismissing workers on the basis of their membership in unions, endorsed the eight-hour day, protected a woman's right to equal pay for equal work, promoted collective bargaining, and backed the worker's right to a "living wage."[77] In exchange for organized labor's support, Wilson informally acknowledged union leaders working on this board as functional representatives of the public good.[78] Although the NWLB had no compulsory powers, it created policies that resembled the corporatist policies constructed, for instance, in the Netherlands and Germany. These countries had enhanced organized labor's position during the war by placing its leaders on a number of tripartite boards that constructed economic and social policy.[79]

Through the Railroad Administration Wilson also extended the same rights to railroad workers and sent the same corporatist message to their leaders.[80] William Gibbs McAdoo and his successor, Walter D. Hines, directors general of the Railroad Administration, used this emergency industrial relations policy to place organized labor in a better position in the railroad industry.[81] McAdoo, for instance, issued General Order No. 8, which stated that workers would not be discriminated against "because of membership or non-membership in labor organizations." [82] He also implemented the working conditions and wage rates that organized labor had been striving to achieve before the war. [83] With a series of orders, McAdoo instituted and enforced the eight-hour day, increased wages, equalized wages between men and women and between African Americans and whites, and, finally, increased the number of workers by 8 percent. [84]

Most important, McAdoo negotiated trade agreements with the railroad union leaders—and in so doing, affirmed their authority to speak for the working class. While the four brotherhoods organized 95 percent of the operating railroad workers, the nonoperating class of railroad workers, the shopcrafts workers, had had less success being organized. Before World War I, the railroad executives prevented the railroad labor unions from organizing a majority of the nonoperating railroad workers. They accepted the operating workers, who had been organized since the 1860s and 1870s, and were willing to negotiate collective bargaining agreements with them. But most railroad executives refused to recognize, let alone bargain with, the nonoperating workers. [85] Much to these executives' dismay, McAdoo offered national trade agreements to the operating *and* the nonoperating unions alike. [86]

The nonoperating unions, organized into system federations primarily affiliated with the Railway Executive Department of the AFL, took advantage of this historic opportunity to increase their membership rolls. The protection offered by General Order No. 8, combined with these national agreements, afforded many nonoperating unions, such as the Maintenance of Way, the chance to increase their membership dramatically during the period of government ownership. [87] In 1917 the Maintenance of Way union had 30,000 members; three years later it had 300,000. Similarly, the Brotherhood of Railway Carmen increased its membership fourfold, the Sheetmetal Workers more than tripled their membership, and the Telegraphers' Organization almost doubled their union membership. [88] Unionization increased across the entire industry, but the greatest gains were made in the national unions representing unskilled, nonoperating railroad workers. In all, union membership rose to unprecedented heights during the war: membership increased from 2,370,000 to 4,000,000. [89] For the first time in American history, the federal government facilitated unionization. The Democratic administration protected organized labor, recognized its leaders as team players, and solicited these leaders' advice and support. [90]

## Labor Arrogance and the Postwar Panic

At World War I's end, the Republicans used the historic increase in union membership figures as evidence of how the wartime labor policies had been overly protective of organized labor. [91] While the Democrats suggested that these policies cultivated a spirit of cooperation between federal government, industry, and organized labor and showed how they could work toward achieving a public good like winning World War I, some old guard Republicans thought these policies made organized labor arrogant and irresponsible.[92] Organized labor's newfound relationship with the Democratic administration, they suggested, caused the equally dramatic surge in industrial unrest in 1918 and 1919.

These Republicans had little problem gaining public support for their position about organized labor's "arrogance." A sense of urgency pervaded the nation in 1918 and 1919 when four million workers went out on strike.[93] The fact that many of the strikes involved large industries further intensified the panic. During 1919 alone, nine strikes erupted involving more than 60,000 workers at a time. Six of these large strikes began between August and November, not only exacerbating the public's fears of industrial unrest but also revealing Wilson's inability to resolve this unrest. Moreover, three of the large strikes involved the vital industries of coal, steel, and the railroads.[94] The *Railway Age* reported that "the three eruptions [might have been] directly traced to the unrest which [was] an aftermath of the war."[95]

The Republicans also pointed to the sympathy strikes in 1919 that disturbed the country as further evidence of the recklessness of organized labor.[96] While the AFL and the conservative railroad labor unions strongly opposed the Seattle general strike, as well as most other sympathy strikes, neither the public nor the two mass political parties distinguished between the reformist and the more radical elements of the American labor movement. These strikes, moreover, underscored how little labor leaders could help during a crisis. Gompers, who led the most conservative part of the labor movement, had great difficulties containing the AFL's rank and file. The Republicans, primarily members from the old guard and the business community, used these labor disputes to show the exclusivity, rather than the mutual inclusivity, of organized labor's interests.[97]

Not surprisingly, the Republican Party made these strikes a primary issue (along with the League of Nations) in the first postwar Congress and the presidential campaign of 1920.[98] Promoting a "return to normalcy," the Republican Party leadership successfully adopted an offensive position against the Democratic administration: without discipline, organized labor obstructed industrial progress and terrorized society; only the GOP could be entrusted to restore the progressive vision of "law and order."[99] The Republicans exploited the public's fear about worker militancy and industrial strife to help them reestablish their party's dominance in the national political arena and to lay the groundwork for moving away from the wartime industrial relations policies.[100]

To make matters worse, members of the Democratic administration responded defensively to their opponents' accusations that the wartime policies had caused the postwar panic.[101] The Democratic Party alienated the AFL and the railroad brotherhoods, among other unions, by breaking its precedent (dating from 1896) of supporting unionization.[102] The 1920 Democratic Party platform ignored the demands of organized labor, the immigrant working class, and the progressive Republicans who had supported the administration's New Freedom policy reforms in 1913 and 1914. Wilson also approved the Palmer raids, or the "Red Scare," which further alienated the Democratic Party both from its northeastern immigrant working-class voters and from organized labor.[103]

Instead of promoting organized labor's wartime record of cooperation with the business community and the federal government, the Democrats abandoned the unions.[104] Wilson did not attempt to prolong the life of his vaguely corporatist wartime industrial relations experiments. By his silence, the president confirmed the Republican perception that organized labor was reckless and irresponsible and would always put its interest above the public interest. It was in this climate of industrial chaos that the Republicans drafted their railroad labor-management relations policy.

### The Plumb Plan

Since the end of World War I President Wilson had been pressuring Congress to resolve the railroad question: Should it be continued as a government operation or returned to private enterprise?[105] In response, the Republican Congress passed the Federal Control Act, specifying that the railroads must be returned to their private owners, not with the end of the hostilities but after not more than twenty-one months of peace elapsed.[106] The old guard and the progressive Republicans purposely postponed drafting legislation in 1918 to ensure that they would be the ones to introduce railroad legislation once the next Congress convened.[107]

In 1919, both the House and the Senate held hearings in their respective Committees of Interstate and Foreign Commerce to formulate legislation for the return of the railroads to private operation. Shippers, manufacturers, farm organizations, labor unions, financiers, economists, security holders, government officials, and other groups and individuals testified at these hearings. Seven plans attracted serious consideration by either the House or the Senate committees.[108] With the exception of the Plumb Plan, all of these plans proposed that the railroads be returned to private operation.[109]

The railroad brotherhoods and Glenn E. Plumb, a Chicago labor lawyer, drew up the Plumb Plan, which emulated Wilson's wartime Railroad Administration labor policy and adjustment machinery: labor unions had the right to organize and bargain collectively in order to establish binding trade agreements for their members.[110] This plan extended Wilson's wartime vision of union leaders as public spokesmen. Railroad labor leaders, for example, represented the workers' interests and, in so doing, made these interests coincide with the employers' interest and therefore serve the public good. Having experienced the effects of positive state interference, the AFL and the railroad brotherhoods, in addition to other unions, willingly broke with their tradition of voluntarism and endorsed the Plumb Plan.[111]

The Plumb Plan received an overwhelmingly negative response from the Republicans, however. The general strike in Seattle, which unfolded just as witnesses were testifying before the hearings, had not created a good climate for this plan. It reminded the Republicans about the dangers associated with establishing a cooperative relationship with organized labor. Less than three weeks after the hearings had been called to order, 110 local unions struck in solidarity with the 35,000 shipyard workers who were protesting low wage rates, which had been set by the shipyards with direction from the federal government.[112] Without federal government contracts, this shipyard would not have been such a large industry that could have employed such a large number of workers in 1919.

Hence, the Republicans' rejection of Wilson's wartime corporatist vision with the Plumb Plan startled few people inside Washington. "I get the distinct impression that even the ardent supporters of permanent government ownership and operation [the progressives]," wrote McAdoo, "feel partially eclipsed and at a disadvantage now because of the vociferous reaction against [the Plumb Plan]."[113] The Republicans were the first to cry that this plan constituted unfair class legislation. Progressives Albert B. Cummins, William E. Borah, Miles Poindexter, William S. Kenyon, and Frank B. Kellogg joined Henry Cabot Lodge, Warren Harding, James Eli Watson, and Joseph Frelinghuysen, members of the old guard, in the battle against all labor relations machinery, like the Plumb Plan, that protected organized labor.[114] Events like the Seattle general strike gave them even more evidence of the foolhardiness of providing unions with any type of governmental protection.

These progressives voted with Norris, Johnson, and LaFollette on agricultural legislation, and they sanctioned organized labor's right to organize and bargain collectively, but they opposed labor legislation that advanced organized labor's position as a private interest group in the economy. In principle, all Republicans rejected any legislation characterized as class legislation.[115] To both factions of the GOP, the whole notion of class was objectionable.[116] It came in conflict with their elitist or trusteeship idea of representation. Only an elite of either impartial administrators or political statesmen could be trusted to rise above the many class interests and push for the public interest.[117] LaFollette and Norris were the only Republicans who supported the Plumb Plan.[118]

### The Remedy for Evils
### of the State Is More State

While most Republicans spurned the wartime experiments and the Plumb Plan, they had no inclination to return to their prewar position—that *no* labor-management relations policy was the best policy. Instead, the Republicans cultivated new ideas about labor law reform that, in turn, some southern Democrats condemned as "experimental, unworkable, expensive, and radical." Edward B. Almon, for instance, alleged that reconstruction presented "no time for [such] untried and dangerous experiments."[119]

Reconstruction signaled the Republicans' new attitude about organized labor. For the first time as a unified party, the Republicans proclaimed that the state must take a greater role in overseeing labor-management relations. Some Republicans thought their labor law reform for the railroads had implications for the entire American workforce. "The principle of the thing," Albert Johnson, a Republican representative from Washington, proclaimed, "affects all labor."[120]

The old guard and the progressive Republicans designed a policy for the railroads that, unlike the Democratic prewar or wartime labor policies, promoted the public good by ensuring industrial peace without pledging the state's commitment to organized labor. Instead of constructing railroad labor-management relations machinery that cultivated a special relationship with organized labor, the Republicans built machinery that ignored it altogether.[121]

The GOP disagreed with the Democrats about what role organized labor should play in relation to the state *and* within society. The Republicans now rejected the two paths Wilson had halfheartedly followed in labor law reform. On the one hand, Wilson made it necessary to pass class legislation during his first administration that provided unions with special aid and protection either as voluntary associations or as representatives of the public good.[122] While it was doubtful that the Republicans would consider passing class legislation that protected organized labor in 1919, they could have included Gompers's concept of voluntarism and business unionism as a justification for the federal government's withdrawal from labor-management relations. A blind eye, then, could have been cast if the railroads started busting the unions, particularly those that had been organized during World War I.

On the other hand, the Republicans rejected President Wilson's vaguely corporatist wartime policies practiced during his second administration because they facilitated cooperation between organized labor, industry, and the federal government. Wilson had little problem giving the AFL center stage during the wartime emergency, especially since other, radical unions and organizations opposed intervention. Likewise, the Republicans might have extended this relationship with organized labor as a means of quelling industrial unrest. The railroad labor-management relations policy could have co-opted the skilled workers in the conservative "labor aristocracy," pitting them against the unskilled workers. This "divide and conquer" strategy had been practiced often by the railroad industry with great success.

The Republicans thought organized labor should be regulated by the state. They chose neither to protect nor co-opt union leaders as functional representatives of the public good. Unlike the Democrats, they insisted that society would profit from making unions accountable to the state for their actions. The old guard and progressive Republicans therefore invented railroad labor relations machinery that made unions responsible to the state, to society, and to their individual members. They tried to answer the general question of union accountability and liability raised by some progressive state and federal courts as well as the conservative Supreme Court. The Republicans erected railroad labor relations machinery that protected the workers' and the employers' freedom to contract, by using worker representatives and safeguarding the privacy of the collective bargaining process. At the same time, this machinery promoted the public interest, by limiting the type of players who could participate in this process.

The Republicans expanded the power and authority of the American state. They did so, however, not in a spirit of reform like the state-building programs implemented during the progressive or New Deal periods. Rather, the Republicans' program bolstered the traditional *liberal* state. It reflected the ontological moment in Locke's vision of state-societal relations in which self-preservation gave life to a state that was normally driven by society. The principles underlying this railroad labor-management relations policy created by a liberal state would become more entrenched than those created by a reform-oriented corporate liberal state. Its opponents changed specific policy provisions that altered its machinery, but they would face grave difficulties dismantling the basic liberal principles underlying it.

### Union Accountability and the
### House Version of the Transportation Act

After the House Committee on Foreign and Interstate Commerce completed its hearings on legislative solutions to the railroad problem, a subcommittee crafted a bill. "In Honor of John J. Esch," the committee named the bill after this progressive Republican.[123] Appointed to chair the committee in December 1918, after the Republicans had reestablished their majority in Congress, Esch became very involved in the railroad dilemma.[124] Esch represented the progressive Republican state of Wisconsin, and like many midwestern and western progressives, he supported the idea of a positive government to protect those victimized by industrial capitalism. Nevertheless, Esch was adamant about what type of legislation could be passed to correct the ills of capitalism.

Esch denounced class legislation that defended one class at the expense of another. Yet Esch's own life experience in the Midwest naturally colored his notion of class. Following the lead of many midwestern progressives, Esch categorized farmers less as a self–interested class and as more deserving of positive state interference than labor, simply because he thought farmers should be rewarded for their contribution to American society. For instance, he supported organized labor's right to organize and bargain collectively, but he believed that a state apparatus, such as a regulatory agency or the federal courts, should make unions responsible to the public; he never would have demanded that farmers be made similarly accountable.[125] When he helped create the Republican railroad labor policy, Esch used the courts to hold organized labor (as well as the railroad carriers) publicly accountable, going so far as to suggest that compulsory arbitration represented a good idea in theory that could not be implemented in practice.[126]

On the surface, Esch and the House Interstate Commerce subcommittee developed labor relations machinery that resembled the machinery provided for by the Railroad Administration. The Esch bill reinstated the national bipartisan adjustment boards that had regulated railroad labor during World War I.[127] This board had three public officials, in addition to its members representing the railroad labor union and the railroad carrier. These public officials, however, had no deciding vote; only the railroad union and the carrier representatives had the power to resolve labor disputes.[128]

Although Esch maintained the bipartisan character of the wartime railroad adjustment boards, the Republican adjustment boards were different in two important respects. First, the Esch adjustment boards settled no disputes between the railroad carriers and the nonoperating railroad workers.[129] Only the operating railroad workers organized by the four brotherhoods could take their disputes to the national adjustment boards. The nonoperating railroad workers, who had made great strides in unionization under the Railroad Administration's protection, could not use the new machinery. Esch had no intention of using it to foster unionization in the railroad industry.

Second, unlike any other Democratic labor relations policy, including that of the Railroad Administration, the National War Labor Board, and the Newlands

Act, the Esch bipartisan adjustment boards did not depend on the "voluntary cooperation" of their constituents. The Republicans abandoned Wilson's ideas of voluntarism. To enforce the permanent adjustment board's decisions, the Esch bill called upon the courts. Offending parties would pay damage awards against all common property, with the exception of insurance or other benefit funds, when the appointed court decided a suit.[130] In effect, the Esch bill's enforcement provision incorporated the railroad brotherhoods and the shopmen. The Republicans created a permanent adjustment board to enforce trade agreements, whereas most state and federal courts had refused to enforce these agreements. The judiciary now sanctioned unions, or other worker representatives, as the railroad workers' legitimate contracting parties.

Taken together, these two provisions made existing unions, namely, the four brotherhoods, accountable for their activities. This labor policy, Esch explained, created "simply an action for civil damages."[131] Although the reformist labor unions, such as the brotherhoods and the AFL, had long supported the idea of strong contractual relations with employers, they opposed this means of holding organized labor accountable. Just as they dismissed the idea of incorporating unions, with the argument that the state and federal courts endangered unionization, these unions spurned the notion of court enforcement. Labor leaders from the AFL and the brotherhoods reproached the courts, especially the federal courts and the Supreme Court, for being the most dangerous antiunion political institution in the United States. They accused the judiciary of upholding discriminatory yellow-dog contracts that both deterred workers from joining unions and promoted the business community's use of injunctions to prevent unionized workers from exercising their right to strike. Why, they asked, would the judiciary now begin to protect organized labor's self-interest during a railroad labor dispute?

Esch and the other members of the Commerce committee paid little heed to the protests of the AFL and the railroad brotherhoods. They thought that the judiciary *should* enforce collective trade agreements and award damages for breaches of these agreements. The courts epitomized a neutral state body, these Republicans believed, and as such could uphold the public interest, and not the special interests of organized labor or the railroad executives.[132] They had no intention of protecting organized labor or promoting its self-interest, as Wilson had done with his wartime industrial relations policies.

## Disagreements within the Progressive Camp

Not all Republican congressmen condoned the enforcement mechanism contained in the Esch bill. J. Stanley Webster, a regular Republican from Washington, and Sidney Anderson, a progressive Republican from Minnesota, proposed two different amendments to change this mechanism. Webster presented an amendment to tighten court sanctions further. He offered a scheme for compulsory arbitration. Although his substitute bill did not prohibit strikes, Webster submitted that the railroad unions and carriers should be liable for violating collective bargaining agreements. Both criminal and civil action could be taken against the railroad workers and their unions.

Anderson presented an amendment that maintained the Esch bill's contractual view of labor relations but struck the courts' role from the bill.[133] Unlike the Esch plan or the Webster amendment, the Anderson amendment made no party liable for a breach of contract in a court of law.[134] Knowing that organized labor opposed any type of court interference, Anderson proposed that the railroad adjustment boards not have the power to enforce their decisions.[135] The courts, he thought, could not be regarded as neutral and so should not enforce the Esch adjustment board decisions.

The three methods of enforcement suggested by the Esch bill and the Webster and Anderson amendments reflected the Republican spectrum of reform and stimulated a great debate in the House. "After all," Esch resolved, "[enforcement] is the crucial question in this labor legislation."[136] The greater question of union liability underlay this debate. The old guard and regular Republicans wanted stricter court sanctions than the Esch bill provided, and the progressives insisted on no sanctions.

Participating in this debate, Nicholas J. Sinnott, a Republican from Oregon, condemned the Webster amendment because of the "difference between the legal sanction and remedy granted against the unions and its members and the legal sanction and remedy granted against the carrier."[137] Since the carriers had been incorporated, and their shareholders enjoyed limited liability, Sinnott argued, the railroad brotherhoods would suffer greater consequences for a breach in contract. The unions' unincorporated status, he noted, would hamper organized labor. "The remedy against the unions," Sinnott said, "is both against the unions and the individual property of the members thereof, even though the member may be wholly innocent, having voted against, and not participating in, the strike or wrongdoing. The remedy and the legal sanction against the carrier is solely against the corporation and not against the members or stockholders of the carriers."[138] Another Republican, William N. Vaile of Colorado, also noted that the unionized railroad worker would be at "the mercy of his associates," since the common-law courts gave unions no limited liability. The Webster amendment "provides that any union which authorizes any member to strike shall be liable for full damages, and . . . the member of the union who might be entirely disposed to abide by the contract." Given what little control individual workers had over determining whether the contract should be upheld, Vaile thought this "result would be very unfair."[139]

Sinnott and Vaile recognized the significance of limited liability, and they constructed an argument about its injustice. Congress, they argued, would never put stockholders in corporations in a similar vulnerable legal position. "If a law were proposed here in this House to abolish the ordinary limitations of liability of a stockholder of a corporation," Sinnott said, "it would not be considered, it would not be tolerated for one moment in this House. Let us treat both labor and capital with even-handed justice."[140] John G. Cooper, a Republican from Ohio, added, "If the amendment of Judge Webster is adopted you shackle and handcuff every laboring man so that if he should in any case decide not to abide by the decision of this board, then the employer can go into court and take his little home from him and everything else he has."[141] M. Clyde Kelly, a Republican from Pennsylvania, also argued, "If any decision is violated[,] members of labor organizations are liable for the full damages to the railroad companies. What does that mean? It means, in the end, absolute destruction of the labor unions. All their common property, buildings, and goods of value are liable to seizure. There would be perpetual litigation and endless lawsuits with their attendant costs."[142]

Rather than ducking these charges, Webster directly challenged them. He asserted that unions and their members *should* be culpable for damages. "The member of a union incurs a burden as well as a benefit," Webster explained, "when he joins the organization, and if his organization, acting in matters pertaining to its jurisdiction, binds him he can not say he has acted against his will."[143] Webster's explanation caused consternation among most Republicans. Johnson protested that under these rules of liability, "the advantages of mutual cooperation and support, of collective bargaining, would be lost, and union members, finding themselves at a disadvantage with nonunion members, would be compelled to quit." The Webster amendment, unlike the Railroad Administration's policies, he thought, included "deliberate discrimination, which [was] unworthy and unjustifiable" against railroad union workers.[144]

The argument over the benefits of collective bargaining agreements and the question of liability contributed greatly to the passage of the Anderson amendment. Although most Republicans thought this amendment offered a second-best solution, they preferred it over either the Esch bill or the Webster amendment. As Johnson said, "Leaders want to keep contracts; sane men will keep contracts. Leave the penalties to the courts."[145] No need for such penalties would arise, because organized labor knew that its best interest resided in abiding by collective bargaining agreements.

Essentially, the Anderson amendment created a public forum that facilitated the negotiation of collective trade agreements and the resolution of disputes about these agreements. Anderson and some progressive Republicans and

Democrats recognized the difficulties facing the railroad workers when they tried enforcing trade agreements. As Robert Luce, a Republican from Massachusetts, explained, the amended Esch bill tried "to meet one very serious question, the question of whether contracts made by organizations of labor or employers shall be kept."[146] Because organized labor voluntarily chose not to incorporate its unions, it lacked legal standing and had weak contractual relations with employers under common law. The progressives, therefore, created a quasi-judicial agency that encouraged unions and employers to form trade agreements without help from the judiciary. The amended Esch bill dealt in what Anderson described as "a complete and positive way with the entire question of labor disputes in connection with the operation of the railroads."[147]

The old guard and the progressives both sponsored national labor-management relations machinery, although they fought over the machinery's design. By contrast, the Democrats who opposed both the Anderson amendment and the Esch bill did so because both pieces of legislation created quasi-judicial labor-management relations machinery. Thetus Sims, a Democrat from Tennessee, said that the enforcement of collective bargaining contracts was "ridiculous," because it involved "a question" of "justice," not "law."[148] The Esch bill created machinery, he claimed, that "smack[ed] of judicial decisions."[149]

On November 17, 1919, the House adopted the Anderson amendment with a vote of 254 to 111.[150] By party, 135 Republicans and 119 Democrats voted for these labor relations provisions. Old guard and regular Republicans constituted 70 of the 111 congressmen opposed; the remaining 41 were antiunion moderate Democrats and progressive Republicans. They contested, however, only the labor relations provisions. When the House later voted for the Esch and conference bills, almost all of these Republican congressmen voted for their passage. The old guard and regular Republicans thus disputed the Anderson amendment, but not the idea of public policies for labor or transportation.

Although the progressives within both parties joined together to pass the Anderson amendment, they voted along party lines when the final Esch bill and conference bill passed. The Esch bill received 108 Republicans votes, and 107 Republicans voted again for the conference bill to pass the Transportation Act. Only 12 Democrats voted for the Esch bill, and 11 Democrats voted for the conference bill. Clearly, the progressive and old guard factions reunited to pass the Transportation Act, while the progressive Democrats who had earlier voted for the Anderson amendment returned to their party fold.

The progressive Republicans passed the Anderson amendment despite the old guard's opposition for three reasons. First, the old guard party leadership had little control over the House progressives. In 1910, the powers of the Speaker of the House diminished because of progressive reforms.[151] Instead of excluding the progressives, as Republican "czar" Joseph Cannon had done during his tenure as Speaker before 1910, Speaker Frederick Gillett, also a Republican, bargained for their support. Second, the amended Esch bill had Anderson's backing; as one of the most powerful representatives of the progressive Republicans, he had easily galvanized their support.[152] Third, after the 1918 congressional elections, the progressive Republicans increased their voting leverage in the House. Of the 135 Republicans voting for the Anderson amendment, 49 were elected in 1918 alone. In contrast, only 9 of the 70 Republicans voting against the Anderson amendment entered Congress in 1918.

### Something Better Than Liberty?:
### The Senate Version of the Transportation Act

While the House debated the Esch bill, the Senate Committee on Interstate and Foreign Commerce drafted its counterpart, the Cummins bill. The Cummins labor relations machinery differed fundamentally from the Esch and the Railroad Administration labor relations machinery because of its emphasis on adjudication as well as its broad jurisdiction. Unlike the Esch bill, whose enforcement provisions engendered opposition in the House, the Cummins bill had support from both the old guard and most progressive Republicans, who thought American labor policy should have courtlike powers to protect the public interest. Taking this one step further, the Senate bill represented more workers, organized *and* unorganized, than the Esch bill. The Republicans behind this policy, however, had no intention of fostering the unionization of the nonoperating railroad workers like the Railroad Administration had done during World War I.

When the Republicans reconstituted the Senate, the old guard chose Cummins, a progressive who had become more conservative after World War I, to head the Interstate and Foreign Commerce Committee.[153] Cummins's appointment, the old guard claimed, could be attributed to the new spirit of Republican reconciliation and reunification. Nonetheless, the old guard gave his selection a good deal of forethought. Cummins, they hoped, would create a national transportation policy that would secure progressive Republican support without giving organized labor any special privileges.[154]

During debate on the labor relations provisions for the Clayton Antitrust Act in 1913, Cummins called for state regulation of organized labor. While he recognized an inherent difference between the business organization and the trade union, Cummins contested the AFL's notion of voluntarism or absolute freedom of association. In the words of one legal historian, he rejected "Gompers' conclusion that the nonviolent exercise of that power should never be subject to state regulation or legal liability. The difference between labor and capital called for a different form of regulation, he believed, but not outright immunity."[155]

Although Cummins had become more conservative after World War I, he still rejected providing unions with immunity under law. As an advocate of the scientific-management ideal of cooperation, Cummins created legislation that he championed as "progressive" despite its punitive labor-management provisions.[156] Although his position seemed contradictory, it corresponded with ideas propagated by the scientific-management community. Critics of this community had accused its converts of grossly neglecting the "human factor" in labor and ignoring the issue of unionization altogether.[157] Cummins's anti-union transportation policy was no exception. He developed a railroad labor policy that pleased the old guard.

At the heart of Cummins's legislation lay the transportation board. This senior professional board was meant to create social harmony by supervising all railroad management functions. While the Interstate Commerce Commission (ICC) would still regulate railroad rates, the transportation board would coordinate management responsibilities, including labor-management relations.[158] Unlike the Railroad Administration or the amended Esch bill, this board was not truly bipartisan. The Cummins bill also instituted a hierarchical system of bipartisan adjustment boards.[159] These adjustment boards differed from those provided by the amended Esch bill or the Railroad Administration because Cummins gave them a regional, rather than a national, outlook and because they were not truly bipartisan.[160]

Providing these boards with such a limited jurisdiction, Cummins understood, would severely undermine organized labor's bargaining power. The railroad executives had already expressed their outrage at the Railroad Administration for helping the nonoperating railroad unions sign five *national* trade agreements. They made no secret of their plans to break these agreements as soon as the railroads were reprivatized. Cummins, moreover, gave these regional adjustment boards no autonomy from the transportation board.[161] His bill would make the regional adjustment boards' decisions legally binding. Then, the transportation board—not the federal courts—would award damages to the railroad workers and the carriers. The courts would be superseded, since they would not determine damage suits or issue injunctions. The Cummins bill gave this one independent administrative agency the task of overseeing labor-management relations.[162] It also gave the transportation board the authority to subjugate labor to the larger economic considerations of the railroads. Wage rates and work conditions would depend on the health of the railroad industry. Finally, the board was to implement compulsory arbitration. As a reporter explained about Cummins's plan, "The whole tendency of organized government is towards compulsion and regimentation: the remedy for the evils of the state is more state." [163]

Cummins gave the transportation board these powers on the grounds that quick resolution of labor disputes on the railroads was imperative. For the same reason, he provided that strikes and lockouts be outlawed. [164] Cummins insisted that workers would be exchanging their right to strike for "an enlightened government" that would resolve all their labor disputes. The board, according to Cummins, would ensure the worker "a fair share of the fruits of his toil." [165]

Not all Republicans agreed with the construction of such a powerful labor-management relations board. When Cummins presented his bill to the Senate, a small group of progressives left the transportation board alone but tried to eliminate these strict accountability measures. Directing his comments to the unions, Owsley Stanley, a Democrat from Kentucky, who authored two amendments to the bill, said that the Senate had offered them "Government tribunals." "We have sugar-coated your servitude. . . . [Cummins and his supporters claim,] 'We will give you something better,' [but,] something better than what? Something better than liberty?" [166] Stanley, LaFollette, Norris, Borah, and Ansel J. Gronna joined 19 progressive Democrats in attempting to drop the antistrike provision from the Cummins bill. The old guard defeated this amendment by a vote of 46 to 25, as well as the second amendment proposed by Stanley. [167] First, Cummins had little doubt about the old guard or the regular Republicans' support, since they never wavered in their position that unions had been privileged before this policy. [168] Second, Cummins maintained enough progressive Republican backing for the labor-management relations provisions, because progressives, too, thought the railroad workers should be held accountable for their actions through some new statutory guidelines. [169] The difference between voting patterns in Stanley amendments and those in the McCormick amendment illustrated the strength of Cummins's lobbying efforts with this faction. [170] Finally, the absence of any strong opposition from Norris and LaFollette, arguably organized labor's greatest champions, provided evidence of Cummins's success. Norris's greatest concern had been that possible collusion between railroad labor and management would hurt consumers. [171] Similarly, LaFollette denounced the antistrike provision and compulsory arbitration, but he spent more time and energy on the farmers' concerns about railroad rates. [172]

The Cummins bill also stripped organized labor of its so-called privileged position by developing the beginnings of the worker representation scheme. While progressive Republicans joined like-minded Democrats in condemning the antistrike provision and compulsory arbitration, they left the bill's broad jurisdiction intact. Unlike the Esch bill, which restricted the labor relations machinery to the operating railroad workers, most of whom belonged to the brotherhoods and the shopmen, the Cummins bill applied to all categories and classes of railroad workers—the operating and nonoperating as well as the organized and unorganized.[173] Furthermore, Selden P. Spence, a Republican from Missouri, introduced and helped pass an amendment that designated subordinate officials, "men who have some supervisory power, although quite a long way down the line, such as yard foremen, track masters, train dispatchers," included as labor, rather than management, and therefore placed them under the jurisdiction of the transportation board.

The inclusivity of the Cummins bill would prove to be a mixed blessing for organized labor. On the one hand, to implement the labor-management relations provisions, a worker representation scheme required construction. This scheme provided the first statutory means of holding unincorporated voluntary associations, like unions, accountable for their actions. Under the common law, unincorporated unions had been released from accountability because they had no legal personality. Unions could not be sued for damages, for instance, incurred during a labor dispute; nor could they establish binding trade agreements without a legal personality. The lack of common-law recourse, in part, gave employers the justification for securing labor injunctions. While the worker representation scheme would not necessarily curb the number of injunctions imposed upon organized labor, it would help regularize the collective bargaining process. Most strikes, moreover, occurred over the issue of union recognition, which the worker representation scheme tried to make conflict-free. If the Cummins labor-management relations policy worked, these employers might not have this recourse readily available for long.

On the other hand, this worker representation scheme gave unions and other voluntary associations only temporary legal personalities. If the railroad workers selected a union as their worker representative, this union would be held responsible for the actions of its members. Further, the Cummins bill did not protect railroad workers from hostile employers, as the Railroad Administration had done during World War I. Also unlike the Railroad Administration, the bill included no provision similar to General Order No. 8, which had guaranteed workers the right to join unions. The implementation of this scheme for worker representation remained ambiguous.

On December 20, 1919, the Cummins bill passed with a secure vote of 47 to 17.[174] Thirty-four Republicans voted in favor of the bill and only 3 progressive Republicans voted against it. In the end, Lodge told Cummins how his bill pleased him.[175] For the first time, Lodge and other old guard Republicans in-dicated that they stood behind a labor policy that, in Cummins's words, "obvi-ously" represented "an advance upon the general course of legislation in the past."[176]

### Statism, Contractualism, and the Transportation Act of 1920

Using the different labor-management relations provisions in the Cummins and Esch bills, in addition to other regulatory provisions such as the voluntary or compulsory consolidation of lines, a joint conference committee drafted a bill amenable to both chambers.[177] During the conference, Esch and the House conferees first demanded that the transportation board be struck from the conference bill. They did not want Cummins's transportation board, authorized by the ICC, to determine wage rates and work conditions. After a long deadlock, the House conferees won. No professional board would coordi-nate all the railroad managerial functions, including labor-management rela-tions, with the ICC. Instead of authorizing the ICC to determine pay scales, for instance, the Republicans redrafted their labor-management relations machin-ery to safeguard private contractual relations between the collective bargain-ing agents and the railroad employers. This machinery, however, did violate the spirit of contractualism in that it recommended policy constraints about work conditions and wage rates.

To further preserve the private character of labor relations, Esch and the House conferees demanded that the Senate conferees drop all the compulsory provisions embedded in the Cummins labor relations machinery. For three weeks, the House and Senate conferees fought about whether this machinery would provide compulsory or voluntary arbitration.[178] The House conferees, moreover, insisted that the new railroad labor policy not prohibit strikes or worker lockouts.[179] Later explaining the labor policy revisions, Cummins said, "The House would not accept that part of the Senate bill which undertook to create tribunals for the adjudication of disputes between railway workers and railway employers; and to make it unlawful, through combination or conspir-acy on the part of either workers or employers, to punish the public in order to maintain their disputes."[180] Senator James E. Watson, an old guard member from Indiana, added, "I sat at the table in the room of the Interstate Commerce Committee and tried by might and main to have teeth put into the Esch-Cummins law. But the House would have none of it."[181] After three weeks, the House conferees won the first round about the design and structure of the Railroad Labor Board: it contained no compulsory provisions.

The Senate conferees grudgingly gave up these compulsory provisions, but in return they demanded that key labor relations provisions in the Esch bill be excluded from the conference bill. In particular, the Senate conferees insisted that membership on the Railroad Labor Board reflect the public interest as well as the private interests of the railroad employers and workers. The Senate conferees clung to their penchant for statism, manifested as a tripartite labor relations agency. Although arbitration would be voluntary, Cummins and the Senate conferees requested that three public members, in addition to three employer and three worker members, sit on the Railroad Labor Board. The Senate conferees also convinced the House conferees to abandon the bipartisan adjustment boards. Either the railroad carriers or one hundred workers acting in concert could carry their labor disputes directly to the Railroad Labor Board. This board, moreover, had the final say in all other general grievances or discipline disputes.

The Railroad Labor Board that was included in the final conference bill protected private contractual relations for the private good rather than for the welfare of its particular constituents. But the House conferees stopped short of providing this public board with any legal authority. Having refused to compromise earlier about compulsory arbitration, the House conferees gave the Railroad Labor Board the power only to investigate disputes, collect evidence, compile testimony, publish hearings, and mandate railroad workers and carriers to appear for judgment. The offending parties involved in a railroad labor dispute would be advised, but not compelled, to abide by the board's rulings.

The absence of enforcement powers, however, furnished the state with more than a minimal role in labor-management relations. In fact, the state, as manifested by the Railroad Labor Board, had greater power over these relations than ever before. As William J. Burke, Republican from Pennsylvania, said, "In so far as a petition [is] signed by 100 unorganized workers . . . the Board [could] interfere in any dispute[;] . . . it leaves the Board free to act of its own accord." [182]

The Railroad Labor Board resembled neither the transportation board created by the Cummins bill nor the bipartisan adjustment boards established by the Esch bill. It implemented neither compulsory arbitration nor bipartisan, voluntary arbitration. The board comprised a quasi-judicial public agency that rendered courtlike decisions about collective bargaining agreements and labor disputes.[183] Although the Railroad Labor Board lacked formal enforcement powers, railroad carriers and organized or unorganized workers could bring to it any concerns about these agreements. As Burke elaborated, "The railroad workers have no choice but to go to the board. . . . Under this bill, [they would have] to accept the findings of the board." [184]

Underlying this idea that a quasi-judicial agency would hand down decisions about collective bargaining agreements was the assumption that the railroad carriers and the workers *should* negotiate such agreements. The joint conference determined that these agreements would best ensure industrial peace in the railroad industry. The Republicans made a crucial linkage between peaceful contractual relations and the public good while avoiding interfering with the common law of contracts. Instead of the judiciary bringing about industrial peace by handing down injunctions against organized labor, all labor disputes would be brought before a professional labor-management relations board.

### A Vote on Both Sides of the Table

Given that this quasi-judicial board recognized collective trade agreements, the joint conference still had to decide who would negotiate these agreements. The Esch bill designated the brotherhoods and the shopmen as the official collective bargaining agents. It restricted the jurisdiction of the labor relations machinery to the unions that had already organized the railroad industry. In contrast, the Cummins bill imposed no limitations on who could use the machinery, but it stopped short of endorsing organized labor. Having given up the compulsory arbitration and the antistrike and lockout provisions, the Senate conferees won this round. The conference yielded no corporatist protection for organized labor; rather, it gave voice to the organized and unorganized workers themselves. The conferees produced the worker representation scheme in the Cummins bill to resolve the issue of agency.

When the Cummins bill had been formulated, the old guard and progressive Republicans cultivated the idea that workers, not organized labor, should be represented by the labor-management relations machinery. They insisted that all workers have access to this machinery. In other words, the old guard rejected the idea that unions alone should become the railroad workers' bargaining agents. They promoted the worker representation scheme with the understanding that it would establish a *temporary* legal relationship between an agent and its members—without any mention of organized labor. In so doing, the old guard Republicans enlisted the principal/agent theory practiced in common law. The progressive Republicans put up little opposition, because they wanted organized labor to have the capacity to negotiate binding trade agreements with the railroad employers. At the same time, they thought unions should be held accountable, though few progressives advocated antistrike provisions or compulsory arbitration.

This worker representation scheme transformed labor law. It shifted the emphasis of Woodrow Wilson's conception of railroad labor law from the unions to the workers. Unlike the wartime railroad labor policy, the conference bill safeguarded the railroad workers' right to representation without specifying who was in the representative pool. The *Monthly Labor Review* noted that "the Act makes no reference to unions, but the commission accepted the representatives of those who were in a position to speak with confidence and authority."[185] The worker representation provisions gave organized labor, like any other association, the opportunity to bargain for railroad workers. The tripartite Railroad Labor Board would then oversee the implementation of worker representation both as a means of resolving labor disputes and as a method of forming lasting contracts.

Furthermore, the Senate conferees deprived the national railroad unions of the authority to nominate who would represent the workers *on* the Railroad Labor Board. When the president appointed three worker representative members to this board, the Senate conferees argued that the nomination process, like the worker representation process, must be expanded. The Senate conferees did not want organized labor to speak for all the railroad workers. Senator Joseph Robinson, a Democrat from Arkansas, explained, "[The] criticism . . . that [the conference bill] does not expressly require that every member of the labor board representing labor shall be a member of a labor union is un-American, unreasonable, and will not justify in public opinion the opposition to this bill."[186] After prolonged debate, the House conferees agreed to eliminate the provision in the Esch bill that gave the brotherhoods and the shopmen's union the power to nominate who would represent the railroad workforce on the Railroad Labor Board and the adjustment boards.[187] The fragile situation regarding the unionization of the nonoperating or shopcrafts unions during World War I underlay this concession.

Thus, the conference bill severed the link, which the Esch bill and the Railroad Administration had cultivated, between the federal government and the national railroad unions—particularly the shopcrafts unions, which benefited greatly from this relationship. The Republicans removed the undercurrent of protectionism that pervaded Wilson's voluntarist and corporatist industrial relations policies. Unions were no longer considered the railroad workers' exclusive bargaining agents, nor would they necessarily represent the railroad workers as a whole by serving as the three worker members on the new tripartite Railroad Labor Board.

The old guard and progressive Republicans' construction of this policy reflected their belief in responsible unionism. The old guard Republicans wanted labor-management relations machinery to hold unions accountable for their activities during labor disputes, yet they exhorted this machinery not to protect these unions.[188] The progressive Republicans, on the other hand, thought that unions could protect the economic interests of their membership as well as the public interest if they negotiated and maintained collective trade agreements with employers. The House and Senate conferees for the Transportation bill built a labor policy that pleased both factions in the GOP, because it made organized labor accountable by redrafting the state and federal courts' principles of agency into a general worker representation scheme.[189]

While the labor policy that emerged from this joint conference was based on a montage of compromises, how the old guard and progressives constructed the montage tells something about organized labor's accountability before law. The Republicans extended a statutory version of responsible unionism similar to the one that materialized in common law. They combined the seemingly contradictory elements of contractualism, maintaining individual rights and freedom to contract, and the public interest or civic virtue. In other words, they created a neutral state-controlled agency—the Railroad Labor Board—to protect the public interest by not granting organized labor the exclusive right to represent the railroad workers.

First, they recognized unions as private interest groups with no special rights and privileges under law. The Esch-Cummins conferees built labor relations machinery that did not interfere with the "private character of the system."[190] The unions (or other private organizations representing the railroad workers) and the employers maintained their freedom to contract during the trade agreement negotiation process. There was no statist control over this process.

Second, when they made restrictions on the number and type of groups allowed to negotiate trade agreements, the Esch-Cummins conferees gave preference to the idea that the public interest should override the employers' and the workers' right to contract. In creating the term *worker representative*, the conferees walked the fine line between traditional and corporate liberalism. Worker representation made unions, and other collective representatives, responsible for their actions without endangering the individual rights of their members. But by controlling who could or could not become such a representative, the American liberal state gained control over labor-management relations. This state safeguarded individualism and kept society free from industrial strife that might jeopardize the public interest.

### Turn Back the Railroads, but Leave the Railroad Men Unfettered

The conference bill satisfied neither organized labor nor the railroad executives. Organized labor registered two main objections: (1) their unofficial positions in the highly unionized railroad industry and (2) the probability that employers would bring in the federal courts to enforce the board's decisions. The bill disappointed the railroad executives as well, because it contained neither compulsory arbitration nor an antistrike provision.

Unlike the wartime labor policies, the conference bill referred to no national labor union per se.[191] Organized labor convinced few Republican policymakers that substantive changes in labor law should be made so that the sixteen railroad unions could bargain for the railroad workers. Even before Congress drafted the Transportation Act, organized labor sent its leaders to lobby Congress. The AFL and brotherhoods, among others, tried to cultivate the same cooperative relationship with Congress that they had shared with the Democratic administration during the Great War.[192] For instance, Gompers assured Congress that "the American Labor movement [would] cooperate with all other agencies to help in this reconstruction time."[193] The AFL's pledges of cooperation fell on deaf ears, however, considering that the Republicans changed the government's position on organized labor as a whole. They imposed no restrictions on the railroad workers, because they did not designate in advance which private interest group could represent them at the collective bargaining table.

Organized labor also feared that since the Railroad Labor Board had such great duties without commensurate enforcement powers, the federal courts would enforce its decisions. Gompers argued that the injunction would serve as the railroad executives' device to enforce board's decisions. In a press conference denouncing the antistrike measure as well as the Association of Railway Executives (ARE), Gompers explained that "the only difference between the anti-strike clause in the Cummins bill and the one in the redrafted conference measure was that in the former a penalty would be imposed by a jury, while in the latter an injunction method would be followed by the penalty and not by a jury."[194] Although the Republican Congress gave the courts no official role in the labor relations provisions, they might still honor the railroad employers' request for injunctive relief in labor disputes. Not only organized labor but also the employers' associations and the railroad executives worked against the compromise labor relations provisions in the Transportation Act. Initially, the employers upheld the rhetoric of contractualism. They implicitly and unwittingly advocated refashioning the judicial principles of agency. But they abandoned their rhetoric of contractualism in protest when the joint conference dropped the compulsory arbitration and antistrike provision. "The bill is far from what we could have wished," one journalist for a trade journal wrote, "and yet [it] embodies a few important essentials and doubtless is the best that could be obtained."[195] The railroad executives counted on using the labor relations machinery to discipline and weaken the railroad labor unions. They insisted that the antistrike measure be included in the Transportation Act.

Most railroad executives resented the "rights" that the Democratic administration had bestowed upon the AFL, the brotherhoods, and, particularly, nonoperating unions when it enacted the National War Labor Board and the Railroad Administration.[196] They argued that organized labor's "arrogance," resulting from the vital role it had played during the war, accounted for postwar industrial unrest.[197] The railroad executives, as well as many members of the business community, expected a Republican Congress to institute labor-management relations machinery that would put organized labor back in its prewar "place" in the economy.

### Conclusion

In all, the Transportation Act demonstrated a return neither to the prewar labor relations policy nor to the wartime labor relations policy. The Republican Congress ensured that railroad unions were no longer perceived as voluntary associations, free to practice all the rights of such an association unhindered by state regulation. At the same time, the railroad labor-management relations policy did not co-opt these unions by making them functional representatives of the public good. The old guard and progressive Republicans portrayed the railroad unions as self-interested organizations that must be regulated to maintain industrial peace, progress, and tranquillity.

Only a state-controlled agency, the Railroad Labor Board, could balance contractualism and the public interest. At once, this state-directed regulatory agency would maintain the employer's and the workers' freedom to contract *and* hold the public interest above the private interests of these contracting parties. The Republican policymakers interwove the normally antithetical ideals of freedom to contract and the public interest and interjected them into responsible unionism. Equating the public interest with industrial stability and tranquillity, the Republicans claimed, was whaat made this view of labor-management relations ideologically appealing and also was what distinguished them from the Democrats.

In general, the Republicans' penchant for promoting statism and the public interest reflected their elitist view of political representation, one of the cornerstones of the GOP's ideology. The old guard believed that statesmen should lead the country, whereas the progressives relied on the advice and guidance of neutral experts. Statesmen or administrative experts could determine the public interest without being swayed by public opinion or the lobbying efforts of private groups and associations.

In the 1920s, interjecting its belief in statism, the Republican Congress brought forth a new vision of labor-management relations. It shifted the emphasis of labor law from the agent to the collective bargaining process and, in so doing, depersonalized this process. Railroad workers were offered representatives who could bargain collectively for them, but the authority to negotiate for these workers was not to be given exclusively or permanently to organized labor; the right to collective bargaining was established without assigning agency. Hence, the Railroad Labor Board protected the individual rights of the railroad workers, not the rights of organized labor.

Although policymakers in the 1930s would again have the same choice of ideologies, namely voluntarism, corporatism, and responsible unionism, the worker representation scheme in the Republican Party's peacetime industrial relations plan, not President Wilson's National War Labor Board or the Railroad Administration, became the primary influence behind the formation of the New Deal National Labor Relations Board. By defeating the Democrats in 1918 and 1920, the Republicans prevented the Democratic Party from extending its policy agenda of New Freedom reforms, including the industrial relations policies, after the war. The political mandate that President Wilson had relied on during the wartime emergency disappeared when the hostilities ended. The Republicans introduced their own reform agenda. The Democratic policymakers experimented with Wilson's voluntaristic notions in implementing section 7(a) of the National Industrial Recovery Act of 1933, but what became the permanent labor policy with the passage of the National Labor Relations Act of 1935 was a product of the Republicans' era of normalcy, or a legislative version of responsible unionism, rather than the Democrats' New Freedom spirit of reform.

CHAPTER **5**

# Collapse or Victory?

*Implementing the Scheme for*
*Worker Representation*

Congress should put a few teeth in the law, and then let us alone.

—Ben Hooper, chairman of the Railroad Labor Board,
to President Warren G. Harding, 1921

From the outset, the AFL and the railroad brotherhoods rallied
against the creation of the Railroad Labor Board. After World War I, they had
lobbied for the Plumb Plan, a labor-management relations policy similar to the
one instituted by the Railroad Administration that bolstered the organization
of shopcrafts workers. The Republican Congress, however, had ignored their
clamoring and established the Railroad Labor Board. A deep antiunion spirit
had gripped the nation after World War I, and the Republicans constructed a
labor policy that stopped just short of possessing this spirit. The Railroad Labor
Board embodied the theory of responsible unionism, which made organized
labor accountable by promoting strong state action. Ironically, this board cultivated one statist measure that helped organized labor—its supervision of the
scheme for worker representation.

Neither labor historians nor political scientists have documented the importance of this scheme for worker representation. The whole history of the Railroad Labor Board has been neglected. What is more, the few scholars who have
examined the board argue that it was an institutional aberration. Supposedly,
the board's operations were a stopgap between those provided by the wartime
labor-management relations machinery and the Railroad Labor Board founded
in 1926. This chapter, by contrast, shows how the Railroad Labor Board shaped
the course of American labor-management relations. Although the board operated for less than five years, the measure on worker representation lived on and
became entrenched in federal labor policy.[1] Indeed, the conflicts that spelled
ruin for the board are also what made this measure so influential in American
labor policy.

The Railroad Labor Board's commitment to implementing the worker representation scheme surprised the railroad executives, who opposed the unionization of shopcrafts workers. Upon the railroads' return to private enterprise, these executives launched an open-shop campaign that targeted specifically the shopcrafts unions that had profited from governmental control. Disappointed that the Transportation Act had included no antistrike provision or compulsory arbitration, railroad executives hoped that the board would not facilitate unionization. Not all board members, moreover, intended their commitment to this scheme to benefit organized labor. Nonetheless, when the board directed the worker representation process, the shopcrafts unions, which had increased their membership rolls during World War I, profited from its action.

In particular, the shopcrafts workers benefited from a battle over worker representation on the Pennsylvania Railroad. When the Railroad Labor Board offered to supervise elections of worker representatives in 1922, the railroad executives challenged its jurisdiction to do so. Although the board gave the Pennsylvania Railroad executives many opportunities to back down, the executives instead escalated this contest over organization of the shopcrafts workers into a battle over state involvement that ultimately had to be decided by the Supreme Court.

In *Pennsylvania Railroad Company v. United States Railroad Labor Board*, the Supreme Court (led by Chief Justice William Howard Taft, a former member of the Republican old guard) ruled that the railroad need not abide by the Railroad Labor Board's decision, since the Transportation Act gave the board no enforcement powers.[2] But then the Court upheld the constitutionality of the board's action in the worker representation process, despite the absence of these powers. According to a unanimous decision by the Taft Court, the Railroad Labor Board had the power and authority to implement the worker representation scheme because the scheme secured procedural rights for workers, not substantive rights that conflicted with employer rights. The Court's ruling disappointed the Pennsylvania Railroad executives.

Meanwhile, the Pennsylvania Railroad, as well as other railroads, led an open-shop campaign against the shopcrafts workers during the 1922 shopmen's strike. During this controversy, the Railroad Labor Board sided with the railroad executives in calling the striking shopmen "outlaws" and allowing the railroads to replace them permanently. The board's activities during the shopmen's strike of 1922 antagonized organized labor. Bert Jewell, president of the AFL Railway Employees Department (RED), also protested the use of labor injunctions, another form of state action initiated by the board.

Although the shopmen felt the full weight of state power during the 1922 strike (whereas executives on the Pennsylvania Railroad who disobeyed the board's decision about their shopcrafts workers did not), both the workers' strike and the executives' disobedience yielded the same result. By 1923, the board had alienated both constituent groups and failed to quiet industrial unrest in the railroad industry. Its operation made for disgruntled progressives and old guard Republicans alike and provided the impetus for reform. President Warren G. Harding pushed for the creation of a new board with enforcement powers; he advocated compulsory arbitration. Although Harding's untimely death in 1923 ended the executive push for compulsory arbitration, the movement for reform remained alive. More than one year later, Republicans in Congress, with the help of the moderate Republican president Calvin Coolidge, started a new board, the U.S. Mediation Board, to direct labor-management relations for the railroads. The old guard and progressive Republicans, who had enacted the Transportation Act, then passed the Railway Labor Act of 1926.

To the dismay of most railroad executives, the Republicans crafted the new labor-management relations machinery so that it emphasized the Railroad Labor Board's preventive capacity. Most notably, they equipped the U.S. Mediation Board with the worker representation scheme. The Republicans followed the Taft Court in instituting labor-management relations machinery that gave the state the authority to make rules determining who spoke for the railroad workers in the collective bargaining process, and they encouraged the railroad executives to participate in this process. The Court's stance on the Railroad Labor Board, not the Harding administration's position of promoting compulsory arbitration, became ingrained in the railroad labor policy.

### Two Tiers of Workers

The passage of the Transportation Act and the subsequent end of governmental control of the railroads placed machinists, boilermakers, carmen, and other railroad workers employed in the shopcrafts in a vulnerable position. Bert Jewell, as the leader of the RED representing federations of these shopcrafts, suspected that key railroad carriers—like the Pennsylvania Railroad, which ran the single largest road—would instigate an open-shop or union-busting campaign.[3] He feared that Samuel Rea, president of the Pennsylvania Railroad, and William W. Atterbury, vice president of operations for the Pennsylvania Railroad, among others, intended to lobby the Railroad Labor Board for the abrogation of the five national agreements that had recognized the AFL unions representing shopcrafts workers under governmental control.

Jewell noted the precarious position of the shopcrafts unions within the railroad labor movement. He had little faith that the "big four" (the Brotherhood of Locomotive Engineers, the Order of Railway Conductors, the Brotherhood of Railroad Trainmen, and the Brotherhood of Locomotive Firemen and Enginemen), which together made up 95 percent of the operating workforce that they organized, would side with the shopcrafts workers against the railroad executives unless they shared the same plight. "They give us their support when it is to their advantage," Jewell explained, "and when it is not to their advantage they do not."[4]

This tension between the shopcrafts unions and the brotherhoods stemmed from the two-tiered workforce that had long structured the railroad industry. Workers in the "running trades," who actually operated the trains, composed the first tier of the "big four." They represented the "labor aristocracy," who, in having the skill to run the railroads, had compelled the railroad executives to establish collective bargaining agreements.[5] Many railroad executives negotiated agreements with the operating workers, but they refused to do so with the nonoperating workers. The shopcrafts workers, who performed clerical and office duties; constructed and maintained tracks, roadways, equipment, rolling stock, signal and telegraph systems, and stations and yards; and saw to the general servicing of the railroad plant, constituted the second, less privileged tier of the railroad workforce.[6] The shopcrafts workers' attempts to organize unions received little recognition from the railroad executives until the period of government control. Then, the AFL organized most of the shopcrafts unions.

Established in the 1860s and 1870s, the four brotherhoods were formed long before the shopcrafts unions.[7] Initially, they neglected the wage issue in favor of guaranteeing their position as skilled laborers on the running trades and obtaining insurance for the widows and children of men who lost their lives in train service.[8] As the federal government's role in the railroad industry increased, the brotherhoods became more active.[9] Over the next ten years, they initiated several concerted efforts to increase wages. The most notable success came in 1916, when President Woodrow Wilson convinced Congress to pass the Adamson Act, reducing the railroad brotherhoods' workday to eight hours without reducing their pay.[10]

As the brotherhoods became more involved in political and economic warfare with the wage movements, they lent more support to the underprivileged shopcrafts workers.[11] The failed fight for the Plumb Plan proposed after World War I marked the high point both of the brotherhoods' political activity and of their cooperation with the AFL unions. The brotherhoods went a full circle; as Selig Perlman described, "The most startling shift has been, of course, in the railway men's organizations, which have changed from a pronounced conservatism to an advocacy of a socialistic plan of railway nationalization under the Plumb plan."[12] The brotherhoods' alliance with the shopcrafts workers was soon ended, however. With reconstruction sparking a union shop drive, the railroad executives targeted the shopcrafts unions but still negotiated with the brotherhoods, in the hope of dividing railroad labor.[13]

The shopcrafts unions had less success organizing than the brotherhoods did, in part because not running the railroads made them expendable. Knowing they could be easily replaced, the shopcrafts workers formed groups called "system federations" as a means of securing more strength.[14] Although these federations first fought for recognition during the Pullman strike of 1894, they remained weak until World War I. The RED emerged in 1908, and a larger federation of system federations was formed in 1912, yet the shopcrafts unions finally acquired political and economic clout under the Railroad Administration.[15] The nationalization of the railroads had helped strengthen these organizations, particularly the RED.

First, General Order No. 8, issued by General William McAdoo, the director of the Railroad Administration, empowered the shopcrafts organizers by providing that "no discrimination would be made in employment because of membership in labor organizations."[16] Already organized, the brotherhoods, by contrast, profited little from this protection. Second, the Railroad Administration facilitated shopcrafts unionization by creating a division of labor that helped coordinate the operation of the railroads, giving shopcrafts workers a voice in the decision-making process. "This at once gave railroad union labor," Walter Hines, a former director of the Railroad Administration, declared, "an aspect of equal participation with railroad officers in labor matters, and consequently a strategic position more advanced than any ever enjoyed before."[17] Finally, the five national agreements for the shopcrafts unions bolstered their strength. Again, the brotherhoods needed no such protection, since they already worked under the shelter of satisfactory agreements negotiated with the railroad executives.

During the war, the railroad executives looked upon the organization of the shopcrafts workers, among other changes made by the Railroad Administration, with distress. When Congress returned the railroads to these executives, they immediately launched an attack to abrogate the five national agreements. They accused the Railroad Administration of giving unfair advantage to the AFL unions of shopcrafts workers. A number of these agreements, the railroad executives emphasized, had been negotiated just before the war's end. Further, Earl H. Morton, president of Railroad Station Agents, phrased his objections in more explosive terms by stating, "The rational, conservative employee may not care to affiliate with the radical element of organized labor, who are the only people who have been given the opportunity to draft national agreements."[18] Atterbury concurred, contending that "the radical rather than the conservative element of organized labor ha[d] been favored by the government through the United States Railroad Administration."[19]

### Democratic Beginnings:
### The First Railroad Labor Board

Given their sudden growth, the nonoperating unions, not the brotherhoods, became the more obvious target of the postwar antiunion campaign. Anticipating this struggle, all parties involved in the railroad industry waited with apprehension as the Wilson administration staffed the first Railroad Labor Board. Would the new board help maintain the AFL unions? Or would it facilitate the railroad executives' open-shop drive? The shopcrafts unions won the first round, since the Wilson administration made the first appointments. The Democrats placed noted supporters of shopcrafts unions on the new Railroad Labor Board.[20]

First, Wilson appointed James J. Forrester, previously the head of the Clerks' Unions; Arthur O. Wharton, a former president of the RED; and Albert Phillips, a former vice president of the Brotherhood of Firemen and Enginemen, to become the board's labor members.[21] Second, he chose G. Wallace W. Hanger, the previous head of the Division of Labor in the defunct wartime Railroad Administration; Henry Hunt, a former mayor of Cincinnati and a trustee of the Cincinnati Southern railway, and R. H. Barton, a former judge on the Tennessee Court of Appeals, to represent the public on the Railroad Labor Board.[22] All three appointees stood behind the organization of the shopcrafts workers.[23] Finally, J. H. Eliot, a former manager of the Texas and Pacific Railroad; Horace Baker, previously a general manager of the Cincinnati, New Orleans, and Texas Pacific Railroad; and William L. Park, a former vice president of the Illinois Central Railroad, became the employer members of the Railroad Labor Board. None of these representatives had records of hostility toward unions like Atterbury on the Pennsylvania Railroad did.[24]

From the outset, both the railroad executives and organized labor fought for the upper hand with the Railroad Labor Board. In the board's first meetings in February 1920, some of the railroad executives rushed to accuse board members of preparing to be lenient with organized labor.[25] The executives set the stage against organized labor in the hope that the board would not raise wage rates, and initially they succeeded, since the board postponed hearing this issue. Wilson suggested that the railroad executives and the railroad unions participate in a conference about wage increases.[26] This conference ended without resolution, however, when the chairman of the Employees' Committee rejected the railroad unions' wage increase demands.

Second, the shopcrafts unions impressed the strength of its demand on the board by staging a wildcat strike in Chicago on April 1, 1920, the day the conference ended. The Chicago, Milwaukee, and St. Paul Railroad fired John Granau, a yard conductor, who organized the Chicago Yardmen's Association.

Seven hundred workers struck to protest to Granau's dismissal, demanding his reinstatement as well as wage increases.[27] In less than a week, this single, newly organized shopcrafts union incapacitated 60 percent of the national railway system. Because Chicago was a hub for the railroads, this wildcat strike affected all industrial centers, especially those in the East and the Midwest.[28] Congress looked to the Railroad Labor Board to settle the strike.[29] Republican senator Medill McCormick of Illinois called for a complete congressional investigation of the wildcat strike.[30] McCormick said that the shopcrafts unions could not be trusted and that because the newly organized board had no enforcement powers, it might not be able to make them behave responsibly.

Cornered, the Railroad Labor Board struck a position between the railroad executives' and the shopcrafts unions' demands. First, the board declared that because the strikers had violated the provisions of the Transportation Act stipulating that they must attempt to confer with their employers before calling the strike, it had no grounds to intervene in this dispute.[31] Then, sending an entirely different message, the board fulfilled the wildcat strikers' central demand—it gave the railroad workers the long-promised wage increase, which incensed most railroad executives.[32] From May 1920 until January 1921, the executives protested the board's wage increase by either laying off employees or reducing wages. By the end of the year, the Pennsylvania Railroad had laid off 30 percent of its workforce. So many railroads followed suit and disobeyed the wage increase decision that, in December 1920, the board officially reprimanded them.[33]

For antiunion railroad executives like Rea and Atterbury, the wage increase was a diversion from what they considered the more serious issue of the existence of national agreements. Rea and Atterbury, as well as other American Railroad Executives (ARE) officials, presented their case against these agreements before the board later in 1921. These agreements with the shopcrafts unions must be terminated, they argued, because the railroads had not been party to the negotiations. How could the federal government force them to abide by an agreement they had not helped to establish? Worker representatives negotiating such agreements, they also claimed, should be affiliated with local organizations, not with a national organization like the RED.[34]

Rather than wait for the Railroad Labor Board's decision about the national agreements, labor leaders immediately lodged their protests with President Wilson. As one leader described, Atterbury "not only violated all decent proprieties by his ultimatum to the Labor Board, [but he] . . . disregarded the transportation laws and flouted existing agencies."[35] In poor health and about to leave office, the president left the dispute in the Railroad Labor Board's hands.[36] Four days later, the board announced that it would not hear the case, explaining that the railroad executives should have first conferred with their workers about wage rates, working conditions, and the national agreements. As a result, the railroad executives dropped the case against the national agreements and held pro forma conferences with worker representatives to fulfill the letter of the law. They anticipated that there would be changes in the board's membership after Harding took office in March 1921, and they planned on bringing the issue of national agreements before the board again.

### The Collapse of the Railroad Labor Board

As the railroad executives hoped, Harding made three new appointments to the board that secured their position about the abrogation of the national agreements. The president used his appointment powers to shape and define the board. He seated an antiunion carrier member, a labor member who had not been nominated by organized labor, and an antiunion public member. First, Samuel Higgins, previously a manager of the New York, New Haven & Hartford Railroad, replaced William L. Park, the only railroad carrier representative who helped with the Railroad Administration.

Second, Harding refused to reappoint James J. Forrester, who spoke for the shopcrafts workers in unions, such as the Maintenance of Way union. Harding gave Forrester's seat to W. L. McMenimen, a vice president of the Brotherhood of Railroad Trainmen, who had the support of neither his union nor the labor community. Labor leaders called McMenimen a "stool pigeon."[37] Further raising these leaders' ire, Harding officially announced that McMenimen represented not the operating or nonoperating railroad workers but the fourth classification of workers—the "subordinate officials." These workers, aside from representing only 5 percent of the industry's workforce, held supervisory jobs that organized labor associated with management.[38]

Finally, Harding appointed Ben W. Hooper to fill Hunt's position as a public representative on the board. Hooper, formerly the governor of Tennessee, took a strong position against organized labor. He wrote articles upholding the Kansas Court of Industrial Arbitration, which had instituted compulsory arbitration, as the model labor board.[39] Compulsory arbitration, Hooper contended, provided the best means available for getting unions to behave "responsibly."[40]

Given the antiunion bias of the three new members, by 1921 the AFL insisted that the Railroad Labor Board could no longer be characterized as a tripartite agency. If these new members voted with the two remaining carrier members, they formed a permanent five-to-four majority. To be sure, the new board's antiunion outlook readily became apparent when it handed down a series of decisions crippling organized labor: it abrogated the wartime national agreements, undermined the power of the national adjustment boards, and lowered wage rates.

## A Faulty Worker Representation Scheme

The status of the five existing national agreements, remnants of the Railroad Administration, was the critical issue facing the Railroad Labor Board.[41] The question of union versus worker representation underlay these agreements.[42] According to the executives, the fact that the newly organized shopcrafts had the agreements gave them an unprecedented amount of bargaining power.[43] As the author of one article in the *Railway Age* described, "the government [had] permitted and even encouraged all classes of employees to organize."[44] Or as a political scientist wrote in 1920, the national agreements "'unionize[d]' all railroad labor, including shop employees many crafts of which had formally worked under local regulations and had not the support of powerful national organizations."[45] The railroad executives resented this.

When the board first met in 1921, the railroad executives demanded that these agreements be broken.[46] "Local" (read nonunion) agents, the carriers proclaimed, could represent these railroad workers.[47] If the national agreements remained valid until their designated expiration date (long after the dismantling of the Railroad Administration), the railroad executives claimed, the shopcrafts unions would unfairly inherit the right to represent the workers. But if the board abolished these agreements, the question of worker representation would become open, which, according to railroad executives like Atterbury, had been the intent of the legislative authors of the Transportation Act. "The railway managers demand the right to deal directly with their own men," one author for the *Railway Age* wrote, "regardless of membership or non-membership in any union. They insist that the men who do not desire to pay tribute in union dues be permitted to have a voice in the working agreements with their own employees as the Transportation Act contemplates they should do."[48]

Clearly, the railroad executives exaggerated the ambiguity of the Transportation Act for their own purposes. On the House and Senate floors, the Republicans avoided openly discussing the status of the five national agreements. Being divided into two factions, the progressives and the old guard, Republicans had fabricated a compromise provision—a scheme for worker representation—that implicitly recognized these agreements by offering any group the authority to become the railroad workers' negotiating agent. When the Railroad Labor Board decided that the system federations of shopcrafts had no automatic authority to negotiate the railroad workers trade agreements, it altered the balance of power in this carefully constructed compromise.[49]

The railroad unions, the RED, strongly opposed dismantling the national agreements. With its decision to do just that, the board destroyed what the AFL described as the most vital aspect of the wartime governmental operation of the railroads. According to the Executive Committee of the AFL, "this decision undid a notable achievement in the direction of justice. It constituted a deliberate step backwards."[50] The board ignored the AFL's protests, however. Indeed, it was precisely because the five national agreements exemplified the most important element of the Railroad Administration's labor policy that the Railroad Labor Board ruled in favor of abrogating these agreements.

To compensate for the loss of the national work condition standards that the national agreements provided, however, the board did impose on the railroads sixteen conditions of its own creation.[51] Jewell influenced the board as it drafted these provisions. He called for the same conditions that he included in a "bill of rights" for labor. Although Jewell, like most labor leaders, would have preferred to maintain the national agreements, the Railroad Labor Board's list of work conditions pleased him. Rules 5 and 15 particularly gratified the shopcrafts workers: they guaranteed these workers the right to select their own representatives, and they prevented the formation of company unions. For the same reason, the ARE condemned the board's imposition of standard work conditions on the grounds that the board had no authority to shape the contents of newly negotiated trade agreements.[52] As one journalist for a trade association magazine summed up most railroad executives' reaction, "[The] Board is magnifying its own powers."[53]

Apart from deciding the controversy over the national trade agreements, by late 1921 the new board became more involved in settling labor disputes. The board members transformed the Republican railroad labor relations machinery by endowing it with quasi-judicial powers and capacities. They made the Senior Railroad Labor Board, rather than the subordinate national adjustment boards, the centerpiece of this machinery. In 1920, the first Railroad Labor Board reprimanded both the railroad executives and the unions for not utilizing the adjustment boards. The board rejected the ARE's first request for a wage decrease, solely on the grounds that the railroad executives had tried to negotiate a settlement directly with employee representatives. But then, in 1921, the board reversed its position, encouraging the railroad executives and the worker representatives to bring their disputes directly before it. Preferring to be judged by the Senior Board, because it had public representatives as well as management and labor representatives, the railroad executives refused to use

the adjustment boards to mediate labor disputes.[54] They thought that circumventing the adjustment boards would be "a defeat for the unions and the principle of free negotiation; a victory for the railroads, who [thought] it to their
advantage to have compulsory arbitration."[55] But, as they slowly realized, the
board's interests were not always their own.[56]

Although neglecting the adjustment boards gave neither the railroad executives nor organized labor an advantage, it did hasten the board's demise. Congress had intended the Railroad Labor Board to hear only appellate cases, but
with parties to a dispute bypassing the adjustment boards, this Senior Board
heard all labor dispute cases, although it had neither the time nor the resources
to resolve them.[57] Despite the board's bias toward the railroad executives, its
decisions about the national agreements and the national work conditions
alienated both these executives and organized labor.

## An Unwarranted Assumption of Authority

Shortly after the Railroad Labor Board issued the decision that terminated the five national agreements between the shopcrafts unions and the
Railroad Administration in 1921, a conflict flared up over the new work conditions.[58] The Pennsylvania Railroad challenged the Railroad Labor Board's
authority to implement Rules 5 and 15, holding that, in effect, the rules operationalized the worker representation scheme without promoting company
unions.[59] Rea and Atterbury demonstrated their preference for company
unions when they refused to negotiate with System Federation No. 90, a federation of shopcrafts affiliated with the RED, despite Rules 5 and 15, which
bound them to meet with these representatives of the railroad workers' "own
choosing."

Recognized as "notorious" for their "anti-union bias," Rea and Atterbury
had every intention of returning to their prewar policy of refusing to negotiate
with any unions other than the Railroad Brotherhood of Train and Engine
Service.[60] Once the Railroad Labor Board ruled for the termination of the national agreements in April 1921, Rea and Atterbury felt that the first step of
their union-busting plan had been satisfied. Then, they implemented the second step: a conference to renegotiate a trade agreement with the shopcrafts
workers that excluded System Federation No. 90.

At this conference, Atterbury announced that System Federation No. 90,
which had been organized in July 1918 and which represented the shopcrafts
under the national agreement, lacked the authorization to negotiate the agreement.[61] In fact, Rea and Atterbury excluded System Federation No. 90 on
the grounds that it had conducted an unfair election. The ballot it used, they

claimed, should not have listed the union by organization; candidates should have been listed without their affiliations. Rea and Atterbury also contested the union's right of regional representation, arguing that worker representatives must be instead chosen from the local railroads. The railroad executives then designed a ballot excluding the System Federation as a representational candidate.

When the Pennsylvania Railroad held the election intended to ensure that System Federation No. 90 would not represent the shopcrafts workers, only 5,236 of 33,104 voted.[62] In protest, the System Federation held its own election, and the shopcrafts workers cast 26,055 votes in its favor.[63] Despite this decisive victory, Rea and Atterbury still refused to acknowledge System Federation No. 90. As C. B. Heiserman, counsel for the Pennsylvania Railroad, said, "Our company refused to negotiate with such officers [affiliated with the RED], . . . recognizing no legal obligation so to do."[64]

At this point, N. B. Good, the president of System Federation No. 90, asked the Railroad Labor Board to intervene. The Railroad Labor Board ruled as follows: both the railroad executives and System Federation had used unfair election guidelines and procedures.[65] Rea and Atterbury had no right to control the process; and similarly, System Federation No. 90 should have offered nonunion representatives a chance to run.[66] Another election, overseen by the Board itself, must be held.[67] The board drafted guidelines for the Pennsylvania Railroad, System Federation No. 90, and the shopcrafts workers to follow, ensuring the election of union or nonunion representatives.[68]

While the shopcrafts workers applauded the board's decision, Rea and Atterbury were outraged. The board had no right, according to Rea, "to indicate the domain of management and to assert jurisdiction over grievances of whatsoever kind and character in connection with the employment, the discipline, and the discharge of its employees."[69] According to Heiserman, his clients were "expressly denying the right and power of the Board to prescribe principles which must in law govern the carrier and its employees in the making of agreements."[70] He elaborated: "The company denied the power of the Board to prescribe an election or any other method, by which the carrier may ascertain who are the authorized representatives of its employees."[71]

In the midst of this conflict, the Railroad Labor Board was assigned a new official leader, Ben Hooper. Under Barton's chairmanship, the board had established national work conditions; with Hooper, expressly hostile toward organized labor, these conditions were not scrupulously enforced. The new chairman had a clear idea about the Pennsylvania Railroad's tactics. "It is perfectly obvious," he wrote to Harding, "that the Pennsylvania [railroad line] has decided to make war upon certain of the labor organizations on its system."

Yet Hooper did little to discourage Rea and Atterbury from practicing their "war making." Attorney General Harry Daughtery, a conservative member of Harding's administration, also sided with the Pennsylvania Railroad by encouraging them to disobey the board's decision. He suggested that they request a delay from the board.[72]

After the board granted them a fifteen-day extension, Rea and Atterbury still refused to meet with System Federation No. 90. Instead, they conferred with the workers elected during the company election and established a new trade agreement.[73] Then, in December 1921, the Pennsylvania Railroad filed a petition with a federal court to stop the Railroad Labor Board from issuing any negative publicity about the company union.[74] Underlying the petition was Rea's and Atterbury's principled protest that the board "laid down general rules of procedures which the railway was ordered to follow in choosing employee representatives. . . . The Board even went so far as to prescribe the form of the ballot."[75] Although the railroad executives had, more often than not, benefited from the board's decisions at the shopcrafts unions' expense, they still undermined the board's power with injunctive relief.[76] Judge J. M. Landis temporarily enjoined the board from "prescribing any regulation relating to rules" about electing the shopcrafts workers' collective bargaining agents.[77]

Despite this attack on its legal authority, the board still refrained from condemning the Pennsylvania Railroad executives' actions until the last moment.[78] According to a journalist for the *New York Times*, "members of the Labor Board showed no surprise when they learned" about the temporary injunction. Indeed, "some [members] expressed themselves as being glad that the matter was to be settled in the courts," since they wanted the "question of the board's legal jurisdiction" settled.

In May 1922, the United States District Court for the Northern District of Illinois upheld the railroad executives' interpretation of the Transportation Act. Judge George T. Page issued a permanent injunction stating that "the appointment or method of election of conferees under section 301 was not one of the functions delegated to the Board, and therefore it ha[d] not the right to make the regulations provided for in Decision No. 218."[79] Imposing a new election on the Pennsylvania carrier, he ruled, "was beyond the powers of the Labor Board."[80] According to the lawyer for the Pennsylvania Railroad, the railroad had a "desire to protect its legal rights and those of its employees from what [the company] deemed to be an unwarranted assumption of authority on the part of the Labor Board."[81]

The board, however, relayed to the journalist from the *New York Times* that it would put up a "vigorous defense." Other members of the Republican administration thought the Pennsylvania Railroad's injunction seriously compromised the board. According to Blackburn Esterlin, special assistant to the

U.S. attorney general, the board "must close shop and transfer all its proceedings if the injunction became permanent."[82] And indeed, once the injunction became permanent, the board took its case to the Seventh Circuit Court of Appeals.[83] Judge Samuel Alschuler overturned the permanent injunction, upholding the board's regulation of the worker representation election process.

According to Judge Alschuler, there was "no question as to the power of the board."[84] He rejected the railroad carriers' argument that "the Board was in no way concerned in the matter of the election" of employee representatives.[85] The board had this preventive power.[86] "It must be within the power of the Board to decide whether the representatives planning to represent the members of organizations do in fact represent them," Henry Hunt, a former public member of the board, said, "if the Board is to function."[87] The Railroad Labor Board "had full jurisdiction" about this "procedural issue" of worker representation.[88] This court of appeals rejected the intention that Hunt suggested had "disembowelled" the Railroad Labor Board.

Judge Alschuler's decision and the public's outcry did little to discourage the Pennsylvania executives from taking the next step of bringing the case before the U.S. Supreme Court. Rea and Atterbury did everything in their power to prevent the shopcrafts workers from obtaining the right to select their own representatives. John J. Dowd, the chairman of the general strike committee overseeing the 1922 shopmen's strike, wrote, "At the very moment that these executives, dominated by General Atterbury, the union hating Vice President, were piously announcing to the Senate Interstate Commerce Committee that they would not grant seniority privileges to union men because the unions are fighting the Government by rejecting a decision of the Labor Board, the Federal Judges in Chicago were writing a decision which allows the board to censure publicly the same Pennsylvania Railroad for having disobeyed one of its most important orders."[89] Rea and Atterbury hoped the Republican-controlled Supreme Court would rule that the Railroad Labor Board had "transcended its power" in overseeing the worker representation process.[90] As Secretary of Commerce Herbert Hoover wrote, "The Supreme Court of the United States is yet to be heard from on the technical question of legality of the ballot. . . . But the merits of the issue between the P.R.R. and the System Federation No. 90 depend upon considerations far deeper than mere legality."[91]

Rea and Atterbury were incensed by the Railroad Labor Board's interference in their conflict with System Federation No. 90. They thought the worker representation process was an open invitation for union busting. The fact that the Republicans had created this board, combined with its reluctance to hold the Pennsylvania Railroad to the same standard that was applied to System Federation No. 90, led them to this conclusion. Yet Rea and Atterbury miscalculated how much faith the Railroad Labor Board put in the scheme for worker representation. Raising questions about the board's capacity to supervise this scheme backfired. While the Supreme Court ruled that the board could not legally enforce its decisions, it presented vitally important dicta in support of the worker representation process that would become the blueprint for the future.

### He Who Seeks Equity Must Come
### into the Court with Clean Hands

On February 19, 1923, the Supreme Court handed down its rulings on *Pennsylvania Railroad v. U.S. Railroad Labor Board* and thereby greatly disappointed the Pennsylvania Railroad.[92] Divided on most labor-management issues, the Court united on this decision. The almost permanent progressive minority of Justices Louis D. Brandeis, Oliver Wendell Holmes, and James R. Clarke voted with its conservative Republican brethren to uphold the Railroad Labor Board's authority to oversee the worker representation scheme. "If the Board has jurisdiction to hear representatives of the employees," Taft wrote, "it must of necessity have the power to determine who are proper representatives of the employees."[93]

What is significant about the board's scheme for worker representation was that the Taft Court relied on the principles of agency for justification. The Court decided that the Transportation Act gave the railroad unions, or any other association, including company-sponsored organizations, only a temporary grant of authority to represent the railroad workers. Since System Federation No. 90 could not be granted this authority on a permanent basis, it was the Railroad Labor Board's obligation to protect the integrity of the worker representation process. In other words, the state, manifested by this board, must safeguard the individual rights of the workers, not the rights of management or organized labor.

The Court's recognition of the worker representation scheme dealt such a severe blow to the Pennsylvania executives because they had brought the case hoping the Court would declare that Congress had *not* intended the national railroad unions to represent the workers.[94] Heiserman, counsel for the Pennsylvania Railroad, argued that the Republican Congress had not intended this system of labor relations to provide unions with protection but rather to exclude them from the worker representation process. Writing the opinion for the unanimous Court, Taft spurned Heiserman's argument. "We find nothing in the act to impose any such limitation if the organization in other respects fulfills the description of the act," he concluded. Organized labor had every right to place its unions *among* the organizations available for workers to secure representation in establishing a trade agreement. "No reason suggests itself," Taft declared, "why such an association, if its membership is properly inclusive[,] may not be regarded as among the organizations of employees referred to in this legislation."[95] Heiserman also grounded the case on Rea and Atterbury's claim that allowing the railroad workers to select worker representatives deprived them of their freedom to contract. Rules 5 and 15 of the Railroad Labor Board's work condition guidelines, these Pennsylvania executives declared, robbed all concerned parties of due process and the right of freedom to contract. Rule 5 stated: "The right of such lawful organization to act toward lawful objects through representatives of its own choice, whether employees of a particular carrier or otherwise, shall be agreed to by the management." And Rule 15 declared that "the majority of any craft or class of employees shall have the right to determine what organization shall represent members of such craft or class."[96] Again, the Taft Court threw out the railroad executives' argument, stating that the board's rules "deprive[d] either side of the rights claimed."[97] In other words, recognizing the workers' right to representation in no way undermined the employers' freedom to contract. No mandate existed that compelled employers to establish collective trade agreements with these representatives.

After dismissing the Pennsylvania executives' particular claims, Taft turned to the question of legislative intent. According to Taft, the worker representation process in the Transportation Act put neither organized labor nor any other group in a privileged position. Congress offered group, not union, representation as a means of giving railroad workers a voice in the collective bargaining process. A group, moreover, considered to be the sum of its members, had the right to ratify or revoke the authority of its contracting agent. The board protected a worker's procedural right to choose a representative, thereby instilling a modicum of individualism in the collective bargaining process.

To the Taft Court, the genius of the worker representation process was three-fold. First, this process never jeopardized the private character of contractual relations. Market relations, not the American state, still governed the conditions of the collective bargaining agreement. Second, the worker representation scheme safeguarded the public interest by giving the Railroad Labor Board the authority to determine who could participate in the collective bargaining process. "If the board has jurisdiction to hear representatives of the employees," Taft wrote, "it must of necessity have the power to determine who are proper representatives of the employees."[98] Third, Congress had the authority to legislate a permanent labor relations agency with just such regulatory powers. A legislatively designed quasi-judicial agency could direct and oversee the election of collective bargaining agents for the railroad employees. "One of the specific powers conferred by Section 308 is to 'make regulations necessary for the efficient execution of the functions vested in it by this title.' This must include the authority to determine who are proper representatives of the employees and to make reasonable rules for ascertaining the will of the employees in the matter."[99] The chief justice insisted that this was "a condition precedent to its effective exercise of judgement at all."

The Taft Court implicitly established the protection of the collective bargaining process in toto. But, in order not to give Congress too much discretionary power after granting it this liberty, Taft differentiated the judiciary's duties from those practiced by the Railroad Labor Board. Such a legislatively established agency could monitor employee representation election procedures, but the judiciary must still determine the legal rights and obligations of the railroad employers and employees. He expounded further: "The Railroad Labor Board did not have the jurisdiction to provide a tribunal to determine what were the legal rights and obligations of railway employers and employees to enforce or protect them. Courts can do that. The Labor Board was created to decide how the parties ought to exercise their legal rights so as to enable them to cooperate in running the railroad."[100] The board, Taft underscored, respected the Pennsylvania Railroad's right to contract because "the statute does not require the Railway Company to recognize or to deal with, or confer with labor unions. It does not require employees to deal with their employers through their fellow employees."[101] The labor relations provisions in the Transportation Act explicitly stated that the railroad executives must recognize worker representatives, not just union representatives. "But," as Taft explained, "we think it does vest the Labor Board with the power to decide how such representatives ought to be chosen with a view to securing a satisfactory cooperation and leaves it to the two sides to accept or reject the decisions."[102]

Showing further support for the representational aspect of the railroad labor relations machinery, Taft emphasized the importance of the adjustment boards. "Undoubtedly the act requires a serious effort by the carrier and his employees," he wrote, "to adjust their differences as the first step in settling a dispute."[103] Taft then admonished the Pennsylvania executives for avoiding these adjustment boards. Albeit indirectly, the Taft Court also reprimanded the Railroad Labor Board for permitting the railroad executives to circumvent the adjustment boards. Committed to arbitration, rather than mediation, the board had allowed the railroad executives to bring their labor disputes directly before it. In contrast, the Taft Court emphasized the usefulness of the adjustment boards and the importance of worker representation.

The Taft Court's endorsement of worker representation indicated its implicit acceptance of the principal/agent idea of collective bargaining buried in the Transportation Act. During the policymaking process, some progressive Republicans in the House of Representatives had been concerned about what legal sanctions this legislation forced on organized labor as well as its membership, since unions enjoyed no limited liability as corporations did. The old guard, by contrast, showed little concern about how these sanctions affected union rights (or the rights of their membership). They advocated instilling the Transportation Act with stronger sanctions, such as compulsory arbitration, to protect the public interest. During the joint conference committee meeting, the progressives compromised with the old guard Republicans by creating a legislative version of the principles of agency. The Transportation Act had not settled whether unions or company-sponsored groups had the right to represent the railroad workers. Rather, the worker representation scheme, like agency law, emphasized the temporary character of the union's legal personality: a union could negotiate collective trade agreements if it had been ratified as the negotiating agent by the railroad workers. This scheme upheld the rights of the railroad workers and the collective bargaining process, not the rights of the unions like System Federation No. 90.

In all, the Taft Court upheld the Republican intent of the Transportation Act, striking a balance between class legislation and compulsory arbitration. Workers had the right to representation free from any type of interference. As the *Washington Post* reported, Taft "held that the labor board did not exceed its powers when it condemned the methods adopted by the Pennsylvania railroad to establish employee representation in dealing with questions of wages and working conditions." [104] At the same time, the Court undermined the old guard Republicans' interpretation of the Railroad Labor Board. Harding and some of his appointees realized that the board had only advisory powers; they nonetheless believed that it should have the power to render legally binding compulsory arbitration decisions. In the Court's opinion, however, the board should not be amended to have this power. Several months later, the Court handed down *Chas. Wolff Packing Company v. Court of Industrial Relations of the State of Kansas*,[105] rendering compulsory arbitration "unconstitutional" in the words of the AFL's new president, William Green.[106] The unanimous Court suggested in dicta in the *Pennsylvania* decision that the worker representation provisions, which promoted trade agreement negotiations, should be strengthened.

### Whose Victory?

When the Court made the *Pennsylvania* decision public, Atterbury applauded, claiming it as the railroad executives' victory.[107] Ignoring the Court's dicta that all parties should abide by the board's decisions voluntarily, the Pennsylvania executives reiterated their refusal to comply.[108] Rea and Atterbury continued negotiating with their company union. With great reluctance, the board issued a final ruling: "If employee representation means anything at all, it signifies right of a class of employees, through majority action, to select their own representatives. . . . That is what Congress said it meant, but the shopcrafts have so far been deprived of this plain, simple, indisputable right." [109]

System Federation No. 90 shared none of the board's patience with the Pennsylvania executives' refusal to recognize their union. In May 1922, they sought an injunction to prevent this conspiracy to defeat the Transportation Act's labor relations, but the United States District Court for the Eastern District of Pennsylvania turned down their request for equity relief. [110] On appeal to the United States Circuit Court of Appeals, System Federation No. 90 gained an injunction against the Pennsylvania railroad. The Supreme Court heard the case in 1924, long after the controversy had ended.

The Taft Court unanimously overturned the labor union's injunction for enforcing the Railroad Labor Board's decision. Although the Pennsylvania Railroad executives ignored the board's decision, the Court ruled that they still could not be enjoined. "We do not think Congress, while it would deprecate such action," Taft noted, "intended to make it criminal or legally actionable. Therefore the bill of complaint does not aver a conspiracy, and without that equitable relief cannot be granted." [111]

Nonetheless, within two years it became apparent that the shopcrafts union had lost this fight against Rea and Atterbury but that the union had won the battle for the worker representation scheme. In 1926, the Republicans made it the centerpiece of the Railway Labor Act. Gompers stated in a press release, "So far as I can see, the Railroad Labor Board has no added strength because of the [*Pennsylvania*] decision but the Pennsylvania Railroad on the contrary stands in a much weakened position and is accused of having adopted a wrong course contrary to the spirit of the law, contrary to the interests of the workers, and intended only to advance the narrow, selfish interests of the railroad." [112]

Gompers's judgment proved true. Rea and Atterbury secured these rulings in the *Pennsylvania* decisions at the expense of the board's prestige, which, after all, promoted their interests more than those of organized labor. "I think there is no question but [that] the Pennsylvania [railroad] refused to accept the jurisdiction of the Labor Board, and the case went to the Supreme Court, and the Supreme Court held that the Labor Board had no power to enforce its decisions," the progressive Republican senator Robert M. LaFollette Jr. wrote; "that is one of the reasons why this new machinery must be set up, if we are going to have any sort of machinery for settling disputes." [113]

## Union Outlaws

While the Taft Court resolved the Pennsylvania dispute, the Railroad Labor Board handed down a decision that sparked the 1922 shopmen's strike that also contributed to the board's collapse.[114] As it had in the first conflict, the Pennsylvania Railroad, being the largest single railroad and the leader of the open-shop campaign against the nonoperating workers, played a large role in this controversy.[115] What changed was that in this second conflict only organized labor was antagonized. To the railroad executives' satisfaction, the board reversed its initial wage increase decision in 1920 and decreased the railroad workers' wages in 1921 and again in 1922.[116] These wage decreases sparked the shopmen's strike in 1922.

The board's decision in 1921 outraged organized labor because it seemed particularly partisan, reflecting the newly established Republican control of the board as well as conservative Republican bias toward the railroad executives. The former Democratic administration had long promised railroad workers a wage increase, not a wage decrease. Labor leaders, like Jewell, contemplated organizing a national strike but at the last moment called it off.[117] The new Republican administration threatened to break this "intolerable public inconvenience."[118] The Department of Justice prepared an injunction to restrain the strikers.[119] The executives, moreover, undermined the railroad unions' solidarity by offering the brotherhoods, the unions for the operating workers, independent wage concessions.[120] "The problem," as Hooper described it, was "to find a way for the Brotherhoods to escape from the strike and save their faces."[121]

Faced with the combined hostility of the Republican administration and the railroad executives, the nonoperating unions abided by the first wage decrease decision.[122] When the board reduced wage rates again in 1922, however, the shopmen struck.[123] Although Hooper claimed that "the decision seemed to impress the labor members of the Board as somewhat drastic, but it is, in fact conservative," nothing the board or the Republican administration said could dissuade the shopmen.[124] On July 1, 1922, four hundred thousand shopmen walked out on the first national strike since the 1894 Pullman strike.[125]

Neither the Railroad Labor Board nor the Republican administration resolved this strike. While the second wage decrease angered union leaders (particularly Jewell, who led the strike), the new comprehensive policy of localization, not the wage decrease, devastated them. Localizing wage rates undermined the shopcrafts.[126] Although the railroad executives established local trade agreements with the brotherhoods, they planned to negotiate no such agreements with the nonoperating unions.[127] Jewell and Gompers saw this decision by the railroad executives as a clear attempt to divide and conquer the shopcrafts unions organized by the AFL.

Revealing its biases against organized labor and in favor of compulsory arbitration, the Railroad Labor Board declared that by the very act of striking the shopmen forfeited all their mediation and arbitration privileges. After just two days, the board responded to the shopmen's strike: by a five-to-two majority (the public members Hanger and McMenimen were absent), the board composed what became known as the outlaw resolution, denouncing this strike. The railroad executives now considered any strikebreakers to be legitimate employees, with all the rights and privileges granted by the labor relations provisions in the Transportation Act.[128]

Pleased by the board's outlaw resolution, the railroad executives adopted it as their own. They characterized the railroad shopmen as "outlaws," arguing that the strike was "against a decision of the Government's own agency" rather than just against the railroads.[129] Further, the railroad executives issued another ultimatum: unless the shopmen returned to work immediately, they forfeited their seniority rights. Adding this second ultimatum to the board's first made the possibility of resolving the shopmen's strike even more remote. Finally, railroads like the Pennsylvania Railroad that were engaged in the open-shop campaign against the shopcrafts unions used the opportunity to negotiate with company unions.[130] Only a few railroads, such as the Baltimore & Ohio, headed by Daniel Willard, agreed to meet with the shopmen in a wage conference.[131] The railroad executives wanted no amicable resolution of this strike—they planned to win the strike by breaking the largest nonoperating railroad union.[132] John J. Dowd, the shopmen's chairman of the general committee, declared, "The 90 per cent are now on strike and will remain on until the Pennsylvania abandons its illegal union-smashing policy, which is now the only obstacle to a settlement."[133]

Realizing that the outlaw resolution was prolonging the strike, the Railroad Labor Board grudgingly rescinded it.[134] By the time the board reversed positions, however, it was too late. The railroad executives balked at giving the shopmen their seniority rights, and the shopmen refused to return to work without them. With the board unable to break the impasse, President Harding stepped forward.[135] To begin with, Harding secretly admonished the board for having passed the now infamous "outlaw resolution." Without the force of law, Harding thought, this type of hard-line resolution was bound to fail. He then began to mediate the strike.

The first Harding plan provided that both parties abide by the board's wage rates, withdraw all lawsuits, and return the shopmen to work with their full seniority rights. The shopmen agreed to this plan, but the railroad executives rejected it, refusing to reinstate the shopmen with seniority rights.[136] In response, Harding developed a second plan that resolved the seniority rights issue. The shopmen would return to work with the promise that the Railroad Labor Board would settle the seniority issue.[137] This time, the railroad executives accepted Harding's plan (knowing the board's inclination to favor the carriers over labor), but the shopmen turned it down.[138]

After Harding's second plan failed, he went so far as to call in Senators

Albert B. Cummins, a progressive Republican from Iowa and chairman of the Senate Interstate Commerce Committee; James Watson, an old guard Republican from Indiana; and Frank Kellogg, a progressive Republican from Minnesota, to meet with the railroad executives about settling the strike.[139] Harding expressed his frustration with the labor unions *and* the railroad executives. He thought both sides were using the seniority issue to prolong the strike.[140]

Harding ultimately used the equity courts to enforce the Railroad Labor Board's wage decrease decision. An injunction forced the shopmen to stop striking and return to work. Harding arrived at this decision, however, only after long deliberation.[141] He was torn between the advice that different cabinet members provided him.[142] The more moderate Republicans—James J. Davis, secretary of labor; Herbert Hoover, secretary of commerce; and Charles E. Hughes, secretary of state—all argued that further negotiations would resolve the strike.[143] The conservative Republican attorney general Daughtery insisted that only an injunction restricting the shopmen would end it.[144] Propounding the old guard Republican line on organized labor—that unions must be prevented from endangering the public interest by striking—Daughtery blamed the shopmen, not the railroad executives, for not complying with the Railroad Labor Board's wage rate decision.[145]

### The Common Law Will Not Help a Fool, but Equity Exists to Help Him

On September 1, 1922, Daughtery secured a temporary injunction from Judge James Wilkerson in the U.S. District Court in Northern Illinois.[146] Yet using the district court to enforce the Railroad Labor Board's decision created an uproar that underscored the weakness of the board.[147] According to the *New Republic*, "the immediate response to Mr. Daughtery's injunction was so indignant that the administration recoiled."[148] Weekly magazines, such as the *Nation* and the *New Republic*, highlighted the Republican administration's bias against organized labor by pointing out that equity relief had not been sought in other cases.[149] The *Literary Digest* reported "criticism coming from conservative daily papers."[150]

Heedless of public outcry against the temporary injunction, Daughtery filed for a permanent one.[151] The temporary injunction, he boasted, had ended the strike, and he added, "No extensive strike tying up Interstate Commerce will ever again take place in this country."[152] But while the injunction stopped the shopmen from striking, no one considered it a victory for the Republican administration.[153] The railroad shopmen's strike represented, at best, only a short-term victory for the Republican administration.[154] The injunction ended the strike, but it also created dissension within the GOP and set the agenda for re-vision of the Railroad Labor Board itself.[155]

Ironically, the president made the first move for reform. Compulsory arbi-tration, Harding believed, was the answer to his frustrations with the shop-men's strike. If the board was to be effective, Harding insisted, the striking shopmen as well as the railroad executives must in the future obey all of its de-cisions. The board had already proved itself incapable of resolving a major rail-road dispute, and Harding doubted that it could avoid a similar strike situation because it lacked the power to enforce its own decisions.[156] "My own theory is that we should make a very complete change in the law creating the Railroad Labor Board," Harding said, "and make provision against suspension of activ-ities, thereby avoiding any menace to maintained transportation."[157] Compul-sory arbitration provided the best remedy for such railroad union unrest, since labor disputes would always be resolved at the constituent groups' expense. The public would never bear the financial burden of resolving a strike.

Once the strike was ended, Harding suggested that Congress give the board enforcement provisions. As Hooper had said one year earlier: "Congress should put a few teeth in the law, and then let us alone."[158] The president pro-posed that the Railroad Labor Board be placed under the Interstate Commerce Commission's (ICC) jurisdiction. Introducing ideas that resembled the Repub-lican progressive Albert Cummins's idea of a transportation board, Harding suggested that labor management relations be subjugated to the economic con-siderations of the entire railroad industry. A professional agency would estab-lish wage rates and working conditions and would have the right to enforce its decisions, thereby avoiding labor disputes. With this type of professional board ensuring fair wage rates and working conditions, disputes between the railroad workers and the carriers would be outlawed. Harding still promoted using compulsory arbitration.

### Conclusion

The shopmen's strike combined with the Pennsylvania Railroad's conflict over the worker representation scheme caused the collapse of the Rail-road Labor Board.[159] Ironically, however, it was the Taft Court's decisions in both *Pennsylvania* cases, not the shopmen's strike, that provided a guideline for Congress to follow. The Court had outlined the limits of the Railroad Labor Board's real and potential constitutional jurisdiction.

Despite Harding's calls for compulsory arbitration, the *Pennsylvania* deci-sions ended the pursuit of this option. Instead of encouraging Congress to give the public Railroad Labor Board enforcement powers, the Taft Court advo-cated that the worker representation scheme be strengthened. Railroad labor disputes could be avoided, the Court maintained, if railroad workers had bona fide representatives negotiating collective trade agreements.

With this emphasis on worker representation, the Court ruled that applying the principles of agency to labor law did not violate its doctrines of due process and freedom to contract. Like the progressive state and federal courts before it, the Taft Court recognized the principal/agent distinction within responsible unionism to promote peaceful contractual relations between railroad unions and their employers. To ensure that the railroad workers chose the principal representing them in good faith, the Court required in dicta that new labor-management relations machinery oversee the worker representation elections. These elections, the Court held, sustained neither the railroad workers' nor the executives' rights, because "the statute [did] not require the Railway Company to recognize or deal with, or confer with labor unions." [160]

The Taft Court's dictum on worker representation was a formal legal construct like the constructs described by Max Weber. It made no mention of concrete ethical values in support of capitalism or liberalism. Nor did it confer substantive rights upon organized labor or business. The rights specified in this dictum, moreover, were devoid of any references to a specific moral position. Instead, the railroad workers received procedural rights, which promoted due process. That is, the railroad workers had the right to fair and equal treatment when they participated in the scheme for worker representation. Neither union leaders nor employers could interfere with their right to determine whether the these workers joined a trade union or an employer-sponsored company union.

The procedural rights embedded within the scheme for worker representation rested upon the value of individualism. This scheme safeguarded the individual rights of the railroad workers not simply for the workers themselves but because they lived in a society that promoted such rights. The worker representation scheme was based on the value of individualism, but because this value was accepted by most everyone, it was not viewed as a value. In other words, individualism was not characterized as what it is—a value—because of its universal appeal.

What is more, the Taft Court's description of worker representation was so compelling because it was perceived as value-free. It explains why the Taft Court's dictum instructed the Republican administration and the Republican Congress when they changed the railroad labor relations machinery in 1926. Like the Railroad Labor Board before it, the U.S. Mediation Board established by the Railway Labor Act of 1926 would protect the procedural rights of all workers and reaffirm the idea that individualism, not any form of collectivism, was tantamount to the public good.

## CHAPTER 6

# Compromises and Concessions

## *The Republicans Revitalize*
## *the Railroad Labor Policy*

The present emergency is this, that the Railroad Labor Board has
broken down.
—Senator James E. Watson, 1926

By 1923, the Railroad Labor Board was in ruins: the conflict over
worker representation on the Pennsylvania Railroad and the shopmen's strike
had all but destroyed its credibility.[1] Nonetheless, the Republicans still supported the idea of state interference in the railroad industry, and they were
anxious for their party to reform the old policy. For this reason, President
Warren G. Harding encouraged the Republican Congress to pass legislation
erecting a new, more efficient board. Yet, although Harding proposed that the
Railroad Labor Board be amended, in part, because the Supreme Court encouraged it, he ignored the dictum offered in the Court's *Pennsylvania* decisions.
Instead of strengthening state involvement in the worker representation process, Harding thought that a new board should use compulsory arbitration—
which organized labor perceived as part of the repressive nature of responsible
unionism—to resolve labor disputes.

According to Harding, the problem with the present Railroad Labor Board
was that it gave the railroad employers and workers too much freedom to contract. Only a public board instituting compulsory arbitration would ensure
that society's interests in peaceful industrial relations would not be sacrificed
to the private interests of the railroad employers, workers, and their representatives. With Harding's untimely death in 1923, however, the Republicans
abandoned their plan for compulsory arbitration. When Calvin Coolidge
succeeded Harding, he, too, advocated reconstructing the old Railroad Labor
Board. President Coolidge, however, was less reluctant to follow the Supreme
Court's dictum in the *Pennsylvania* decisions.

Trying to establish himself as the new Republican Party leader, Coolidge committed his party to revising the labor-management relations machinery. Coolidge realized that he must bring the progressive and old guard Republicans together if the GOP was to make the Railroad Labor Board an effective labor-management relations agency. The progressive Republicans, sympathetic to the worker's plight, wanted national labor unions recognized as autonomous players authorized to participate in the collective bargaining process. Initially, they sponsored the Howell-Barkley bill, which officially made sixteen national unions the railroad workers' exclusive contractual agents. But the progressives backed down when the old guard tried to block this bill by arguing that it was class legislation.

Having almost lost their battle to stop the Howell-Barkley bill from coming to a vote in either the House or the Senate, the old guard concluded that they could not single-handedly quash the progressive Republicans' and Democrats' effort to change the Railroad Labor Board. For the board to retain its Republican identity, the old guard realized they must cooperate with the progressive Republicans; only old guard participation in this policymaking process would guarantee that the sixteen standard railroad unions, which included shopcrafts unions, would receive no exclusive rights to represent the railroad workers. Acting as the conciliatory agent, Coolidge brought these Republican factions together to draft another proposal to amend the board.

With President Coolidge's encouragement, the Republicans wrote new legislation even before the defeat of the first measure. The Railway Labor Act of 1926 spurned any pretensions of compulsory arbitration and created a mediation board with the power to bind its decisions legally, thus finally rectifying the structural flaw of unenforceability embedded in the original Transportation Act, which included the Railroad Labor Board.[2] These adjustments in the labor-management relations machinery, however, took a back seat to the debate that stormed over the scheme for worker representation.

Should railroad labor relations machinery give specific national unions the right to represent the railroad workers? Or should the worker representation scheme implemented by the Transportation Act be extended? Over the course of negotiations, the Republican policymakers decided against assigning national labor unions exclusive agency. Yet, to better run the scheme for worker representation, they did impose a duty on employers and workers' representatives: the railroad executives had a duty to sit down with representatives of the workers' "own choosing."

What was significant about this debate over exclusive or unrestricted agency in the railroad labor policy was, first, that it shifted the focus of labor law from organized labor to the collective bargaining process and, second, that it furnished the state with a continual role for interference in the regulation of this process. The U.S. Mediation Board did not give unions either the freedom to associate as voluntary associations or the right to become functional representatives of the public good in the collective bargaining process. Rather, this new policy legitimized labor's right to organize as one organization among many that could bargain for the railroad workers. The Supreme Court upheld this unrestricted notion of agency after ruling that it left the employers' right to freedom of contract and due process undisturbed.

This scheme for worker representation also resolved a fundamental problem that had plagued not only the railroad unions, most notably the shopcrafts unions, but organized labor in general. The Railway Labor Act circumvented the legal dilemma resulting from organized labor's status as an unincorporated association. Organized labor had trouble negotiating binding trade agreements with employers, because most state and federal courts refused to enforce them. Without a legal personality provided by a charter of incorporation, unions had no authority to negotiate contracts for a collective of workers. The new labor legislation, however, embraced the idea of representation, albeit not exclusively union representation, for railroad workers, and it gave representatives the authority to negotiate trade agreements and resolve labor conflicts. Once they received the right to representation, with quasi-judicial agencies enforcing the ensuing trade agreements, unions no longer needed charters of incorporation. Yet, unlike charters of incorporation, this legislation gave unions the competence to negotiate these agreements only temporarily. At any time, railroad workers or employers could ask for another worker representation election.

Organized labor paid a price for the opportunity to negotiate enforceable collective bargaining agreements: because the AFL's and the railroad brotherhoods' lobbying efforts failed to secure exclusive union representation, their unions had to compete with employers who established company unions to provide collective representation for the workers. Hence, the Railway Labor Act underscored the importance of state control in this competitive collective bargaining process.

### Intraparty Conflict: The First Attempt to
### Revise the Railroad Labor Board

By 1922, demands for the Railroad Labor Board's repeal grew stronger.[3] Consequently, Harding encouraged Congress to establish a new labor board by emphasizing the present board's inability to enforce its own decisions. In his 1922 State of the Union address, Harding proposed replacing the Railroad Labor Board with an "impartial tribunal" with strong enforcement powers.[4] He suggested that railroad labor-management relations machinery be placed under the Interstate Commerce Committee's (ICC) jurisdiction. In a speech to Congress, Harding stated, "There ought to be contact with the Interstate Commerce Commission. . . . Theoretically, a fair and living wage should be determined quite apart from the employer's earning capability, but in practice, in the railway service, they are inseparable."[5]

Firmly behind the theory of administrative politics and technocratic expertise, Harding thought that the ICC could best determine wage rates and work conditions for the railroad workers. Describing a plan that resembled Senator Albert B. Cummins's transportation board, Harding suggested that labor-management relations be subjugated to the economic considerations of the entire railroad industry. A professional agency of public representatives would determine wage rates and work conditions. This new agency would enforce all its decisions, thereby preventing an outbreak of labor disputes in the railroad industry. In other words, the ICC would oversee compulsory arbitration. Harding again expressed his support for disciplining organized labor. In 1920, as an old guard Republican in the Senate, Harding had voted for a ban on strikes and lockouts in the labor relations provisions of the Transportation Act. However, Harding did not live long enough to see any changes.

Harding's successor, Calvin Coolidge, also maintained that Congress must amend the Railroad Labor Board. In his inaugural address in 1923, Coolidge suggested that the Republican Congress legislate a better solution for the "labor problem" in the railroad industry, but he dropped Harding's ideas about extending the ICC's jurisdiction to resolve labor disputes with compulsory arbitration. Coolidge sought legislation creating a new independent agency that directly involved the parties engaged in labor disputes. This agency would provide mediation, rather than compulsory arbitration.

Coolidge promoted a voluntary scheme of mediation and voluntary arbitration for two reasons. First, Coolidge was not a member of the old guard or the progressive faction of the GOP. He shared neither the old guard's commitment to compulsory arbitration and desire to discipline organized labor nor the progressives' support for organized labor. Instead, he took a moderate position— labor-management relations machinery should encourage worker representation (though not exclusively union representation) in order to establish and maintain trade agreements with employers. Unlike the first Railroad Labor Board, which was developed after the progressive and old guard Republican leaders in Congress had settled on a series of intraparty compromise positions, the second board was created only after Coolidge built a Republican coalition.

Coolidge believed that unless he adopted a moderate position between these two factions, neither the old guard nor the progressive Republicans would give him the support necessary to amend the Railroad Labor Board.

Second, Coolidge relied on the moderate Republican members of his administration to help pass legislation to create the final U.S. Mediation Board. He solicited help and advice from Secretary of Commerce Herbert Hoover and Secretary of Labor James J. Davis, who both believed that mediation and voluntary arbitration worked better than compulsory arbitration. President Harding, in contrast, had relied more on the advice of the old guard congressional Republicans and Attorney General Harry D. Daughtery, both of whom promoted the use of extreme labor relations measures like the labor injunction.

From the beginning, Coolidge worked behind the scenes to bring the old guard and the progressives together to amend the Railroad Labor Board.[6] If he could force the railroad unions and the carriers to agree to legislation amending the board, Coolidge believed, the two dominant Republican factions would fall in line.[7] In a State of the Union address in 1923, Coolidge said, "If a substantial agreement can be reached among the groups interested, there should be no hesitation in enacting it into law."[8] Coolidge then asked Secretary of Commerce Hoover and Secretary of Labor Davis to orchestrate a meeting between organized labor and the railroad executives. The president understood that these two constituent parties only would agree to labor-management relations provisions that neither protected organized labor nor imposed compulsory arbitration on it. The railroad executives, after they had fought so vehemently against Wilson's protective wartime Railroad Administration, would not support labor relations machinery that made organized labor the railroad workers' exclusive bargaining agents; organized labor would never endorse compulsory arbitration.[9]

Coolidge also asked his cabinet members to provide those meeting with recommendations for revising the labor relations provisions of the Transportation Act. In one memorandum, Hoover wrote, "The President has suggested the importance and the desirability of some agreement upon this question [reorganization of the Railroad Labor Board] as a basis for amendment to the act."[10] Coolidge's efforts showed his clear commitment to new labor-management relations machinery. Nevertheless, he took no credit for the passage of what came to be the Railway Labor Act of 1926.[11] If either the progressive or the old guard Republicans believed that he supported organized labor at the railroad employers' expense, or vice versa, Coolidge risked alienating one of these factions. Thus, in order to reunify the progressive and old guard Republicans, the president maintained a neutral position about railroad labor relations. He preferred to help shape the Republican policymaking process from afar.[12] In fact, a report from the Commerce Department mentioned that the administration's involvement must be kept secret. The memorandum informed Hoover:

> [A] report has reached me that an effort is being made to commit the Administration to some method of adjusting labor disputes, on the mistaken representation that the railroad presidents have refused to confer with labor representatives in an effort to reach a solution mutually satisfactory. . . . Steps are now being taken. . . . I am expecting to succeed in being at a conference in the near future. . . . The reason I impart this information to you, to be treated for the present as strictly confidential, is that I believe premature publicity will injure, and would perhaps destroy, the chances of success.[13]

Coolidge, Hoover, and Davis proceeded with great caution so as not to create a public debate about a new railroad labor policy.[14]

Despite the Republican administration's attempt to keep its negotiations with organized labor and the railroad executives a secret, its first effort to amend the Railroad Labor Board failed. Hoover met with organized labor and the railroad executives separately, and both gave him recommendations on how to amend the Railroad Labor Board. But Hoover failed to get the two groups together.[15] "[Hoover] made an effort to get Mr. Holden and the representatives of the railroads to confer with the employees, but was unable to get them to do so."[16] Only organized labor was convinced to draft such amendments. Of course, this group needed no encouragement, since it had always advocated amending the Railroad Labor Board.

Not surprisingly, after the railroad unions drafted legislation creating a new labor policy, the Republican administration withdrew its support. The Republicans backed away from their promise to amend the Railroad Labor Board, however, not simply because organized labor's suggestions dissatisfied them. Hoover reviewed the unions' draft of legislation and "made two suggestions for changes and explanations he did not insist upon."[17] Rather, the Republican administration refused to sponsor legislation for amending the Railroad Labor Board that had the support of only organized labor, the progressive Republicans, and the progressive Democrats. Coolidge would not back legislation that did not have the old guard Republicans' support. The Republican administration anticipated correctly that the old guard would denounce any legislation introduced by these parties.

In the Sixty-eighth Congress, therefore, the Republican administration failed to build a new adjustment board for the railroad industry. Indeed, once Coolidge understood the old guard's position on this issue, he encouraged the pro-administration Republicans and the old guard to reject organized labor's attempt to revise the board. This labor-backed legislation, the Howell-

Barkley bill, was defeated—first, because the Republican administration withdrew its support and, second, because of the Republican old guard's obstructionist tactics.

## A Progressive Triumph

The AFL and the brotherhoods had long hoped to revise the Transportation Act, although they delayed proposing legislation until 1923, when they believed it had a realistic chance of passing.[18] The midterm elections of 1922 supplied these unions, or so they thought, with the opportunity to amend the Railroad Labor Board. As the brotherhoods' journal, *Labor*, explained, the election "wasn't a 'Democratic landslide,' but it was a Progressive triumph."[19]

However, organized labor leaders overestimated the strength of the progressive movement and underestimated the Republican Party leaders' ability to build a coalition with their progressive brethren and amend the Railroad Labor Board to their satisfaction. No bipartisan progressive coalition emerged after the 1922 congressional elections. Instead, these elections gave the progressive Republicans more institutional leverage, initially within Congress and later with President Coolidge.

In the 1922 congressional elections, the progressives won more seats in both the House and the Senate. The off-year election produced a backlash against the old guard, which had been hostile to organized labor's demands when the Transportation Act had passed Congress in 1920. In the Republican primaries, the progressive Albert J. Beveridge defeated the incumbent senator Harry S. New of Indiana, a close friend of President Harding's; the progressive Lynn J. Frazier defeated the incumbent old guard senator Porter J. McCumber of North Dakota; the progressive candidate Smith W. Brookhart won the party's nomination in Iowa when William S. Kenyon became a federal court judge; and Robert M. LaFollette Jr. won the Republican nomination in Wisconsin without any trouble.[20] The progressive leader Gifford Pinchot, moreover, defeated the Republican-backed candidate for the gubernatorial nomination of Pennsylvania.

While the old guard and regular Republicans lost their strong majorities in Congress, the progressive Republicans strengthened their position of governance. In the Senate, the GOP lost 7 seats, reducing their majority of 59 to 37 in 1920 to 51 to 43 in 1922. For instance, Senator Joseph S. Frelinghuysen of New Jersey, President Harding's friend and a strong member of the old guard, lost his race to Governor Edward I. Edwards, an anti-Prohibition Democrat. The two old guard Senate leaders from Pennsylvania, Philander C. Knox and Boies Penrose, died shortly after the election. At the same time, the Wisconsin electorate reelected the progressive Republican senator Robert M. LaFollette by a plurality of votes in Wisconsin. The progressive Republican Hiram Johnson from California also maintained his position in the Senate. In Minnesota, the moderate progressive Republican Frank B. Kellogg lost his Senate race to the more progressive-minded Henrik K. Shipstead, a Farmer-Laborite. Finally, Brookhart, a member of the progressive Republican faction from Iowa, won the 1922 election.

The contests in the House of Representatives also reduced the Republican majority. The all-time-high Republican majority of 303 to 132 dropped in 1920 to 225 to 207. The Democrats gained 76 seats, and the Farmer-Laborites and Socialists picked up 3 seats. Moreover, two old guard members in the House, Joseph W. Fordney and Frank W. Mondell, lost their seats in the 1922 congressional elections.[21]

The first session of the Sixty-eighth Congress convened in 1923. These Republican losses helped the progressive faction of the GOP more than they did the Democratic Party, since the latter never managed to create a congressional party program in preparation for the 1924 presidential election.[22] The midterm elections broke the southern Democrats' control of the party from a high of 70.3 percent in the Senate to 60.5 percent, and 82 percent in the House to 55.8 percent, but the newly elected Democrats from other regions found it difficult to coalesce.[23] By contrast, the 1922 congressional election results elated the progressive Republicans. According to William Allen White, "The discontented farmer and the aspiring laborer have got together."

Secretary of Commerce Hoover, moreover, concurred. Disappointed by the 1922 results, he blamed the progressive Republicans for the GOP's poor election returns. And indeed, when Congress reconvened, the progressive Republicans were more powerful than ever.

### A Coalition of Labor Unions Lobbies for a New Railroad Labor Board

These midterm election results caused organized labor to believe, mistakenly, that bipartisan legislation amending the Railroad Labor Board would now have a greater chance at passage. The AFL predicted "that the general attitude of the members of the 68th Congress [would] be of a more liberal nature and that it [would] not be as difficult" to revise the Railroad Labor Board.[24] President Coolidge also encouraged Congress to revise the Railroad Labor Board: "The settlement of railroad labor disputes is a matter of grave public concern. The Labor Board was established to protect the public in the enjoyment of continuous service by attempting to insure justice between the companies and their employees. It has been a great help, but it is not altogether satisfactory to the public, the employees, or the companies."[25] Consequently, a coalition of labor unions met to draft such legislation and solicited the support of two progressives in Congress to introduce the legislation, the Republican senator Robert Howell and the Democratic congressman Alben Barkley.[26]

The railroad brotherhoods hired Glen Plumb's assistant, Donald R. Richberg, to draft this first legislative alternative to the Railroad Labor Board.[27] When Richberg and David Lilenthal completed their draft of suggestions for a new labor board, they submitted it to Howell and Barkley, who wrote a final draft and presented it before Congress.[28] In its final form, the Howell-Barkley bill reestablished the voluntary features of the Erdman and Newlands Acts, mandated that the railroad carriers and the representatives of the railroad workers rely on adjustment boards (unlike the provisions in the Transportation Act), and strengthened the provision forcing the railroad executives and the representatives of the railroad workers to meet in conferences.[29] The bill relied on mediation rather than arbitration to adjust labor disputes, with a national board of mediation—composed of employees and employers, and no public representatives—constituting the centerpiece of the bill. Most important, the worker representatives on this mediation board were to be chosen from the sixteen recognized national railroad labor unions, "thus underwriting their legality and undermining the company unions."[30] In other words, the Howell-Barkley bill assigned exclusive agency to organized labor. In contrast to the labor relations provisions in the Transportation Act, this bill would make sixteen railroad unions the workers' permanent collective bargaining agents.

Howell and Barkley immediately brought this legislation to their colleagues' attention. Howell consulted with members of his party about its passage, but they refused to sponsor this so-called class legislation. "Conferences were had with Senator Howell regarding his efforts to obtain a position for the Howell-Barkley bill on the Senate program," a memorandum from Richberg's office explained, "in support of which he had numerous discussions with Senator Charles Curtis and other members of the Steering Committee. Eventually, however, the Committee declined to advance the Howell-Barkley bill."[31] Further, some leading members of the old guard, Senators Simeon Fess of Ohio, James E. Watson of Indiana, and Charles Beecher Warren of Michigan, in addition to the conservative Democratic senator William C. Bruce of Maryland, led the opposition to this legislation.

Although the old guard Republican leadership rejected the Howell-Barkley bill, progressive Republicans championed it. Norris, LaFollette, and Brookhart, along with the Democratic progressive Clarence Dill of Washington and the Farmer-Laborite Shipstead, joined Howell to fight for the bill's passage. In the House, Barkley obtained support for the legislation primarily from his progressive colleagues. Although Howell and Barkley, in theory, led a bipartisan progressive campaign for their labor legislation, the progressive Republicans were the real leaders behind it.

Indeed, Howell, Norris, LaFollette, and Brookhart more often than not took the lead in guiding progressive legislation through Congress throughout the 1920s—in part because no progressive Democrats had the same standing in the Republican Congress. The progressive Republicans chaired Senate and House committees, whereas the progressive Democrats, being in the minority party, could not. These progressive Republicans also held pivotal congressional positions because their votes determined legislative outcomes in partisan debates. Finally, although the Democrats consistently voted for the Howell and Barkley bills, the Democratic Party elite never took any real interest in amending the Republican-constructed Railroad Labor Board.

Throughout the 1920s, aside from the few progressive Democrats, the ruling Democratic elite never sponsored pro-labor legislation. From 1918 until 1930, more than half of the Democratic members in both the Senate and the House were conservative southerners who stood behind Prohibition, the Ku Klux Klan, and fundamentalist religion. When William G. McAdoo, the former secretary of the treasury and head of the wartime Railroad Administration under Woodrow Wilson, was implicated in the Harding administration's Tea Pot Dome scandal, the New Freedom progressives lost all hope of revitalizing their agenda. By 1923, most of the progressive Democrats, who supported organized labor, aligned themselves with the Conference for Progressive Political Action (CPPA).[32] Amending the Railroad Labor Board was at the top of the CPPA's list of reforms. In the Sixty-eighth Congress in 1924, all but the staunchest southern Democrats joined the large number of progressive Republicans and the few progressive Democrats to defeat the Coolidge administration's Republican policies. Nonetheless, in the 1920s, the Democrats essentially retreated from their former pro-labor leadership position. A plank for collective bargaining did not appear until the formulation of the 1936 campaign platform. Hence, the active participants in the battle over the Howell-Barkley bill were the progressive Republicans (in alliance with a few progressive Democrats, such as Clarence Dill) and the old guard party elite.

### Coolidge Leads the Republican Congress

By 1924, the intraparty conflicts between the progressive and old guard Republicans over amending the Railroad Labor Board had taken a form different from the conflicts in 1919 and 1920. Although embroiled in battles in the beginning years of Republican ascendancy, both factions had made an effort to maintain party loyalty. They had compromised their respective positions to pass a Republican national transportation policy as part of the postwar reconstruction effort and had made concessions to reunite the GOP in order to win the 1920 presidential election. But, in the winter and spring of 1924, with the Democratic Party in complete disarray, the progressives and the old guard no longer worried about maintaining party loyalty. Instead, the Republican old guard feared that their progressive colleagues' bid for the presidential election in 1924 might succeed.

Struggling to maintain their dominance in the Republican Party, the old guard Republicans tried to quash the progressives' attempt to revise the Railroad Labor Board. They presented their colleagues with no compromises or concessions, and they began filibustering as well as using other obstructionist tactics to defeat the progressive legislation. Likewise, the progressive Republicans no longer hesitated to throw their support to the Democratic Party.

Denouncing the Howell-Barkley bill as class legislation, the old guard in the Senate and the House defeated it. Although the Coolidge administration wanted to amend the Railroad Labor Board, it worked with the old guard congressional Republicans to kill the Howell-Barkley bill, both groups condemning this measure as class legislation.[33] In a letter to Coolidge, Secretary of Labor Davis said, "I frankly gave my opinion [to the committee considering the Howell-Barkley bill] that it would be difficult to secure the enactment of this legislation, and even if it did pass as originally planned I did not think it would solve the problem of securing satisfactory railway adjustment machinery."[34]

By 1924, the old guard Republicans and the Coolidge administration defeated the Howell-Barkley bill.[35] Yet they killed the bill only after arranging meetings between the railway executives and the railroad unions to formulate new legislation.[36] As part of trying to persuade the progressives and organized labor to drop the Howell-Barkley bill, the Coolidge administration promised to sponsor legislation in the next Congress.[37]

The battle against the Howell-Barkley bill began when Howell took his bill to the Senate Interstate and Foreign Commerce Committee. He tried to strike appropriations for the current Railroad Labor Board, but he lost the vote by a count of 42 to 21.[38] The old guard Republican leadership called for a vote on the amendment before the progressives could rally troops on the Senate floor; 14 progressives "regarded as favorable to the bill" were absent.[39] Of the 42 voting against Howell's measure to eliminate the board's funds, 31 were old guard and regular Republicans.

After failing to cut appropriations for the present Railroad Labor Board, Howell brought out his bill for a new board to the Senate Interstate and Foreign Commerce Committee. Beginning on February 28, the committee heard testimony from outside groups and individuals who almost unanimously denounced the proposed legislation.[40] The sole voice of support came from organized labor.[41] Collectively, the railroad executives thought it was premature to alter the board.[42] These executives had no concrete policy ideas about how to amend the Railroad Labor Board, although they harbored many objections to the Howell-Barkley bill.[43] In particular, the railroad executives were alarmed that sixteen national railway unions might be entitled to represent the railroad workers in national adjustment boards and might "close shop" the entire industry.[44] Unionization of shopcrafts workers, not of the brotherhoods, disturbed them. The bill's opponents also maintained that it would not protect the public from industrial unrest.[45]

Representatives from the American Railway Executives (ARE) tried to persuade the Senate committee that the Howell-Barkley bill, providing for national adjustment and mediation boards, was a piece of restrictive class legislation.[46] One railroad executive claimed,

> There is a plain inconsistency between the principle of "voluntary" settlements. The Howell-Barkley would establish national adjustment boards, the members of which would be composed equally of representatives of the national labor unions and the railways. The railroads do not want these boards established. . . . The bill would also indirectly apply force to railway employees who do not belong to the national labor unions. Only employees belonging to the national unions would be represented on the boards. Therefore, employees who do not belong to the national union would be forced either to go out without representation or to join the national union.[47]

The progressive Republicans had anticipated this criticism and had been concerned about it. Howell warned the coalition of labor unions supporting the Howell-Barkley bill about the dangers associated with making organized labor the railroad workers' only bargaining agent.[48] Meeting with union leaders, Howell even tried to dissuade them from such an assignment, but they would not back down from their position.[49]

Although the Coolidge administration withdrew its support and the Senate old guard voiced its opposition, the Senate Committee on Interstate and Foreign Commerce recommended the Howell-Barkley bill to the Senate at large. With only three members of the old guard on the committee voting in opposition, the committee wrote a favorable report.

Reacting to this report, the old guard and the Republican administration feared that the progressive Republicans, in alliance with the Democrats, might pass these amendments. The Republican leadership, therefore, rallied its troops to fight the bill when it hit the Senate floor. The leadership devised a multitude of ways to delay the vote on the bill. First, a number of old guard senators presented amendments so objectionable to the progressive Republicans that they felt compelled to fight them, expending much time and energy trying to defeat them before Congress adjourned for the 1924 presidential and congressional elections in June. The AFL reported that "efforts to secure the favorable consideration of the Howell-Barkley bill came to naught. Because certain members of the Senate had suggested a compromise no attempt was made to have the bill acted upon."[50] Second, the old guard Republican leadership called roll-call votes when most members were absent. After sixteen roll-call votes, the Senate adjourned, preventing the Howell-Barkley bill from coming to a vote.[51]

The Barkley bill encountered the same obstructionist tactics in the House Committee on Interstate and Foreign Commerce and on the House floor that the Howell bill faced in the Senate. Forewarned, the old guard Republican leadership in the House worked with regular Republicans to kill the Barkley bill before it, too, came up for a vote. Speaker of the House Frederick Gillett, floor manager Nicholas Longworth, and the chairman of the House Committee on Interstate and Foreign Commerce, Samuel Winslow, led the opposition.

Unlike the Howell bill, however, the Barkley bill was never reported out of its committee. From February 28 until May 5, the old guard leadership in the House pigeonholed the bill in the Foreign and Interstate Commerce Committee. Acting as chairman of this committee, Winslow kept the bill from being discussed. Barkley responded to Winslow's obstructionist tactics by petitioning the bill out of the Interstate and Foreign Commerce Committee. The progressives had devised this reform measure to reduce the old guard's control in the House. An article explained that "the Howell-Barkley bill was forced before the House of Representatives by resorting to a new rule adopted. This provides that if a committee fails to act upon a bill it can be discharged from further consideration if 150 members of the House sign a petition to that effect."[52] Barkley had long since acknowledged the probability that he would have to petition the Howell-Barkley bill out of the Interstate and Foreign Commerce Committee to get it onto the House floor for a vote, and he had already informed the union representatives supporting the bill of this fact.[53]

The House passed the petition by a vote of 194 to 181.[54] Forty-six progressive Republicans, Farmer-Laborites, and a socialist voted with 148 Democrats to pass it; 152 old guard and regular Republicans and 29 Democrats rejected it.[55]

Thus, the Barkley bill finally reached the House floor after the petition vote, and Congress received it favorably. The old guard Republican leadership therefore had to resort to a different obstructionist tactic to prevent the bill from coming to a vote. As counsel for the railroad labor unions described,

> on May 5 a decisive majority of the House decided to discharge the committee on interstate and foreign commerce from further consideration of the Barkley bill. . . . An obstructive minority thereupon prevented any consideration of the bill on its merits and the House was compelled to remain in session until 11:45 P.M. in order to reach a vote limiting the de-

bate to three hours. This bill came before the House again on May 19 and filibustering tactics were again resorted to so that after the three hours' debate was concluded no further consideration of the bill or amendments could be obtained before the House adjourned at 10:17 P.M. By roll-call after roll-call the majority of the House again demonstrated that it desired to give the bill consideration and arrive eventually at a final vote.[56]

Furthermore, Congressmen Longworth, Gillette, and Everett Sanders (who was later appointed Calvin Coolidge's private secretary) filibustered the bill and rendered it "pending business," limiting discussion to two days.[57] Ultimately, the old guard Republican leadership defeated the Barkley bill by blocking the progressives' last effort to have it come to a final vote before the House adjourned. When they called twenty-four roll-call votes, Barkley finally pulled the bill from consideration, though he denounced the Republican leadership's obstructive tactics. As Barkley declared: "We have spent 24 hours and 24 roll-calls during two days' consideration of the measure, and although a substantial majority of the members of this House on every roll-call demonstrated its desire to consider and pass the bill, a conservative, obstructive, and filibustering minority, led by the Republican leader, his steering committee, and some of the minor constellations in the Republican firmament, have been able, by methods not often heretofore adopted, to prevent the passage."[58] He added that they "feared to permit it to come to a vote."[59] Indeed, not daring to test how close the vote would be, Winslow, the chairman of the Interstate and Foreign Commerce Committee, refused to schedule hearings.[60]

Neither the Howell bill nor the Barkley bill passed the Sixty-eighth Congress.[61] Still, progressives in both the Republican and Democratic Parties found the support for the Howell-Barkley bill "surprising." Barkley saw a "legislative vitality" about the progressives' plan to construct a new labor board. The bill, he argued, was "acting upon the political pronouncements of all three parties in the last campaign and upon the suggestion of the President."[62] Thus, the progressives considered their attempt to pass the bill a partial victory. Barkley explained, "It may [be] reported as the outstanding achievement of this session of Congress that a general understanding of the uselessness and menacing qualities of the Railroad Labor Board now prevails at least in Congress, if not with the public at large."[63] And indeed, progressives persuaded the Republican administration to pledge its support for legislation. Coolidge placed the Railroad Labor Board issue on the Republican Party's agenda.

## A Competitive Labor Relations Policy

After Congress adjourned to prepare for the 1924 congressional and presidential elections, the progressive and old guard Republicans reconsidered their respective positions on the Howell-Barkley amendments to the Railroad Labor Board. Fearing the old guard might obstruct their efforts to pass protective labor legislation, the progressive Republicans conceded assigning exclusive agency to organized labor in exchange for the Coolidge administration's sponsorship of another bill. The old guard, on the other hand, worried that the progressive Republicans, with ever increasing support from the progressive Democrats and the Republican administration, would amend the Railroad Labor Board despite old guard opposition.

Instructed by the Republican Party leader President Coolidge and lobbied by "the affected parties," the progressive and old guard Republicans worked to pass the Railway Labor Act of 1926. Together, they drafted a new Republican railroad labor-management relations policy that depended on the worker representation process. Like the Transportation Act, the new Railway Labor Act contained no protective provisions for organized labor. The Republicans insisted that a state-operated agency be used to guarantee individual employment rights and to safeguard the public good of industrial peace and tranquillity, not to protect organized labor.

Having advocated amending the Railroad Labor Board from the outset of his administration, Coolidge wanted the board to retain its Republican character. However, unlike the old guard Republican president Harding, Coolidge compromised with the progressive Republicans—because he fear they might bolt from the GOP during the 1924 elections.[64] He thought LaFollette's bid for president as a third-party candidate (sponsored by the CPPA) posed more of a threat to his election than the Democrats' campaign. Coolidge's fear did prove to be well grounded, since most congressional progressive Republicans supported LaFollette's campaign.

In 1924, as part of his plan to entice the progressive Republicans back into the party fold, Coolidge dispatched Hoover to persuade the railroad executives and organized labor to develop a new railroad labor policy.[65] Knowing that organized labor would meet to discuss legislation at any time, Hoover set out to secure the railroad executives' cooperation. In March 1925, the ARE finally formed an official committee to meet with organized labor to propose new legislation.[66] Secretary Hoover impressed upon the railroad executives that they had no choice but to amend the Railroad Labor Board. They must either face the Howell-Barkley bill as a law or help draft a different law amenable to their interests. And by December 1925, little more than six months after the railroad executives had lobbied to prevent the passage of the Howell-Barkley bill, they met with organized labor, and the two jointly wrote this policy.[67]

Unlike the Howell-Barkley bill, this legislation upheld on the Republican consensus that unions should be awarded no special privileges—it was not class legislation. Company unions still survived under this legislation, since it neither limited their jurisdiction nor outlawed them. The issue of authorization within agency law directed the new railroad labor legislation.

With the Coolidge administration, the Republican and Democratic progressives, and both organized labor and the railroad executives supporting this legislation, the old guard had to back it as well. They realized that participating in the Republican coalition and drafting this legislation would be better than accepting legislation drafted by a bipartisan coalition. The congressional old guard agreed with the Coolidge administration that the Railway Labor Act should be drafted by Republicans. Hence, a key member of the old guard and chairman of the Interstate and Foreign Commerce Committee, Senator James E. Watson of Indiana, sponsored the bill in the Senate. In the House, the chairman of the Interstate and Foreign Commerce Committee, James Parker of Indiana, also sponsored it.[68] Both Watson and Parker had themselves opposed the Howell-Barkley bill in the previous session of Congress.

With these two members of the old guard leading the way, the Interstate and Foreign Commerce Committee reported the Watson bill out of committee without any revisions. The bill passed the Senate with no amendments on May 11, 1926, by a vote of 69 to 13.[69] The House, too, reported the Parker bill out of committee without revisions, and it passed without amendments on March 1, 1926, by a vote of 381 to 13. As the *Railway Age* reported, "all efforts to amend the bill failed by large majorities."[70]

Because the labor relations controversy between the old guard and progressive Republicans had run its course in the fight over the Howell-Barkley bill, once the progressives endorsed the key provision—the scheme for worker representation—the Watson-Parker bill passed with a strong majority and almost universal Republican support. But why did the Republican old guard finally agree to support the new amendments to the Railroad Labor Board?

### The Old Guard Changes Its Colors

When the old guard Republicans changed their position on amending the Railroad Labor Board, they hid the real reasons for their dramatic turnabout. Publicly, they argued that the board needed grave repairs to become an efficient labor relations machine.[71] Watson characterized the Railway Labor Act as an emergency measure by stating, "The present emergency is this, that the Railroad Labor Board has broken down."[72] Watson and the old guard began echoing what the progressives had said during the debate about the Howell-Barkley bill. For instance, in 1924 Congressman George Huddleston, a progressive Democrat from Alabama, argued that the Howell-Barkley bill should be enacted, since the board rarely settled labor disputes. In the Committee on Interstate and Foreign Commerce Hearings, Huddleston stated, "In view of the decision of the Supreme Court as to the lack of power on the part of the Labor Board and the general irritation and dissatisfaction with the board existing on behalf of labor, I want to ask you [Alfred Thom, the ARE general counsel] if you do not think that in future the labor organization will be practically unanimous in declining to pay any attention to the Labor Board whatever?"[73] (Thom answered affirmatively.)

The old guard suggested, furthermore, that the Supreme Court's *Pennsylvania* decisions had destabilized the board.[74] The Court's affirmation that the Railroad Labor Board did not have the power to enforce its own decisions, they maintained, played an important part in the decision to pass the amendments to the Transportation Act. Attitudes about the board had also changed after the fiasco of the 1922 shopmen's strike.[75] The board was not effective when it had to resort to either the courts of equity or the Supreme Court to resolve its disputes.

From the old guard's perspective, to run an effective operation the board needed protection from judicial interference and support from its constituents. "The facts are that all the organizations of labor squarely state that they never again will appeal to the Railroad Labor Board in any case," claimed Watson. "Four-fifths of the railway managers of the country state that they never again will appeal to it in any case; and if neither side appeals to the board, it has no jurisdiction over anything."[76] Watson and Parker emphasized the fact that the two historically antagonistic groups had finally accepted, and even helped draft, legislation enacting a permanent bureaucratic apparatus for labor relations.

All this—the general inefficiencies of the Railroad Labor Board (including the absence of constituent support), the *Pennsylvania* decisions, and the shopmen's strike—however, does not truly explain why the old guard changed its position about amending the board. The Supreme Court had handed down the *Pennsylvania* decisions, and the shopmen's strike had been resolved, *before* the progressives introduced the Howell-Barkley bill. The old guard supported this second piece of legislation only because the progressives, who had expressed a willingness to compromise and cooperate with the old guard about the legislation, amassed considerable institutional leverage within the Republican Party.

After the 1924 race for the presidency, the progressives still held the swing vote in both the House and the Senate. Although the Republicans had a majority of 247 to 183 in the House, more than 20 of the progressive Republicans often sided with the Democrats, sometimes giving the latter a majority. Even though Nicholas Longworth, the Speaker of the House, tried to discipline these insurgents, they prevented the Republicans from controlling a working majority.

The old guard leadership in the Senate had even more trouble convincing the progressive Republicans to vote with their party members. When Senator Henry Cabot Lodge died in 1924, the old guard lost its most effective leader. William Butler, the new Senate leader, had great difficulty commanding Republican majorities, primarily because he was not a member of the old guard. Butler became the unofficial Senate leader only after Coolidge's landslide victory and Lodge's death. As Coolidge's spokesman, Butler was an outsider who had problems convincing either the progressives or the old guard to pass the president's legislative agenda.

In addition to this weakness, in the Senate the Republicans had a tenuous majority of 56 Republicans, 39 Democrats, and 1 Farmer-Laborite. And of these 56 Republicans 5 to 7 progressives would break ranks to vote with the Democrats. No longer under pressure to maintain Republican unity to elect a president, as they had been during the legislative debate over the Transportation Act, the progressives made it clear that they would work with the Democrats to amend the board.

The progressives' actions during the debate over the Howell-Barkley bill made their position clear. With or without the support of the old guard and the regular Republicans, the progressives intended passing legislation amending the Railroad Labor Board. This legislation would undoubtedly offer the sixteen standard national railroad unions the exclusive right to represent the railroad workers. While the progressives could hope for only a slim majority for the Watson-Parker bill, Coolidge, now being conciliatory to the progressive Republicans, had no plans to veto it. Thus, the old guard decided it had better participate in the policymaking process when the Sixty-ninth Congress considered the bill. As a result, the national unions gained no special privileges or absolute rights to represent the railroad workers. Instead, the scheme for worker representation became the centerpiece of this legislative effort.

### The Railway Labor Act of 1926

When the two Republican factions began working together, their legislation created a labor-management relations policy that ensured strong contractual relations between employers and collectives of railroad workers. Unlike the labor relations policy developed in 1920, this contractual policy contained no incompatible elements that would lead to its demise. It operationalized an effective conception of responsible unionism—not because of the changes in labor-management relations but because the scheme for worker representation also imposed a duty to bargain on the railroad executives and these worker representatives. This made collective bargaining a certainty, albeit not necessarily with organized labor. At the same time, the supervision necessary to implement this scheme gave the state an ongoing role in railroad labor-management relations.

The Watson-Parker bill established more elaborate mediation machinery than its failed precursor. As in the Transportation Act, the railroad workers and their employers would have a duty to try to settle disputes before using a board, although the new labor board differed from the old one in several important respects: board composition, mediation procedures, and trade agreement negotiations. First, no public members would sit on the Mediation Board, only members nominated by the railroad carriers and the railroad workers.[77] This provision was included to prevent both sides from claiming that the board rendered biased decisions. Second, the new board, the Mediation Board, had no powers to investigate and adjudicate disputes but rather helped mediate or voluntarily arbitrate disputes at the request of both the railroad carriers and the representatives of the railroad workers.[78] Third, the Watson-Parker bill included adjustment boards that would help the railroad executives and the representatives of the railroad workers renegotiate trade agreements and settle any disputes about these agreements.[79]

Like the old railroad labor policy, the new policy put contractualism, or the process of collective bargaining, above resolving labor disputes. This policy fulfilled the six characteristics of contractualism that the legal historian Tamar Lothian has delineated. First, it portrayed trade unions as private interest groups. In other words, unions received no special privileges or rights when they negotiated collective bargaining agreements. Second, very few limitations were imposed on the number of private interest groups that could negotiate these agreements. Third, this policy did not specify what should be included in the agreements. The collective bargaining agent and employers were not hindered by policy constraints about wage rates and working conditions—they retained their fundamental freedom to contract. Fourth, a policy grounded in contractualism had external forces, such as worker militancy or the economy, that influenced the trade agreement negotiation process. There could be no ban on strikes, for example. Fifth, the policy could not be compulsory despite the fact that it facilitated industrial peace and harmony. Finally, this policy was developed to ensure this peace and harmony, but it was not to influence what went into the state's economic policy program.[80]

Unlike the old policy, the new railroad labor policy made contractualism possible. On the one hand, this was due to the new mediation machinery that was included in this policy. On the other hand, it was possible because the Republicans built a more detailed plan for worker representation. The Watson-Parker bill made it the railroad executives' and the worker representatives' *duty* to meet in conferences to negotiate or renegotiate trade agreements; the Mediation Board was to enforce these agreements.

Although the Watson-Parker bill resembled the Howell-Barkley bill on the surface, it had been altered significantly to accommodate the old guard Republicans. When the progressives and the railroad labor leaders drafted the Howell-Barkley bill, they developed machinery for the adjustment of labor disputes between labor unions and their employers, not between worker representatives and their employers. With the Watson-Parker bill, the railroad labor unions compromised this position.[81] The Republicans deleted the protectionist element in the Howell-Barkley bill, designating that not one of the sixteen railroad unions become the workers' exclusive collective bargaining agent.

Moreover, although the representatives of the railroad workers and the executives had to meet in adjustment boards in the Watson-Parker bill, these boards differed from those proposed in the Howell-Barkley bill. The Watson-Parker bill assigned the adjustment boards national, regional, or local jurisdiction. The railroad executives had opposed the adjustment boards in the Transportation Act because of their national jurisdiction. National adjustment boards could institute national agreements with national labor unions. Local adjustment boards, by contrast, gave organized labor no assured role in the collective bargaining process. Labor unions constituted merely one group among many, including company unions, that could represent the railroad workers.

The Watson-Parker bill also contained a proclamation that protected company unions: "Nothing in this Act shall be construed to prohibit individual carriers and their workers from agreeing on the settlement of disputes through such machinery of contract and adjustment as they may mutually establish." Moreover, in a separate paragraph an additional assurance was inserted: "Nothing in this paragraph shall be construed to supersede the provisions of any agreements (as to conference) then in effect between the parties."[82]

These provisions in the Watson-Parker bill gave organized labor no special role in the labor-management relations machinery. To revise the Railroad Labor Board, the progressive Republicans compromised their position by eliminating all the clauses that had protected organized labor in the Howell-Barkley bill.[83] Meyer Jacobstein, a Democratic progressive congressman from New York, stated, "I want you to know that labor gave up something in the bill. Do you know what they gave up? Do you know, according to this bill, that the employers can deal with labor on their own roads and make a contract with them? For instance, the Pennsylvania Railroad system can do such a thing with their own employees without opposition from organized labor. This bill does not preclude the employer from dealing with his own labor if he so desires and if labor so desires."[84]

A comparison of the Howell-Barkley and Watson-Parker bills indicates that the old guard forced organized labor, not the railroad executives, to make the most fundamental concession: in principle, labor unions, company unions, or any other type of local unions could represent the railroad workers at the collective bargaining negotiation table. Providing that the newly created adjustment boards could renegotiate trade agreements meant that the railroad executives' existing company unions could survive under the Railway Labor Act.

But why would organized labor, legislatively coached by the progressive Republicans, settle for a board based on this worker representation scheme? Essentially, the union leaders and the progressive Republicans faced the choice of living with the old Railroad Labor Board or creating the U.S. Mediation Board; they decided on the latter alternative despite its obvious flaws.

## A New Deal for Organized Labor?

Although the debates on the Watson-Parker bill produced no amendments, they nevertheless revealed the significant impact this legislation would have on organized labor. Except for the brief wartime emergency period, during which union leaders had been functional representatives of the public good within a corporatist industrial relations policy framework, organized labor had long proclaimed its ideology of voluntarism and opposed any type of institutional regulation sponsored by the old guard Republicans or by the progressives of either political party. Indeed, since the latter part of the nineteenth century, the AFL had avoided establishing strong contractual relations with employers, because of its opposition to incorporation. The AFL hoped to avoid the common-law state and federal courts altogether. Organized labor had supported the Arbitration Act of 1888, the Erdman Act, and the Newlands Act, but only because they implemented *temporary* means of settling disputes using mediation and voluntary arbitration boards. The boards developed by the various acts created no permanent institutional state apparatus to interfere with the AFL's organizational autonomy.[85]

Following this same reasoning, from the very beginning the AFL and the railroad brotherhoods denounced the erection of the Railroad Labor Board instituted by the Transportation Act. This board was a permanent, quasi-judicial agency that imposed unsolicited decisions on bargaining agents. Being antistatist, the AFL condemned the first Railroad Labor Board as an invasive institution.

The AFL and the railroad brotherhoods' support of the Watson-Parker bill, albeit as a "second-best" substitute for the Howell-Barkley bill, marked the beginning of a new era. Union leaders did not stand on street corners and announce the death of voluntarism, but their acceptance of this Republican labor policy demonstrated their willingness to accept a statist policy for the railroads. Organized labor, however, had never been categorically opposed to governmental intervention in labor disputes. Instead, it spurned the American judiciary's direct interference in the disputes. Gompers's notion of voluntarism was based more on maintaining the privacy and self-interest of unions and their members than protecting them from any type of state interference. As long as the labor policy did not restrict organized labor's autonomy, the AFL and the railroad brotherhoods could accept such interference.

In 1926, the AFL and the railroad brotherhoods thought that the Railway Labor Act strengthened contractual relations with the railroad executives, despite that fact that the act did not specify who could negotiate these relations. During the House hearings on the Watson-Parker bill, the progressive railroad labor lawyer Donald Richberg explained what he considered to be the ultimate purpose of the legislation: "Why should the government set up tribunals in aid of this agreement of private parties to work out a harmonious solution of their industrial relations? The answer, in a word, is that the courts of the land are set up not for the purpose of making contracts for the parties; but for the purpose of interpreting contracts of the parties and enforcing the obligations that men voluntarily assume to one another." [86] Richberg recommended that the Watson-Parker bill establish permanent agencies—the adjustment boards and the Mediation Board—to aid the railroad executives and the railroad workers' representatives in making and abiding by contracts. He thought the federal courts' enforcement of these agreements posed little threat to organized labor.

Oddly enough, the old guard Republican senator Simeon D. Fess endorsed Richberg's reading of the Watson-Parker bill in the Senate debate: "This bill is written in accordance with the proper theory of adjustment and contracts. The first principle is to respect the building force of a contract," and, he added, "[to] allow the parties making a contract to go to their fullest limit to reach an agreement by negotiation or conference." [87] Thus, the Watson-Parker bill, according to the old guard, the progressives, and the railroad labor unions, provided the means for railroad worker organizations and associations to establish binding trade agreements with the railway executives, namely, (1) the workers' right to representation and (2) the duty imposed on the railroad executives and the representatives of the railroad workers to meet in conferences for the purpose of negotiating trade agreements. If a labor dispute erupted over the trade agreement negotiated in this conference, the involved parties would carry the dispute to mediation and arbitration boards. The president, moreover, would have the option to compel these parties to cease participating in a dispute while an emergency board worked to resolve the dispute grievances. "[The Railway Labor Act] provides that if the agreements, which both parties are pledged to respect, are not sufficient to adjust a dispute which arises, then there shall be a Government body." In short, the new Mediation Board and adjustment boards enforced trade agreements negotiated by unincorporated voluntary associations of workers with arbitration awards. Organized labor was pleased with the very idea that the railroad executives would sit at a collective bargaining table.

The AFL and the railroad brotherhoods were confident enough in this new Mediation Board that they did not mind working in cooperation with the courts. Unaware that organized labor felt so beleaguered by "government by injunction," some senators puzzled over the court enforcement provision in the bill. The AFL, for instance, had long taken the position that the courts must not be allowed to interfere in labor disputes; now, it accepted this provision.[88]

The issue of the courts' role led some congressmen to question organized labor's new position toward institutional regulation as a whole. They went so far as to query whether the courts would be imposing involuntary servitude on individual workers by the very act of enforcing these arbitration awards. Having anticipated this problem when the legislation was being drafted, Richberg explained that the legislative authors had no intention of imposing involuntary servitude on the railroad workers. "What we want to do is make it perfectly clear that these acts may come before the State courts in matters of litigation and contract between employers and employees," Richberg stated during the hearings, and "to make it perfectly clear that these provisions do not imply any obligations to render service without the consent of the individual."[89]

Richberg further explained that railroad workers would not be forced into any type of involuntary servitude or work that entailed unacceptable conditions. Instead, he saw the Railway Labor Act as extending the law of contracts in a beneficial way for organized labor. In the hearings for the Watson-Parker bill, Richberg enumerated how the courts would, in all likelihood, do this. "Well, as I read the laws that have been written quite clearly in recent years, not only in the lower courts, but in the Supreme Court of the United States, a conspiracy to induce men to violate a contract has been quite persistently and consistently enjoined and prohibited under dire penalties by the courts and certainly this law does not make any change in that law." Richberg maintained, "Now here is a contract, here is an award under a contract, an agreement to abide by it, and certainly a concerted movement to break that is just like conspiracy to break any other kind of contract, subject to the same law[;] . . . perhaps, we have enlarged the field out of which contracts may be created."[90]

During the floor debates, many members of Congress discussed questions about contract law and whether the Railway Labor Act extended or interfered with it. Some congressmen cited *Coppage v. Kansas* and *Adair v. United States*, among other cases, as evidence for opposing any legislation or amendments that proposed any type of direct interference with the contractual relations of employers and employees.[91] But progressive and old guard Republicans alike brought home the point that the act *extended* the law of contracts rather than *interfering* with it.

This extension, moreover, embraced the principles underlying the doctrine of actual agency. The act allowed workers to select their own representatives. This meant that collective bargaining could be accomplished without pre-assigning agency; no duty to negotiate with any two specific agents existed. More than three years after the Railway Labor Act passed Congress, Richberg himself emphasized the difference between contracts and representation: "I have found there is much confusion created because many persons mistakenly think that a right to select their own representatives grants a right to make a contract or grants rights in certain contracts. It should be made clear that rights of representation and rights of contract are entirely different things."[92] The Railway Labor Act included the notion of authorization essential to the doctrine of actual agency.

In another memorandum written the same year, Richberg continued to explain, "This policy recognizes that labor relations should be governed by contract and that such contracts are only possible and enforceable where employe[e]s[,] being individually helpless, act collectively through self-selected representatives."[93] The legislative authors circumvented the problem of interfering with the employers' and workers' freedom to contract, not by forcing the two to negotiate contracts, but by encouraging them to meet in conferences with representatives to negotiate these contracts.

In essence, the worker representation provision in the Watson–Parker bill was the legislative counterpart to the principles of agency. Congress ensured that individual workers had the right to representation and imposed the duty to confer on their representatives and the railroad employers. By so doing, Congress institutionalized the principles of agency—that union accountability stemmed from the union's authority to represent its members—upheld by the Taft Court throughout the 1920s in its labor dispute cases. By using the idea of worker representation, the legislative authors, the old guard congressmen Watson and Parker, aided by Richberg and Thom, circumvented the problems the courts faced of enforcing trade agreements between unincorporated labor unions and railroad executives.

More important, without the worker representation provision, the newly established board would have no authority to promote responsible unionism. With it, the board had the power to forestall worker militancy by determining who could represent the railroad workers at the collective bargaining table.

In regulating the workers' freedom to choose representation, the board was meant to safeguard both the individual rights of these workers and the idea of individualism that pervaded American society. Union certification, in principle, could be only temporary in nature. A shift in labor law occurred when the authors of the Railway Labor Act transferred power from the agent to the collective bargaining process. Coupling the worker representation scheme with the state-controlled U.S. Mediation Board meant that this labor law protected the collective bargaining process, not the specific players in it. Organized labor was now at the mercy of the U.S. Mediation Board.

### A Fresh Start: The Supreme Court Upholds the Railway Labor Act

The Supreme Court determined the constitutionality of the Railway Labor Act in 1928 in *Texas & New Orleans Railroad Company v. Brotherhood of Railway & Steamship Clerks*.[94] In this case, the Supreme Court, now led by Chief Justice Charles Evans Hughes, affirmed Congress's new role as the permanent policymaking institution for industrial relations. The unanimous Court upheld the duties of the Mediation and Arbitration Boards. More important, the Hughes Court affirmed the worker representation scheme that the Taft Court had endorsed earlier in the *Pennsylvania* cases, because it provided for the public interest *and* the freedom to contract.[95]

In the *Texas* case, the Railway and Steamship Clerks had secured an injunction against the Texas & New Orleans Railroad Company for interfering with its workers' right to representation. During a wage dispute, the Texas & New Orleans system had discharged members of the Railway and Steamship Clerks and attempted to organize a company union. A Texas court issued an injunction to prohibit the company from interfering with the employees' right to representation. The Texas & New Orleans system then challenged the issuance of the court's injunction and the constitutionality of the Railway Labor Act itself.

The employers in the *Texas* case tried to convince the justices that the Railway Labor Act violated freedom to contract and due process of law. First, they purported that the Court must follow the precedent established in the *Pennsylvania* cases in their case as well. In other words, the Supreme Court should find that the Mediation Board had no power to force the Texas & New Orleans system "to determine an abstract right," and to sustain an injunction would violate "an inherent and inalienable right" addressed by the *Adair*, *Coppage*, and *Hitchman* cases. Counsel for the Texas & New Orleans system insisted that the Railway Labor Act must not limit their right to discharge labor union members from acting as worker representatives. Counsel also argued for the railroad's right to interfere: "[The] mere suggestion or advice by officers and agents of the railroad to employees with respect to their organization or selection of representatives, is not unlawful."[96]

Writing a unanimous decision for the Court, Chief Justice Hughes sustained the railroad labor union's injunction against the Texas & New Orleans Railroad. The Court held that the injunction did not impinge on the employers' right to contract or due process of law. Directly addressing the issues presented by counsel for the Texas & New Orleans system, Hughes stated, first, that the *Pennsylvania* cases had no relevance to the case at bar. These cases were not germane, he argued, because the statutory differences distinguished the first Railroad Labor Board, established by the Transportation Act, from the second, enacted by the Railway Labor Act. "It was with clear appreciation of the infirmity of the existing legislation, and in the endeavor to establish a more practicable plan in order to accomplish the desired result, that Congress enacted the Railway Labor Act of 1926. It was decided to make a fresh start."[97]

A second legal obligation distinguished the labor-management relations provisions in the Transportation Act from those in the Railway Labor Act. In the latter act, Congress instituted an emergency board to act after all efforts of settlement by mediation and arbitration had failed. Once the president appointed this emergency board of investigation, both the railroad executives and the workers were prohibited from altering the existing trade agreement. During these emergency situations, no one less powerful than the president could be entrusted with safeguarding the public interest. According to Hughes, "This prohibition, in order to safeguard the vital interests of the country while an investigation is in progress, manifestly imports a legal obligation."[98] Hughes therefore concluded that although the *Pennsylvania* cases involved the question of enforceability, they did not provide a precedent for prohibiting the use of an injunction against the Texas & New Orleans Railroad.

After addressing that railroad's specific objections, Hughes expressed the more general yet primary reason why the Court upheld the constitutionality of the Railway Labor Act. Hughes proclaimed that the Railway Labor Act did not violate the "inherent and inalienable" right of the carrier to hire or discharge its workers. The worker representation provision sustained the act.

Unions were not recognized as the sole agents for worker representation, because worker representation, not union representation, constituted the primary element of the act. Accordingly, Hughes wrote, "Freedom of choice in the selection of representatives on each side of the dispute is the essential foundation of the statutory scheme. . . . Such collective action would be a mockery if representation were made futile by interference with freedom of choice. The Railway Labor Act of 1926 does not interfere with the normal exercise of the right of the carrier to select its employees or to discharge them."[99] He maintained, "The statute is not aimed at this right of the employers but at the interference with the right of employees to have representatives of their own choosing."[100]

In no passage of the *Texas* decision did Hughes indicate that unions had a new legal identity. Following the precedents established by *Adair*, *Coppage*, *Pennsylvania*, and other decisions, the Supreme Court considered unions to be one among many possible organizations entitled to represent employee interests.[101] With the *Texas* decision, the Court recognized the constitutionality of the first legislatively designed agency for mediating and arbitrating labor disputes. Thus, both the Republican-controlled majority in Congress and the Supreme Court supported the representational aspect of labor policy in the Railway Labor Act.

Finally, the railroad employer's rights had not been violated, according to Hughes, because the act encouraged worker representatives to prohibit any interference in the flow of interstate commerce: "Congress may facilitate the amicable settlement of disputes which threaten the service of the necessary agencies of interstate transportation."[102] Congress had the right and authority to promote the railroad workers' representation, since industrial conflicts interrupt interstate commerce. The Court had changed its emphasis: it no longer placed labor relations under the law of contracts.

### Conclusion

The worker representation scheme in the Railway Labor Act—which was initially a compromise provision in the Transportation Act because it wed the republican ideal of the public good to contractualism in a theory of responsible unionism—became the mainstay of American labor policy. These two ideals, however, produced an odd marriage. On the one hand, a public good is normally associated with a tangible outcome, like the prohibition of child labor. Children under the age of fifteen, for example, can no longer work. Contractualism, on the other hand, constructs a procedure. It ensures that all parties follow this procedure. If the outcome is predetermined, it would corrupt the process.

By making a process into a public good, the Republicans produced a policy that was filled with irony. First, they introduced a railroad labor-management relations policy that would become the blueprint for American labor policy, yet it was a policy that did not officially recognize organized labor. This policy, in other words, acknowledged a worker's right to labor union representation without giving organized labor any special privileges or even a specific role in the labor-management relations process. Second, the worker representation process gave the newly established state apparatus the ability to determine the nature of industrial conflict. While the Republicans' scheme for worker representation gave organized labor no special role, it did develop a new role for the state, which increased its power and authority.

The conclusion that the railroad labor-management relations policy made organized labor dependent on the state is contrary to the argument about American exceptionalism. A weak labor movement does not help account for the creation of a weak modern welfare state. Nor does it provide evidence in support of the counterargument that the power and authority of a strong state accounts for the weakness of the American labor movement. Instead, the Republicans' worker representation scheme meant that organized labor's fate would fluctuate in accordance with the will and the whim of the state. Sometimes, this dependence would strengthen the railroad unions; at other times, it would not.

Finally, the Republicans' emphasis on procedure and organized labor's dependence on the state helps explain why this labor legislation had the support of both organized labor and the railroad executives. Contrary to their past behavior, these two antagonistic groups consciously surrendered their autonomy and accepted these solutions. The railroad employers supported the Railway Labor Act because they hoped to maintain or establish trade agreements with employer-sponsored company unions and thereby exclude the newly established shopcrafts unions from the labor-management relations process. Organized labor, on the other hand, supported the Railway Labor Act because it strengthened Congress's role in labor-management relations at the expense of the Supreme Court and the federal equity courts. The unions believed legislation such as this would preclude judicial interference in labor disputes. The railroad employers and the union leaders each thought they could manipulate the worker representation process to their advantage.

## CHAPTER 7

# The Progressive Response to the Iron Cage of the Injunction

The extraordinary remedy of injunction has become the ordinary remedy.

—Felix Frankfurter and Nathan Greene,
*The Labor Injunction*, 1930

Organized labor railed against the "iron cage" of injunctions more in the 1920s than in any other decade.[1] It was during this time that the Taft Court expanded the scope and jurisdiction of the labor injunction. A rash of injunctions were also issued by the state and federal courts. At the same time, the old guard Republicans in Congress applauded the judiciary's use of the labor injunction; and even though they helped establish the U.S. Mediation Board in 1926 for the railroad industry, thinking that this labor-management relations machinery codified organized labor's responsibility during labor disputes, they still rejected all plans of limiting "government by injunction."[2]

The progressive Republicans held an entirely different view of organized labor's responsibility under law. They preferred legislative solutions to labor-management relations and wanted to limit the judiciary's use of labor injunctions. After the institution of the U.S. Mediation Board, the progressive Republicans thought they saw a window of opportunity for such reform. Beginning in 1928, with their Democratic brethren, they formed a bipartisan bloc known as "the coalition" and fought for anti-injunction legislation.[3] With President Herbert Hoover and his Republican-backed administration obstructing the passage of this legislation, the Norris-LaGuardia Anti-Injunction Act did not become law until 1932.

But while a bipartisan coalition fought for anti-injunction legislation, the principles behind it were not bipartisan. The progressive Republicans grounded the Norris-LaGuardia Anti-Injunction Act in the notion of responsible unionism they had cultivated with the old guard Republicans. They shifted the focus of anti-injunction legislation from the agent, or the union seeking immunity, to the activities associated with the collective bargaining process. Just as the Republican scheme for worker representation emphasized the collective bargaining process and not the agent, so the Norris-LaGuardia Act withdrew equitable relief for certain types of activities or conduct and not for special classes or agents. Borrowing the fiduciary term "the principles of agency," the Norris-LaGuardia Act assigned unions responsibility because of their activities. Therefore, injunctions could not be issued against "certain defined conduct" that occurred during most labor disputes.

Making injunctive relief dependent on conduct rather than agency, however, extended the emphasis on procedural law that underlay the Republicans' scheme for worker representation in the railroad labor legislation. The Norris-LaGuardia Act, like the Transportation Act and the Railway Labor Act before it, eroded the union's status as a private, voluntary association. This anti-injunction legislation undermined organized labor's theory of voluntarism, which placed unions outside the reach of equity law or any other type of state interference. Unions were not immune from being enjoined or given rights as special entities or legal persons, like those rights enjoyed by business corporations.[4] The progressives codified agency law in what one law student described as a "legislative" attempt "to clarify the basis of union liability."[5] Ironically, the Norris-LaGuardia Act limited the use of the labor injunction by containing "responsibility sections" for organized labor.

A sectarian battle raged between the AFL and the progressive Republicans and Democrats over the passage of anti-injunction legislation precisely because of this notion of union responsibility. Union leaders wanted substantive changes in labor law that would give unions immunity from equitable relief. In contrast, the bipartisan coalition of progressives thought that anti-injunction legislation must contain procedural changes in equity law that would make unions less vulnerable to the labor injunction. To maximize support for the Norris-LaGuardia Act as well as to make it consistent with their own ideological beliefs, the progressive Republicans drafted legislation that built upon the 1920s notion of agency law underlying the worker representation scheme that, after all, a Republican Congress had passed and the Taft Court had upheld.

This sectarian battle, moreover, highlights how members of the bipartisan coalition acted as semiautonomous state agents when they formulated and passed the Norris-LaGuardia Anti-Injunction Act. The business community simply opposed it. And the AFL, even at the eleventh hour, kept drafting its own legislation to curb injunctive abuse; union leaders accepted only the Norris-LaGuardia bill when its passage was imminent. Similarly, this anti-injunction legislation became law only after the progressive faction of Republicans increased their institutional leverage in Congress by forming an alliance with the progressive Democrats that made a presidential veto futile.

### Substantive or Procedural Anti-Injunction Legislation

While the progressive Republicans formulated and reformulated what became the Norris-LaGuardia Act, organized labor clung to its own ideas about anti-injunction legislation. From 1900 until 1929, the AFL consistently drafted anti-injunction proposals that substantively altered labor law by making either conspiracy doctrine or antitrust regulations inapplicable to unions.[6] Despite evidence to the contrary—namely, the failure of the Clayton Act— the AFL still argued that anti-injunction legislative restrictions should be the vehicle by which to change labor law. Only on the insistence of progressive legal experts, and, more important, of the progressive Republicans who guided bills through Congress beginning in 1929, did organized labor abandon its position on such substantive legal reform.

After President Woodrow Wilson's defeat, the AFL appealed to progressive Republicans rather than to progressive Democrats for help drafting anti-injunction legislation. Throughout the 1920s, the AFL asked for help from progressive Republican leaders such as George W. Norris of Nebraska, John J. Blaine of Wisconsin, Robert B. Howell of Nebraska, and Robert M. LaFollette Jr. of Wisconsin, rather than their progressive Democratic counterparts. Few progressive Democrats who had advanced the New Freedom legislative agenda returned to Congress. In 1918 and 1920, Senators Lee S. Overman of North Carolina, James K. Vardamen of Mississippi, William H. Thompson of Kansas, Henry F. Hollis of New Hampshire, John Kern of Indiana, and John F. Shafroth of Colorado no longer sat in Congress; and by 1925, Senators Atlee Pomerene of Ohio and Robert L. Owen of Oklahoma also had left office.[7] The progressive Democrats who returned after Wilson lost his bid for reelection— namely, Senators Henry F. Ashurst of Arizona, John B. Kendrick of Wyoming, James A. Reed of Missouri, and Joseph T. Robinson of Arkansas and Congressmen Carter Glass of Virginia and Oscar D. Underwood of Alabama, among others—no longer fought for a progressive Democratic agenda, although they voted for progressive measures such as the 1924 Howell-Barkley bill.[8] Moreover, the Democrats still actively involved in the passage of a progressive program, such as Edward Costigan of Colorado, Thomas J. Walsh of Montana, Alben Barkley of Kentucky, and Burton K. Wheeler of Montana, played second fiddle to their progressive leaders—LaFollette and Norris. In the 1920s, Republican insurgents, not Democratic insurgents, carried progressivism in Congress.

The progressive Republicans also received support from most progressive lawyers and law professors sympathetic to organized labor's plight. By the 1920s, these legal experts recognized the Democrats' effort to curb injunctive abuse—the Clayton Act—as a failure. The Clayton Act did not limit the reach of the labor injunction, they argued, because it protected organized labor from prosecution for restraint of trade. For instance, Edwin E. Witte, a progressive expert on the labor injunction, initially argued for changes in labor law similar to those in the Clayton Act. Legislation modeled after the 1906 British Trade Disputes Act, which secured immunity for organized labor, might, he believed, free American unions from injunctive abuse. But by the 1920s Witte, among other progressive legal experts, agreed that the Supreme Court would overrule such substantive changes in labor law.[9] The *Bedford Cut Stone v. Journeymen Stone Cutters' Association of North America* ruling, the last of a series of decisions undermining the Clayton Act, convinced Witte and other progressive jurists that injunctive abuse could be checked only by procedural reforms in labor law.[10]

In September 1923, the AFL Executive Council asked Jackson H. Ralston, regular counsel for the AFL, to consult with Francis B. Sayre, a Harvard law professor, about drafting anti-injunction legislation. In Sayre, the AFL got help from someone who shared the progressive Republican conviction about labor law reform.[11] Knowing that the AFL wanted substantive alterations in labor law, Sayre and Ralston suggested that it lobby for the introduction of two separate bills.[12] If the Supreme Court struck down the first bill, containing substantive changes, they reasoned, it might sustain the second bill, providing procedural changes. "When the bills are presented in Congress [*sic*] we want them to be Supreme Court proof," said Ralston and Sayre, "and we know of no way in which that can be done except to submit them to those who we believe are most competent to pass upon them."[13]

Neither the House nor the Senate Judiciary Committee heard these bills, and in December 1925 the AFL again solicited help from progressive legal experts. At this time the Executive Committee, at its annual AFL convention, had William Green, the AFL's newly elected president, hire Witte, the progressive legal expert, to study equity relief and the legal rights of wage earners.[14] Like Sayre before him, Witte recommended that anti-injunction legislation "limit the equity jurisdiction of the federal courts, . . . [to] remove nearly all the major complaints that labor finds in the issuance of injunctions involving or arising out of labor contracts." He continued, "Nevertheless, this legislation proposal does not embrace labor's complaint with reference to the doctrine of 'conspiracy'[;] . . . the remedy for this complaint involves quite a different principle of law."[15] Witte concluded that the AFL should submit two separate bills:

first, anti-injunction legislation that limited the reach of the federal courts' equity arm in labor disputes; second, general labor legislation that provided a system for incorporating unions. The latter would be modeled after the 1906 British Trade Disputes Act, Witte explained, to regulate labor-management relations in all industries.[16]

Not pleased with Witte's advice, the AFL cast it aside and convinced Henrik Shipstead, a Farmer-Laborite from Minnesota, to introduce a bill that made only substantive changes in labor law.[17] As a favor to his friend Andrew Furuseth, the head of the International Seaman's Union, Shipstead introduced anti-injunction legislation that redefined the meaning of private property in order to exempt unions from federal equity orders. The Shipstead bill provided that "nothing shall be held to be property unless it is exclusive, tangible and transferable."[18] According to a spokesman for the AFL, "The labor injunction issue can be summed up in these two points: If business and labor is [sic] property, the labor injunction is right. . . . If business and labor are human relations, and have no connection with property, the labor injunction judge has usurped his powers."[19] During the annual AFL convention in 1926, Furuseth argued that anti-injunction legislation must correct "the real trouble [that] is the misuse and extension of the word 'property.'"[20] The Thirteenth Amendment outlawing slavery and involuntary servitude, Shipstead and Furuseth claimed, could be used to limit injunctive abuse. According to Furuseth, in compelling strikers to return to work, the labor injunction forced them into involuntary servitude.

Disturbed that the Taft Court had rendered the labor relations provisions in the Clayton Act worthless, the AFL had stood fast to its position that unions must be exempted from antitrust statutes.[21] Green, Furuseth, and other labor leaders kept lobbying for substantive changes in labor law that would destroy the labor injunction per se. Yet these leaders had no indication that the Taft Court would change course and support substantive alterations in labor law.[22]

Given the Taft Court's general denunciation of this type of labor legislation, the Republican progressives thought that the AFL leaders were fooling themselves. Undoubtedly, the Court would strike down the Shipstead bill. Senator John J. Blaine (who would serve on the Senate Judiciary subcommittee that heard the Shipstead bill and the Norris substitute bill) observed that Shipstead and union leaders proposed to solve the problem of injunctive abuse "by redefining property—property to be defined as tangible and transferable, thereby going upon the assumption that a restraining order could not be issued and that all workers would be entitled to a remedy in an action at law."[23] Grounded in the same principle that underpinned the Clayton Act, the Shipstead bill exempted organized labor from accountability under equity law. The bill also emphasized that the Thirteenth Amendment, outlawing slavery and involuntary servitude, constitutionally substantiated this exemption.[24] Dismissing the bill, Felix Frankfurter said, "The talk about the Thirteenth Amendment is too silly for any practical lawyer's use and would only nullify the aim that lay behind the formation of the 'public policy.'"[25]

### The Progressive Procedural Alternative to Equity Relief

Believing that the Shipstead bill included unconstitutional and ineffective labor provisions, the progressive Republican leaders lined up against it. Senators Norris, Blaine, and Walsh, who formed the subcommittee that heard the Shipstead bill, thought that again the AFL had pursued the wrong path for reform.[26] Sitting through two months of hearings in February and March 1928 only solidified their perspective that the Shipstead bill offered the same sweeping protection from judicial interference that the Democrats had offered organized labor under the Clayton Act. By redefining labor as human relations rather than property, Senator Blaine wrote to Witte, Shipstead and the union leaders had not "touched the problem at all from the legal standpoint."[27] Sayre also argued, "If labor believes the Shipstead bill will save all, [it] will be bitterly disappointed."[28] The progressive Republicans thought that collectively the AFL labor leaders had put their heads in the sand: they ignored the Taft Court's rulings in the *Duplex* and *Bedford* decisions that had rendered the exemption in the Clayton Act worthless.[29]

Likening the Shipstead bill to the Clayton Act, the progressive Republicans argued that antitrust exemptions or redefinitions of labor as "non-property" were simply empty phrases. "The Shipstead bill would probably be held unconstitutional," Witte said, "because it discriminates in the degree of protection accorded to different classes of property."[30] Hence, the three progressive senators on the Judiciary Committee—Blaine, Norris, and the Democrat Walsh—wanted to draft a substitute for the Shipstead bill.

In May 1928, Norris asked progressive legal experts who shared his views on anti-injunction proposals to craft the first Norris substitute bill.[31] Witte, Frankfurter, and labor lawyers Herman Oliphant, who represented the Rapid Transit workers in *Interborough Rapid Transit Co.*, and Donald R. Richberg, counsel for the railroad brotherhoods, spent three years writing and rewriting the Norris bill.[32] In 1932, Congress passed it as the Norris-LaGuardia Anti-Injunction Act.

Formulating the first Norris substitute bill in 1928, the progressive drafting committee reiterated the complaints of Norris, Blaine, and Walsh against the

AFL's proposals to restrict "government by injunction." Witte, Frankfurter, Oliphant, and Richberg wrote that "the solution of this problem [could not] be found in any short, sweeping prohibition."[33] Legislation that limited the reach of the labor injunction, they wrote, must be rooted in procedural changes in equity law.[34] "I think there is better chance of passage of a procedural measure and better likelihood of securing its fair interpretation and observance by the courts," Frankfurter stated, "if we do not overload it either with doubtful substantive provisions, or at all events, provisions which run counter to the deeper hostilities of the judges."[35] Rather than relying on the Thirteenth Amendment, the drafting committee studied the due process clause in the Fourteenth Amendment and developed subtle procedural changes consistent with the Taft Court's interpretation of this clause.

The Norris substitute bill reflected an approach to injunctive relief entirely different from the Clayton Act or the Shipstead bill. Instead of categorically prohibiting federal courts from enjoining a union or its membership, this bill dictated *when* an injunction could be used during a labor dispute. These progressives put forth procedural reforms concerning the federal courts' jurisdiction, not substantive alterations in labor law that freed organized labor from responsibility under interstate commerce.

At the same time, the Norris substitute bill limited injunctive abuse by clearly defining the principles of agency to circumscribe the grounds for equity relief. Yellow-dog contracts, which bound a worker not to join a union, and the union's lack of personality no longer sufficed as reasons to enjoin strikers.[36] The bill provided, first, a public statement purporting that, because of their "helplessness," individual workers needed representation at the bargaining table; second, a section invalidating yellow-dog contracts; third, restrictions on the use of injunctions; and fourth, a narrow interpretation of union responsibility.

### The Helplessness of Individual Workers

The Norris bill's public policy statement about the "helplessness of the individual unorganized worker" would, its authors hoped, discourage the Supreme Court from misconstruing the bill's legislative intent, for while avoiding any association with class legislation, this bill expanded the common-law conception of the liberty of contract. First, it recognized the helplessness of individual unorganized workers. Second, it enabled the union, or any other voluntary association, to help these individual unorganized workers negotiate a collective bargaining agreement.[37] "The proposed declaration of public policy based on the helplessness of the individual unorganized worker (which has been declared a fact by the Supreme Court and which is a fact)," a memoran-

dum circulating in Senator Norris's office explained, "states the obvious necessity of full freedom of association and freedom from interference, restraint
or coercion of employers of labor in the designation of representatives or other
concerted activities 'for the purpose of collective bargaining or other mutual
aid or protection.'" [38] (The legislative authors never completed the syllogism
that if the union protected the helpless workers, the union would receive the
anti-injunction relief).[39] Instead of making organized labor the beneficiary of
this legislation, and making itself vulnerable to the assertion that it constituted
class legislation, this bill relied on agency law. It recognized unions as competent collective bargaining agents without assigning them exclusive agency.

The progressive legislators built into this legislation the same concept of
agency law as in the Transportation Act of 1920 and the Railway Labor Act of
1926. In these pieces of labor legislation, workers had the right to representation, be it union or nonunion. As one of the legislative authors, Frankfurter,
declared: "This public policy in respect to railroad employees has already been
declared by Congress and there is no apparent reason why the same public policy should not be applied to all other employees who may be subject to the authority of the Federal Courts." [40]

### Yellow-Dog Contracts Invalidated

The Norris substitute bill also provided that yellow-dog contracts
be invalidated and rendered "innocuous as a ground for injunction." [41] Congress circumscribed the federal courts' jurisdiction so that they could no
longer grant employers injunctions against third parties who interfered with
yellow-dog contracts, which prohibited workers from joining unions.[42] How
could the due process of an employer be denied, Frankfurter asked rhetorically,
if the federal courts merely chose not to enforce yellow-dog contracts? [43] Employers could still ask their workers to sign yellow-dog contracts, but the federal courts could no longer enjoin unions for inducing workers to breach these
contracts. To no longer find third parties liable effectively nullified the yellow-
dog contract, since employers secured them not as a means of making individual workers accountable but for their interference value.

### Withdrawing the Labor Injunction

To ensure that the labor injunction could not be applied, the Norris
bill defined what type of conduct required equitable relief. The bill stipulated,
"All possible plaintiffs have the same number of remedies, regardless of who
they are and who the defendant may be," and "All possible defendants have the

same protections no matter who they are and who the plaintiff may be." It limited the labor injunction by describing the scope of activities that deserved one. "Certain defined conduct is not remediable by injunction and that protection is applicable *to all* and *against all* equally." [44]

Changing the focus from the agent itself to the conduct of this agent meant that the legislative authors avoided giving organized labor its long-sought-after immunity. "To attempt to destroy judicial power to grant injunctive relief in labor disputes would be both wrong and futile," they explained, "because, first, this power can be and ought to be exercised for the protection of many recognized rights, and, second, the withholding of relief against wrong in one class of classes and permitting relief against the same wrong in another class of classes is subject to grave constitutional objection." [45] The Norris substitute bill withdrew accountability on the basis of activity or conduct, not agency. [46] It withdrew "the injunctive remedy from all litigants based upon certain defined conduct." The bill issued few prohibitions, giving the Supreme Court little leeway to declare that it protected the class of organized labor in violation of the rights of all other classes.

### Union Accountability, Not Protection

The "sound law of agency" constituted the fourth procedural reform that put "a further restraint upon judicial interference with freedom of association." [47] It explicitly limited union accountability in order to circumscribe the federal courts' injunctive arm. [48] "Persons and associations shall not be held responsible for the unlawful acts of individuals," the Norris bill provided, "except upon clear proof of actual participation or authorization or ratification of such acts." [49] Forcing the federal courts to apply actual agency law meant that unions would no longer be penalized for their unincorporated legal status. [50] These courts could enjoin only specific union members or specific union officials. Unlawful or threatening activity by a few nonunion participants was no longer grounds for issuing an injunction.

At the time, employers were engaged in the "common practice of employing industrial spies and private detectives to do violence and provoke violence," Frankfurter noted, "thereby creating the occasion for enlisting the aid of law." [51] The bill's agency section, he reasoned, was "no more than a statement of the governing principles of the law of agency as they are applied in litigations other than labor." Yet Frankfurter's emphasis on agency law substantiated the applicability of the doctrine of "actual" agency, not "apparent" agency, to labor law. "Those principles call for *a full quantum of proof*," he noted, "before fixing responsibility upon one person for the acts of another." [52] Otherwise, as Frankfurter explained, "presumptions of guilt and easy inferences in labor cases have created the result that an organization engaged in an industrial struggle by legal means is held answerable in law for all violence and unlawful conduct done by anyone at all." [53]

The progressive legislative authors of the Norris bill derived their emphasis on agency from two sources. First, according to Frankfurter, the Supreme Court had relied on agency in rendering the first *Coronado* decision in 1922.[54] In an important article for the *New Republic*, he focused on how this conservative Court used the doctrine of "actual" agency to determine union liability under common law.[55] The Court secured the votes of the almost permanent members of the minority—Louis D. Brandeis, Oliver Wendell Holmes, and Harlan Fiske Stone—when it relied on these principles to define and thereby to limit union accountability. Following the same logic as established by the doctrine of actual agency, the progressive drafting committee thought the Taft Court would accept restrictions on the labor injunction that clarified the union's responsibility under law.

Second, from the 1890s through the 1920s, progressive state and federal court judges relied on the principles of agency to explain why unions could negotiate binding trade agreements. These progressive judges applied agency law to labor law because the dominant conservative state and federal court judges refused to uphold collective trade agreements negotiated by unincorporated labor unions. But as progressive legal jurists noted, the courts' refusal to enforce such agreements represented a matter of policy, not precedent. In reference to yellow-dog contracts, these jurists noted that trade agreements "are frequently 'more honored in the breach than in the observance.'" Wesley Sturges further underscored the hypocrisy of the state and federal courts in not enforcing collective trade agreements by writing, "On the evidence it seems most consistent to say that the formula that 'an unincorporated association is not a legal entity separate from its members' has been employed by the courts only as a *method of statement* of the real reasons for their decisions . . . that to sue and be sued in the association name are exclusively 'corporate relations.'" [56]

Finally, the progressive legislators recognized that by using agency law to limit organized labor's vulnerability to the labor injunction, they created policy that recognized the complexity of this unwieldy organization. Agency law worked well. It depended on "the liability of the union and its members for the acts of its officers, or of the members for the acts of the union." [57]

For the first time, a statute identified the union as a legitimate bargaining agency for workers in all industries. In 1926, the Railway Labor Act allowed unincorporated unions to represent employees during the trade agreement negotiation and enforcement processes.[58] The Railway Labor Act, then, defined union accountability and liability by relying on agency law. This became the integral part of the worker representation scheme. Two years later, progressive legislators and lawyers defined the extent of union responsibility to render yellow-dog contracts nonenforceable and to limit the reach of the labor injunction. They thought that the principles of agency upheld union and union-member rights without violating due process.[59]

Clearly, the committee drafting the Norris bill adopted an entirely different approach to limiting injunctive abuse than that taken by the committee drafting the labor-sponsored Shipstead bill. Furuseth and Green still advocated anti-injunction legislation that withdrew equity relief against unions, their members, and potential members; by contrast, the Norris bill made procedural changes in labor law, such as rendering the yellow-dog contract unenforceable, withdrawing injunctions imposed on any person participating in certain defined labor disputes, and offering a new definition of the union. In turn, these types of provisions in the Norris bill deprived the federal courts of their most common justifications for enjoining unions and their members and thereby limited the number of injunctions these courts could award.

Although the primary purpose of the Norris bill was to liberate organized labor from "government by injunction," agency law and the bill's public policy statement expanded the Hughes Court's rationale about due process, freedom to contract, and the worker representation scheme in the railroad industry to all industries. Unlike the Shipstead bill, which relied explicitly on the Wilsonian idea of protectionism for underprivileged groups, the Norris bill followed the labor-management relations path of responsible unionism laid out by the Republican railroad labor legislation. As one law student wrote for the *Columbia Law Review*, agency law constituted "the 'responsibility' section's" anti-injunction legislation.[60]

## The Second Norris Bill and the Second Failure

The progressive lawyers and legislators drafting the Norris substitute bill expended great effort, but the Senate Judiciary Committee did not hold hearings until 1929, after the presidential election of 1928, which brought Herbert Hoover into office.[61] Norris, Blaine, and Walsh had to reintroduce the Norris substitute bill in the first session of the Seventieth Congress. Norris, moreover, had trouble reporting this bill to the Senate as a whole. The AFL did not pledge its support until the fall of 1929, and union leaders spent the rest of this year and the next wrangling over revisions. The old guard Republican members of the Judiciary Committee were also obstructive.[62] As Norris explained, the substitute bill was "criticized by both sides . . . very severely."[63]

In 1926, when the old guard and progressive Republicans supported the Railway Labor Act, the old guard did so with the understanding that the administrative agency implementing labor-management relations would discipline organized labor. The railroad labor policy, however, proved to be no detriment to organized labor. By 1928, the old guard Republicans realized that the worker representation scheme they had so carefully crafted with the progressive Republicans benefited organized labor; they quickly abandoned their quest for developing a "new order" in labor relations based on responsible unionism. Besides, the old guard Republicans never thought that the creation of railroad labor-management relations machinery would obviate the need for the labor injunction that they still supported. Meanwhile, the progressive Republicans observing the same phenomenon continued to carry the Republican flag for this type of unionism. A labor policy based on a worker representation scheme and contractualism had a better chance of passage in Congress.

Aside from this battle within the Republican Party, the Senate Judiciary Committee faced a conflict with the AFL. Although it no longer considered the Shipstead bill a viable legislative option, the AFL refused to support the Norris substitute bill.[64] When it finally agreed to back the Norris bill in the fall of 1929, the AFL fought with the progressive Republicans over revisions. The AFL insisted that the Norris bill be expanded to take all remedies for damages in labor disputes away from the federal courts and to overwrite the "indirect criminal contempt clause" with a clause that would withdraw the remedy for *all* contempt cases.[65] In protest to the AFL's suggestions, the legislative authors immediately warned Norris, "[While] it is one thing . . . merely to withdraw the remedy of injunction for a given act, it is a wholly different thing to take away all remedies, including civil action for damages which sub-section J does."[66] The AFL's revisions proposed "a serious constitutional doubt" and incurred "needless risks for no particular gain."[67]

Furthermore, the conflict between the AFL union leaders and the progressive legislative authors within and outside the Senate Judiciary Committee went beyond the scope of these specific labor relations provisions. Each group accused the other of misunderstanding the issue of general equity abuse.[68] For instance, AFL president Green said that Norris "dealt with the very controversial subject of the use of injunctions in labor disputes in a very conservative and moderate way." He continued, "I am not sure from a reading of your address that you favor the modification of the power of the equity courts to issue injunctions in labor disputes or whether you favor a continuation of the policy now pursued by equity courts."[69]

The AFL's intransigence upset Norris, Blaine, and Walsh because they knew how hard the old guard and pro-administration Republicans had worked to defeat their bill.[70] The bipartisan progressives and organized labor, they thought, must present a united front. As it was, with the AFL arguing for revisions and Norris, Blaine, Walsh, and Borah backing the original Norris bill, anti-injunction legislation never left the Judiciary Committee in 1929. Bogged down by these sectarian battles, the committee brought the Norris anti-injunction bill to the Senate only when the Republican Party itself began to crumble.

## Herbert Hoover, the Progressive Republicans, and Judge John J. Parker

After the Wall Street market crash, Hoover's honeymoon with Congress ended, and the progressive Republicans left the GOP. Rejecting the Republican Party's reaction to the Great Depression, the progressive Republicans formed an alliance with the progressive Democrats to undermine the Republican Party. Norris led this bipartisan coalition, while the Republicans LaFollette, Borah, Blaine, Brookhart, Howell, and Johnson; the Democrats Wheeler, Walsh, and Wagner; and the Farmer-Laborite Shipstead became some of the coalition's most active members. The progressive Republicans led the opposition to Hoover's administration.

Even before the midterm congressional elections in 1930, the progressive Republicans and Democrats tested their institutional strength by opposing President Hoover's depression policy program. In early 1930, the progressive Republicans voted, albeit unsuccessfully, with the Democrats in opposition to Charles Evans Hughes's confirmation to succeed the late William Howard Taft as chief justice. Then, in April 1930, the progressive Republicans worked again with the progressive Democrats to reject Judge John J. Parker's nomination to the Supreme Court. The death of Justice Edward T. Sanford had created another vacancy on the Court. After convincing the majority in the Senate that Judge Parker must be denied confirmation because of his use of the labor injunction, the progressive Republicans and Democrats realized that the Norris substitute bill could finally be reported out of the Judiciary Committee and passed by Congress.[71]

The progressive Republicans and Democrats used this confirmation battle to test their effectiveness as a coalition. With Norris chairing the Judiciary Committee, the progressive Republicans and Democrats on the committee asked Judge Parker questions that focused attention on his antiunion, racist judicial record. In particular, Norris, Borah, Blaine, Walsh, and Dill emphasized Parker's role in issuing injunctions against organized labor. Parker's antiunion record, these progressives thought, might help them publicize the need for anti-injunction legislation.

During the confirmation hearings, Parker came under attack by the progressive Republicans and Democrats for upholding a yellow-dog contract in the *Red Jacket Coal* case.[72] Parker had affirmed a series of equity complaints in 1927 that encompassed the southwestern nonunion coal fields in West Virginia, and approximately three hundred coal companies had received injunctions.[73] Parker, however, defended his position, stating, "It must be obvious to anyone that, as a member of the Court in the *Red Jacket* case, I had no latitude or discretion in expressing any opinion or views of my own."[74] He added that he had "followed the law as laid down by the Supreme Court" in the 1917 *Hitchman Coal & Coke Co. v. Mitchell* decision, which upheld an injunction against union leaders as third parties in the potential inducement of a breach of a yellow-dog contract. "Any other course," Parker insisted, "would result in chaos."[75]

Parker's response played poorly during the confirmation hearings. Not helping Parker's chances for confirmation, Hoover adopted the same defensive strategy. Hoover asked Attorney General James E. Mitchell to go public with his opinion of the legal merit of the nominee's *Red Jacket Coal* decision. According to Mitchell, the Supreme Court's decision obliged Parker to enjoin the UMW for inducing the miners to violate their yellow-dog contracts.[76] The UMW leaders, the attorney general added, were "maliciously endeavoring to cause the employees of the plaintiffs to violate their contracts of employment with the plaintiffs, and were, by force, intimidation, and violation, endeavoring to compel the plaintiffs' employees to cease work, and enjoined [the union leaders] these acts."[77] Bringing public attention to the fact that employers secured injunctions against unions on these meager grounds, however, only increased the public outcry against Parker's confirmation in particular and the labor injunction in general.

Attorney General Mitchell's press statement about the *Red Jacket Coal* case underscored how state and federal courts used yellow-dog contracts to rationalize their offering equity relief to employers when the public perceived this type of contract as unfair. Not a single Judiciary Committee member voted for Parker's nomination. Even Senator Frederick Steiwer of Oregon, who opposed the Norris bill, refused to support his nomination.[78]

Against the advice of the old guard Republicans, Hoover himself entered the confirmation battle.[79] He issued a public statement denouncing the progressive Republicans on the Judiciary Committee for making Parker's appointment a political issue.[80] In so doing, Hoover argued, these progressives usurped his constitutionally given power. "Shall the legislative branch," he asked, "control the decisions of the Supreme Court?"[81] Hoover's statements fell on deaf ears, however, and on May 7, 1930, Parker lost the nomination for the Supreme Court by a vote of 41 to 39.[82] As the popular press explained, "a nominee for justice of the Supreme Court of the United States was denied confirmation by the Senate, largely, if not almost entirely, upon the basis that as a circuit judge he had upheld the validity of a yellow-dog contract."[83] The political strength of the progressive Republicans and the Democrats in the Senate, in addition to organized labor's strenuous lobbying efforts, stopped Parker from reaching the Supreme Bench.[84]

### The Old Guard Prevents the Passage of the Norris Substitute Bill

Reinvigorated by their success in the Parker confirmation hearings, the progressive Republicans and Democrats held hearings on the Norris substitute bill. Although they opposed Parker's Supreme Court nomination, the old guard Republicans on the Judiciary Committee led the battle against this bill. In 1926, President Coolidge and the progressive Republicans had induced the old guard to help draft the Railway Labor Act. But, by 1930, the old guard no longer endorsed collective bargaining, even if agency was not assigned specifically to organized labor. Anti-injunction legislation, they thought, primarily benefited organized labor—and for this reason, they opposed it.

Senators Charles S. Deneen of Illinois, Frederick H. Gillett of Massachusetts, Frederick Steiwer of Oregon, and Arthur R. Robinson of Indiana led the old guard Republican campaign against this bill. When the Senate was reorganized after Hoover's election, these four old guardsmen and three regular Republicans—Felix Hebert of Rhode Island, Daniel O. Hastings of Delaware, and Charles W. Waterman of Colorado—sat on the Judiciary Committee. Steiwer, Deneen, Gillett, and Robinson had little trouble persuading these Republicans to vote against recommending the Norris bill. The Democrats Hubert D. Stephens of Mississippi, William H. King of Utah, and Lee S. Overman of North Carolina also voted against the Norris bill.[85] On June 20, 1930, the old guard Republicans carried the day when the Judiciary Committee voted 10 to 7 for an unfavorable report.[86]

Writing an unfavorable majority report, Senator Steiwer challenged Congress's right to control the "Federal Courts, by indirection to impose one pattern of industrial relationships upon the industry of the country, regardless of local conditions."[87] Frankfurter, observing the legislative process closely, ridiculed Steiwer's position, proclaiming, "'States rights' as a slogan has the vitality of a low organism. . . . [The federal courts] have always refused to follow state policy and have intervened in such local affairs on the basis of their conception of some transcending national policy . . . [They] can invade state policy by judge-made law," Frankfurter argued, "but Congress is impotent to define law for the general guidance of its own creations."[88]

In the majority report, Steiwer further contested the idea that anti-injunction legislation would prohibit the federal courts from enforcing yellow-dog contracts. Although Steiwer and the conservative majority stopped short of endorsing these contracts, they wrote, "However distasteful such contracts may be to us, yet the fact remains that the Supreme Court in the three cases [*Hitchman Coal & Coke Co. v. Mitchell, Coppage v. Kansas,* and *Adair v. U.S.*] has held that there is no legislative power, state or federal, to inhibit or outlaw employment contracts providing against union membership."[89] Ignoring the difference between the Shipstead bill and the Norris substitute bill, Steiwer predicted that the Supreme Court would strike down this anti-injunction legislation as class legislation that violated freedom to contract and due process.

The coalition of progressive Republican and Democratic senators wrote a minority report responding to Steiwer's "misrepresentations."[90] Neither due process nor freedom to contract were disturbed, according to these progressives, since the bill abolished injunctive relief in all cases, rather than in a defined class of cases.[91]

Fearing that the progressive coalition of Republicans and Democrats might convince the Senate to pass this legislation despite the unfavorable majority report, the old guard Republicans prolonged the Judiciary Committee's work until Congress adjourned for the 1930 congressional elections in June. They consulted James E. Mitchell for his comments on the constitutionality of the Norris bill.[92] The Republicans Deneen, Gillett, and Waterman and the Democrats Hastings, Overman, and Robinson voted with Steiwer to pass the motion to send the bill to the attorney general; the progressive Republicans Borah, Blaine, Norris, and Ashurst voted against it.[93] Receiving the bill for review, Mitchell responded, "The Attorney General is not authorized to give his official opinion upon the call of either House of Congress or any committee or member thereof."[94] Mitchell served his purpose: no time remained for the Norris bill to be reported to the Senate before adjournment.[95]

### The Progressives Prevail

Recognizing that the progressive Republicans posed a greater threat to GOP policymaking than the Democrats, the old guard party elite spent most of its campaign energy at the primaries. In particular, members from the Republican old guard wanted Norris, the leader of the bipartisan progressive alliance, unseated. In a desperate attempt to defeat Norris, the GOP party leaders tried tricking the Nebraskan population into voting for the wrong George W. Norris—in the Republican primary, they ran an unknown Norris against the incumbent Senator Norris.[96] The old guard party elite also sought to defeat the progressive Senate leader from Idaho, William E. Borah.[97] They spent large sums of money attempting to get rid of these key progressive Republicans.

In fact, the 1930 midterm elections bolstered the progressive Republicans' strength. All the important incumbent progressive senators and congressmen won the Republican primaries, whereas two friends of the Hoover administration, Representatives Ruth Hanna McCormack and B. Carroll Reece, lost their seats to Democrats. At the same time, one key old guard local party machine, the Philadelphia machine, collapsed when the old Progressive Party leader Gifford Pinchot became the governor of Pennsylvania. In a last-ditch effort to unseat Pinchot, the old guard Republican leaders William S. Vare and William W. Atterbury went so far as to support the Democratic candidate.[98]

In all, the old guard and regular Republicans took a beating at the midterm congressional elections. In 1928, the Republicans had majorities of 267 to 163 in the House of Representatives and 56 to 39 in the Senate. Just two years later, they lost both control of the House and their strong majority in the Senate. The 1930 election left 218 Republicans, 216 Democrats, and 1 Farmer-Laborite in the House. By the time the seventy-second session met, the Republicans in the House had lost 4 more seats to the Democrats in special elections.[99] The Democrats became the majority party with 219 members, in contrast to 214 Republican members and 1 Farmer-Laborite. In the Senate, the Republicans maintained a slim majority of 48, compared with 47 Democrats and 1 Farmer-Laborite.[100]

The midterm elections spelled further disaster for the old guard and regular Republicans because the Democratic Party underwent a significant change in composition. Many of the newly elected Democrats were northern urban liberals or midwestern progressives. For instance, 6 of the 11 Democrats entering the Senate in 1930—namely, Marcus A. Coolidge (Massachusetts), Edward P. Costigan (Colorado), Cordell Hull (Tennessee), J. Hamilton Lewis (Illinois), Robert J. Bulkley (Ohio), and George McGill (Kansas)—were progressives. The percentage of congressional Democrats from the South, moreover, decreased for the first time since 1922. From 1918 until 1928, representatives from the South dominated the Democratic Party. But the percentage of southern Democrats dropped from 63 percent of the party in 1928 to 53 percent in 1930, with northern liberal progressive Democrats and midwestern progressive Democrats filling their seats.[101]

Two major demographic changes account for this transformation in the Democratic Party. First, between 1910 and 1930, the majority of the population moved from the rural areas to the urban areas.[102] Second, 17 million people became eligible to vote between the years 1920 and 1928.[103] Beginning in 1928, what political scientists have called the "Al Smith Revolution" occurred, as the Republicans lost their dominant position in the industrial centers to the Democrats.[104] Between 1928 and 1932, the Democratic net plurality in the twelve largest cities increased from 210,000 to 1,791,000. Just four years earlier, in 1924, the Republicans had enjoyed a net plurality of 1,308,000 in these urban centers.[105] Clearly, the 1930 midterm congressional elections were part of this voting realignment.

### Institutional Leverage

In 1931 and 1932, because of the slim majorities in Congress, the progressive Republicans, working with the progressive Democrats, played the crucial role in congressional policymaking. This bipartisan coalition, led by progressive Republicans, compelled the Republican administration and the old guard Republican elite to help pass a policy item that had long been on the progressive reform agenda—anti-injunction legislation. In 1932, the progressive Republicans and Democrats guided the Norris-LaGuardia Act through Congress.

Throughout the 1920s, the progressive Republicans had constituted an important voting bloc. In 1931, they formed an alliance with the progressive Democrats and became the controlling bloc. In the Senate, 31 senators labeled themselves progressives or voted with this progressive bloc: 15 Republican progressives, 15 Democratic progressives, and 1 Farmer-Laborite.[106] The election of these progressive senators was critical for the passage of the Norris-LaGuardia Anti-Injunction Act, moreover, because the Senate, not the House, guided it through Congress. Progressive representatives in the House played only a supporting role in the battle for anti-injunction legislation. In fact, the progressive Republican Fiorello LaGuardia, the House sponsor of this legislation, accepted the Norris bill in toto and at the last moment began fighting for its passage.

Flexing their newfound muscle in the House and Senate after the 1930 congressional elections, three progressive Republican senators, Norris, LaFollette, and Bronson Cutting of New Mexico, and two progressive Democratic senators, Costigan and Wheeler, called a nonpartisan conference in Washington, D.C., to plan legislative strategies to be employed during the lame-duck session. Still trying to maintain party loyalty, the old guard leader Senator James E. Watson of Indiana denounced Norris for leading the Republican insurgents away from the party fold and into this conference.[107]

Although the progressive Republicans applauded the old guard's efforts at reconciliation, they no longer shared much of a common ideology with the old guard Republicans. After the Great Depression, the old guard Republicans backed away from their ideology of economic nationalism and elitism. At the same time, the new progressive Democrats abandoned their position on states' rights and pluralism. The northeastern urban Democrats embraced economic nationalism and advocated building a new administrative state. During this emergency period caused by the depression, the progressive Republicans discovered that they shared more with the progressive Democrats than with their own party.

Further, the progressive Republicans increased institutional leverage through their "coalition" with the progressive Democrats.[108] The two groups had first discovered the effectiveness of such an alliance in the opposition to Judge Parker's confirmation. In 1931 and 1932, the progressive Republicans voted with the coalition of northeastern and midwestern progressive Democrats on social and agricultural issues, rather than with their fellow Republicans. For instance, in 1931, the progressive Republicans worked with the Democrats on the most important legislation of that year—the Smoot-Hawley tariff. In addition, the progressive Republicans almost replaced the old guard president pro tempore, George H. Moses of New Hampshire, with a more progressive Republican.[109] Finally, the progressive Republicans voted with the Democrats to elect the Texas Democrat John N. Garner Speaker of the House. By a vote of 218 to 207 they ousted Bernard Snell, the regular Republican.[110]

By 1931, almost all the progressive Republicans had bolted from the GOP: Norris, Blaine, Johnson, Borah, LaFollette, Cutting, Brookhart, Peter Norbeck of South Dakota, Lynn J. Frazier of North Dakota, Thomas D. Schall of Minnesota, and Peter Nye of North Dakota voted consistently against policies sponsored by President Hoover. All this dissension in the Republican ranks meant that Hoover had failed to unite the GOP. "Whoever controlled the Republican party during the second session of the 71st Congress," said the historian Harris Gaylord Warren, "it was not Herbert Hoover."[111] Hoover thought "the Norris group" planned to "destroy the Republican party and to erect a new party on its ruins."[112]

The president, moreover, never created strong bonds with the old guard Republican Party elite who had controlled Congress under the administrations of Harding and Coolidge. Hoover preferred to surround himself with independent-minded Republicans not connected with Washington politics; thus not one member of the old guard sat on Hoover's cabinet. Hoover also tried to deprive the old guard party leadership of its right to reorganize the Senate. The 1930 congressional election, Hoover maintained, repudiated the congressional GOP, not his administration. With the House and Senate now under the progressive coalition's control, Hoover wanted the regular and old guard Republicans to vote for Democratic leadership.

In a last-ditch effort to destroy the bipartisan progressive coalition, this Republican president abandoned his party. The president's plot to divide and conquer Congress failed, however. As the Democratic senator Carter Glass explained, Hoover wanted the "opportunity to charge [the Democrats] with obstructing the wise policies of the administration."[113] But the Democrats chose not to reorganize the House, and the old guard Republicans refused to sacrifice their majority rights to reorganize the Senate. Neither the Republicans in the Senate nor the Democrats in the House enjoyed an effective majority: the 31 Senate Democrats and the 30-odd House progressives could swing the vote for or against a policy in either chamber. The progressive Republicans took advantage of the wedge Hoover had driven between his administration and the old guard Republicans and in effect became the opposition movement against Hoover's administration.

In 1931, the coalition immediately developed a policy program for economic recovery, including unemployment relief, unemployment insurance, higher taxes, lower tariff rates, expanded credit facilities for farmers and business owners, and new stock exchange regulations.[114] Along with the junior Democratic progressive senators Robert F. Wagner and Edward Costigan, the senior progressive Republicans again led the way with this policy, advocating governmental intervention in the economy. Hoover vetoed most of these policies, but the coalition did force the Republican administration and the old guard Republicans to pass the Norris-LaGuardia Anti-Injunction Act. Since 1928, the old guard Republicans had successfully obstructed the passage of anti-injunction legislation sponsored by Senator Norris, who led the progressive Republicans. In 1932, however, strengthened by the influx of progressive Democrats entering after 1930 and bolstered by their alliance with all the progressive Democrats, the progressive Republicans were no longer hindered by the Republican administration's and the old guard Republicans' obstructionist tactics. The history of the anti-injunction legislation shows how, by working as an alliance, the progressive Republicans and Democrats forced the Republican administration and the old guard Republican Party elite to vote for this type of labor legislation.

## The Norris-LaGuardia Act of 1932

The progressive Republicans and Democrats and organized labor deliberated about whether to reintroduce the Norris anti-injunction bill in 1931 or in 1932.[115] Preoccupied with the Smoot-Hawley tariff bill, Norris suggested that the Judiciary Committee delay a year before reintroducing the legislation. Waiting until the first session of the Seventy-second Congress in 1932 would give them a better chance of passing this anti-injunction legislation, since the old guard Republicans on the committee would not obstruct its passage with delays.[116]

So, in 1932, Norris reintroduced the bill. By this time, the composition of the Judiciary Committee itself had changed. The most obstructive old guard Republicans had lost their positions on the committee. "Quite a change in the membership of the Senate Judiciary Committee" occurred. Norris explained that "Senators Deneen and Gillett, Republicans, did not return to the Senate and Senator Steiwer was no longer on the committee. In addition to this the membership of the two parties was so close that the Democrats were entitled to a larger representation than they formerly had on this committee. The new Democratic members were favorable to the anti-injunction bill." [117]

The publicity about the labor injunction engendered by the Parker confirmation hearings also gained the Norris bill more public support than ever before. The progressive governors—such as Democrat Franklin D. Roosevelt of New York, Democrat Joseph B. Ely of Massachusetts, and Republican governor LaFollette of Wisconsin—all endorsed anti-injunction legislation.[118] The Judiciary Committee heard impressive testimony about the labor injunction from progressives of many professions.[119] Finally, Alexander Fleisher of the Committee of Labor Injunctions organized by the American Civil Liberties Union brought some of the progressives together with the AFL union leaders.[120] "As a result of [a] conference between Norris, Donald R. Richberg, Felix Frankfurter and the AFL," Fleisher, explained, "the suggested amendments were ironed out so that the A.F. of L. agreed to the elimination of almost all of them leaving only a few suggestions that [might] be brought in by the way of amendments in committee." [121] On February 23, 1932, the Norris substitute bill received a favorable report from the Judiciary Committee. It passed by a vote of 9 to 5: the progressive Republicans Norris, Blaine, Borah; the progressive Democrats Dill, Ashurst, and Walsh; and the regular Democrats King, Bratton, and Stephens voted in support. The old guard and regular Republicans Robinson, Hastings, Hebert, Austin, and Waterman voted in opposition to the Norris bill.

After the Judiciary Committee finally released the Norris substitute bill, less than one week elapsed before the Senate as a whole passed it by a vote of 75 to 5.[122] On March 1, 1932, only the most staunch members of the old guard— Warren Robinson Austin (Vermont), Hiram Bingham (Connecticut), Frederick

Hale (Maine), Henry Wilder Keyes (New Hampshire), and George Moses (New Hampshire)—voted against the legislation.[123] During the debate, Senator Hebert led the opposition with amendments that would have lessened the impact of the legislation.[124] All his amendments, however, were overruled by a voice vote.[125]

Explaining why the Norris bill passed in 1932, when it had not been reported to the Senate in either 1930 or 1931, Norris stated that "there was that impenetrable wall of opposition, an opposition not voiced, not out in the open, but under cover, silent and effective. . . . Many of those previously opposed had changed their attitude [by 1932], and a majority of the members of the Judiciary Committee this time favored the bill." [126] Steiwer, who had obstructed the bill's passage in 1930 by delaying committee consideration and convincing a majority on the Judiciary Committee to hand down an unfavorable report, no longer opposed this bill.[127] "Not only did he drop his opposition," Norris relayed, "but he voted for the bill in exactly the same language which he had previously opposed." [128]

Anti-injunction legislation received the same degree of support in the House. The progressive Republican LaGuardia sponsored an anti-injunction bill that resembled the Norris bill. Unlike Norris, LaGuardia had spent little time preparing anti-injunction legislation.[129] Norris enlisted LaGuardia's help because of his credentials as a strong progressive Republican.[130] Under his guidance, the House passed the LaGuardia bill 363 to 13. The LaGuardia bill was subject to even less debate than the Norris bill. This bill differed from the Norris bill on a few minor points: first, it had no amendment on mandatory clauses; second, the LaGuardia bill restricted jury trials to contempt cases.[131] In all other respects, the LaGuardia bill resembled the Norris bill.[132] Just one week after the Senate passed the Norris bill, only members of the Republican old guard voted against it.[133]

When the bill came before the Senate, Norris braced himself for a fight with the old guard, who after all had sabotaged his previous attempts to pass anti-injunction legislation. This time, however, they remained silent, and the Senate gave its unanimous consent. Realizing that their obstructionist tactics would no longer succeed, most of the old guard and regular Republicans grudgingly voted for the legislation. Moreover, Norris, Blaine, and Walsh, the subcommittee members who had drafted the original Norris substitute bill, represented the Senate during the conference committee. Not hindered by the old guard, the conference committee redrafted a joint bill that resembled the Norris bill.[134] On March 17 and March 18, 1932, the House and the Senate, respectively, passed the final Norris-LaGuardia bill by a voice vote.

### Hoover's Hypocrisy

Given the large majorities that passed the preconference Norris and LaGuardia bills and the adoption of the conference bill by voice vote, Hoover thought it judicious to sign the bill into law. The coalition could muster a two-thirds vote to override the president's veto. Hoover came to this conclusion, however, only after two desperate final efforts to obstruct the Norris-LaGuardia Act failed.

First, Hoover asked Attorney General James E. Mitchell to review the final conference bill and write a public letter explaining which provisions might be overruled by the Supreme Court. Second, Hoover asked his secretary of labor, William Doak, to persuade the labor lawyer Donald Richberg, who had helped draft the Norris substitute bill, to declare his opposition to this anti-injunction legislation. Secretary Doak essentially offered Richberg a bribe to drop this legislation. Richberg wrote,

> When I met Secretary Doak . . . he explained that the President was worried over the possibility that the Anti-Injunction Bill might be pressed for passage in the Congress then in session and on account of strong opposition thereto wished to see whether some compromises might not be worked out. Therefore, Secretary Doak had arranged for a conference that day at luncheon and in the afternoon between Mr. James A. Emery, counsel for the National Manufacturers Association, Mr. Walter Gordon Merritt, counsel for the League of Industrial Rights and myself, which would be attended also by Mr. Doak and a lawyer from his department. I protested vigorously that such a conference would be wholly useless; that Emery and Merritt were the two principal advocates of the use of injunctions in labor disputes[;] . . . it seemed apparent to me that a conference such as suggested would be wholly useless and that it could only serve as the means for confusing the whole situation and possibly put me in a very false position.[135]

He continued, "Perhaps I should add one further fact which may or may not have any connection with the Anti-Injunction Bill. During my conference with Secretary Doak he asked me whether I would be interested in an appointment to the Federal bench, indicating that he might be able to exert considerable influence in this direction. I told him very frankly that I was not interested. . . . I do not think he was trying to offer me a judgeship in exchange for aid in scuttling the Anti-Injunction Bill. I only mention the incident to show the pressure of one sort of another which was exerted."[136] When both of these attempts to abort the Norris-LaGuardia bill failed, Hoover had no choice but to sign it into law.

Then, during the presidential campaign in 1932, Hoover claimed the bill as his own legislative victory. He argued that the Republicans were responsible for the passage of the Norris-LaGuardia Act.[137] Having fought against the obstructionist tactics of the Hoover administration and the old guard Republicans for three years, Norris was outraged by Hoover's attempt to take credit for the passage of the Norris-LaGuardia Act. Norris wanted the progressive Republicans, who had bolted from the GOP in 1930, and the progressive Democrats to be recognized as the true sponsors of this anti-injunction legislation.[138] Thus, Norris wanted the congressional coalition (the driving force behind Roosevelt's campaign)—not Hoover—to be recognized for the passage of the Norris-LaGuardia Act.

If Hoover's response to the Great Depression represented the overriding issue, still Norris's battle against Hoover contributed to Roosevelt's success in 1932. In newspaper articles and speeches, calling attention to what he dubbed as "Hoover's hypocrisy," the progressive Republican senator Norris explained that the progressive Republicans had spent no less than three years fighting delays imposed by the old guard and pro-administration Republicans. The strong majorities behind the Norris-LaGuardia bill, Norris argued, had forced the president's hand.[139] "From the very beginning," said the progressive leader, "the Administration was bitterly opposed to this bill." Norris went on to state that during the hearings for the first substitute bill in 1930, "the Administration Senators bitterly opposed this measure. They obstructed its passage at every opportunity."[140]

### Conclusion

With the passage of the Norris-LaGuardia Act, Congress limited the power of the Supreme Court and the lower federal courts in industrial relations. The American judiciary could no longer freely issue its most effective "lever," as Taft described the injunction, against organized labor. The bipartisan coalition of progressive Republicans and Democrats, in effect, ended the judiciary's monopoly in labor-management relations.

The contents of the Norris-LaGuardia Anti-Injunction Act showed that the AFL had entered a new age in labor-management relations in which the union's duties and privileges were determined by its activities rather than its agency. Imposing tests for causality and requirements for responsibility during labor disputes essentially depersonalized labor-management relations. Not only labor unions but any group or association conducting a labor dispute was freed from enjoinment. Because the legal personality of the organization orchestrating a labor dispute was no longer germane, labor-management relations were becoming a process that would soon require fully developed machinery to discern group accountability. The progressive principles of agency, which the Taft Court elevated to a new level in its vision of labor-management relations, were the foundation for the construction of the statist regulatory apparatus—namely, the National Labor Relations Board (NLRB)—passed during the New Deal.

Relying on the principles of agency to provide the logic of union accountability under law had a great impact on the development of organized labor. Put simply, these principles were developed into a theory of responsible unionism that undermined the AFL's ideology of voluntarism. By offering unions temporary legal relationships through the principles of agency, the federal courts and Congress gave themselves the authority to regulate union activities. Organized labor essentially lost its autonomy by sacrificing privacy for protection from "government by injunction." Further, in 1935, organized labor abandoned its theory of voluntarism by accepting the NLRB. Once they became defined by their activities, unions thereafter had to be certified by this board in order to obtain the temporary legal relationship with its membership necessary for representing them at the collective bargaining table.

CHAPTER **8**

# The Republican Origins of the Wagner Act

It would be folly to rely on such a law [the Wagner Act] to create for labor a power that can come only from action and organization.

—*Nation*, May 22, 1935

On May 16, 1935, eleven days before the Supreme Court rendered the *Schechter Poultry Corp. v. United States* decision, which undermined the so-called first New Deal policy program, the Senate passed the Wagner bill.[1] Shortly thereafter, the Wagner bill passed the House of Representatives, and President Franklin D. Roosevelt signed the National Labor Relations Act (NLRA), or what is commonly called the Wagner Act, into law. This was a watershed. Collective bargaining became a public process: the National Labor Relations Board (NLRB) conducted worker representation elections and protected workers from unfair labor activities. Upholding the workers' right to join unions as well as other labor organizations, the NLRB relied on the majority rule principle to determine which organization would become a collective bargaining agent. The board determined the size of the bargaining unit and then supervised a worker representation election. With these powers, the Wagner Act simultaneously promoted collective bargaining and furthered unionization— but at the expense of union autonomy.

The passage of the Wagner Act completed the construction of American labor policy. Although Congress has modified and amended this policy, the essential structure it erected in 1935 guides labor-management relations today.[2] For this reason, historians and political scientists have been preoccupied with locating the origins of the Wagner Act. Uncovering these origins, they assume, will help explain the development of American liberalism.[3] Indeed, conventional wisdom holds that the American state gave organized labor the right to organize and bargain collectively as part of its New Deal package of reform.[4]

Associating the roots of the Wagner Act with such a significant reform period supposedly provides one with evidence that American liberalism has become more democratic over time. Just as women were enfranchised during the progressive era of reform, organized labor was freed from economic oppression and given the right to unionize during the New Deal period.

What triggered the democratic spirit that led to the creation of American labor policy, however, is still up for dispute. Some political scientists and labor historians suggest that the NLRB emerged because of external forces like labor unrest, whereas others focus on the internal policymaking process, determining the origins of particular provisions and then demonstrating how they account for the history of this board as well as the American labor movement. Kenneth Finegold and Theda Skocpol, for instance, question state motivation, arguing that state managers running the National Recovery Administration lacked the bureaucratic capacity to implement section 7(a), the primary labor relations provision in the National Industrial Recovery Act (NIRA).[5] When Roosevelt and the Democratic Party recognized the state's incapacity, Wagner had the opportunity to pass a permanent labor policy. By contrast, Michael Goldfield suggests that it was not a question of state capacity but the activities of a social movement that manifested massive industrial unrest in 1934 and convinced President Roosevelt to establish the NLRB.[6]

This book transcends the state/societal dichotomy by arguing that the origins of the Wagner Act predated the New Deal. The Democratic administration and the Republican Supreme Court severely hampered Wagner, inducing him to extend existing labor relations policies. Wagner modeled his labor legislation after statutory and common-law ideas of responsible unionism that were formulated before the New Deal reform era. Particular legal ideologies, judicial doctrines, and legislative precedents set up an institutional framework of responsible unionism that helped him mold the Wagner Act.[7] The Republicans' and Democrats' struggle over the labor problem instigated a formal legal system in labor-management relations that was relatively autonomous and self-sustaining.[8]

American labor policy could be described as formal because this policy developed its own rationale and logic.[9] "Juridical formalism," Max Weber wrote, "enables the legal system to operate like a technically rational machine. Thus it guarantees to individuals and groups within the system a relative maximum of freedom. . . . Procedure becomes a specific type of aspiring contest, bound to fixed and inviolable 'rules of the game.'"[10] In the United States, this type of policy became dominant not because it was supported by those it ruled— organized labor and employers—but because it had gained public support.

More specifically, a formal system of law emerged when two factions within the Republican Party—the old guard and the progressives—constructed the first and second labor-management relations boards in the Transportation Act of 1920 and the Railway Labor Act of 1926, respectively. These boards built what Weber called a "general rule" around a scheme for worker, as opposed to union, representation. That is, workers had a right to representation that was associated with neither a specific representative nor a predetermined goal within a collective bargaining agreement. The board developed a rule that protected the worker's procedural right to select a representative. Who these workers chose—a friend of management or a union leader antagonistic to management—was not in question. No substantive or ethical value overtly embraced or rejected unionization.

It was this self-sustaining legal precedent that Wagner and his legislative assistants relied on when they crafted labor legislation. Initially, they accepted the Democrats' position on organized labor. Wagner helped the Roosevelt administration draft section 7(a) of the NIRA, which emphasized the workers' right to representation without giving either the unions exclusive right to representation or the state strong control over the representation process. When this labor policy failed to protect organized labor effectively, given the rise of company unions, Wagner and his legislative assistants searched for an alternative. First, in 1934, they drafted the Trade Disputes bill, which furnished section 7(a) with more enforcement powers. However, the Roosevelt administration undermined the passage of this bill, forcing Wagner to create yet another approach to labor law.

In his second attempt, Wagner was influenced by the labor disputes that erupted over minority representation and plurality rule beginning in 1933. He decided that a statist policy would be the most effective, because it used majority rule to control access to the workers' representation process. Wagner and his legislative assistants understood, moreover, that even if they convinced the Roosevelt administration to pass legislation that gave organized labor sufficient statutory protection to associate, the Supreme Court might strike it down as class legislation. By making statism and the scheme for worker representation the foundation for labor reform, Wagner's group circumvented the problems associated with the Roosevelt administration's proposals for such reform and addressed the Court's concerns about class legislation violating due process of law. But they failed to anticipate how this Republican approach would not always help organized labor.

Making majority rule the centerpiece of the Wagner Act meant that Wagner facilitated state intervention in labor-management relations that did not always make organized labor the benefactor of such intervention. The Transportation Act and the Railway Labor Act suffered from the same flaw. The NLRB used majority rule to ensure the public interest and shield the individual interests of the workers, not organized labor's interests and rights, from employers. Governed by this state-operated regulatory agency, organized labor no longer shaped its own destiny—it was dependent on this agency.

American labor policy cannot be defined in terms of the state/societal dichotomy that Finegold, Skocpol, and Goldfield, among others, have identified. The formal legal constructs developed in responsible unionism influenced the identities and the strategies of the Democratic and Republican policymakers wherever they were located in a public-private continuum, transcending this dichotomy. What is more, the Wagner Act did little to sustain the linkage between state-expansive policies, reform, and progress in the United States. This act, as well as the Transportation Act and the Railway Labor Act before it, created a competitive labor-management relations structure in which organized labor battled with employers to gain the loyalty of individual employees and therefore the temporary authorization to represent these workers at the collective bargaining table. This competitive labor-management relations policy would later prove problematic for organized labor.

### The First Democratic Labor Principles

Beginning with Woodrow Wilson's administration in 1913, Democratic labor legislation had roughly reflected a private conception of power. In other words, private groups and organizations shared and shaped the public sphere of law and authority. Labor legislation empowered (or enfeebled) organized labor by offering it freedom to associate and to establish collective trade agreements. Democratic labor legislation had recognized the collective bargaining rights of the players but had left the actual process of negotiating such rights into collective bargaining agreements alone. The union exemption provided for in the labor relations provisions of the Clayton Act of 1914, the centerpiece of Wilson's labor policy, had affirmed organized labor's right to bargain collectively and had partially exempted unions from prosecution under antitrust laws by altering the statutory definition of a labor union.[11]

President Wilson and the Democrats who designed the labor relations provisions in the Clayton Act had hoped to identify this partial exemption with the AFL's theory of voluntarism for one reason: they thought that it would please organized labor yet could be enacted in Congress with little cost. Although the AFL repeatedly requested that unions have full immunity from antitrust liability, Wilson gave them only a partial exemption from such liability.[12] And he did it knowing that the burden of interpreting this exemption would be imposed on the courts;[13] Wilson realized that neither he nor the

Democratic Congress could be held accountable if the judiciary emasculated this exemption. Indeed, the AFL heralded the labor-management relations provisions in the Clayton Act as its "industrial Magna Charta,"[14] despite the fact that the Supreme Court rendered these provisions all but ineffective in the early 1920s.[15]

During the next three years, Wilson undergirded this theory of voluntarism with an element of protectionism when he enacted two more pieces of labor legislation, the Seamen's Act and the Adamson Act, into law. First, Wilson signed into law the Seamen's Act of 1915, which provided safe work conditions for seamen. Second, the Wilson administration gave workers in the railroad industry an eight-hour day by passing the Adamson Act of 1916.[16] Without such special aid and assistance, Wilson claimed, organized labor would be at a competitive disadvantage in its battle with the business community.[17]

In all, the labor policy sponsored by the Democrats during the New Freedom period harbored voluntarism, protectionism, and a pluralistic notion of power: private groups influenced the public sphere of power and authority.[18] Competing groups, like organized labor and business, each fought to shape the federal government's policies on market relations. The government awarded itself the responsibility to umpire these groups, guaranteeing that they all competed on a level playing field. Neither Wilson nor his administration had tried fully to protect organized labor's privacy from judicial interference. Although the New Freedom labor policy, notably the Clayton Act, reflected the AFL's theory of voluntarism, it did little to combat the activities of the historically hostile judiciary. In fact, a cadre of progressive Republicans in the Senate who also sympathized with the AFL's attempt to bargain collectively considered Wilson's refusal to challenge the courts as evidence that his labor policy was a "sham."[19]

It was not until the eve of World War I that Wilson made labor policy a priority in his legislative program. At this time, he thought that organized labor, particularly the AFL, could help him pull the United States out of its isolationist position. Wilson co-opted union leaders like Samuel Gompers into supporting the Great War by giving them a corporatist role to play in politics and economics. He specifically established the War Labor Conference Board so that these labor leaders, as well as business leaders, could help design a wartime labor policy. For the first time in American history, labor leaders sat alongside business leaders to help formulate a wartime industrial relations policy for unionized and nonunionized workers alike.[20] Later that year, Wilson institutionalized this conference by setting up the National War Labor Board (NWLB) to implement the policies it had endorsed.[21]

The duties and powers assigned to the NWLB, however, attempted not to redefine organized labor's status before the law. Under the wartime labor policy, unions were still regarded as voluntary associations, endowed with no special rights or public duties. Thus, the primary difference between peacetime and wartime labor policies was that Wilson publicly asked for the voluntary cooperation of organized labor and the business community, and he made union leaders functional representatives of the public good by furnishing them with the voice to speak for the whole American workforce.[22]

### Roosevelt, the First New Deal, and Voluntarism

Between 1933 and 1935, when Franklin D. Roosevelt developed the first package of New Deal reforms, he also built a labor policy consistent with organized labor's vision of voluntarism. Unlike Wilson, however, Roosevelt put less emphasis on organized labor's ability to help during a crisis. Roosevelt's reliance on the AFL's ideology of voluntarism also proved more opportunistic than Wilson's earlier reliance on this ideology in gaining the labor vote. In theory, President Roosevelt and key members of his administration endorsed the workers' freedom to organize unions, but in practice, they allowed business and industry to circumvent that freedom. Roosevelt even went so far as to legitimize the ideas of plurality rule and minority representation, which management used to create company unions, under the protective guise that these unions constituted the worker's right to associate.

Three episodes in New Deal history illustrate how Roosevelt and key members of his administration relied on a loose interpretation of voluntarism to explain their attitude toward labor. First, the Roosevelt administration participated reluctantly in the creation of section 7(a) of the NIRA. Second, this administration tacitly supported plurality rule and minority representation, culminating in its response to the automobile strike of 1934. Finally, key members of the Roosevelt administration had a hand in the construction of the Walsh Adjustment Industrial bill, which promoted the idea of the employee's freedom to associate instead of collective bargaining.

### Labor and Economic Recovery

Section 7(a) of the NIRA encapsulated the labor policy under the New Deal. This section gave employees the right to join unions and to engage in collective bargaining.[23] The New Deal policymakers roughly borrowed it from the worker representation sections in the Railway Labor Act of 1926 and the Norris-LaGuardia Anti-Injunction Act of 1932.[24] Section 7(a) stipulated

(1) [that] employees shall have the right to organize and bargain collectively through representatives of their own choosing,

(2) that no employee and no one seeking employment shall be required as a condition of employment to join any organization or to refrain from joining a labor organization of his own choosing.[25]

The idea that workers should enjoy the freedom to associate was the heart of the labor relations policy in the NIRA: they had the right to organize and to bargain collectively, in exchange for supporting industrial codes that freed whole industries from prosecution for trade practices that would otherwise have been construed as antitrust violations.[26] The scheme for worker representation was therefore voluntary, just as participation in the National Recovery Administration (NRA) was voluntary. The NIRA imposed no duty on employers to bargain collectively with worker representatives or unions. Moreover, a weak institutional apparatus safeguarded these workers' right to representation. The primary difference between section 7(a) and the public policy statement in the 1932 Norris-LaGuardia Anti-Injunction Act was that the former prevented employers from driving their workers into labor organizations.[27]

Section 7(a) in the NIRA did little to expand the legislative boundaries around worker representation forged by the Norris-LaGuardia Act—in part, because Roosevelt's support for this section reflected his commitment to the urban-liberal Democrats and the progressive Republicans behind it more than any pledge to please organized labor. Roosevelt reluctantly included it at the urging of the pro-labor senators Wagner and Robert M. LaFollette Jr., a progressive Republican, after his administration struck down organized labor's attempt to associate labor law reform with economic recovery.[28]

Initially, the AFL had endorsed Senator Hugo Black's thirty-hours bill in 1932 and 1933, arguing that unionization helped end economic decline.[29] The Black bill proposed the institution of a thirty-hour workweek to stimulate business and curb unemployment. But Roosevelt and his inner circle of so-called Brain Trusters, who designed the first New Deal program, challenged this idea. Unlike business and trade associations, which in their view simultaneously served a public and a private interest, union organizations served only the private interests of their membership.[30] Roosevelt included section 7(a) in the first New Deal program policy grudgingly, as compensation for his rejection of the Black bill. He thought that neither union leaders nor unionization could help revitalize the economy.[31]

Roosevelt's first labor policy was therefore based on voluntarism and pluralism, with no element of protectionism or corporatism. He did not go as far as Wilson had by explicitly asking for organized labor's advice and cooperation

during the depression emergency period. Nor did he offer it special aid or protection. Ironically, Roosevelt might have instituted protectionist labor legislation without being accused of programmatic or ideological inconsistency. But,
unlike Wilson, Roosevelt thought economic reform occurred only with the
protection of members of the business community. Businesses should no longer
compete with their neighbors. The first New Deal structurally reordered
business–government relations: a corporate state relaxed antitrust regulations
because business and the federal government collaborated on how to bring
about economic recovery.[32] Given the new ethic extended between big business
and the federal government, that the Roosevelt administration had awarded organized labor a secondary position was even more glaring under the first New
Deal reform program than it had been during the New Freedom reform period.

### Voluntarism Gone Awry: Plurality Rule and
### the Automobile Strike of 1934

After the passage of the NIRA in March 1933, a large number of industries participated in what the chief administrator, General Hugh S. Johnson, called the Blue Eagle program of economic recovery, administered by the
NRA. Many members of the business community greeted this program with
enthusiasm. Although they had less fervor for section 7a of the NIRA—the
employee representation clause—most businesses decided that the economic
benefits of drafting industry-by-industry codes outweighed the detriments
associated with this section, particularly after they discovered that critical
members in the Roosevelt administration did not fully support it.[33]

Initially, the business community regarded the Roosevelt administration
with suspicion, simply because it had included section 7(a) in the NIRA. Roosevelt also met with this community's disfavor when he established the National Labor Board (NLB) to mediate labor disputes arising from the ambiguity about how to implement this section. Finally, the business community was
wary of Roosevelt because he had appointed Wagner, a well-known union advocate, to run the bipartisan NLB, which mediated labor disputes involving
employees and employers participating in the Blue Eagle program.[34]

Many prominent members of this community were relieved, however, when
it became apparent that Roosevelt rarely promoted the rights of labor organizations over those of company unions.[35] Offering their own interpretation of
section 7(a), employers insisted that worker representation meant they could
form company unions that thwarted unionization; workers thought this type of
representation gave them the opportunity to organize bona fide trade unions.[36]
Forced to settle these disputes over representation, Roosevelt and members

of his administration, most notably General Johnson and Donald Richberg, general counsel for the NRA, interpreted section 7(a) in favor of company unions more often than in favor of bona fide labor unions.[37] To do so, they relied on the ideas of minority representation and plurality rule, which employers used to subvert unionization, claiming that these principles should be regarded as a form of pluralism that governed the workplace.[38]

The conflict over union or company union representation first became heated, however, when Wagner, acting as chair of the NLB, rejected minority representation and plurality rule in favor of majority rule. Wagner preferred majority rule because it was the guiding principle behind the labor relations provisions operating under the U.S. Mediation Board upheld by the Republican-dominated Supreme Court. Adopting this position, he convinced ten thousand striking hosiery workers to return to work with the promise that the board would use the majority rule principle to determine the worker representation election. Then, relying on a secret ballot, the NLB supervised such an election.[39] Not surprisingly—with Roosevelt, Johnson, and Richberg in support of plurality rule and minority representation—the board found majority rule difficult to enforce.

By November 1933, the board failed to convince the Budd Manufacturing Company and the Weirton Steel Company to abide by the results of their respective worker representation elections.[40] These companies knew that the NLB had no enforcement powers and they could ignore its rulings with impunity.[41] In response, the Democratic administration and Democrats in Congress took sides on the issue of plurality versus majority rule. Administrators from the NRA, the Justice Department, the Labor Department, and the NLB fought over what course labor-management relations should follow.

First, Johnson and Richberg complicated the question of implementation by publicly denouncing majority rule and promoting the idea of operating labor-management machinery on the bases of minority representation and plurality rule.[42] As Johnson and Richberg interpreted the meaning of section 7(a) as it should be included in the industrial codes, a union and a company union could coexist in the same plant or factory.[43] The idea that employees have the right to self-organization without interference from their company, they argued, meant "only one thing, which is that employees can choose anyone they desire to represent them, or they can choose to represent themselves. . . . But neither employers or employees are required by law to agree to any particular contract, whether proposed as an individual or collective agreement."[44] If one worker refused union representation, this union could not force the company to bargain exclusively with its negotiating agents.[45] Second, the Justice Department and the Labor Department undermined the NLB by stalling its efforts to litigate the Budd and Weirton employers involved in the strike dispute. These departments, however, had few suggestions about what type of labor policy would be most appropriate.[46] Third, William Leiserson, the executive secretary of the NLB, opposed plurality rule and recommended that a stronger mediatory agency be created.[47] Milton Handler, general counsel at the NLB, advocated majority rule and adjudication, as opposed to mediation.

Entering the fray, ostensibly to resolve the Budd Manufacturing and Weirton Steel disputes, Roosevelt issued a series of executive orders that eventually supported the plurality rule and minority representation position adopted by Johnson and Richberg. First, on December 16, 1933, Roosevelt issued Executive Order 6511, giving the board a stronger directive to enforce worker representation elections. This executive order endorsed the board's past rulings but stopped short of supplying it with enforcement powers or standing squarely behind the principle of majority rule.[48] Two months later, Roosevelt issued Executive Order 6580, indicating his support for the NLB's attempts to force the Budd Manufacturing Company and the Weirton Steel Company to abide by its decisions. This order, drafted by Milton Handler, endorsed majority rule and gave the NLB the explicit power to conduct worker representation elections. The board would "hold an election whenever a 'substantial number of employees' (as defined by the Board) or any specific *group* of employees of any *plant* or enterprise or *industrial unit* or any employer subject to a Code . . . requested it." But then, Roosevelt qualified his own executive order and sided with the advocates of plurality rule. Three days after he issued his executive order, Johnson and Richberg condoned plurality, not majority, rule—without being reprimanded in public or in private for undermining this order. They released a statement to "correct the press interpretation of Executive Order 6580," claiming the "order merely provided a method of selecting representatives to act for the majority, but did not interfere with the right of minority groups or individual employers to deal with their employer."[49] Johnson and Richberg tried to protect company unions from being displaced by regular unions.

Roosevelt's quiet endorsement of plurality rule and minority representation had a tremendous impact on unionization during the first New Deal period, from 1933 until 1935.[50] With plurality rule, employers established company unions. If a majority of the workers voted for union representation rather than company union representation, according to Johnson and Richberg, the NLB still had no cause to acknowledge the former as the exclusive collective bargaining agent.[51]

Roosevelt again lent legitimacy to plurality rule and minority representation in March 1934, when he helped resolve a strike in the automobile industry.

Early on, the automobile executives in Michigan realized that they could never convince their workers to vote for a company union under the scheme for worker representation. But they could rely on the notion of plurality representation and minority rule to prevent unionization. For employers to bargain with regular unions, they insisted, would be unfair to the few workers who had enrolled in company unions and who therefore had no representation at the collective bargaining table. Much to organized labor's dismay, Roosevelt sided with the automobile industry on this point. Although Roosevelt had supported the majority rule principle with Executive Order 6580, he now threw his political weight behind minority rule and allied himself with the automobile companies.[52] As a member of the Petroleum Labor Policy Board explained to Secretary of Labor Frances Perkins, "I think very serious errors have been made in the handling of the automobile labor disputes, and apparently no one in the Administration is aware of the mistake in policy that is the real cause of the difficulties in Detroit. . . . The failure of the Automobile Board to settle the strikes and disputes [is] not so important as the feeling in the minds of wage-earners that lies back of those failures. Even though the strikes are settled, the feeling is bound to remain. From all over the country letters are coming that read like these: 'It begins to look like we can be fired for joining the union,' and 'the government backs down when it has to make a finding that big interests have violated section 7(a).'"[53]

Section 7(a) floundered not because this bureaucratic apparatus lacked state capacity, as Skocpol and Finegold have argued.[54] Instead, this provision lost legitimacy as a result of Roosevelt's intervention in how the Petroleum Labor Policy Board implemented it. The automobile workers felt betrayed by what Roosevelt did. Along with many other workers, they had assumed that section 7(a) had been included in the NIRA in response to the demands of their labor leaders. Roosevelt's action, however, exposed just how tenuous his commitment was to the labor movement.[55] At the same time, the language used in Executive Order 6580 showed how adamant Roosevelt was about making the worker representation scheme a scheme that would not only benefit organized labor.

Roosevelt's support for constructing separate labor boards for each industry participating in the National Industrial Recovery program was his concession to the automobile workers during this strike. These boards had the capacity to mediate labor disputes erupting over union recognition.[56] But they did not implement majority rule. They protected only the workers' freedom of association, not collective bargaining. Hence, Roosevelt embraced no labor-management relations machinery that might lead to what Charles Wyzanski later described as "collectivization."[57] In fact, he tacitly opposed the idea that employers had a duty to bargain collectively with worker representatives.

Despite all the confusion about majority or plurality rule, one side of the bargaining table—the employers' side—won the battle over the interpretation of section 7(a). More than two-thirds of all manufacturing companies participating in the NRA used company unions, rather than regular labor unions, to fulfill the employee representation clause in the NIRA.[58] The Roosevelt administration's overt and covert support for plurality rule and minority representation greatly hindered unionization during the NIRA's lifetime.

### Formulating the Trade Disputes Bill

In the late fall of 1933, realizing that the problem of plurality versus majority rule continued to plague labor-management relations, Wagner abandoned all hopes for the success of the labor policy provided by the NIRA and introduced a comprehensive labor-management relations policy. The Trade Disputes bill encapsulating this policy, which he wrote primarily with Leon D. Keyserling, created a tripartite National Labor Relations Board to mediate, arbitrate, and adjudicate labor disputes in all industries.[59] Unlike the National Labor Board, the new NLRB would try to *prevent* labor disputes by supervising worker representation elections. The NLRB would help determine such representatives by monitoring elections or using "other appropriate method[s]."[60]

The Trade Disputes bill fell short, however, of implementing majority rule. Instead, it stipulated that since company-dominated unions had caused most labor disputes with their demands for plurality rule and minority representation, they should be prohibited. Wagner and Keyserling drafted a list of unfair labor practices that employers would be forbidden to engage in when workers sought representation.[61] Without inserting provisions to protect union activity itself, Wagner and Keyserling developed legislation that prevented company-dominated unions from controlling worker representation elections and the trade agreement negotiating process. Wagner said, "The bill which I have introduced forbids employers from dominating labor organizations but defines labor organizations as associations of employees for the purposes of collective bargaining in regard to wages and hours of employment."[62] Specifying what would be considered interference in worker relations, the Trade Disputes bill stated: "Employers could not interfere with the worker's right to self-organization, disturb a labor organization's autonomy, offer financial assistance to employee representatives or their organizations, and discriminate against employees involved, or not involved, in a labor organization."

To justify further the prohibition of company-dominated unions, Wagner and Keyserling associated the Trade Disputes bill with the Keynesian theory of economic recovery.[63] Given the tremendous transformation in the structure of the economy from industrialization to mass industrialization, workers, they argued, could no longer represent themselves before the employers of large businesses and conglomerates. Without collective bargaining, workers stood no chance of regaining their balance in bargaining power. Yet strikes over union recognition disrupted interstate commerce and affected economic recovery. Hence, Congress needed to pass labor legislation preventing the grievances that caused these strikes. The purchasing power provided by stable wage rates resulting from collective bargaining agreements, Wagner and Keyserling added, would also stimulate the economy.

With the Trade Disputes bill, Wagner and Keyserling constructed a labor policy that facilitated collective bargaining by thwarting company unions. But this did not mean that the bill represented a "qualitative" departure from the Transportation Act of 1920 and the Railway Labor Act of 1926. The Trade Disputes bill was not the first piece of labor legislation that gave "unambiguous public support to independent unionism as a means to promote collective bargaining," as Tomlins argued. The Trade Disputes bill could have simply recognized the existing national unions.[64] But Wagner knew that his legislation would have little chance of being upheld as constitutional by the Supreme Court if he gave workers the right to select their representatives from among only bona fide unions, such as the AFL.

Like the legislative authors of the Transportation Act and the Railway Labor Act before them, Wagner and Keyserling carefully avoided making organized labor the direct beneficiaries of the Trade Disputes bill, knowing that the federal courts might categorize such as class legislation.[65] While the authors of the Trade Disputes bill hoped to hinder the formation of company unions, whereas not all the authors of the railroad legislation harbored the same intent, it still employed the scheme for worker, as opposed to union, representation embodied in the Transportation Act and the Railway Labor Act. The Trade Disputes bill shared two essential features with that precedent-setting railroad legislation.

First, the Trade Disputes bill maintained that collective bargaining never endangered employers' liberty or freedom to contract, because the contracts resulting from this type of bargaining must be classified as merely an extension of individual employment contracts. Tomlins also explained that the Trade Disputes bill "made collective bargaining an expression of the public interest in the terms of individual contacts of employment." Yet he deemphasizes how the preceding *American Steel Foundries v. Tri-City Council* and the Railway Labor Act had both been built on this type of contract.[66] During the House and Senate floor debates about the Railway Labor Act, many members of Congress discussed questions about collective bargaining and contract law. Did this type of bargaining extend or interfere with either the workers' or the employers' freedom to contract? Some congressmen cited *Coppage v. Kansas* and *Adair v. United States*, among other cases, as justifying their opposition to legislation that interfered with the contractual relations of employers and workers.[67] The progressive and old guard Republicans behind the Railway Labor Act offset this opposition with the point that their legislation *extended*, rather than interfered with, the law of contracts.

Second, in the Railway Labor Act this extension operated in conjunction with the worker representation scheme. Freedom to contract and collective bargaining became compatible by law if this scheme for representation in no way hindered the question of agency or changed the law of personality. More than three years after the Railway Labor Act passed Congress, Donald Richberg, then legal counsel for the brotherhoods and an author of this act, emphasized this difference between contracts and representation. "This policy recognizes that labor relations should be governed by contract," he wrote, "and that such contracts are only possible and enforceable where employe[e]s, being individually helpless, act collectively through self-selected representatives."[68] The legislative authors circumvented the problem of interfering with the employers' and workers' freedom to contract, not by forcing the two to negotiate contracts, but by requiring them to meet in conferences with representatives to negotiate these contracts.

In essence, the worker representation provision in the Watson–Parker bill and the Trade Disputes bill was the legislative counterpart to the principles of agency. These principles emerged slowly in labor law, between the late 1890s and the 1920s, to trace union accountability during labor disputes. Judges and justices in state and federal courts ruled in progressive decisions that because the unions' legal status was that of voluntary, unincorporated associations, they had no legal identity as competent collective bargaining agents. This meant trade agreements could not be enforced. These judges and justices therefore used agency law to make unions competent contracting parties. Instead of granting unions fictitious corporate personality, agency offered a means to hold unions accountable (without assigning the status of agent specifically to the union) on the basis of the relationships they entered into both with and on behalf of their members. Under these principles, the labor union, or indeed any voluntary association, was allowed a *temporary* legal relationship with its members. Congress codified agency law and circumvented the law of personality (that union accountability stemmed from the union's authority to represent its members), upheld by the Taft Court throughout the 1920s in its labor dispute cases. As Sturges wrote, agency law in the 1922 *Coronado* decision held unions liable as organizations and intertwined this notion of agency with union representation.[69]

Describing the type of struggle that would ensue because of this temporary relationship, Wagner told Congressman William Kelley of New York:

> The bill does not deal with the subject of organization by employers by their own side or by employees by their own side. So far as violence or intimidation are concerned, they are adequately prohibited by common law, and the bill does not refer to them. Insofar as moral coercion or economic pressure are concerned, employers should be allowed to exercise this force upon other employers in organizing trade associations, and employees should be allowed to exercise it upon other employees in forming labor associations. Otherwise self-organization in any realistic sense is impossible. *The only kind of coercion that is prohibited by my bill is interference by employers with the self-organization of employees or by employees with the self-organization of employers.* This is the real problem that we have to face in connection with industrial discontent at the present time and the bill is absolutely neutral and impartial on this question.[70]

Kelley thought that the labor-management relations policy must be free from the partisan wishes of organized labor and business. That is, organized labor could no more profit from this policy than organized business. Of course, Kelley understood that unions and employers would undoubtedly be locked in a perpetual conflict over who represented the workers.

### The Roosevelt Administration Minimizes Wagner's Efforts

Having carefully crafted the Trade Disputes bill along these circuitous lines to pass judicial review by the still Republican-controlled Supreme Court, Wagner was surprised by the Roosevelt administration's refusal to support it.[71] Roosevelt, critical members in his administration, and the bulk of pro-administration Democratic congressmen and southern Democratic congressmen opposed the bill.[72] Indeed, working behind the scenes during the hearings, they combined successfully to sabotage it. Officials from the Department of Labor and the NRA, as well as pro-administration Democrats in Congress, offered a substitute bill.[73] David I. Walsh, the chairman of the Senate Committee on Education and Labor, appointed Charles E. Wyzanski, solicitor general of the Labor Department, to draft this substitute bill.

To begin with, Wyzanski renamed the new bill the Walsh Industrial Adjustment bill, disassociating it from the Wagner Trade Disputes bill. Wyzanski then proceeded to erase the most important provisions from the Trade Disputes bill. First, he deleted the public policy statement that recognized the relationship between labor and the problems associated with economic concentration. Second, he eliminated the employers' duty to negotiate with their workers' representatives.[74] As he described it, in the substitute bill the workers' right to join a union, or any other labor organization, was founded on basic civil liberties: every individual has the right to belong to associations of his or her own choosing. He echoed the AFL's theory of voluntarism in an attempt to explain why American labor policy should recognize the organizational autonomy of the union, knowing that its autonomy would only hurt organized labor.

Wyzanski's approach to the workers' right to join a voluntary association showed so little regard for the special characteristics that defined labor-management relations—namely, the inequalities between workers and their representatives and employers—that Edwin E. Witte, a progressive lawyer who had helped write the Norris-LaGuardia Anti-Injunction Act, thought that in this bill the workers' right to association would be turned against them. As Witte explained, "As it now stands employers are authorized to enter into closed shop agreements with company unions. If they continue this, they can in effect bring back the yellow-dog contract, because they can require that their employe[e]s must belong to a company union."[75] The Walsh Industrial Adjustment bill contained a blanket "right to association" clause without recognizing the inherent inequality between workers and their employers.

At the same time, this substitute bill rejected the preference Wagner gave to collective trade agreements over individual trade agreements. Whereas the original Trade Disputes bill made it the employer's obligation to bargain with worker representatives and provided that the NLRB would supervise worker representation elections to ensure that these workers secured their "actual" liberty to contract, the Walsh Industrial Adjustment bill did not. Wyzanski eliminated Wagner and Keyserling's idea that the American state *should* promote collective contractualism in order to protect the public interest. In other words, the Walsh Adjustment Industrial bill did not recognize that collective bargaining reduced industrial strife and, for this reason, should be considered a public good. Further following these ideological lines, the Walsh Adjustment Industrial bill maintained the moribund Conciliation Service to ensure that private parties of employers and workers resolved their disputes. Again, the Walsh substitute bill inverted the emphasis of the Wagner labor relations machinery, substituting the resolution of labor disputes for their prevention.

Outraged that he had no opportunity to revise his own creation, Wagner sponsored several amendments that restored the heart of his original bill. Yet, by a vote of 9 to 2, the committee approved Wyzanski's revisions without Wagner's amendments. Only Wagner and the progressive Republican senator

Robert M. LaFollette Jr. voted against the Walsh bill. To Wagner's chagrin, Roosevelt pledged his support for the Walsh bill.[76]

Although members of the Roosevelt administration and the pro-administration Democrats succeeded in railroading the Walsh bill through the Labor and Education Committee, they failed to convince either prominent labor leaders or business leaders to back it. The AFL, which had supported the Trade Disputes bill, offered no public endorsement of the Walsh bill. In private, members of the AFL claimed that the Walsh bill short-changed labor unions.[77] President Green of the AFL said, "We firmly hoped and believed that the Wagner Disputes Act would be *passed* at this session of Congress. Why a bill which was so thoroughly considered and analyzed should be set aside for a new measure, little understood, vague and indefinite as to its scope and meaning, substituted at the closing days of Congress, is difficult to understand."[78] On the other hand, the business community gave the Walsh bill no support, on the grounds that it supplied organized labor with too much protection. Sensing Roosevelt's reluctance to promote unionism categorically, business groups like the national Chamber of Commerce and the National Association of Manufacturers thought they could afford to oppose any legislative package that threatened the existence of company unions.

Before the Walsh Industrial Adjustment bill came up for debate, however, events outside Washington forced Roosevelt to reexamine his position. In particular, a crisis in the steel industry loomed large in the spring of 1934.[79] Thinking it would be too difficult to pass without excessive delay, Roosevelt abandoned the Walsh Industrial Adjustment bill. Instead, he asked Wyzanski to develop another labor board; it went into effect as part of Public Resolution #44. Initially created through emergency legislation to respond to the impending steel strike, this new board operated on the premise that workers had the freedom to associate, but not necessarily the right to engage in collective bargaining.[80] Again, Roosevelt revealed his position on majority rule, although in this case he did so by accepting its absence.

Unsure that Public Resolution #44 would pass Congress, Roosevelt took steps to isolate the main proponents of the Wagner Trade Disputes bill—the bipartisan coalition of urban-liberal Democrats and progressive Republicans. He struck a deal with the regular Republicans in the Senate, giving them the opportunity to amend this public resolution.[81] An ad hoc Republican committee, including some of the most vigorous opponents of unionism, sent back Public Resolution #44 with six amendments.[82] Then, to gain a Democratic consensus in favor of this amended resolution, Roosevelt called a conference with leading Democrats. Labor Secretary Perkins, Wyzanski, Richberg, Walsh,

Wagner, and Senate majority leaders Joseph Robinson and Joseph Byrns met and discussed it.[83] Outnumbered six to one, Wagner reluctantly gave his support to Public Resolution #44.

### Formal Legal Systems, Legal Domination, and the Republican Legacy

During its period of operations, between July 1, 1934, and March 1, 1935, the National Labor Relations Board established by Public Resolution #44 resolved few labor disputes. The board heard a good number of industrial conflicts, but because it lacked the power to enforce judgments, not one set of employers or employees complied with its rulings.[84] Yet the board's failure to resolve these conflicts presented Wagner with the opportunity to introduce new labor legislation. The 1934 congressional elections, which greatly strengthened the liberal Democrats, also contributed to Wagner's decision.

### Dodging Plurality Rule

When they brought forth the National Labor Relations bill, Wagner and his legislative assistants did not try to reintroduce the Trade Disputes bill. They had learned some hard lessons from the failure of this earlier bill. After seeing how the Democratic administration doggedly promoted plurality representation and minority rule, they recognized that prohibiting company unions gave workers no guarantee that they had the right to select their own collective bargaining agents. If labor legislation gave employees the freedom to associate without defining the size of the bargaining unit, Wagner and his legislative assistants now realized, employers could undermine the collective bargaining process simply by encouraging the formation of more than one labor organization. As Henry I. Harriman, the president of the Chamber of Commerce, conveyed to Richberg, the business community made the following resolution: "Rights for minority groups and individuals in collective bargaining: 1822 for, 67 against."[85]

The authors of the Wagner Act also understood that the passage of such labor legislation was not the last hurdle. The Republican Supreme Court, which had emasculated labor legislation before, could render the Wagner Act ineffective. Indeed, after the passage of Public Resolution #44, Keyserling wrote a long memorandum addressing the "knotty legal points [that] must necessarily be avoided."[86]

Faced with both of these problems, Wagner and Keyserling based their legislation on the Republican ideological foundation for labor law. They thought that this foundation, which gave an administrative agency determinative powers, would best be able to eliminate company unionism and facilitate collective bargaining. Thus, Wagner traded his party's association with voluntarism, which had become tainted by plurality rule and minority representation, for the Republicans' conception of statism and made majority rule the centerpiece of the National Labor Relations bill. He modeled this legislation on a statist ideology for another reason as well. Like the Republicans and the coalition of progressive Republicans and Democrats who had engineered the Transportation Act, the Railway Labor Act, and the Norris-LaGuardia Anti-Injunction Act, Wagner thought the worker representation scheme would withstand judicial scrutiny.

## Wagner and the Battle against Class Legislation

Since the turn of the century, the Supreme Court had cast a shadow over progressive reform. Legislation that served one class would be interpreted by the Court as class legislation and therefore struck down as unconstitutional or rendered ineffective. For this reason, Wagner and Keyserling thought it foolhardy to stipulate that organized labor represented the workers' only outlet for collective bargaining. They did not advocate awarding unions any special privileges or permanent duties that made their labor legislation vulnerable to the claim that it protected one class at the expense of all others. As Wagner explained during the battle over the Trade Disputes bill, "The worker is left absolutely free to determine whether he will bargain individually or collectively, whether he will join a union or remain outside of one."[87] In fact, since the failure of the Howell-Barkley Railroad Labor Board bill (which had protected sixteen railroad unions), shortly before the passage of the 1926 Railway Labor Act, no member of Congress had seriously reopened the debate about unions becoming workers' exclusive bargaining agents. The legislative authors of the Wagner Act did not entertain the idea of promoting or protecting free labor-management relations: unions could be protected only indirectly as the emphasis in labor-management relations was transferred from the players to the collective bargaining process. In deciding to design the National Labor Relations bill after the Republican ideal that the American state must supervise and regulate industrial relations, they were essentially following the "path of least resistance."

Wagner, moreover, had had firsthand experience in the 1920s trying to maneuver labor law so that it could not be considered class legislation. As the labor historian Christopher Tomlins correctly points out, Wagner derived the idea that a union could serve the public as a collective bargaining unit from his work as a progressive when he sat on the state supreme court in New York.[88] In the 1923 *Schlesinger v. Quinto* decision, which upheld an injunction against an employer who breached a collective trade agreement negotiated by a labor union, Wagner had written that unions were agents for their principals—union members. Working within the narrow margins of the common law about labor-management relations, Wagner upheld the injunction not because he saw the union possessing the legal personality necessary to negotiate such a binding trade agreement but because he recognized the union's temporary legal relationship with its members. Forty thousand workers had authorized the union to enter into the agreement. Hence, Wagner did not challenge whether the category of class legislation could be applied to organized labor. Rather, he circumvented it by recognizing the public role the union, or any other vehicle for worker representation, played in the collective bargaining process.

Wagner cannot be credited, however, with developing this interpretation of unionization.[89] The idea that unions had no rights independent of those of their members culminated in the 1920s. The state and federal courts repeatedly ruled that unions, lacking a legal personality, could not negotiate binding trade agreements for their members.[90] Like Wagner, other progressive state and federal court judges upheld collective trade agreements by using the theory of agency to demonstrate union accountability. Some progressive judges had relied on custom and usage as well as third-party beneficiary theory for the same reason. Agency theory, or the principles of agency, received its greatest recognition when the Republican-dominated Supreme Court upheld its application in labor law.

As demonstrated in chapter 3, a unanimous Supreme Court had used the principal/agent distinction to trace union liability during a labor dispute in the *Coronado* decisions.[91] In concluding that the United Mine Workers were at fault, the Taft Court ruled that the existence of a legal relationship had to be proved. Taft wrote that

> a corporation is responsible for the wrongs committed by its agents in the course of this business and this principle is enforced against the contention that torts are *ultra vires* of the corporation. But it must be shown that it is in the business of the corporation. Surely no stricter rule can be enforced against an unincorporated organization like this. Here it is not a question of contract or of holding out an appearance of authority on which some third person acts. It is a mere question of actual agency which the constitutions of the two bodies settled conclusively.[92]

Observers at the time noted that a general theory of agency was applied to trace the United Mine Workers' accountability.[93] In a long legal memorandum written in preparation for the Wagner Act, Keyserling reported that the Court had found the "international union was held not to be implicated, so that only the individual members and the central funds of districts No. 21 could be reached by judgement."[94]

The Supreme Court also followed the logic underlying agency theory when it upheld the constitutionality of the Mediation Board in *Texas & New Orleans Railroad Company v. Brotherhood of Railway & Steamship Clerks.*[95] The unanimous Court, now led by Charles Evans Hughes, ruled that the worker representation scheme did not interfere with the railroad executives' due process or with their freedom to contract, because the scheme had not specified that organized labor represented the railroad employees. Hughes maintained, "The Railway Labor Act of 1926 does not interfere with the normal exercise of the right of the carrier to select its employees or to discharge them. The statute is not aimed at this right of the employers but at the interference with the right of employees to have representatives of their own choosing."[96] In no part of the *Texas* decision did Hughes indicate that unions had a new legal identity.[97] Rather, they derived their temporary authority to represent the railroad employees from the Railroad Labor Board. By extending this temporary authority, which could in effect be issued permanently, the rules and regulations that bound normal contract theory were circumvented as the board made collective trade agreements enforceable.

The Court's influence extended beyond these rulings. Under the leadership of Chief Justice Taft, the Court had helped shape this Republican-created labor legislation. Between 1920 and 1926, progressive Republicans and Democrats alike contributed to the development of the scheme for worker representation. In the late 1920s and early 1930s, both factions discovered the utility of this worker representation scheme, realizing that it could help organized labor *and* withstand scrutiny of the Republican Supreme Court.

### The Republicans' Legacy— the National Labor Relations Act of 1935

By 1935, the legal authority of agency theory reached across political eras, including the National Labor Relations bill, commonly known as the Wagner Act. To recognize a policy continuum in labor legislation between the 1920s and the 1930s is not to say that the Republican Party supported the Wagner Act or that Wagner himself wanted to hinder unionization. All but the progressive Republicans opposed the Wagner Act, and Wagner was long a champion of organized labor. What made the labor policymaking process a continuum were the legal developments that emerged between the late 1890s and 1935. Common-law precedents and Supreme Court rulings about class legislation and agency theory defined labor legislation in the 1920s and 1930s. The momentum behind the choice made by Wagner and his legislative assistants was not just the relative autonomy of the state but also that of the law.

Wagner's first attempt to pass a permanent labor policy, the Trade Disputes bill, had included the Republican scheme for worker representation, which, in effect, extended contract law to collective bargaining agreements.[98] This bill, however, concentrated on protecting the players involved in collective bargaining rather than regulating their access to the entire process. The Trade Disputes bill banned company-dominated unions and used mediation and arbitration to resolve labor disputes on a case-by-case basis. By 1935, Wagner and his legislative assistants realized that labor-management relations could be made effective if the National Labor Relations bill adopted a more comprehensive role in the process. While Wagner's second bill, like his first bill, still listed five prohibitions designed with antiunion employers in mind, his new legislation built a strong administrative agency, providing it with independent, discretionary powers. The NLRB would control the most important aspect in labor-management relations: it would determine who had access to the bargaining table. In this way, Wagner and his legislative assistants thought, they could facilitate collective bargaining.

Wagner, Keyserling, Philip Levy, and the other legislative assistants who helped formulate the Wagner Act put great enforcement powers in the hands of this administrative agency in the hope that antiunion businesses and industries would no longer have the capacity to obstruct the collective bargaining process.[99] As shown earlier, the primary problem associated with section 7(a) was the emergence of company unions because the NRA recognized plurality rule. Between 1933 and 1935, many businesses and industries formed company unions as a foil. With the intent of obstructing meaningful negotiations with bona fide unions, they insisted that collective bargaining negotiations include these company unions.

Wagner could have extended the logic underlying the Trade Disputes bill—drafting an ironclad definition of what constituted a company-dominated union and then prohibiting it. But, over time, antiunion businesses and industries would have found the legislative loophole giving them the opportunity to circumvent this prohibition. When Wagner, Keyserling, and others began drafting the second Wagner bill, they defended themselves against the idea that the NLRB include a "prohibition against coercion of employees by employers or by unions." As Keyserling explained, this type of prohibition on employees in the organization of their own side would "be a joker. It would enable many courts that have shown themselves unfavorable to the legitimate activities of labor to defeat the very objectives of this bill."[100]

Hence, Wagner and his legislative assistants instead provided the NLRB with its own discretionary powers.[101] To do so, they made section 9—the principle of majority rule and of the NLRB implementing it—the heart of American labor relations policy.[102] The NLRB would regulate labor-management relations by offering authorized negotiating agents access to the collective bargaining process: it would determine who could negotiate these agreements. The board was not to shape the content of these agreements. Nor did it umpire the negotiating agents involved in the collective bargaining process, which mediation and conciliation boards had done. Rather, the NLRB drafted a legal formula for determining these agents and controlling the size of their bargaining units. "The bill leaves the kind of voting unit to the discretion of the Board," wrote a Labor Department official.[103] "Section 9(a) is from Section 10(a) of last year's Bill," another Labor Department official explained in a memorandum comparing the 1934 Walsh bill with the new Wagner bill. "In last year's Bill, however, the Board was given discretion as to whether or not to apply majority rule; but in this year's Bill majority rule is made mandatory, not permissive."[104]

Before an agent could represent workers at the collective bargaining table, the NLRB was to establish a clear pattern of agency. Like the Railway Labor Act, the National Labor Relations Act relied on the principles of agency: union accountability stemmed from the members of a union explicitly extending authorization to it with the majority rule provision. This provision, however, only offered unions or any other collective bargaining agent the temporary authority to negotiate for a union's members.[105] Knowing that the Supreme Court opposed class legislation, Wagner and his legislative assistants were careful that the NLRB did not create and protect a new "class" of such agents.

Wagner and his legislative assistants also remade the tripartite board into a public board that reflected the public interest, and not merely a compromise of public and private interests.[106] With the NLRB given authority to investigate and adjudicate labor disputes, including the power to determine who the workers had elected to represent them, Wagner's group decided that all sides of the labor dispute must be present during the election hearings. Employers could provide evidence at these hearings. This meant that the hearings were to be adversarial in format, with employers, unions, and workers arguing their cases before the NLRB. Unlike the board established by the Trade Disputes bill, the NLRB could not mediate or arbitrate a labor dispute; it had to represent the public interest.

Because the public as well as the private interest was now invested in collective bargaining, Wagner and his legislative assistants obliged employers to participate in such bargaining. Here they followed the legal reasoning provided by the Supreme Court in *Texas & New Orleans Railroad Company v. Brother-*

*hood of Railway & Steamship Clerks*.[107] In 1930, Chief Justice Charles Evans
Hughes, with a unanimous Court behind him, upheld the constitutionality of
the Mediation Board. While this board did not have quasi-judicial powers, the
Court declared that it had been constructed to facilitate collective bargaining
and that this type of bargaining, as long as it included a scheme for worker representation, posed no threat to either the employers' or the workers' freedom to
contract. Indeed, the Court upheld an injunction against employers who tried
to obstruct the collective bargaining process.

Likewise, Wagner and his legislative assistants stipulated that as long as the
NLRB did not single out organized labor, a duty could be imposed on employers to bargain in good faith with their workers' representatives. To protect the
freedom to contract, however, the NLRB had to stop short of determining what
would be contained within these contracts. Labor legislation had to protect the
process or procedures involved with collective bargaining without specifically
helping organized labor, the historically recognized player in this process. They
developed what a labor historian describes as a strong professional agency that
had determinative powers.[108]

The creation of this type of agency should be regarded, however, less as a
legislative departure and more as the culmination of the slow evolution of labor law from the late 1890s until 1935. Wagner did not change his position from
the mediation to the prevention of labor disputes.[109] All along, Wagner wanted
to prevent labor disputes and encourage collective bargaining. But he also understood the limits of American liberalism. The state, in either the Republican-
dominated 1920s or the Democratic-led 1930s, would not change its substantive position about organized labor. In other words, organized labor stood little
chance of being perceived as having mutually inclusive interests, like the business corporations did, with the rest of American society. Collective bargaining
was established because the individual worker, not the union, should have the
right to participate in this type of bargaining. The NLRB was to guard this individual's right without taking a position about organized labor itself. As Keyserling stated, "The object of the bill is to give employees the same type of
freedom of self-organization that employers already have. Just as employers
are now absolutely free from coercion by employees in the organization of trade
associations, so should employees be protected from coercion by employers
in the organization of labor associations."[110] Wagner therefore addressed the
problem—how best to provide the individual with this right and facilitate collective bargaining—by building a strong quasi-judicial agency.

Wagner and his legislative assistants' statist approach to labor-management
relations constituted what Max Weber would have categorized as a formal legal system. It began as a minor trend or common-law conception about apply-

ing the principles of agency in labor law to ensure that organized labor had the authority to represent workers during a collective bargaining process; it was transformed first into a worker representation scheme under the Railroad Labor Board and finally into the majority rule provision established by the NLRB. These boards developed rules that protected the workers' procedural right to representation. Whether these workers chose a friend of management or a union leader antagonistic to management could not be questioned. No substantive or ethical value embracing or rejecting unionization would be expressed. But it became the American state's prerogative to regulate the collective bargaining process.

First in his capacity as a progressive justice and then as an experienced legislative author, Wagner had learned of the dangers associated with a labor policy based on voluntarism—providing workers with the freedom to associate—but little protection to ensure that employers did not obstruct or manipulate this freedom to their advantage with policies such as minority rule and plurality representation. Similarly, they saw the advantages of relying on the judicial doctrine underscoring agency law or the formal worker representation scheme developed by the Republicans in the 1920s. Restricted by the Republican Supreme Court's anticlass legislation position, Wagner and his legislative assistants created an independent, quasi-judicial agency that had the power to investigate and judge labor disputes, create procedures for worker representation elections, and determine who won these elections as the only effective means of enforcing the workers' right to representation and facilitating the collective bargaining process. While the AFL balked at providing the NLRB with such great powers, Wagner and his legislative assistants thought that the success of a labor-management relations policy depended on them.

### Conclusion

The significance of Wagner's departure from the Democrats' policy toward organized labor was underscored once again when he introduced the National Labor Relations Act before Congress. At every turn, Roosevelt's administration revealed its deep ambivalence about organized labor by not supporting the second bill.[111] First, Roosevelt suggested that such a policy was unnecessary. Despite that board's dismal record in resolving labor disputes, the president proposed that Congress extend the life of the NLRB established by Public Resolution #44. Second, when Wagner's bill arrived on the Senate floor, a number of conservative Democrats offered amendments that undermined the bill's intent.[112] Third, after realizing that Wagner had secured enough legislative support for his National Labor Relations bill that it could pass despite a veto, Roosevelt decided to appeal personally to the senator to change some of its main provisions. The president called Wagner, Perkins, Richberg, Assistant Attorney General Harold M. Stephens, and union leaders Green and Sidney Hillman to a White House meeting for this purpose.[113] During this meeting, Roosevelt asked Wagner to work on a compromise bill with Stephens and Richberg.[114]

Three days after this meeting Stephens drafted a memorandum recommending, among other provisos, that the NLRB not be given the discretionary power to determine bargaining units. Stephens wrote: "Mr. Richberg has suggested that certain questions of policy, with the probability of widespread administrative enforcement complications, may arise from this section [9b]. Among these are the following: *First, employees have heretofore selected their own unit for collective bargaining through self-organization; perhaps they should continue to exercise this choice. Secondly, an unsympathetic Board could use this power to discriminate against employee organizations.*"[115] Meanwhile, Perkins opposed the construction of the NLRB as an independent regulatory agency. In a memorandum from the Labor Department, an official wrote that the "orderly administration of government requires the grouping of agencies under cabinet heads responsible to the President. Loosely knit independent units cause public confusion and make coordinated policy impossible."[116]

Then, before Wagner could reject Stephens's and Richberg's suggestions, as he planned to do, the Supreme Court overruled the constitutionality of the NIRA in the *Schechter Poultry Corp. v. United States* decision, causing Roosevelt to change his mind about the unamended Wagner bill.[117] Roosevelt stopped the negotiations between Stephens, Richberg, and Wagner and suggested that Congress pass the bill posthaste. The Roosevelt administration suddenly saw Wagner's bill as an excellent test case for challenging the Supreme Court's authority to undermine the New Deal with the *Schechter* opinion, especially since nothing else suitable was in the legislative pipeline.[118] At long last, Roosevelt stopped obstructing Wagner.[119] Less than one month after the Supreme Court rendered the *Schechter* decision, the House and Senate passed the National Labor Relations bill with little opposition.[120]

# Responsible Unionism and the Republicans' Venture across Policy Time Frames

No greater disservice has been rendered to political science than the statement that the liberal state was a "weak" state.

—Franz L. Neumann, *Democratic and Authoritarian States*, 1957

Political scientists often explain American political development in terms of dialectics and teleological ethics. The course of American history supposedly consists of a series of reform periods. A dialectical transformation occurs as a crisis sparks the construction of a new policy regime; then this regime collapses as a subsequent crisis makes the erection of yet another policy regime essential; and so forth. At the same time, teleological ethics are manifest in theories of political development. American liberalism became more and more tolerant and inclusive as it unfolded over two hundred years of history: the revolutionary era established the first representational democracy in the modern world; the Jacksonian era extended mass suffrage to the common man; the Civil War freed African American slaves; the progressive era gave women suffrage; the New Deal period recognized labor's right to organize and bargain collectively; and finally, the civil rights era enforced liberties for all.[1]

This book has traced the development of American labor policy in order to test the limits of the dialectical and teleological perceptions of periodization in United States history. First, while labor policy was an important, state-expansive policy, it was founded in a different political environment than most state-building policies. The origins of this policy cannot be located in one reform era. The formation of labor policy crossed two policy regimes—the era of normalcy and the New Deal era of reform. Policymakers after World War I developed it, in part, as a repudiation of the labor-management relations experiments used in the progressive era, another policy regime. American labor policy was not the product of one policy era or another, let alone of a specific "crisis."

The origins of this policy emerged slowly between the 1880s and 1935. The ideas underlying it were not bound by the intent of one actor or constrained to one period. Rather, they were part of a formal legal system that was governed by institutional rules and regulations that the American political culture had helped perpetuate.[2] American labor policy reflects the reciprocity of relations between the state and political culture.[3] The primary expression of this reciprocity was exhibited when the state sustained the value of individualism with agency law and the scheme for worker representation. State apparatuses, the U.S. Mediation Board and the NLRB, resembled the technical, rational machines that Max Weber described in his definition of legal formalism, which could simultaneously constrain *and* liberate organized labor.[4]

Second, the creation and implementation of American labor policy was not teleological. This policy proved to be exclusionary rather than inclusionary. Whereas other state-building policies, like mass suffrage during the Jacksonian period, were driven by the reformers' impulse to make the democratic process more open and inclusive, labor policy made this process more restrictive and exclusive. American labor policy weakened the links between reform, liberal democracy, and state expansion. It showed the liberal democratic state's intolerance toward different groups and associations that supposedly threatened the basic tenets of American liberalism.

### From the Era of Normalcy to the New Deal: Crossing Policy Time Frames

In the late 1880s, the AFL first debated the issue of governmental intervention in labor relations. Samuel Gompers believed that registering labor organizations as singular entities, with legal personalities like those assumed by business corporations, would promote collective bargaining. The primary benefit of such a move, he thought, would be to make collective trade agreements legally binding. But the combination of the federal and state judiciaries' animosity toward organized labor and the knowledge that these charters made unions themselves accountable for their members' actions under these trade agreements caused Gompers to reverse his position. By the late 1890s, he feared that employers would win suits against unions for any damages inflicted by their members. These damage suits, he worried, might contribute to organized labor's early demise. Hence, the AFL refused to incorporate its unions, closing off the first path to federal governmental intervention in labor-management relations.

From 1900 onward, no common-law doctrines or statutory laws altered organized labor's legal standing. Yet in 1906 and 1907, some progressive state and federal courts tentatively resolved some problems associated with organized labor's ambiguous legal position. They used three doctrines, each embodying the principles of agency, to enforce collective trade agreements. Rather than offering labor a fictitious personality, these principles ignored this issue and constructed a legal mechanism that assessed accountability without assigning agency. The Supreme Court also relied on agency law in the 1922 *Coronado* decision. The conservative and progressive justices applied the doctrine of "actual" agency to determine the extent of the United Mine Workers' liability.[5] The Taft Court legitimized the progressive state and federal courts' use of agency by relying on it as a general means of holding unincorporated unions accountable for their activities.

After World War I, the Republican Congress faced the choice of extending the wartime policy, returning to the prewar absence of a cohesive policy, or constructing a new policy. It chose the last, creating a labor policy based on the principles of agency. In order to prevent the national railroad unions from becoming the workers' exclusive collective bargaining agents (particularly the shopcrafts workers, who organized primarily during the time of governmental control in World War I), the Republicans developed legislation based on a fluid conception of worker representation: either a labor union or a company-sponsored union could represent the employees at the negotiating table. The old guard and progressive Republican factions in Congress recast agency law into statute in the labor relations provisions of the Transportation Act of 1920. Both Republican factions drafted this particular labor relations machinery, in part, to repudiate Woodrow Wilson's wartime labor policy. Wilson had given unions the opportunity to participate in the decision-making process surrounding the wartime labor relations machinery during the Great War, by making them exclusive agents for negotiating collective bargaining agreements. When the war ended, the old guard Republicans sought new labor relations machinery that would hold national railroad unions strictly accountable to the public. Progressive Republicans wanted a labor policy that offered workers "the right to select representatives of their own choosing" and that ran little risk of being rejected by the Supreme Court as class legislation.

When the Railroad Labor Board collapsed by 1924, the Republicans, in 1926, rather than abandon railroad labor legislation altogether, constructed a new board, the U.S. Mediation Board. While the machinery changed from nonenforceable arbitration to mediation, this second board had a better scheme for worker representation. This scheme imposed a duty on employers to negotiate collective trade agreements with worker representatives. But when they found that it proved more beneficial to the national unions than to the railroad companies, the old guard Republicans could no longer support this type of governmental intervention. They retreated to their pre-1920 position that the laissez-faire economy, and not federal labor relations machinery, best governed labor-management relations. Meanwhile, the success of the worker representation scheme encouraged the progressive Republicans, particularly after the Taft Court and Hughes Court endorsed it in *Pennsylvania Railroad Company v. United States Railroad Labor Board* and the *Texas & New Orleans v. Brotherhood & Steamship Clerks*, respectively.[6] The progressives also included the rationale behind this scheme in the Norris-LaGuardia Anti-Injunction Act of 1932. Instead of making the union immune to the labor injunction, the progressive Republicans circumscribed the activity that organized labor could be held accountable for during a labor dispute.

In making the majority rule provision the centerpiece of the National Labor Relations Act, Senator Robert F. Wagner also built labor legislation on the state-supervised scheme for worker representation. What began as the old guard Republicans' attempt to discipline organized labor by making unions accountable for their actions under the labor relations provisions in the 1920 Transportation Act was turned by Wagner (with the full support of progressive Democrats and Republicans) into the primary means of recognizing unions as collective bargaining agents. The majority rule principle operationalized the Republican idea of worker representation. The NLRB used majority rule as a means of determining whether a union or any other organization could be certified or decertified as a worker representative and therefore be given the authority to negotiate collective bargaining contracts.

The Wagner Act created a competitive atmosphere in which the union, the employer, and any other collective bargaining organization were never assured of their position vis-à-vis the individual worker or within society in general. Unions, for instance, fought to become the workers' representative, while employers battled to overturn the possibility of negotiating with such a representative. The only permanent player was the NLRB—always on hand to determine which group or association had won the authority to represent the workers. While the NLRB might repeatedly identify a national labor union as the workers' chosen representative in a given dispute, it never acknowledged it as a permanent bargaining representative. Having to be certified by their membership meant that these representatives could also be decertified.

On the one hand, the NLRB supplied unions with much-needed protection from the unfair labor practices of employers who had heretofore obstructed unionization. The results of this protection became visible after the NLRB had provided only three years of service. By 1938, the union membership rolls had doubled.[7] By 1947, they had increased seven times, with 14 million workers organized in unions.[8] On the other hand, the logic behind the Wagner Act could not safeguard organized labor from antiunion lawyers. By offering organized labor only the temporary privilege of representing workers at the collective bargaining table, American labor policy sent one clear message: the union, like the employer, threatened the individual worker's right to choose a representative and therefore should be watched and treated with suspicion by state-operated regulatory agencies.

### A Help and a Hindrance

The state supervision imposed by the Wagner Act, although intended to prevent employers from using company unions to fulfill their obligation to bargain with their workers, could be used against organized labor. This is what happened with the passage of the Taft-Hartley Labor-Management Relations Act in 1947. The Republicans leading the Eightieth Congress used the same rhetoric Wagner had employed about safeguarding the public interest and individual workers. Wagner himself captured the tenor of the legislative debate in 1947 when he explained, "This erroneously conceived mutuality argument is that since employers are to be prohibited from interfering with the organization of workers, employees and labor organizations should also be prohibited from engaging in such activities . . . [and] this would defeat the very objects of the bill." [9] Whereas Wagner relied on this reciprocal interpretation to prevent his labor legislation from being struck down by a conservative Supreme Court, the Republicans and southern Democrats drafting the Taft-Hartley Act relied on it to undermine organized labor's strength.

The shift in focus from the agent to the collective bargaining process, although necessary to pass the railroad labor legislation, the anti-injunction legislation, and the Wagner Act, made organized labor vulnerable to state control. State supervision could take the form of the NLRB describing external regulations about the size of the unit seeking certification to represent workers, as well as prescribing internal rules of conduct for this unit after its certification. In particular, the Taft-Hartley Act made organized labor accountable for unfair labor practices. [10] As several labor lawyers described, "The [Taft-Hartley Act] seems to be designed for the *fluidity of attack and counterattack* rather than for the evolution of stable relationships. It invites a *constant shifting in the bargaining agent, in its composition (the unit), in its personnel (the union), in its implementation (the union-shop contract) and in its very life (decertification).*" [11] Equating unions with employers, this act provided that the NLRB would protect individual workers from unfair labor practices instigated by organized labor. Unions could not be trusted. Only the state-controlled regulatory agencies truly safeguarded individual workers' rights. The NLRB acted as a seemingly neutral umpire for the state although it had the "very life" of the union in its hands.

The Taft-Hartley Act, however, did not strangle organized labor. After all, the numbers of workers joining unions peaked almost a decade after its passage. Just as the policymakers behind the passage of the Wagner Act were constrained by formal legal constructs, so too were the policymakers responsible for the enactment of the Taft-Hartley Act.[12] American labor policy was a formal legal system governed largely by procedural rules and regulations, which could alternatively be a help or a hindrance to organized labor and employers. The NLRB, in other words, was never consistently pro-union or pro-employer.

Yet this is not to say that American labor policy was value-free. Rather, it was based on a value that was so universally supported that it became an assumption. Employers and workers alike could not imagine that the public interest might be tantamount to the private interests of organized labor. They thought that unions primarily promoted the self-interests of their members. Organized labor indeed differed from most other movements in that it placed almost no emphasis on the broad, public interest.

American labor policy made it progressively more difficult for organized labor to establish worker solidarity. A diminished sense of worker solidarity in the United States, in turn, contributed to a duality of working-class consciousness. That is, because the statist labor-management relations agencies took credit for safeguarding the public interest, the nonunion individual employee, as well as the public, identified with the dominant value propagated by these agencies: that organized labor free of regulation could not be trusted. By contrast, union employees, who directly benefited from unionization, accepted what became a deviant value, that unionization was in the public interest. Or these union employees could also accept the dominant value that they should not have much faith in the union leadership.

Hence, by casting doubt on the union's integrity as an organization acting in the public interest, or at least the working-class interest, American labor policy consciously encouraged the creation of a rift between the individual worker and the union. Workers joined unions to further their self-interest. Labor leaders therefore fulfilled these interests and neglected the public interest as this value embedded within American labor policy produced a self-fulfilling prophecy. The policy that led to its expression, moreover, became self-sustaining. Future Democrats and Republicans might subtly tinker with it, but they would not change the competitive spirit that the labor-management relations machinery instilled between organized labor and employers.

The final irony about American labor policy was that the AFL, which had not been involved in developing the fundamental principles behind this policy, embraced the very same conception of individualism that would stunt its growth. In practicing business unionism before the New Deal, the AFL had placed less emphasis on public interest politics than most other organizations in the labor movement. Voluntarism was based on the workers' collective pursuit of self-interest. What distinguished voluntarism from responsible unionism was state involvement in the labor-management relations process. The freedom of association that the AFL wanted was part of American labor policy. Yet Gompers had only sought freedom of association to further the self-interest of the AFL's membership. The American state therefore constrained not only those at the margins of the labor movement but also the AFL and the brotherhoods, who came closest to sharing its values.

This book has laid bare the limits of American liberalism. It has not recounted the oft told story about the betrayal of this type of liberalism. The origins of American labor policy cannot be explained by either the Republicans' or the New Deal Democrats' lack of foresight or duplicity. These policymakers carefully and consciously denied a specific group—the trade union—liberty and equality of opportunity as a voluntary association. The labor-management relations machinery constructed would alternatively bolster and limit organized labor's participation in politics and the economy. Although this machinery would not disempower organized labor, it did ensure that the labor movement remained weak and the state maintained tight control over the labor-management relations process.

# NOTES

## Preface

1. Eisenach, "Reconstituting the Study of American Political Thought," 170.

## Chapter 1

1. See Piven, "Decline of Labor Parties," 1–19; Shafer, *Is America Different?*; Hattam, *Labor Visions and State Power*; and Forbath, *Law and the Shaping of the American Labor Movement*. See also Orren, *Belated Feudalism*, for a provocative refutation of "American exceptionalism."

2. See Sombart, *Why Is There No Socialism?*, and Perlman, *History of Trade Unionism*, for the classic interpretation of American exceptionalism. For the modern debate, see Foner, "Why Is There No Socialism?"; Lipset, "Radicalism or Reformism"; and Voss, *Making of American Exceptionalism*, 231–49. For a good overview of this debate, see also Mink, *Old Labor and the New Immigrants*, 25–44.

3. This term is generally associated with the quest of the conservative coalition of Republicans and southern Democrats for the passage of the Taft-Hartley Labor-Management Relations Act of 1947, which amended and substantively changed the National Labor Relations Act of 1935 by placing unions and employers on equal footing before the National Labor Relations Board. See Tomlins, *State and the Unions*, 282–316, and Lichtenstein, *Labor's War at Home*.

4. See Orren, *Belated Feudalism*, 19–28. Although the idea of "belated feudalism" recently advanced by Orren embraces the liberal state, thereby going beyond the absences persistent in "American exceptionalism," it does not account for the role of liberal ideology. In her discovery that the remnants of feudalism helped shape the development of the liberal state, Orren ignores how liberalism constrained this state when it established the modern framework for labor-management relations. As a result, she focuses on the legislative and voluntary aspects of labor-management relations and neglects the restrictive and disciplinary aspects of these relations that have limited organized labor and dampened worker solidarity.

5. Locke, *Political Writings*, 272.

6. See Furner, "Knowing Capitalism," 244, and Gerber, "Corporatism in Comparative Perspective," 94, for good definitions of functional representation. Both see functional representation as a key component of corporate liberalism. According to

Furner, the groups that participate in modern society as an "organic structure of functional, specialized, interdependent social segments . . . each [have] legitimate needs and each [are] entitled to representation." Or as Gerber describes, functional representation is the "legitimization of the power and authority of private business corporations and the use these corporate bodies have made of state power to maintain their control over the political economy."

7. Ironically, this policy implemented by the National Recovery Administration (NRA) made business a full partner but only gave organized labor a small role in the collective decision making of the corporate liberal state. See Fine, *Automobile under the Blue Eagle*.

8. The Supreme Court's interpretation of section 10 of the 1898 Arbitration Act brought home this lesson. Although Stromquist writes that for "the first time important legal protections . . . were provided to organized labor, and it was supported by the brotherhoods," the Court rendered some of these unconstitutional as class legislation. See Stromquist, *Generation of Boomers*, 262, and *Adair v. United States*, 208 U.S. 161 (1908). See also Zakson, "Railway Labor Legislation," 327–32, and Cushman, "Doctrinal Synergies and Liberal Dilemmas," 264–65.

9. The National War Labor Board (NWLB) introduced the concept of worker representation. The early representation elections emphasized Wilson's ambiguous commitment to voluntarism, not responsible unionism, since they never disturbed "private interests." Unlike the worker representation scheme that evolved under the Transportation Act and the Railway Labor Act, the NWLB respected the autonomy of employers and labor organizations. It maintained the status quo: if employers established an open shop or a union shop, the American state, manifested by the NWLB, had a weak supervisory role in the collective bargaining process. Most important, the NWLB had little effect on organized labor's freedom of association because the labor-management relations grievance structure—shop committees—existed independent of these employers and national unions. See Conner, *National War Labor Board*, 5, 3–17, and Troy, "Labor Representation on American Railways," 297. Dubofsky correctly points out that Wilson's wartime policy was confused. It had elements of both corporatism and voluntarism. Dubofsky, "Abortive Reform."

10. See Forbath, "Courts, Constitutions, and Labor Politics"; Hattam, *Labor Visions and State Power*, 30–75; and Bernstein, *The Lean Years*, 190–242.

11. Weber's conception of ideology combined with the consensual view of American history provides the theoretical construction for this book. First, Weber's notion of ideology explains how responsible unionism, not the AFL's ideology of voluntarism, influenced the creation of federal labor policy. Although this type of unionism was not explicitly articulated until 1947 with the passage of the Taft-Hartley Act, it still reflected a cohesive set of values and beliefs that had their own history. The development of federal labor policy exhibits what Weber described as "a dualism of the autonomously created law between groups, and the norms determinative of disputes among groups members." Quoted from Feldman, "Interpretation of Max Weber's Theory of Laws," 211–12. In other words, Weber recognizes a dualism or dichotomy that captures "the distinction between, on the one hand, subjectively created laws that regulated activities between social groups or communities, and, on the other hand, preexisting or natural norms, rooted in tradition from the 'time out of mind,' that

regulated members within a group." "Because of Weber's sensitivity to the tensions within Western society," Feldman explains, "he can recognize and sensibly argue that capitalism simultaneously has distinct advantages and dehumanizing disadvantages." Second, the ideology of responsible unionism that captured the tension within liberalism and capitalism also embodies a consensual view of American history. It explores how conservative and progressive thought alike with a conception of justice based on procedural due process, which in turn is premised on a theory of individualism that exhibits an innate fear of group power, collectivism, and mass movements. As Thomas Bender describes, consensus history has an "emphasis on continuity, the reenactment of 'classic' patterns." Unlike traditional consensus history, my argument in no way attempts to undermine the plethora of histories established by the new social history. Instead, it makes a case for the coexistence of the "wholes and the parts" that Bender outlines. See Bender, "Wholes and Parts."

12. Feldman, "Interpretation of Max Weber's Theory of Laws," 206. See also Tomlins, *Law, Labor, and Ideology*, 29–34, for a provocative and insightful explanation of Weber's legal sociology and its application to American legal history despite the problems of categorization normally associated with the common law.

13. Weber, *Economy and Society*, 2:811.

14. Ibid.

15. Ibid.

16. See Trubek, "Reconstructing Max Weber's Sociology of Law," and Kronman, *Max Weber*, for two important interpretations of Weber's notion of the autonomy of law.

17. See Dubofsky, *State and Labor in Modern America*, xi–xvii, 207. Dubofsky also examines the role of the state in the formation of federal labor policy. Instead of illustrating the reciprocal relationship between the state and culture, Dubofsky separates the two. His study then depends on the traditional conception of organized labor as he concludes that "the persistence of individualistic patterns of behavior added to the ethnic, racial, and gender divisions that fragmented the working class insured that American workers would hit no home runs socially, economically, or politically." See also Leuchtenburg, "Pertinence of Political History." Not all historians maintain this position, particularly not those writing legal and institutional histories. Political scientists and legal scholars writing on the state and new institutionalism, like Hattam and Forbath, are indebted to Wilentz, *Chantz Democracy*, and Fink, *Workingmen's Democracy*. See Forbath, *Law and the Shaping of the American Labor Movement*, and Hattam, *Labor Visions and State Power*. They have shown that American workers were not all conservative and oblivious to class. This has led Forbath, among others, to question where American workers "end[ed] up supporting unions and political parties that were more conservative than those embraced by their counterparts abroad." Hattam also takes ideology and culture into account in her statist explanation of the origins of business unionism in the United States. My argument also addresses the state's role in the creation of individualism *within* political culture, departing from Dubofsky's notion that the working-class propensity for individualism explains state behavior and, in turn, the development of labor policy.

18. See Feldman, "Interpretation of Max Weber's Theory of Laws," 208, and Cotterrell, "Legality and Political Legitimacy," 69–93.

19. Dubofsky also captures the ambiguity of state intervention. He notes that the

first studies that take the state into account focus on its repressive capacity. See Dubofsky, *State and Labor in Modern America*, xvii. Tomlins, *State and the Unions*, drew on Klare, "Judicial Deradicalization," and Stone, "Post-war Paradigm."

20. Casebeer, "Drafting Wagner's Act"; Casebeer, "Holder of the Pen"; and Barenburg, "Political Economy of the Wagner Act," highlight the statement of legislative intent behind the Wagner Act instead of the operating provisions. Casebeer emphasizes the neo-Keynesian underpinnings in the Wagner Act, whereas Barenburg focuses on the vision of labor-management cooperation behind the act.

21. See Skocpol, *Protecting Soldiers and Mothers*, 48, for an excellent account of the reciprocal nature of the American state.

22. The first scholarly accounts of the AFL's theory of voluntarism provided an explanation of American exceptionalism. See Perlman, *History of Trade Unionism*. Perlman, a member of John R. Commons's school of labor economics at the University of Wisconsin, suggested that voluntarism was promoted by skilled craftsmen or members of the labor aristocracy. It is a pragmatic philosophy that helped workers achieve their goals by relying on their own voluntary associations and defended the autonomy of the international craft union against the coercive interference of the state. Rogin explored voluntarism as an organizational ideology in "Voluntarism." He contests the idea that voluntarism arose out of labor's unfavorable experience with the state. Beginning in the 1960s, the new labor history reexamined the development of the American working class, challenging the inherent conservatism expressed by voluntarism. See Gutman, *Work, Culture, and Society*; Montgomery, *Citizen Worker*; Montgomery, *Workers' Control in America*; and Fink, *In Search of the Working Class*. In turn, the new labor history provoked new institutionalists to explore why the working class became conservative in the twentieth century. See Hattam, *Labor Visions and State Power*, and Forbath, *Law and the Shaping of the American Labor Movement*.

23. See Horowitz, *Political Ideologies of Organized Labor*.

24. See Gompers, *Seventy Years of Life and Labor*.

25. *A Verbatum [sic] Report of the Discussion on the Political Programme at the Denver Convention of the American Federation of Labor, December 14, 15, 1894* (New York: Freytag Press, 1895), 19–21; Samuel Gompers, "The Strenuous Struggle of Labor," *American Federationist* 9 (1902): 178; and Samuel Gompers, "The American Labor Movement: Its Makeup, Achievements, Aspirations," *American Federationist* (1914): 357–58.

26. Not all historians and political scientists agree about the AFL's participation in progressive reform. See Lubove, *Struggle for Social Security*, and Skocpol, *Protecting Soldiers and Mothers*. For the conventional argument about the AFL's reluctance to participate in progressive reform, see Hattam, *Labor Visions and State Power*, 165.

27. Perlman, *History of Trade Unionism*, 185–86; Zieger, "From Antagonism to Accord," 25–28; and Troy, "Labor Representation on American Railways," 295–300.

28. Perlman, *History of Trade Unionism*, 259.

29. Murray, *Politics of Normalcy*, ix. See Murray for a review of the standard historiography of the 1920s. See also Hicks, *Republican Ascendancy*.

30. See Hicks, *Republican Ascendancy*; Mayer, *Republican Party*; and Schlesinger, *Crisis of the Old Order*.

31. See Burnham, "Party Systems," 298–302; Ashby, *The Spearless Leader*; Nye,

*Midwestern Progressive Politics*; Robertson, *No Third Choice*; and Lowitt, *George W. Norris.*

32. Kutler, "Judicial Philosophy," and Forbath, *Law and the Shaping of the American Labor Movement.*

33. A group of historians and legal historians have challenged this perspective, offering a revisionist interpretation of this history. See Ernst, "Free Labor"; Kens, "Source of a Myth"; Urofsky, "Myth and Reality"; Les Benedict, "Laissez-Faire and Liberty"; and Porter, "That Commerce Shall be Free."

34. See Eisenach, *Lost Promise of Progressivism*; Filene, "Obituary," 20–34; and Link, "What Happened to the Progressive Movement?"

35. See Dubofsky, *Industrialism and the American Worker*, 134–41, and Bernstein, *The Lean Years.*

36. Zieger, *Republicans and Labor*, and Zieger, "From Hostility to Moderation." My argument that the origins of federal labor policy should be attributed to an ideology constructed by the Republicans and progressive legal realists represents a departure from Zieger's argument that the GOP modified its approach to labor-management relations because of external factors such as the labor vote.

37. Glad, "Progressives and the Business Culture," 75–89.

38. See Orren, *Belated Feudalism*, and McDonagh, "Representative Democracy," for counterexamples that emphasize continuous political change in the United States.

39. See Andersen, *Creation of a Democratic Majority*; Sinclair, *Congressional Realignments*, 4–5; and Sinclair, "Party Realignment." See also Brady, "Reevaluation of Realignments"; Clubb, Flanigan and Zingale, *Partisan Realignment.*

40. Burnham, "Party Systems," 298–302.

41. Skowronek, *Building a New American State*, 283–88, and Weinstein, *Corporate Ideal*, 3.

42. See Wiebe, *Businessmen and Reform*, 1–5; Wiebe, *Search for Order*, 286–302; Hays, "The Organizational Society"; Jacoby, *Employing Bureaucracy*, 167–205; Galambos, "Emerging Organizational Synthesis"; and Galambos, "Technology, Political Economy, and Professionalization." See also Berk, "Constituting Corporations and Markets," for a provocative critique of the organizational synthesis school of thought.

43. Chandler, *The Visible Hand*, 484–97; Noble, *America by Design*; McCraw, *Regulation in Perspective*; and Kolko, *Railroads and Regulations.*

44. Sklar, *Corporate Reconstruction*, 3.

45. The introductory essay by Weir, Orloff, and Skocpol in *The Politics of Social Policy in the United States*, 22. See also Krasner, *Defending the National Interest*; Skowronek, *Building a New American State*; Stephan, *State and Society*; Finegold and Skocpol, "State, Party, and Industry"; Skocpol, "Political Response to Capitalist Crisis"; and Skocpol and Finegold, "State Capacity and Economic Intervention."

46. See Klare, "Judicial Deradicalization"; Stone, "Post-war Paradigm"; and Tomlins, *State and the Unions.*

47. Stone, "Post-war Paradigm," 1514–16.

48. See Hawley, *New Deal and the Problem of Monopoly*, and Hawley, "Discovery and Study," 309–320; Hawley, "Herbert Hoover"; Himmelberg, "Business, Antitrust Policy, and the Industrial Board"; and Colin Gordon, *New Deals.*

49. Hawley, *New Deal and the Problem of Monopoly*, 9.

50. See Hawley, "Discovery and Study."

51. Hawley, *New Deal and the Problem of Monopoly*.

52. See Tomlins, *State and the Unions*, and Zieger, "Herbert Hoover."

53. See Tomlins, *State and the Unions*, 102, and Gregory, *Labor and the Law*, 186, 197.

54. Tomlins, *State and the Unions*, 102.

55. Brody, *Workers in Industrial America*, 138–46.

56. The Edward D. White and Melville W. Fuller Courts began designing the judicial solution in the respective *Adair v. United States*, 208 U.S. 161 (1908), and *Coppage v. Kansas*, 236 U.S. 1 (1913), cases.

57. The decisions of the *Duplex v. Deering*, 254 U.S. 443 (1921); *Truax v. Corrigan*, 257 U.S. 312 (1921); *American Steel Foundries v. Tri-City Central Trades Council*, 257 U.S. 184 (1921); *Bedford Co. v. Stone Cutters Association*, 274 U.S. 37 (1927); *United Mine Workers of America v. Coronado Coal Co.*, 259 U.S. 344 (1922); and *Coronado Co. v. United Mine Workers*, 268 U.S. 295 (1925), cases expanded the federal and state equity courts' power to resolve labor disputes by injunction.

58. *Pennsylvania R. Co. v. United States Railroad Labor Board*, 261 U.S. 72 (1922).

59. Louis Stark, "Democracy—and Responsibility—in Unions," *New York Times Magazine*, May 5, 1947.

## Chapter 2

1. "Protest against Injunction Abuse," *American Federationist* 9 (1902): 303–4.

2. Johnson, *National Party Platforms*, vol. 1.

3. See Cook, "Privileges of Labor Unions," 779–800; Pound, "Liberty of Contract," 481–83; Frankfurter and Greene, *The Labor Injunction*; and Sayre, "Labor and the Courts." See Twining, *Karl Llewellyn*, for a history of legal realism that includes these participants. For an excellent article on the different progressive positions on labor law reform, see also Ernst, "Common Laborers?"

4. See Hattam, *Labor Visions and State Power*, 204–8; Forbath, *Law and the Shaping of the American Labor Movement*; Voss, *Making of American Exceptionalism*, 240–45; and Mink, *Old Labor and the New Immigrants*, 24–25, 37–38.

5. Few scholars have examined how the AFL's and the progressives' ideological differences stopped them from forging an effective coalition against the conservative courts. See McCormick, "Progressivism"; Wiebe, *Search for Order*; and Hays, *Response to Industrialism*.

6. See Schlegel, *American Legal Realism*; Kalman, *Legal Realism at Yale*; and Rumble, *American Legal Realism*. Legal realists, as well as the broader category of legal progressives, involved themselves in the study of law and its applications. They disliked formalism, deductions, and abstractions in classical legal orthodoxy. The sociological jurisprudence of Roscoe Pound and Oliver Wendell Holmes as well as the philosophy of pragmatism developed by John Dewey and William James "shaped the climate of progressive juristic opinion which formed the background to the realist movement." Quoted from Rumble, *American Legal Realism*, 5.

7. Horwitz, *Transformation of American Law*, 4–11.

8. This is not to say that other labor movements would have had a greater chance of success in battling the conservative courts with the progressives. For instance, the progressives were no more supportive of the Knights of Labor or the Industrial Workers of the World (IWW), which had ideologies even further afield from the American liberalism than the AFL's ideology of voluntarism.

9. Few historians and political scientists agree on a definition of voluntarism. John R. Commons's Wisconsin school of labor economics offered the first explanation in scholarship. See Commons et al., *History of Labor in the United States*, and Perlman, *History of Trade Unionism*, for the classic explanation that voluntarism was a pragmatic philosophy that helped workers achieve their goals by relying on their own voluntary associations but should not be taken seriously as an ideology. See also Rogin, "Voluntarism," 521–35. Rogin suggests that voluntarism conflicted with some of the ideas underlying the progressive labor economists' own political agenda, namely, legal realism. Beginning in the 1960s, the new labor history directly challenged the Commons school. Labor historians no longer reduced the labor movement to the study of the AFL and the railroad brotherhoods. Influenced greatly by Thompson's book *The Making of the English Working Class*, they studied the organized and unorganized workers and presented a different picture of the American working class that rejected that voluntarism was inherently conservative. See Gutman, *Work, Culture, and Society*; Montgomery, *Citizen Worker*; Montgomery, *Workers' Control in America*; Fink, *In Search of the Working Class*. By the early 1980s, the new labor history provoked a new genre in law and political science—new institutionalism—to explore why the working class became conservative in the twentieth century. See Mink, *Old Labor and the New Immigrants*; Hattam, *Labor Visions and State Power*; and Forbath, *Law and the Shaping of the American Labor Movement*. The new institutionalists use the information mined by the new labor historians to explain the transition from the nineteenth to the twentieth century. Hattam and Forbath, for instance, argue that the AFL developed voluntarism and American exceptionalism as a defensive strategy against the repressive state, manifested primarily by the hostile judiciary using its monopoly of power against organized labor. My argument does not attempt to explain the origins of voluntarism. Rather, informed by Rogin's work on voluntarism, it traces the distinct development of this ideology in comparison to the progressives' jurisprudence and ideas about the reform of labor law. Whether the AFL formulated voluntarism as a defensive strategy becomes less important as the debate over labor law shifted. The progressive ideology of responsible unionism, not voluntarism, becomes the operative ideology in the debate over labor law. The conservative courts, most notably the Supreme Court, depended on voluntarism as a foil to justify their position against labor reform.

10. See Voss, *Making of American Exceptionalism*, and Fink, *Workingmen's Democracy*.

11. John Spargo, "The Passing of Gompers and the Future of Organized Labor," *North American Review* 22 (1925): 411.

12. Samuel Gompers, "Views of Labor Advocates," *American Federationist* 9 (1903): 120.

13. Fink, "Labor, Liberty, and the Law."

14. Commons, "Karl Marx and Samuel Gompers," 284.

15. Gompers, *Seventy Years of Life and Labor*.

16. Ibid.

17. Horowitz, *Political Ideologies of Organized Labor*, 28−29.

18. Samuel Gompers, "Labor's Protest to Congress," *American Federationist* 15 (1908): 261−66.

19. Samuel Gompers, "The Strenuous Struggle of Labor," *American Federationist* 9 (1902), 178.

20. Ibid.

21. According to Rogin, Gompers used voluntarism to challenge classical legal orthodoxy. But he did so with positivistic conceptions of freedom of association that alienated members of the progressive movement. Rogin shows the difference between the AFL's theory of voluntarism and the progressives' notion of deficit under labor law. Rogin, "Voluntarism," 521−35.

22. "Historical Review of Trade-Union Incorporation," *Monthly Labor Review* 40 (1935): 39.

23. Ibid., 40−43.

24. Ibid., 41.

25. See Pollock and Maitland, *History of English Law*, 486−511; Pound, "Liberty of Contract," 456−58.

26. Tomlins, *State and the Unions*, 23. *Black's Law Dictionary* defines incorporation as "the act or process of forming or creating a corporation. The formation of a legal or political body, with the quality of perpetual existences and succession, unless limited by the act of incorporation."

27. Dodd, *American Business Corporations until 1860*. Legislative power of incorporation was first tested by the courts with *Terrett v. Taylor*, 9 Cranch 43 (1815), and *Trustees of Dartmouth College v. Woodward*, 1 N.H. 111 (1817).

28. Pound, "Liberty of Contract," and Dodd, "Dogma and Practice," 986.

29. Until the 1850s, incorporation occurred "on a modest scale." By 1904, three hundred industrial corporations controlled 20 percent of all manufacturing that affected 80 percent of all industries in the United States. In 1929, two hundred barge corporations had 48 percent of corporate assets and 58 percent of net capital, like machinery and buildings. See Trachtenberg, *Incorporation of America*, 4.

30. See Horwitz, *Transformation of American Law*, 71−75, and Hall, *The Magic Mirror*, 97−98.

31. Horwitz, *Transformation of American Law*, 71−75. See also Hager, "Bodies Politic," for an explanation of the dominant theories of corporate personality.

32. *Santa Clara v. Southern Pacific R.*, 118 U.S. 394 (1886).

33. Historians argue over whether or not the Supreme Court decision *Santa Clara v. Southern Pacific R.* produced "natural entity theory" or whether it emerged in social fact a decade later. See Horwitz, *Transformation of American Law*, 71−75.

34. Wiecek, *Liberty under Law*, 115−29; Gillman, *The Constitution Besieged*, 104−14. See also Hager, "Bodies Politic," 629−30. Hager notes that "surprisingly enough, virtually no one [progressive legal jurists] linked this doctrine theoretically with the rise of real entity theory" or natural entity theory.

35. See Wiecek, *Liberty under Law*, 118.

36. See McCormick, *Party Period and Public Policy*, 36−37.

37. Gompers, "Labor's Protest to Congress," 264, and Samuel Gompers, "Industrial Warfare: Its Costs and Its Lessons," *American Federationist* 15 (1908): 31.

38. In 1900, the AFL declared, "A Federal Congress enacted a law for the incorporation of trade unions. Beyond question the advocates of the bill believed they were doing the organized workers a real service, but at the same time, and since, we have repeatedly warned our fellow unions to refrain from seeking the so-called protection of that law." Lay, "Coronado Coal Case," 167.

39. In 1901, American labor union leaders saw their greatest fears realized when a British court handed down the Taff Vale opinion. The British court ruled that a union, as a quasi-corporate body, could sue or be sued in a court of law. See *Monthly Labor Review* 40 (1935): 41; Trade Disputes Act of 1906, *Statutes of the Realm* 6 Edw. 7, c. 47 (1906), sec. 3; Wright, "Consolidated Labor," 42–45.

40. "Incorporation for Unions in Massachusetts," *Literary Digest*, November 1, 1902, 544, and "Labor Press about the Taff-Vale Decision," *Literary Digest*, January 17, 1903, 76–77. Gompers went so far as to predict that incorporation could make the judiciary's newly favorite antistrike remedy, the injunction, easier to obtain. See also Gompers, *Labor and the Employer*.

41. Samuel Gompers, "Trade Unions Do Not Desire Incorporation," *American Federationist* 10 (1903): 103. See also Clarence S. Darrow, "Should Trade Unions Incorporate?" *American Federationist* 10 (1903): 79–80.

42. Atkins and Kitchen, "Some Problems," 167.

43. Tomlins, *State and the Unions*, 87–88.

44. Quoted from Rogin, "Voluntarism," 524.

45. Samuel Gompers, "Labor by Law, not by Discretion," *American Federationist* 21 (1913): 45.

46. Leon Fink describes that the AFL wanted an "outright proscription on legal intervention in peaceful labor disputes." See Fink, "Labor, Liberty, and the Law," 917.

47. Samuel Gompers, "Invading Labor's Rights," *American Federationist* 12 (1904): 129, and Samuel Gompers, "Labor and Equal Rights," *American Federationist* 2 (1900): 165; Rogin, "Voluntarism," 526.

48. Symposium by Professor John R. Commons et al., "Amend the Sherman Antitrust Law," *American Federationist* 6 (1908): 354–65. See also Ross, *A Muted Fury*, for an excellent account of the AFL's position against the courts. Ross argues that lacking an inherent hostility toward the judiciary, the AFL conducted a narrow campaign against injunctions that interfered with the practice of "pure and simple unionism" (11–12).

49. Fink, "Labor, Liberty, and the Law," 908.

50. *Loewe v. Lawlor*, 208 U.S. 274 (1908); Samuel Gompers, "Labor Organizations Must Not Be Outlawed: The Supreme Court's Decision in the Hatters' Case," *American Federationist* 15 (1908): 180–92; Samuel Gompers, "Labor's Political Campaign," *American Federationist* 15 (1908): 341–53; John B. Lennon et al., "Supreme Court Decision in the Hatters' Case," *American Federationist* 15 (1908): 161–78.

51. As Robert Wiebe maintains, the progressives' conception of social justice demanded that "reforms should come to the workers, not through them." In particular, they opposed the so-called closed shop that mandated that all workers joined the union. Wiebe, *Businessmen and Reform*, 162.

52. See Eisenach, *Lost Promise of Progressivism*, 142–45.

53. "Labor in Politics," *New Republic*, February 25, 1919, 377.

54. See Mowry, "California Progressive and His Rationale"; Nye, *Midwestern Progressive Politics*; Hofstadter, *Age of Reform*.

55. Ashby, *The Spearless Leader*, 62.

56. See Ross, *Origins of American Social Science*, and Fitzpatrick, *Endless Crusade*.

57. See Link, "What Happened to the Progressive Movement?"

58. Davis, "Welfare, Reform, and World War I," 516 – 17.

59. See Kerr, *American Railroad Politics*, and Hicks, *Republican Ascendancy*, 7 – 8.

60. See Davis, "Welfare, Reform, and World War I," 516 – 33, and Brandes, *American Welfare Capitalism*.

61. Among the prominent progressive Republicans in the Congress were William E. Borah (Idaho), Coe Crawford (South Dakota), Moses Clapp (Minnesota), Asle Gronna (North Dakota), George W. Norris (Nebraska), Robert M. LaFollette (Wisconsin), Hiram W. Johnson (California), William S. Kenyon (Iowa), Albert B. Cummins (Iowa), Miles Poindexter (Washington), and Joseph Bristow (Kansas). See Holt, *Congressional Insurgents*, 3 – 5, and Mowry, *The California Progressives*.

62. See Buenker, *Urban Liberalism and Progressive Reform*.

63. Lowitt, *George W. Norris*, 8, 40 – 41.

64. DeWitt, *The Progressive Movement*, 26 – 29.

65. Link, "What Happened to the Progressive Movement?," 833 – 51.

66. The progressives' attitude about organized labor is best displayed in the *Nation*, the *New Republic*, and *Yale Law Review* during these years. Even general counsel for the railroad brotherhoods, Donald Richberg, supported the public interest concerns over private interests. In part, this also explains Richberg's conservatism during the New Deal. See Vadney, *The Wayward Liberal*.

67. "Direct Action and the Plumb Plan," *New Republic*, August 20, 1919, 70.

68. Ernst, "Common Laborers?," 62 – 68.

69. Commons, "Law and Economics," 375; Commons, *Institutional Economics*; Rutherford, "J. R. Commons's Institutional Economics."

70. Commons, "Karl Marx and Samuel Gompers," 285.

71. Quoted from Mitchell, "Commons on Institutional Economics," 650. See also Chasse, "John R. Commons and the Democratic State," and Rutherford, "J. R. Commons's Institutional Economics."

72. I refer to these jurists as legal progressives rather than the more narrow category of legal realists because of the debate about legal realism. See Schlegel, *American Legal Realism*.

73. Zucker, *George W. Norris*, x.

74. See Ernst, "Common Laborers?," 69 – 75. See also Oliphant, "Return to Stare Decisis"; Cook, "Privileges of Labor Unions"; and Frankfurter and Greene, *The Labor Injunction*.

75. Ernst, "Common Laborers?," 69 – 75.

76. Cook, "Privileges of Labor Unions," 800 – 801.

77. See ibid., 779 – 800; Atkins and Kitchen, "Some Problems," 162; Pound, "Liberty of Contract," 481 – 83; Frankfurter and Greene, *The Labor Injunction*; Sayre, "Labor and the Courts," 682 – 705; Sturges, "Unincorporated Associations"; and Magill and Magill, "Suability of Labor Unions." See also Laski, "Personality of Associations"; Geldart, "Legal Personality"; Dewey, "Historic Background"; Dodd, "Dogma and Practice"; and Chafee, "Internal Affairs," for general articles on the issue of the legal personality. These progressive law professors, some of whom associate themselves with sociological jurisprudence or the philosophy of pragmatism, others with legal re-

alism, referred to the issue of the legal status of the labor union. They made organized labor a second thought, however, in comparison to their primary preoccupation with the fictitious personality of the business corporation.

78. *United Mine Workers of America v. Coronado Coal Co.*, 259 U.S. 344 (1922).

79. See Frankfurter and Greene, *The Labor Injunction*, and Witte, *Government in Labor Disputes*.

80. Gompers and Brandeis debated the subject in a public forum on December 4, 1902. See Strum, *Louis D. Brandeis*, 104, and Tomlins, *State and the Unions*, 87.

81. See Hovenkamp, "Labor Conspiracies in American Law," 960 – 62.

82. "Incorporation for Unions in Massachusetts," 544.

83. Brandeis to Jacob Nathan, June 27, 1916, Brandeis Papers, University of Louisville Archives (microfilm, University of Wisconsin, Madison).

84. *Monthly Labor Review* 40 (1935): 42.

85. Quoted from Mason, *Brandeis*, 142.

86. According to Horwitz, this progressive jurisprudence reacted to the emergence of a complex organizational society and of obdurate social crises in the late nineteenth and early twentieth centuries by challenging the reigning "classical" legal orthodoxy that divided law into two separate spheres of private and public. See Horwitz, *Transformation of American Law*, 4, 11.

87. Brandeis to Jacob Nathan, June 27, 1916, Brandeis Papers, University of Louisville Archives (microfilm, University of Wisconsin, Madison).

88. In England, progressive legal jurists like Harold Laski as well as Sidney and Beatrice Webb supported the *Taff Vale Ry. Co. v. Amalgamated Society of Ry. Servants*, App. Case 426 (1901), despite the labor movement's outrage. They applied the paradigm of Otto Gierke, one of the leading theorists of real or natural entity theory, to organized labor. The Webbs, for instance, wrote that Gierke's theory was "only common sense . . . considering that Trade Unions were now in fact social entities." Quoted from Hager, "Bodies Politic," 623.

89. See Cooper, *Warrior and the Priest*, xii.

90. See Fine, *Laissez-Faire and the General Welfare State*, 128.

91. See Gillman, *The Constitution Besieged*.

92. See Warren, *Supreme Court*, 3:422–24, and Hall, *The Magic Mirror*, 190. For revisionist history that adds greater complexity to this perspective, see Ernst, "Free Labor"; Kens, "Source of a Myth"; Urofsky, "Myth and Reality"; Porter, "That Commerce Shall Be Free"; and Cushman, "Doctrinal Synergies and Liberal Dilemmas."

93. *In re Debs*, 158 U.S. 564 (1895). The Sherman Act was not applied to the trade union until *Loewe v. Lawlor* in 1908.

94. These courts, moreover, developed a "freedom to contract" doctrine, based on the due process clause, in which employers and workers had the right to contract at will without any legislative guidelines. The state courts first used this doctrine in the mid-1880s in *Jones v. People*, 110 Ill. 590 (1884); *Millett v. People*, 117 Ill. 294 (1886).

95. Horwitz, *Transformation of American Law*, 17, and Hall, *The Magic Mirror*, 22.

96. Pound, "End of Law." Pound associates equity and natural law "with the identification of law with morals in English law."

97. Horwitz explains, "It was marked by a series of basic dichotomies: between means and ends, procedures and substance, processes and consequences." Horwitz, *Transformation of American Law*, 16.

98. See Frankfurter and Greene, *The Labor Injunction*, and Witte, *Government in Labor Disputes*. According to Chief Justice Field, the "practice of issuing injunctions in cases of this kind [was] of very recent origin." See *Vegelahn v. Guntner*, 167 Mass. 92, 100 (1896). Frankfurter and Greene also noted that William Howard Taft wrote the "pioneer" federal decision basing federal relief in labor dispute. *Toledo, A.A. & N.M. Ry. Co. v. Pennsylvania Co.*, 54 Fed. 746 (N. D. Ohio, 1893).

99. Frankfurter and Greene, *The Labor Injunction*, 52.

100. Book review of Edward Berman's book entitled *Labor and the Sherman Act* (New York: Harper & Brothers, 1930), *American Federationist* 37 (1930): 876.

101. See Witte, *Government in Labor Disputes*; Forbath, "Shaping of the American Labor Movement," 1151; Ernst, "Yellow-Dog Contract and Liberal Reform"; and Petro, "Injunctions and Labor Disputes," 351–53.

102. Frankfurter and Greene, *The Labor Injunction*, 5.

103. According to Hattam, the federal courts had three courses of action. First, they could follow the conservative state courts' predilection for criminal conspiracy cases and risk the chance, given the increase in industrial conflicts, that they might undermine their own legitimacy. Second, they could recognize legislative protection. Third, the legal remedy at hand could be transformed from civil to equity law. "The third option is the one courts and employers pursued after 1885." See Hattam, *Labor Visions and State Power*, 162.

104. Powell, "Protecting Property and Liberty"; Kens, "Source of a Myth," 70–98; and Urofsky, "Myth and Reality," 53–72.

105. Book review of Berman's *Labor and the Sherman Act, American Federationist*, 876.

106. Gompers requested that the Clayton Act provide a legal definition of a labor union. Mason, "Labor Clauses of the Clayton Act," 494. Section 6 and section 20 composed the main body of labor relations provisions in the Clayton Act. Under section 6, the Clayton Act freed unions from accountability by redefining the term "labor organizations." It said "that the labor of a human being is not a commodity or article of commerce." Complementing section 6, section 20 prevented the federal courts from enjoining organized labor. According to its authors, the Clayton Act amended the Sherman Act to the effect that labor organizations and their members, unless committing irreparable damages, could not be enjoined for participating in legal strikes or primary boycotts that restrained interstate trade.

107. Samuel Gompers, "The Charter of Industrial Freedom," *American Federationist* 21 (1914): 971–72.

108. *Congressional Record*, 53d Cong., 2d sess., 1914, 51, pt. 14:13965.

109. Ashby, *The Spearless Leader*, 78; McKenna, *Borah*, 133; and Mason, *Organized Labor and the Law*, 180.

110. Schlabach, *Edwin E. Witte*, 56.

111. Link, *Wilson, the New Freedom*, 444; *Congressional Record*, 63d Cong., 2d sess., 1914, 51, pt. 16:16042, 16050, 16051. In early 1914, the Clayton Act passed Congress by a vote of 35 to 24 in the Senate and a vote of 245 to 52 in the House of Representatives. In the Senate, not one progressive Republican voted for the measure. Likewise, in the House few progressive Republicans voted for its passage. Lowitt, *George W. Norris*, 15.

112. Less than one month after his election in 1912, Wilson asked the Democratic

congressional leaders, not the progressive Republicans, for suggestions about how to amend the Sherman Act. Link, *Wilson, the New Freedom*, 425–44.

113. *Congressional Record*, 63d Cong. 2d sess., 1914, 51, pt. 10:9566.

114. Ernst, "Labor Exemption," 1169–70. Ernst offers a compelling interpretation of the labor relations provisions in the Clayton Act that also emphasized the participation of Albert B. Cummins, a Republican from Iowa, in the congressional debate.

115. Jones, "Wilson Administration and Organized Labor."

116. Wilson, however, decided not to bring the attorney general's conclusion to the attention of Congress. See Sarasohn, *Party of Reform*, 169. See also Jones, "Enigma of the Clayton Act," 201–21.

117. See Ernst, "Labor Exemption," 1166. According to Ernst, Taft "recognized that Wickersham's reading of the statute was plausible" but he thought the Supreme Court would merely render the act ineffective, not unconstitutional.

118. Gompers, "Charter of Industrial Freedom," 971–72, and Ernst, "Labor Exemption," 1167.

119. Taft, *Anti-trust Act*, 98–99.

120. In a letter to Judge Jeremiah Smith on December 24, 1914, Taft stated that President Woodrow Wilson presented organized labor with a "gold brick" to buy their vote. Taft to Judge Jeremiah Smith, December 24, 1914, Taft Papers, Library of Congress (microfilm, Herbert Hoover Presidential Library).

121. See Mason, "Labor Clauses of the Clayton Act," 494, and Murray, "Public Opinion, Labor, and a Clayton Act."

122. The AFL, in particular, hoped that section 6 would prohibit the outcome of a case similar to *Loewe v. Lawlor* or the Danbury Hatters' case. This case illustrates, however, that section 6 offered organized labor an ineffectual definition of a labor union. See *Loewe v. Lawlor*.

123. Taft to George Wickersham, n.d., Taft Papers, Library of Congress (microfilm, Herbert Hoover Presidential Library). See also Taft, *Anti-trust Act*, 98.

124. Hovenkamp, "Labor Conspiracies in American Law," 960–62.

125. *Duplex v. Deering*, 254 U.S. 443 (1921); *Truax v. Corrigan*, 257 U.S. 312 (1921); *American Steel Foundries v. Tri-City Central Trades Council*, 257 U.S. 184 (1921). See also Cushman, "Doctrinal Synergies and Liberal Dilemmas," 235–93.

126. Memorandum, n.d., Norris Papers, Library of Congress.

127. As Oliver Wendell Holmes Jr. wrote, "When a responsible defendant seeks to escape from liability for an Act which he had notice was likely to cause temporal damage to another, and which has caused such damage in fact, he must show a justification." See Holmes, "Privilege, Malice, and Intent," 9.

128. Frankfurter and Greene, *The Labor Injunction*, 25.

129. Ibid., 26–27.

130. Llewellyn, "Effect of Legal Institutions upon Economics," 666.

131. Cook, "Privileges of Labor Unions," 801.

## Chapter 3

1. *United Mine Workers of America v. Coronado Coal Co.*, 259 U.S. 344 (1922).

2. "Labor Unions Liable to Pay for Strike Damages," *Literary Digest*, June 17, 1922, 8.

3. Ibid., 7.

4. Ibid., 9.

5. See Tomlins, *State and the Unions*, and Lichtenstein, *Labor's War at Home*.

6. Brandeis's influence is seen in law and letters.

7. Felix Frankfurter, "The Coronado Case," *New Republic*, February 25, 1922, 328–29.

8. As John R. Commons, a progressive economist, explained in 1924, "'A new equity' is needed—an equity that will protect the job as the older equity protected the business." Quoted from Mitchell, "Commons on Institutional Economics," 642.

9. Rogin, "Voluntarism."

10. Holmes, "Privilege, Malice, and Intent," 3.

11. For the progressives' preoccupation with legislative solutions, see Ross, *A Muted Fury*.

12. For an explanation of the state that also includes theories of culture, see Hall, "Toad in the Garden," 35–74.

13. See Orren, *Belated Feudalism*, and Tomlins, *State and the Unions*, for excellent histories of the development of the common law of labor relations in the United States.

14. *A. R. Barnes & Co. v. Berry*, 169 Fed. 225 (1909); *Goyette v. C. V. Watson Co.*, 245 Mass. 577, 140 N.E. 285 (1923); Witmer, "Collective Labor Agreements in the Courts," 196; and Christenson, "Legally Enforceable Interests," 73. See also, e.g., *Burnetta v. Marceline Coal Co.*, 180 Mo. 241, 79 S.W. 136 (1904); *West v. Baltimore & Ohio R. Co.*, 137 S.E. 654 (1927); *Gary v. Central of Georgia Ry. Co.*, 141 S.E. 819 (1928); and *Ruggles v. International Association of Iron Workers*, 331 Mo. 20, 52 S.W. (2d) 869 (1932), for cases in which trade agreements were not viewed by the courts as contracts.

15. See Hoxie, *Trade Unions in the United States*, 216, and Duguit, "Collective Acts," 755. See, e.g., *Chambers v. Davis*, 128 Miss. 613, 91 So. 346 (1922).

16. Lack of mutuality, which has fallen into disuse, stems from the *Lumley v. Wagner*, 1 De Gax, M. & G. 604 (1852), decision in England. The courts used lack of mutuality and did not enforce collective trade agreements in the following cases: *Howard Peterson v. United Engraving Co.* (Minn. Dist. Ct. 1922); *St. Louis, Iron Mountain and So. Ry. v. Matthews*, 64 Ark. 398, 406, 42 S.W. 902, 904 (1897); *St. Louis Brownville & Mexico Ry. v. Booker*, 5 S.W. (2d) 856, 859 (Tex. Civ. App. 1929), Cert. denied, 279 S.W. 852 (1929); *Epstein v. Gluckin*, 233 N.Y. 490, 135 N.E. 861 (1922). See also Cook, *Cases and Other Authorities*, 151; Cook, "Present Status," 897; Ames, "Mutuality in Specific Performance"; Stone, "'Mutuality' Rule in New York," 443; and Witmer, "Collective Labor Agreements in the Courts," 204. See also *St. Louis, I. M. & S. Ry. Co. v. Mathews*, 42 S.W. 906 (1897). The Supreme Court of Arkansas cited the *Railroad v. Scott*, (Tex. Supp.) 10 S.W. 99 (1888); *Bolles v. Sachs*, 37 Minn. 315, 33 N.W. 862 (1887). See, e.g., *A. R. Barnes & Co. v. Berry*.

17. See Sturges, "Unincorporated Associations," 399, for an explanation of enabling statutes that recognized unions as organizations.

18. Dewey, "Historic Background." See also Laski, "Personality of Associations," and Geldhardt, "Legal Personality," for the debate on legal personality.

19. See, e.g., *Hudson v. Cincinnati*, 152 Ky. 711, 154 S.W. 47 (1913); *West v. Baltimore & Ohio*; *Young v. Canadian Northern R.*, 4 D.L.R. 452, 2 W.W.R. 385 (1929), and

3 D.L.R. 352, 1 W.W.R. 446 (1930); *Gregg v. Starks*, 188 Ky. 834, 224 S.W. 459 (1920); *Keysaw v. Dotterseich Brewing Co.*, 121 App. Div. 58, 105 N.Y. Supp. 562, 4th Dept. (1907); *Moody v. Model Glass Co.*, 145 Ark. 197, 224 S.W. 436 (1920); *Cross Mountain Coal Co. v. Ault*, 157 Tenn. 461, 9 S.W. (2d) 692 (1928); *U.S. Daily Publishing Corporation v. Nicholas*, 32 Fed. (2d) 834 (App. D.C. 1929); *Mastell v. Salo*, 140 Ark. 408, 215 S.W. 583 (1919); *Langmade v. Olean Brewing Co.*, 137 App. Div. 355 (121 N.Y. Supp. 388, 4th Dept. 1910); *Gulickson v. Seglin Construction Co.*, 273 N.Y. Supp. 908 (County Ct. 1934); *Kessel v. Great No. R.*, 51 Fed. (2d) 304 (W. D. Washington 1931); *Yazoo & M.V.R.R. v. Webb*, 64 Fed. (2d) 902 (C.C.A. 5th 1933); *Burnetta v. Marceline*. See also Commons and Andrews, *Principles of Labor Legislation*, 389.

20. *Byrd v. Beall*, 150 Ala. 122, 43 So. 749, 124 Am. St. Rep. 60 (1907).

21. Ibid.

22. *West v. Baltimore & Ohio*; *Keysaw v. Dotterweich Brewing Co.*; *Gary v. Central of Georgia R. Co.*, 37 Ga. App. 744, 141 S.E. 819 (1928).

23. Dewey, "Historic Background," 655.

24. *Hudson v. Cincinnati*; *Burnetta v. Marceline*; *West v. Baltimore & Ohio*; *Ribner & Webber v. Gilchnstr. Metal Polishers Union*, 113 Atl. 320 (N.J. Ch. 1919).

25. See, e.g., *Burnetta v. Marceline*; *West v. Baltimore & Ohio*; *Cross Mountain Coal Co. v. Ault*; *Mastell v. Salo*.

26. Quoted from Rice, "Collective Labor Agreements," 584.

27. *Piercy v. Louisville & Nashville R. Co.*, 248 S.W. 1042 (1923).

28. See, e.g., *Gulla v. Barton*, 164 App. Div. 293, 149 N.Y. Supp. 952 (1914); *Mueller v. Chicago and N. Western R. Co.*, 194 Minn. 83, 259 N.W. 798 (1935); *Yazoo and M. Valley R. v. Sideboard*, 161 Miss. 4, 133 So. 669 (1931); *Rentschler v. Missouri Pacific RR*, 126 Neb. 493, 253 N.W. 644 (1934); *Johnson v. American R. Exp. Co.*, 163 S.C. 191, 161 S.E. 473 (1931); *Marshall v. Charleston and WC R.*, 164 S.C. 283, 162 S.E. 348 (1931); *Hall v. St. Louis San Francisco Co. R.*, 28 S.W. 687 (Mo. App 1930); *Donavon v. Travers*, 285 Mass. 167, 188 N.E. 705 (1934).

29. *Gulla v. Barton*, 953.

30. Ibid. The court held, "Evidence does not show any act of the plaintiff, made with the knowledge of the facts, which would waive the benefit of the company with the union on his behalf."

31. Affirming this case in 1926, a progressive judge on the Ohio Court of Appeals held in the *H. Blum & Co. v. Landau* decision, "It clearly appears that the contract between the Garment Manufacturers' Association and the International Ladies' Garment Workers' Union was a contract made for the benefit of third parties." Judge John J. Sullivan, a Rooseveltian progressive Republican, delivering the opinion, declared, "That such a contract as the one at bar is enforceable there can be no question." *H. Blum & Co. v. Landau*, 23 Ohio App. 426, 155 N.E. 154 (1926).

32. See, e.g., *Whiting Milk Co. v. Grondin*, 282 Mass. 41, 184 N.E. 379 (1933); Hamilton, "Individual Rights," 256; "Collective Labor Agreements," 1160; Anderson, "Collective Bargaining Agreements," 241.

33. Christenson, "Legally Enforceable Interests," 93.

34. See, e.g., *Schlesinger v. Quinto*, 194 N.Y. Supp. 401 (1922); *Gary v. Central of Georgia R.*, 44 Ga. App. 120, 160 S.E. 716 (1931); *Hall v. St. Louis–San Francisco R.*, 244 Mo. App. 431, 28 S.W. (2d) 687 (1930); *McCoy v. St. Joseph Belt R.*, 77 S.W. (2d)

175, 179 (Mo. App. 1934); *Piercy v. Louisville & N. R.*, 198 Ky. 477, 248 S.W. 1042 (1923); *West v. Baltimore & Ohio R.*, 103 W. Va. 417, 137 S.E. 654 (1927); *Snow Iron Works v. Chadwick*, 227 Mass. 382, 390, 116 N.E. 801, 806 (1917); *Mosshamer v. Wabash R.*, 221 Mich. 407, 408, 191 N.W. 210, 211 (1922); *Boucher v. Godfrey*, 119 Conn. 622, 178 Atl. 655 (1935).

35. *Barnes v. Berry.*

36. Anderson, "Collective Bargaining Agreements," 240.

37. *Barnes v. Berry*; Rice, "Collective Labor Agreements," 594.

38. *Schlesinger v. Quinto.* The union involved negotiated a collective trade agreement with the Cloak, Suit and Skirt Manufacturers' Protective Association, which the latter association violated.

39. Ibid., 410.

40. See Horwitz, *Transformation of American Law*, 47–48.

41. Cook, "Agency by Estoppel," 40.

42. Corbin, "Contracts for the Benefit of Third Persons," 1008. See also Corbin, "Does a Pre-existing Duty Defeat Consideration?"

43. Ibid.

44. Priest, "Invention of Enterprise Liability," and Landes and Posner, "Positive Economic Theory," 871–77.

45. Horwitz, *Transformation of American Law*, 48.

46. Ibid., 74.

47. For an explanation of the British labor movement and the question of incorporation, see Hager, "Bodies Politic," 617–25.

48. Ernst, "The Labor Exemption," 1151–73, and Ernst, "Free Labor," 19–35.

49. See Rice, "Collective Labor Agreements," 607, and Agger, "Equitable Relief," 258.

50. Atkins and Kitchen, "Some Problems," 168.

51. "Legal Consequences Flowing from Trade Agreements," 411.

52. "Responsibility of Labor Unions for Acts of Members," 469.

53. *United Mine Workers of America v. Coronado Coal Co.* and *Coronado Coal Co. v. United Mine Workers of America*, 268 U.S. 295 (1925).

54. Frankfurter, "The Coronado Case," 328.

55. The local paid only $27,500, since it was not held liable for triple damages under the Sherman Act. Bickel, *Unpublished Opinions*, 99.

56. Magill and Magill, "Suability of Labor Unions," 81.

57. "Labor Unions Liable to Pay for Strike Damages," 7–9.

58. "Gompers Attacks Coronado Decision," *New York Times*, June 7, 1922, and *Letters of Louis D. Brandeis*, 5:57.

59. Frankfurter, "The Coronado Case," and Sturges, "Unincorporated Associations," 382–405; Cook, "Privileges of Labor Unions," 800.

60. *Letters of Louis D. Brandeis*, 5:57.

61. Sturges, "Unincorporated Associations," 385.

62. When Warren G. Harding became president, one of his first concerns was to ensure that the Supreme Court remained an old guard stronghold. Harding had little trouble maintaining the conservative character of the Court, since the four justices preceding Taft had been appointed by Republican presidents. Justices William Rufus

Day and Joseph McKenna had been appointed by William McKinley and Theodore Roosevelt, respectively. Two of Taft's appointments from his own term as president, Willis Van Devanter and Mahlon Pitney, were still on the Court in 1921. President Woodrow Wilson's three appointments to the Court, Louis D. Brandeis, James C. Clarke, and James R. McReynolds, had little impact on the conservative majority. McReynolds joined this conservative majority in most of his opinions, while only Brandeis and Clarke voted with Oliver Wendell Holmes, becoming part of a permanent minority. Harding had the opportunity to appoint more old guard Republicans during his three-year administration when Justices William Rufus Day and Mahlon Pitney retired in 1922 and 1923, respectively. Harding placed the "eminently conservative" Pierce Butler and Edward T. Sanford on the Taft Court. Justice Clarke, a progressive Democrat appointed by Wilson, left the Court in 1922, permitting Harding to nominate George Sutherland, a western old guard Republican, who believed in the legal equivalent of "rugged individualism" and gave the Court an even stronger conservative majority. Finally, McKenna stepped down in 1925, and Harding's successor, Calvin Coolidge, nominated his attorney general, the then conservative Harlan Fiske Stone. Taft to Justice Edward Sanford, January 25, 1927, and Taft to Horace Taft, December 1, 1929, Taft Papers, Library of Congress (microfilm, Herbert Hoover Presidential Library). See Mason, "William Howard Taft," 3:2108, and Burner, "John H. Clarke," 3:2078, 2081-82.

63. *United Mine Workers of America v. Coronado Coal Co.*; and *Coronado Coal Co. v. United Mine Workers of America*.

64. See Sayre, "Labor and the Courts," 682-705.

65. Atkins and Kitchen, "Some Problems," 162.

66. Ibid.

67. Ibid., 164.

68. *United States v. E. C. Knight*, 158 U.S. 1 (1895), and *Hammer v. Dagenhart*, 247 U.S. 375 (1918), limited the reach of the federal government.

69. Sturges, "Unincorporated Associations," 396-99.

70. Hattam, *Labor Visions and State Power*, 161-66.

71. Sturges, "Unincorporated Associations," 387.

72. "Notes," *Columbia Law Review* 38 (1938): 471-72.

73. Ibid.

74. Mason, *Organized Labor and the Law*, 218.

75. Taft to Horace D. Taft, June 16, 1922, Taft Papers, Library of Congress (microfilm, Herbert Hoover Presidential Library), and Mason, "William Howard Taft," 3:2114.

76. *United Mine Workers of America v. Coronado Coal Co.*, 390.

77. Ibid., 385-86, 391.

78. Ibid., 391.

79. Lay, "Coronado Coal Case," 164.

80. *Taff Vale Ry. Co. v. Amalgamated Society of Ry. Service*, A.C. 426 (1901).

81. Justices Brandeis, Holmes, Clarke, and Day were initially in the minority. Taft to Horace D. Taft, June 16, 1922.

82. Quoted from Mason, *Brandeis*, 142.

83. Bickel, *Unpublished Opinions*, 97.

84. Ibid.

85. Taft to Horace D. Taft, June 16, 1922.

86. Bickel, *Unpublished Opinions*, 85.

87. Ibid., 96.

88. Ibid., 99.

89. Frankfurter, "The Coronado Case," 329.

90. Ibid.

91. Ibid., 328.

92. Ibid.

93. Ibid.

94. "Notes," *Columbia Law Review* (1938), 468.

95. *Coronado Coal Co. v. United Mine Workers of America*.

96. See, e.g., *Aluminum Casting Co. v. Local International Molders Union*, 197 Fed. 221 (1912).

97. *Coronado Coal Co. v. United Mine Workers of America*, 300, 304.

98. "Notes," *Columbia Law Review* (1938), 455. This commentary on the second *Coronado* case explained "that in an action for damages against a voluntary unincorporated association, facts must be alleged and proved rendering all members of the association liable, that liability of members may be established by public acts of association itself or by acts of its officers."

99. Taft cites *Loewe v. Lawlor*, 208 U.S. 274 (1908), which made workers liable for conspiracy in restraint of trade under the Sherman Act.

100. "Notes," *Columbia Law Review* (1938), 455.

101. Ibid., 457.

102. *United Mine Workers of America v. Coronado Coal Co.*, 390.

103. The potential dangers of organized labor's newly established suable status were never realized, however. Only one state, which did not have an enabling statute ensuring that organized labor could be sued, used the *Coronado* precedent. No increase in the number of common-law cases in which employers sued unions or unions sued employers was recorded in the 1920s or the early 1930s. See, e.g., *Varado v. Whitney*, 166 Miss. 663, 147 So. 479 (1933); Laurent, "Labor Law," 523; and "Notes," *Columbia Law Review* 31 (1931): 257.

104. "Comments on the decision of the United States Supreme Court in the case of the United Mine Workers of America vs. the Coronado Coal Company," n.d., AFL Papers, State Historical Society of Wisconsin.

105. Sturges, "Unincorporated Associations," 405; *United Mine Workers of America v. Coronado Coal Co.*, 390; and "Notes," *Columbia Law Review* (1938), 459.

106. "Comments on the decision of the United States Supreme Court in the case of the United Mine Workers of America vs. the Coronado Coal Company," n.d., AFL Papers, State Historical Society of Wisconsin.

107. "Labor Unions Liable to Pay for Strike Damages," 7.

108. See Hattam, *Labor Visions and State Power*, 167.

109. Ibid., 200–202.

110. Edwin E. Witte to Roger N. Baldwin, December 24, 1931, Witte Papers, State Historical Society of Wisconsin.

111. Gompers to Horace W. Glasgow, December 18, 1923, AFL Papers, State Historical Society of Wisconsin.

112. Ibid.

113. Samuel Gompers to Executive Council, American Federation of Labor, February 8, 1922, AFL Papers, State Historical Society of Wisconsin.

114. Ibid.

115. In a letter, Gompers discussed Samuel Untermyer's proposal for incorporation after the first *Coronado* decision. Samuel Gompers to Charles C. Lockwood, July 3, 1922, AFL Papers, State Historical Society of Wisconsin.

116. "Labor Unions Liable to Pay for Strike Damages," 9.

117. Quoted from Lay, "Coronado Coal Case," 167-68.

118. Frankfurter, "The Coronado Case," 330.

119. "Labor Unions Liable to Pay for Strike Damages," 9.

120. Atkins and Kitchen, "Some Problems," 167-68.

121. Frankfurter, "The Coronado Case," 329.

122. "Civil Liabilities of Members of Unincorporated Labor Unions," 551.

## Chapter 4

1. For an excellent discussion about the tension within the progressive movement, the alternative paths of development for American liberalism, and the labor question, see Furner, "Knowing Capitalism."

2. See Conner, *National War Labor Board*. Although worker representation existed under the National War Labor Board, these elections depended on the voluntary cooperation of the employers, the workers, and the national unions. Instead of implementing the scheme with a provision for majority rule, the NWLB facilitated the status quo: it never rendered opinions compelling employers to negotiate with worker representatives. The shop committees, moreover, were independent of the national labor organizations. The NWLB had a weak supervisory role in the collective bargaining process because it held no elections on providing the workers with the right to representation. See also Dubofsky, "Abortive Reform," and Troy, "Labor Representation on American Railways," 297.

3. Labor historians and legal scholars generally regard the labor relations provisions in the Transportation Act as a makeshift measure that had little bearing on the construction of the subsequent railroad labor legislation. The Railroad Labor Board was a quasi-judicial agency with no enforcement powers, whereas the U.S. Mediation Board established by the Railway Labor Act and amended in 1934 provided voluntary mediation and arbitration. See Zakson, "Railway Labor Legislation"; Stone, "Labor Relations on the Airlines," 1485-92; and Lecht, *Experience under Railway Labor Legislation*. See also Zieger, *Republicans and Labor*, for the most comprehensive explanation of both the formation and the implementation of the railroad labor legislation in the 1920s. By deemphasizing the importance of the specific labor relations machinery (the issue of quasi-judicial adjudication or arbitration and mediation), my argument takes issue with these interpretations of the railroad labor legislation. I suggest that the worker representation scheme and the role of the state agency implementing this scheme in the 1920 Transportation Act are important elements that have been ignored despite the help they offered in shaping the construction of the 1926 Railway Labor Act and the majority rule provision in the Wagner Act. While Zakson correctly notes that the U.S. Mediation Board represented "a return to voluntarism," the process that

worker representatives underwent as parties to this mediation reflected responsible unionism.

4. Anthony Downs suggests that political parties "formulate public policies in order to win elections rather than win elections to formulate policies." See Downs, *Economic Theory of Democracy*, 28, and Schlesinger, "New American Political Party," 1153.

5. For the classic argument about state managers, see Block, "Ruling Class Does Not Rule."

6. See Skocpol, "Political Response to Capitalism Crisis."

7. Palmer, *British Industrial Relations*, 127; Wrigley, *Lloyd George*, 130–42; Cronin, *Labour and Society in Britain*, 46. The postwar period in Great Britain represented a turning point in labor history precisely because it reestablished the prewar labor policy and did not extend the wartime policy. While the wartime experience made unions and employers more dependant on the state, the 1920s industrial policy was noncorporatist. Indeed, after the failure of the general strike in 1926, Parliament passed the Trade Disputes Act of 1927, which strictly enforced a code of voluntarism. Although this act was punitive, making employees "contract in" before their dues could be contributed to political candidates and prohibiting sympathy strikes, it reinstated the system of voluntarism for one reason. Since the Trades Union Congress and employers preferred voluntarism, they both circumvented this act altogether. From 1927 until the 1960s, they negotiated collective bargaining agreements without legal guidance or governmental supervision. In Great Britain, collective bargaining, not labor law, governed wages and employment conditions. Gerber, by contrast, emphasizes British nationalization immediately after World War I with corporatism. He compares this reconstruction corporatist strategy with the defeat of the Plumb Plan, arguing that the United States stood at the crossroads of liberalism and corporate liberalism after World War I.

8. See Windmuller, *Labor Relations in the Netherlands*; Slomp, *Labor Relations in Europe*; Feldman, *Army, Industry, and Labor*; Braunthal, *Socialist Labor and Politics*; and Streeck, "Organizational Consequences," 35–36.

9. For an explanation of the Plumb Plan in context with British postwar nationalization plans, see Gerber, "Corporatism in Comparative Perspective."

10. For the Republican Party's postwar position against organized labor, see Zieger, "From Hostility to Moderation." A strong economy and the potential labor vote convinced the Republican Party "to adopt a far more moderate approach to the labor problem" by the end of the decade. Zieger maintains that the GOP modified its position because of political expediency, whereas this chapter suggests that despite shifting patterns in intraparty politics, primarily caused by the struggle between the old guard and progressives, the GOP left an ideological imprint on the railroad labor legislation in 1920 and 1926.

11. The progressive party leaders in Congress at this time were Senators William E. Borah (Idaho), George W. Norris (Nebraska), Robert M. LaFollette (Wisconsin), Hiram W. Johnson (California), Charles McNary (Oregon), Irvine L. Lenroot (Wisconsin), and Knute Nelson (Minnesota). The following senators were considered moderate progressive Republicans (they would vote with the progressives on legislation involving agriculture but would vote with the old guard on issues such as the tariff or

labor): Frank B. Kellogg (Minnesota), William S. Kenyon (Iowa), Albert B. Cummins (Iowa), Miles Poindexter (Washington), and Wesley L. Jones (Washington). In the House, some of the progressive leaders were Sidney Anderson (Minnesota), Royal Cleves Johnson (South Dakota), James William Husted (New York), Elijan C. Hutchinson (New Jersey), and Ira Clifton Copley (Illinois). Outside Congress, progressive leaders were George M. Perkins, Philip LaFollette, George L. Record, Theodore Roosevelt, Amos Pinchot, Gifford Pinchot, Harold Ickes, Walter Brown, James Garfield, William Allen White, Raymond Robins, Everett Colby, Oscar S. Straus, Chester Rowell, Peter Norbeck, Bronson Cutting, Arthur Capper, Truman Newberry, and Robert Howell. The following members of Congress considered themselves part of the old guard: Senators Frank Brandegee (Connecticut), Lewis Ball (Delaware), Charles Curtis (Kansas), Joseph E. Watson (Indiana), Joseph S. Frelinghuysen (New Jersey), Boies Penrose (Pennsylvania), James W. Wadsworth (New York), William Calder (New York), Philander C. Knox (Pennsylvania), Walter Edge (Maine), Reed Smoot (Utah), and Frances E. Warren (Wyoming) and Congressmen Frederick H. Gillett (Massachusetts), George Washington Edmonds (Pennsylvania), Joseph Warren Fordney (Michigan), and Franklin Mondell (Wyoming). Outside Congress, William Howard Taft, Nicholas Murray Butler, James T. Adams, John T. King, and Charles Nagel were influential members of the old guard.

12. See Robertson, *No Third Choice*, 107–8; Livermore, *Politics Is Adjourned*, 245; and Mayer, *Republican Party*, 351.

13. See Wilensky, *Conservatives in the Progressive Era*; Sundquist, *Dynamics of the Party System*; Burnham, "Party Systems"; Noble, *Progressive Mind*; Blum *The Progressive Presidents*; Blum, *The Republican Roosevelt*.

14. As early as the 1916 presidential campaign, the eastern or what was known as George Perkins's group of progressives, led by the former Bull Moosers Perkins, Theodore Roosevelt, and Hiram W. Johnson, had begun negotiating with the old guard. Although their first bid failed, these progressives bargained with the old guard about reinstatement again in 1917. After Charles Evans Hughes's defeat in the 1916 presidential election, the old guard welcomed the insurgents back into the party fold. Bringing these insurgents back into the Republican Party fold, the old guard believed, would give them electoral support from the rural Midwest and the West, where Hughes had clearly been defeated. See Robertson, *No Third Choice*, 14–21; Sarasohn, *Party of Reform*, 194–95; and Burner, *Politics of Provincialism*, 10.

15. Teddy Roosevelt wrote a public letter stating, "Taft and I are now in absolute accord about present needs and about our failures and shortcomings and the cause of them during the past years." Quoted from Livermore, *Politics Is Adjourned*, 151.

16. To discredit Adams, William M. Calder read a damaging article the candidate had written for the *Dubuque Telegraph Herald* in 1914 that threw his patriotism into doubt. The next day, the old guard party leaders, calling for Republican Party unity and harmony, supported the progressives' favorite candidate, Hays, instead of Adams. Robertson, *No Third Choice*, 50–57, and Livermore, *Politics Is Adjourned*, 70–76, 107–8.

17. The chairman of the GOP would have to remain neutral when the party made its presidential nomination in 1920; the Advisory Committee, which had progressive representation unlike any other Republican national committees, would be dissolved;

and the chairman would no longer choose who sat on the Executive Committee. The National Committee, which was controlled by the old guard, would have this privilege. See Robertson, *No Third Choice*, 50.

18. Ibid., 98–100. In Rhode Island, for instance, Governor R. Livingston Beeckman, a progressive, campaigned for the old guard's candidate, Le Baron B. Colt. Applauding Beeckman's effort, Lodge proclaimed his pleasure that "personal desires [had been] subordinated to the interests of the party."

19. Arthur Capper (Kansas) and Truman Newberry (Michigan) were elected to the Senate for the first time in 1918. Newberry was a moderate progressive, evenly dividing his votes with the progressive insurgents and the old guard. Progressive Republican governors Peter Norbeck (South Dakota), Robert Carey (Wyoming), and Henry Allen (Kansas) also won in 1918. See *Official Congressional Directory*, 66th Cong., 1st sess. (Washington, D.C.: Government Printing Office, 1920).

20. Nagel, *Speeches and Writings*, 17–19.

21. Ibid.

22. Herbert Croly, Walter Lippmann, and Walter Weyl developed this notion of elitism in the *New Republic*, a progressive weekly. See also O'Leary, "Herbert Croly."

23. See McCormick, *Party Period and Public Policy*, 178–80.

24. Ibid. See also Eisenach, *Lost Promise of Progressivism*, 111–21, for an explanation of how the progressives' critique of political parties in the early twentieth century represented a rejection of state and local party organizations, not national party organizations. The progressives did view the national party, independent of local interests, as a vehicle for reform.

25. Ashby, *The Spearless Leader*, 87; Lowitt, *George W. Norris*, 8, 40–41; and Buenker, *Urban Liberalism and Progressive Reform*.

26. Land grants, the Homestead Act, loans to railroads for construction, the Blair Education Act, and protective tariffs all constituted a significant part of the Republican policy agenda. See Burner, *Politics of Provincialism*, 18, and Gienapp, *Origins of the Republican Party*, 172.

27. Oddly enough, the Republican Party's success cannot be attributed to the charisma of its leaders. William McKinley, Thomas B. Reed, and John Sherman had no special attributes, such as William Jennings Bryan's powers of oratory. The Republicans, moreover, did not come to power by virtue of a new policy agenda. The major campaign policy, the Republican Party's opposition to free silver, could hardly be said to have attracted a new constituency. Instead, the Republicans' success in 1894 and 1896 resulted from having a national party organization that reacted quickly to the profound industrial changes that swept the country beginning in the 1880s. See Degler, "The Nineteenth Century," 36–37.

28. See Skowronek, *Building a New American State*, 168.

29. See Degler, "American Political Parties," 949–68; Burner, *Politics of Provincialism*; and Ladd, *American Political Parties*.

30. Sarasohn, *Party of Reform*, 165.

31. Nye, *Midwestern Progressive Politics*, 183–84.

32. Wilensky, *Conservatives in the Progressive Era*, 45.

33. Weinstein, *Corporate Ideal*, and Wiebe, *Search for Order*.

34. Broesamle, "The Democrats," 113; Degler, "The Nineteenth Century," 953.

35. Because William Jennings Bryan captured the Democratic nomination in 1896,

1900, and 1908, the provincial rural factions dominated the Democratic Party. Bryan represented the radical agrarian populists in the Midwest and the South. The Democratic Party elites upheld the agrarian life as a symbol of the good life, and states' rights took precedence over building a unified nation-state. Burner, *Politics of Provincialism*, 10, and Perry Belmont, "The Plight of the Democratic Party," *North American Review* 172 (1901): 268.

36. Skowronek, *Building the New American State*, 174-75.

37. As a congressional party leader, Wilson had generally managed to serve all the sections of party elites in his national Democratic coalition. But when he became the national administrative authority operating the entire wartime apparatus, he made decisions that pitted one section against another section of Democratic Party elites. See Burner, *Politics of Provincialism*, 10, 29, 35.

38. For example, in Missouri, the Democratic state machine fought with the administration about Joe Folk's candidacy for the Senate, and a Republican won the seat. See Livermore, *Politics Is Adjourned*, 231.

39. "Towards a New Party," *New Republic*, August 18, 1918, 41; "Why the President Did It," *New Republic*, November 2, 1918, 3-4.

40. Since the electoral realignment of 1896, the Republicans controlled this region of the country by holding 79 of 96 of the seats. The biggest drop in seats occurred in 1912 with Wilson's election. At this time, the Republicans carried only 42 of 119. The Republicans' victory reasserted their longtime dominance in the Northeast. See data from Ewing, *Congressional Elections*, 83.

41. Ibid., 91.

42. Livermore, *Politics Is Adjourned*, 231.

43. Schlesinger, "New American Political Party," 1160. See also Burnham, "Party Systems and the Political Process," 301.

44. The Democrats also lost all the close races for the House of Representatives and the Senate in the midwestern and the western states. Republicans defeated the Democratic senatorial candidates in Missouri, Nebraska, Oregon, Colorado, Wyoming, Kansas, Indiana, Idaho, and South Dakota. In each case the Democratic vote dropped anywhere from 25 to 42 percent. See Livermore, *Politics Is Adjourned*, 225.

45. See *Guide to Congressional Elections* (Washington, D.C.: Congressional Quarterly Press, 1988), 892-96, for the popular vote returns.

46. Livermore, *Politics Is Adjourned*, 206-23, 227. Angry that Wilson made an "appeal" that a Democratic majority be returned to Congress while he characterized himself as "above politics," many members of his party did not go to the polls. The Republican vote also dropped by 16 percent, with 4,158,000 voting in 1914 and 1916 in contrast to 3,494,000 voting in 1918.

47. Ibid.

48. Ibid., 206-23.

49. Ibid., 226.

50. Eagles, *Democracy Delayed*, 32-84, and Boinville, *Origins and Development of Congress*, 142-44.

51. Robertson, *No Third Choice*, 105.

52. Quoted from ibid., 167.

53. Livermore, *Politics Is Adjourned*, 224.

54. By 1916, the progressive Republicans expressed their disillusionment with his

New Freedom reform program. See Lowitt, *George W. Norris*, 56; Greenbaum, *Robert Marion LaFollette*, 174−77; Nye, *Midwestern Progressive Politics*, 286; Feinman, *Twilight of Progressivism*, 2; Robertson, *No Third Choice*, 107; and Garraty, *Henry Cabot Lodge*, 355−56.

55. See Wilensky, *Conservatives in the Progressive Era*, 52−53, and Robertson, *No Third Choice*, 90−116.

56. Hays took the unusual step of helping Lodge and other congressional party leaders reorganize Congress. See Robertson, *No Third Choice*, 72−74.

57. Ripley, "Functions of the Party Leaders," 114.

58. Ripley, *Congress*, 50.

59. Smith and Deering, *Committees in Congress*, 23.

60. Ripley, *Majority Party Leadership*, 96.

61. Franklin Mondell of Wyoming, the majority leader, and four other majority party members ran the sixty-sixth and sixty-seventh sessions of the House, while it has been contended that Frederick H. Gillett of Massachusetts, the Speaker of the House, was a figurehead. Chiu, *Speaker of the House*, 331−43.

62. Ripley, *Majority Party Leadership*, 100.

63. See Robertson, *No Third Choice*, 152; Lowitt, *George W. Norris*, 221−25; and Ashby, *The Spearless Leader*.

64. See Robertson, *No Third Choice*, 114−15.

65. The three most important committees, Foreign Relations, Finance, and Appropriations, went to the old guard senator leaders Lodge, Boeis Penrose of Pennsylvania, and Francis E. Warren of Wyoming, respectively. Old guard member Charles Curtis of Kansas also became the majority whip. *Official Congressional Directory*, 66th Cong., 1st sess., 1920.

66. Although Lodge said that the progressives would be given "full recognition" for rejoining the GOP, he assigned only the moderate progressives committee chairmanships, like Albert B. Cummins, who became chair of the Interstate and Foreign Commerce Committee. Some progressive senators, such as Hiram Johnson, said the old guard's tactic of appointing moderate progressives to chair important committees was simply an attempt to "buy-off" these Senators at the expense of their more militant colleagues. Robertson, *No Third Choice*, 171−72.

67. Norris sponsored a resolution to reform the Senate rules about reorganizing the chamber after an election. He had the backing of most progressive Republicans until the old guard convinced the moderate progressive Cummins to sponsor a modification of Norris's resolution that undermined its most important provisions. Escalating the conflict, Borah announced to the press that the progressives would "align themselves with the Democrats" if Senators Penrose and Warren were given these seats. These progressives received no important committee assignments. *New York Times*, November 16, 1918. See also Lowitt, *George W. Norris*, 222−25.

68. See George and George, *Woodrow Wilson*, and Cuff, *War Industries Board*, 243.

69. Lowitt, *George W. Norris*, 59−60.

70. See Johnson, *National Party Platforms*, 231.

71. Goldstein, *Political Repression*, 123. See also Shapiro, "Great War and Reform," 323.

72. See Samuel Gompers, "America's Labor Convention in War Time," *American*

*Federationist* 25 (1918): 29–39; Dubofsky, *Industrialism and the American Worker*, 124; and Conner, *National War Labor Board*, ix.

73. See Goldstein, *Political Repression*, 122–24. See also Taft, *American Federation of Labor*, 362.

74. Wehle, "War Labor Policies," 329. To appease the business community, the board also upheld the "open shop" (antiunion shop) where it already existed and followed local customs for work conditions in all of its rulings. See also Preston, *Aliens and Dissenters*.

75. Conference in office of President Gompers, May 27, 1921, AFL Papers, State Historical Society of Wisconsin.

76. President Wilson appointed Frank B. Walsh and William Howard Taft to co-chair the National War Labor Board. Taft served as the general counsel for the board. Wilson appointed his son-in-law William G. McAdoo to serve as the director general of the Railroad Administration. McAdoo Papers, Library of Congress. See Conner, *National War Labor Board*, 18–34; Dubofsky, "Abortive Reform"; and Boemke, "Wilson Administration."

77. See Goldstein, *Political Repression*, 122.

78. Grant, *Bernard M. Baruch*, 145, 169.

79. See Windmuller, *Labor Relations in the Netherlands*; Markovits, *Politics of West German Trade Unions*; and Lehmbruch and Schmitter, "Introduction," 1–28.

80. Wehle, "War Labor Policies," 331.

81. See Willard, "Railroads on a Sound Basis," 137, and Johnson, "Problem of Railroad Control," 355.

82. Wolf, *Railroad Labor Board*, 49.

83. Wehle, "War Labor Policies," 331.

84. "Labor Conditions during Federal Control," *Railway Age* 66 (1919): 181–86.

85. See Zieger, "From Antagonism to Accord," 25–28, and Troy, "Labor Representation on American Railways," 295–300.

86. Zakson, "Railway Labor Legislation," 340–46.

87. Troy, "Labor Representation on American Railways," 295–300.

88. See Wolf, *Railroad Labor Board*, for membership figures, 58.

89. Dubofsky, *Industrialism and the American Worker*, 129.

90. Conference in office of Samuel Gompers, May 27, 1921.

91. See Bernstein, *The Lean Years*.

92. Goldstein, *Political Repression*, 123.

93. Ibid., 134.

94. The bituminous coal strike involved 435,000 workers, the shopmen's strike involved 250,000 workers, and the steel strike had 367,000 workers disputing their management. In comparison with these large strikes between 1916 and 1918, only two such large strikes occurred. Industrial strife also increased dramatically in 1918 and 1919; 4 million workers participated in strikes. *Monthly Labor Review* 10 (1920): 199–207. See also "Railroad Strikes and High Cost of Living," *Iron Age*, May 20, 1920, 1455.

95. See "Features of Railroad, Coal, and Steel Strikes," *Iron Age*, May 20, 1920, 1455.

96. "The General Strike," memorandum written by McGrady of the Legislative

Committee, n.d., and "Statement by President Gompers to William F. Spencer and Mr. J. J. Forrester, Fraternal Delegates from the American Federation of Labor to the British Trades Union Congress," June 7, 1921, AFL Papers, State Historical Society of Wisconsin; Schriftgiesser, *This Was Normalcy*; Gilfond, *Rise of Saint Calvin*; and "Coolidge's Police Strike Record," *New Republic*, September 19, 1923, 103.

97. See Greenbaum, *Fighting Progressive*, and Ashby, *The Spearless Leader*, 86.

98. See Montgomery, *Worker's Control in America*, 113–38.

99. Moore, "Directions of Thought," 53.

100. Zieger, "From Hostility to Moderation," 25–26.

101. Wilson's attorney general, Mitchell Palmer, had federal agents arrest five thousand to ten thousand people in thirty cities on January 2, 1920. See Goldstein, *Political Repression*, 149; Leuchtenburg, *Perils of Prosperity*, 66–83; Murray, *Red Scare*; Robertson, *No Third Choice*; Ashby, *The Spearless Leader*; Livermore, *Politics Is Adjourned*; Feinman, *Twilight of Progressivism*; and Mayer, *Republican Party*.

102. Buenker, *Urban Liberalism and Progressive Reform*, 83–85.

103. Murray, *Red Scare*.

104. Lincoln Colcord, "The Administration Adrift," *Nation*, November 15, 1919, 635.

105. Neither Wilson nor members of his administration were willing to fight for an extension of the wartime Railroad Administration. The president, moreover, did not develop a postwar labor policy. McAdoo to Frederic C. Howe, December 15, 1919, McAdoo Papers, Library of Congress; Wolf, *Railroad Labor Board*, 79.

106. *Congressional Record*, 65th Cong., 2d sess., 1918, 56, pt. 11:11532.

107. Samuel Gompers, "The President's Message," *American Federationist* 28 (1920): 63.

108. See *Congressional Record*, 66th Cong., 1st sess., 1919, 58, pt. 6:5359–62. The Senate Committee on Interstate Commerce met from January 3 until February 21, 1919, to hold hearings about extending federal control and alternative plans.

109. See Robertson, *No Third Choice*, 200.

110. The railroad brotherhoods and Plumb also started an "educational campaign" for the public about nationalization. They founded a journal, called *Railroad Democracy* (later changed to *Labor*). Untitled memorandum, August 30, 1919; "Memorandum to the Railroad Committee of the Executive Council of the American Federation of Labor," c. 1919, AFL Papers, State Historical Society of Wisconsin. See also *Congressional Record*, 66th Cong., 1st sess., 1919, 58, pt. 6:3586, and "Railroad Labor Reaching for the Throttle," *Literary Digest*, August 16, 1919, 9–11.

111. See Shepherd, "Federal Railway Labor Policy," 183; "Railroad Labor Reaching for the Throttle," *Literary Digest*, August 16, 1919, 10; *American Labor Yearbook, 1919–1920*, vol. 4 (New York: Rand School of Social Science, 1920), 276–80; "Strikes," *Nation*, December 6, 1919, 707; American Federation of Labor, Convention, *Proceedings* 39 (1919): 328–29; "Railroad Hearings before Senate Committee," *Railway Age* 66 (1919): 397.

112. Brecher, *Strike!*, 104–5.

113. McAdoo to Walter D. Hines, February 24, 1920, Wilson Papers, Historical Society of Pennsylvania.

114. Robertson, *No Third Choice*, 110–35.

115. Greenbaum, *Fighting Progressive*, 2–3.

116. See Ashby, *The Spearless Leader*, 85–86.

117. Robertson, *No Third Choice*, 251–52.

118. Norris and LaFollette suffered the consequences of their "disloyalty" when the old guard excluded them from any important committee seats in the new Republican Senate. McAdoo to Frederic C. Howe, December 15, 1919, McAdoo Papers, Library of Congress; Wolf, *Railroad Labor Board*, 79; and Shepherd, "Federal Railway Labor Policy," 188; Robertson, *No Third Choice*, 176–77; "Railroad Labor Organizes Co-operative Commission," *Railway Age* 68 (1920): 255.

119. Edward B. Almon (D.-Ala.) said this during the legislative date in the House. *Congressional Record*, 66th Cong., 2d sess., 1919, 58, pt. 9:8514.

120. Ibid., 8511.

121. See Cooper, *Warrior and the Priest*, xii.

122. Wilson's attempts could be described as halfhearted, since he openly recognized labor legislation as inconsistent with his New Freedom measures, which were designed to restore fair market relations. Yet Wilson also believed that the protectionist labor policy established during the New Freedom years did not endanger these fair market relations. Sklar, *Corporate Reconstruction*, 408, 412.

123. Esch worked on a substitute bill (H.R. 10453) with Republicans Edward L. Hamilton (Michigan) and Samuel E. Winslow (Massachusetts) as well as Democrats Alben W. Barkley (Kentucky) and Thetus Sims (Tennessee). *Congressional Record*, 66th Cong., 1st sess., 1919, 58, pt. 5:4594.

124. J. J. Esch to David Moore, August 9, 1919, and J. J. Esch to William P. Welsh, August 11, 1919, Esch Papers, State Historical Society of Wisconsin.

125. J. J. Esch to David Moore, August 9, 1919, and J. J. Esch to William P. Welsh, August 11, 1919. Esch, for instance, opposed government ownership of the railroads, and yet he advocated stronger powers for the ICC to encourage industrial stability.

126. *Congressional Record*, 66th Cong., 1st sess., 1919, 58, pt. 5:8481.

127. A board would be composed of thirty members—fifteen to be appointed by the railroad brotherhoods and the shopmen and fifteen by the Association of Railway Executives (ARE), the American Railway Express Company, and Pullman Carlines. The ARE was to appoint fifteen members, whereas these last two groups, representing fewer employers, were to each appoint one representative. When the railroad carriers and union representatives brought a labor dispute involving wages, hours, or work conditions to this board, a two-thirds vote of the board's members would be required to settle the dispute. In case of deadlock, a state-controlled tripartite Appeals Board of nine members would hear the dispute. See MacVeagh, *The Transportation Act*, 150–51.

128. Ibid. The permanent board had additional powers to investigate and publish its findings.

129. Sigmund, "Federal Laws Concerning Railroad Labor Disputes," 101–19.

130. Ibid.

131. *Congressional Record*, 66th Cong., 1st sess., 1919, 58, pt. 8:8481.

132. Esch studied the effectiveness of compulsory arbitration in France, Germany, and Italy. He concluded that it would not work even if "it should be enacted into law." *Congressional Record*, 66th Cong., 2d sess., 1919, 58, pt. 5:3270.

133. See *Congressional Record*, 66th Cong., 2d sess., 1920, 59, pt. 4:3304–8, for statements contrasting Representative Sidney Anderson's amendment to the final version of the Transportation Act.

134. Ibid., 66th Cong., 1st sess., 1919, 58, pt. 8:8483–85.
135. Ibid., 8483.
136. Ibid., 8481.
137. Ibid., 8518.
138. Ibid.
139. Ibid.
140. Ibid.
141. Ibid., 8483.
142. Ibid., 8503.
143. Ibid.
144. Ibid.
145. Ibid., 8511.
146. Ibid., 8449.
147. Ibid., 8481.
148. Ibid., 8506.
149. Ibid., 8507.
150. Ibid, 8479–80, 8520–21, 8989–90. When the Esch bill first arrived on the House floor for discussion, a conservative Republican faction tried to pass an amendment implementing compulsory arbitration and ban labor unions from striking the railroads. Republican J. Stanley Webster offered the amendment to protect the public with a system of compulsory arbitration and a ban against strikes and lockouts. As Esch predicted, the House did not have the votes to pass more "drastic" legislation. The amendment failed by a vote of 203 to 189. A coalition of progressive Republicans and Democrats defeated the Webster amendment.
151. The Speaker lost the power to appoint committee members, chair the omnipotent Rules Committee, and control all legislative considerations that hit the House floor.
152. Evidence of Anderson's power materialized several months later when he was placed, as the token progressive Republican, on the all-powerful Steering Committee. Anderson would not have received this seat unless the old guard felt threatened by his leadership abilities.
153. Although Cummins still thought of himself as progressive, "when he died he was thought of by many as a conservative." See Harrington, "Political Ideas of Albert B. Cummins," 392. *Congressional Record*, 66th Cong., 1st sess., 1919, 58, pt. 5:4594. The Cummins bill (S.R. 2906) was drafted with the help of Republican senators Miles Poindexter (Washington) and Frank B. Kellogg (Minnesota) as well as Democrat senators Atlee Pomerene (Ohio) and Joseph T. Robinson (Arkansas).
154. Before entering the Senate, Cummins had been a progressive governor in Iowa. He helped institute the direct primary, passed a law abolishing corporate campaign contributions, and considered himself an enemy of the railroad monopolies. Yet after World War I, Cummins's idea of progressivism changed. He adopted a more conciliatory view of the large-scale corporation as an advocate of the scientific management. See Kerr, *American Railroad Politics*, 144.
155. See Ernst, "Labor Exemption," 1169–70, for an enlightening explanation of the complex formulation and passage of the labor relations provisions in the Clayton Act.

156. See Harrington, "Political Ideas of Albert B. Cummins," 392.

157. Jacoby, *Employing Bureaucracy*, 46 – 47, 101.

158. The two agencies would guarantee the railroad a minimum income to ensure that the national railroad services remained in tact, and excessive earnings from the stronger roads would then be used to support the weaker roads. Kerr, *American Railroad Politics*, 143 – 49.

159. First, a board composed of representatives for the railroad executives and the railroad workers was to arbitrate disputes about wages and working conditions. Both the national railroad unions and the railroad workers' nonunion representatives would suggest who should be appointed to sit on this board, but the public transportation board would then make appointments. The national railroad unions had no guarantee that their representatives would be appointed to the board of wages and working conditions. Second, regional bipartisan adjustment boards would resolve all other labor disputes. See Sigmund, "Federal Laws Concerning Railroad Labor Disputes," 105 – 18, and Kerr, *American Railroad Politics*, 148.

160. *Congressional Record*, 66th Cong., 1st sess., 1919, 58, pt. 5: 5497 – 99.

161. Ibid.

162. Ibid.

163. "Cummins versus Plumb," *Nation*, September 13, 1919, 361.

164. See "The Cummins Bill," *New Republic*, September 24, 1919, 220 – 21. See also Zieger, *Republicans and Labor*, 51, and Lowitt, *George W. Norris*, 222 – 23. Two or more persons could not "enter into any combination or agreement with the intent substantially to hinder, restrain, or prevent the operation of trains." Senator Oscar Underwood (Alabama) and Joseph T. Robinson (Arkansas) were the sponsors of the antistrike provision of the Cummins bill. See *Congressional Record*, 66th Cong., 1st sess., 1919, 58, pt. 5:4828 – 33. Cummins also made it illegal for any person knowingly and with like intent to "aid, abet, counsel, command, induce or procure the commission or performance of such an act."

165. *Congressional Record*, 66th Cong., 1st sess., 1919, 59, pt. 5:4599.

166. *Congressional Record*, 66th Cong., 2d sess., 1920, 59 pt. 1:896.

167. When Stanley proposed a second amendment to abolish this provision, it also met defeat with a vote of 39 to 24. In addition, Senator Medill McCormick of Illinois, a moderate progressive, put forth a compromise provision that would have substituted a sixty-day "cooling off" period for the ban on strikes and lockouts. Again, this amendment failed to pass the Senate, though with a closer vote of 33 to 30. Cummins defended his bill from any changes that would have protected organized labor as the wartime labor policy had done. *Congressional Record*, 66th Cong., 2d sess., 1920, 59, pt. 1:896; *Congressional Record*, 66th Cong., 1st sess., 1919, 58, pt. 5:4599; "Railroad Hearings before Senate Committee," 398.

168. "Esch-Cummins Bill Passed by Senate and House," *Railway Age* 68 (1920): 621; "Senator Harding on Anti-strike Bill," *Railway Age* 68 (1920): 166.

169. Cummins did not believe that the railroad workers had a right to quit at any time. He insisted that the prohibition of strikes would only prevent conspiracies plotting a strike rather than the individual's actual right to leave his employment. See Kerr, *American Railroad Politics*, 148.

170. Ten progressive Republicans and three regular Republicans voted for the

McCormick amendment, as opposed to only five Republicans who voted for the first and the second Stanley amendments to erase the antistrike provision from the bill.

171. *Congressional Record*, 66th Cong., 1st sess., 1919, pt. 5:4598.

172. Ibid.

173. Spence purported that the Cummins bill covered the estimated 425,000 unorganized workers. Ibid., pt. 1:545.

174. A minority report written by the progressive Republican senator Robert M. LaFollette of the Interstate Commerce Committee had also been submitted to the Senate to contest the Cummins bill. The progressive Democratic senator David T. Walsh (Massachusetts) was another member of the Interstate Commerce Commission who opposed the Cummins bill. LaFollette and Walsh attempted to delete the antistrike clause and the Cummins bill in its entirety. The Cummins bill was passed on December 20, 1919, by a vote of 46 to 30. Republican senator Medill McCormick (Illinois) also tried to pass an amendment to the Cummins bill to strengthen the antistrike provision and provide for compulsory arbitration. He modeled his amendment after the Canadian Disputes Act, which provided a system of compulsory arbitration. This amendment also failed to pass by a vote of 33 to 30. See *Congressional Record*, 66th Cong., 2d sess., 1920, 59, pt. 1:809−11, 821, 896−98. *Congressional Record*, 66th Cong., 1st sess., 1919, 58, pt. 4:3349−50; "Committees to Prepare for Return of Roads," *Railway Age* 68 (1920): 241.

175. Robertson, *No Third Choice*, 166.

176. *Congressional Record*, 66th Cong., 1st sess., 1919, 58, pt. 5:4597.

177. Cummins, Poindexter, Kellogg, Pomerene, and Robinson were the Senate representatives; Esch, Hamilton, Winslow, Sims, and Barkley were the House representatives for the Conference Committee. The committee met from January 2 until February 18, 1920. See "Federal Control of Railroads," *House Conference Report No. 650*, 66th Cong., 2d sess., 1920, 59, pt. 1:6−21, 58−61.

178. Johnson, "Problem of Railroad Control," 365.

179. See "Anti-Strike Bill Passed by Senate," *Railway Age* 69 (1920): 1127.

180. *Congressional Record*, 69th Cong., 1st sess., 1926, 67, pt. 8:8817, and *Congressional Record*, 66th Cong., 2d sess., 1928, 59, pt. 4:3328.

181. Ibid.

182. Ibid., 3280.

183. Willard, "Transportation Act of 1920," 84.

184. Ibid.

185. "New System of Wage Adjustment for Railways," *Monthly Labor Review* 10 (1920): 46−47.

186. *Congressional Record*, 66th Cong., 2d sess., 1920, 59, pt. 4:3333.

187. "Subordinate officials" would be designated to represent nonunion employees. See Wolf, *Railroad Labor Board*, 89, and MacVeagh, *The Transportation Act*, 148−49.

188. According to Zieger, "the establishment of the new Board represented a sharp rebuke to the rail unions." Zieger, "From Hostility to Moderation," 27.

189. The compromise version of the bill became law on March 20, 1920. It passed both chambers of Congress with a clear Republican majority and little debate. What little debate was generated in both the Senate and the House centered simply on defending the compromises made by the conferees. The House voted 250 to 150 (204 Republicans for vs. 125 Democrats against the bill). The Senate passed the bill by a vote

of 47 to 17 (32 Republicans for vs. 14 Democrats against the bill). See *Congressional Record*, 66th Cong., 2d sess., 1920, 59, pt. 4:3316, for when the bill passed the House, and *Congressional Record*, 66th Cong., 2d sess., 1920, 59, pt. 4:3272–77.

190. Labor relations machinery based on contractualism, as the legal historian Tamar Lothian describes, contains six components. First, such a policy defines organized labor as a private interest group. No special privileges or rights are given to the union or any other private group negotiating collective bargaining. As Lothian explains, the "government facilitates collective self-organization by guaranteeing the right to organize and granting legal recognition to unions as agents for their membership group." Second, contractualism imposes few restrictions on the number of private interest groups or unions allowed to negotiate collective trade agreements. Third, a contractualist labor policy does not direct what type of provisions should be included in these trade agreements. The two parties involved, the collective bargaining agent and employers, remain unfettered by policy constraints about wage rates and working conditions—they retain their fundamental freedom to contract. In other words, as Lothian concludes the "model of private exchange reigns supreme." Fourth, contractualism allows external forces, such as worker militancy or the tide of the economy, to influence the trade agreement negotiation process. No ban on strikes, for instance, would be implemented as part of an industrial relations policy. Fifth, while the contractualist model of labor relations would help private interest groups and employers resolve disputes, it cannot be compulsory. Finally, this model of labor-management relations is confined to the prevention and resolution of labor disputes. Neither the business community nor organized labor is invited to participate in the state's economic policymaking process. See Lothian, "Political Consequences of Labor Law Regimes," 1003–8.

191. See Dubofsky, *Industrialism and the American Worker*, 124, and Conner, *National War Labor Board*, ix.

192. Partial minutes concerning the 1920 presidential campaign and "Labor's Political Campaign," press release, February 9, 1920; Gompers to President Warren G. Harding, August 19, 1921, AFL Papers, State Historical Society of Wisconsin.

193. See "Reconstruction Program of the American Federation of Labor," *Monthly Labor Review* 8 (1919): 63.

194. "The 'Return' of the Railroads," *New Republic*, March 3, 1920, 8.

195. "Financial Situation," *Commercial and Financial Chronicle*, February 28, 1920, 792. See also George A. Anderson, "Our Railroad Problem," *Atlantic Monthly* 124 (1919): 850.

196. George Soule, "Unions and the Public," *Atlantic Monthly* 133 (1924): 213; Slichter, "Current Labor Policies," 397; Schwab, "Capital and Labor," 158; Elbert H. Gary, "The Menace of the Closed Shop," *American Industries* 20 (1920): 31–32.

197. See "Labor Principles of the National Association of Manufacturers," *Monthly Labor Review* 11 (1920): 39.

## Chapter 5

1. For the conventional position that the Railroad Labor Board was a temporary measure and that the Railway Labor Act constituted a return to voluntarism, see Zakson, "Railway Labor Legislation."

2. *Pennsylvania R. Co. v. United States Railroad Labor Board*, 261 U.S. 72 (1922).

3. Memorandum entitled "Minutes of conference held in the Executive Council Chamber of the American Federation of Labor," January 15, 1920, AFL Papers, State Historical Society of Wisconsin.

4. "Conference with Representatives of the Department: A.F. of L." June 5, 1921, AFL Papers, State Historical Society of Wisconsin.

5. Arnesen, "'Like Banquo's Ghost, It Will Not Down.'"

6. See Zieger, "From Antagonism to Accord," 25–28, and Troy, "Labor Representation on American Railways," 295–300.

7. When the four brotherhoods first emerged, they replicated the great "amalgamated" unions that formed in England in the 1850s and 1860s. Perlman, *History of Trade Unionism*, 181.

8. For this reason, the brotherhoods offered a conciliatory model of collective bargaining that stressed mutual insurance and benefits and discouraged the use of strikes. Despite their trepidation about strikes, a series of bloody strikes from the 1870s through the 1890s, culminating with the Pullman strike, helped transform the brotherhoods into labor organizations that resembled other unions. The Sherman Act precipitated another significant transformation. Witnesses to the Pullman strike, which had been instigated by the American Railway Union (ARU), an industrial union led by the Socialist Eugene Debs, the brotherhoods realized that the state could bolster or break a union. See Salvatore, *Eugene V. Debs*, 88–146. By the end of 1894, the federal government incarcerated Debs, and the ARU folded. The Pullman strike underscored the power of the state in labor-management relations and induced the brotherhoods to seek political solutions to resolve industrial conflicts. Stromquist, *Generation of Boomers*, 49, 97–99.

9. In 1906, Congress passed the Mann-Elkins Act, for instance, tightening railroad regulation. Stromquist, *Generation of Boomers*, 182.

10. Link, *Woodrow Wilson and the Progressive Era*, 236–37; Zakson, "Railway Labor Legislation," 335–38; and Kerr, "Decision for Federal Control," 550.

11. See Zieger, *Republicans and Labor*, 24, 118. Zieger writes that the operating and nonoperating unions, for instance, cooperated to the extent that they lobbied for the Plumb Plan and published *Labor*, a journal about railroad workers edited by Edward Keating after World War I.

12. Perlman, *History of Trade Unionism*, 259.

13. Zieger, *Republicans and Labor*, 11.

14. Davis, "1922 Railroad Shopmen's Strike," 113.

15. Perlman, *History of Trade Unionism*, 185–86.

16. Hines, *War History*, 7, and Zakson, "Railway Labor Legislation," 341.

17. Kaufmann, *Collective Bargaining*, 57.

18. "Labor Head Criticizes Railroad Administration," *Railway Age* 69 (1920): 1119.

19. Ibid.

20. While the Democratic administration alone determined who represented the public on the Railroad Labor Board, the Transportation Act provided that the railroad executives and workers nominate who could represent their interests. The Transportation Act, however, made no mention of which group of employers and employees had authority to make these nominations. Yet it did provide the Interstate Commerce Commission, not the president, with the power to "prescribe" nomination rules,

regulations, and procedures. Rushed by the thirty-day deadline, the ICC handed the nomination privileges for employer representatives directly over to the Association of Railway Executives, the primary railroad executive association and the national railroad unions. More than 90 percent of the railroad employers, after all, belonged to this trade association. Since 90 percent of the railroad employees belonged to the national railroad unions, the ICC reasoned, they could nominate who should become the Labor Board members. Categorizing all the railroad employees into four groups, the ICC asked only the first three groups, which belonged to the national railroad unions, for nominees. The four brotherhoods, the shopcrafts unions, and the nonoperating unions each submitted two nominations. The ICC excluded the fourth group, the so-called subordinate officials, who were not represented by national unions, from this nomination process. Before the fourth category of workers could make nominations, the ICC decided, hearings would determine who belonged in this category. The ICC recognized that the progressive and old guard Republicans had long argued about this fourth category during the House and Senate floor debates. The progressives protested its very creation, believing that their old guard colleagues developed it only to undermine railroad unionization. By contrast, the old guard insisted that if the Railroad Labor Board was equitable, the nonunion employees would be given representation, despite their minority status. See Wolf, *Railroad Labor Board*, 96–100; "New Epoch for American Railways," *Current History* 12 (1920): 37; Sharfman, *Interstate Commerce Commission*; and Fuess, *Joseph B. Eastman*, 89–90, 107–8.

21. Wolf, *Railroad Labor Board*, 98.

22. Ibid., 98–99.

23. Ibid. Hanger headed the Railroad Administration Division of Labor. Before serving on this wartime agency, moreover, he had been the assistant commissioner on the Board of Mediation and Conciliation in 1913 and the chief statistician at the Bureau of Labor Statistics.

24. Ibid., 99. The employer member Park also had helped out the Railroad Administration during the war by managing the Chicago–Great Western Railroad.

25. "Remarks of Samuel Gompers before Conference of the Executives of the Railroad Organizations Affiliated with the A.F. of L. and the Four Brotherhoods," February 10, 1920, Conferences File, AFL Papers, State Historical Society of Wisconsin; "Returning the Railroads," *Current History* 11 (1920): 412; "The Public's Representation on the Labor Board," *Railway Age* 70 (1921): 778.

26. On March 10, the former director of the Railroad Administration, Walter D. Hines, opened this conference with a letter from Wilson, urging the railroad executives and union leaders to negotiate a new wage settlement. "Conference with Representatives of the Railway Department of the A.F. of L.," June 5, 1921, AFL Papers, State Historical Society of Wisconsin, and "The Public's Representation on the Labor Board," 777.

27. Wolf, *Railroad Labor Board*, 103–5.

28. Ibid.

29. Although the Railroad Labor Board did not intervene during the strike, its first decisions involved this strike as well as the underlying motivation for the strike, the employees' year-and-a-half-old demand for an increase in wages to compensate for the high cost of living. See Shepherd, "Federal Railway Labor Policy," 218.

30. *Congressional Record*, 66th Cong., 1st sess., 1919, 59, pt. 5:5335–36.

31. The decision was quoted from "Railroad Labor Board Will Not Consider Demands Made by Men on Strike," *Commercial and Financial Chronicle* 110 (1920): 1714.

32. Effective on May 1, 1920, railroad workers received increases varying from 12.5 percent for supervisory personnel to 26.2 percent for stationary engineers and firemen. Wolf, *Railroad Labor Board*, 129; "The Situation before the Labor Board," *Commercial and Financial Chronicle* 110 (1920): 1792−93; "The Railroad Wage Cut," *Literary Digest*, March 26, 1921, 10−11; *Congressional Record*, 67th Cong., 2d sess., 1922, 62, pt. 2: 1554−56.

33. Hoover to Harding, July 2, 1921, Commerce Papers, Railroads: Problems; "How the Railroads Propose to Bring About a Reduction in Rates," reprint from Association of Railway Executives in Commerce Papers, n.d., Railroads, Rates File, Hoover Papers, Herbert Hoover Presidential Library, West Branch, Iowa.

34. The ARE also challenged the standardization of wages, hours, and work conditions instituted by these agreements. Wage rates and working conditions should vary from region to region, the railroad executives maintained, in accordance with the cost of living, which varied across the country. S. Davies Warfield Statement, February 6, 1922, Hoover Papers, Herbert Hoover Presidential Library, West Branch, Iowa; J. R. Smaltze to Harding, July 11, 1921; Byers to Harding, July 8, 1921; J. C. Blair to Harding, August 3, 1921, Harding Papers, Library of Congress (microfilm, Herbert Hoover Presidential Library); Ralph Budd to Coolidge, October 6, 1923, Coolidge Papers, Library of Congress (microfilm, Herbert Hoover Presidential Library).

35. Wolf, *Railroad Labor Board*, 142.

36. Ibid., 143. On February 6, he sent a telegram to union leaders and the ARE explaining that the ICC and the Railroad Labor Board, not his administration, had the authority to resolve it.

37. Executive Council Meeting, statement by President Samuel Gompers about Railroads, Cincinnati, Ohio, May 9, 1921, AFL Papers, State Historical Society of Wisconsin.

38. To Chief Executives of Standard Recognized Railroad Labor Organizations from Samuel Gompers, December 21, 1921, AFL Papers, State Historical Society of Wisconsin, and Fuess, *Joseph B. Eastman*, 108. The newly appointed Interstate Commerce Commission, moreover, voiced no objections about McMenimen's appointment. In contrast to how the ICC had behaved one year earlier when Wilson appointed the first Railroad Labor Board members, the new ICC gave Harding few directions about how to make his appointments. He was given more autonomy than his Democratic predecessor, in part, because of the new composition of the ICC. Harding had appointed John J. Esch, the coauthor of the Esch-Cummins Transportation Act, to the ICC, who had only grudgingly supported bipartisan representation. When the Transportation Act had been passed, Esch supported the antistrike provisions and the idea of compulsory arbitration, though he doubted the feasibility of putting these ideas into practice.

39. Hooper, *The Unwanted Boy*; Hooper, "Labor, Railroads, and the Public," 15−18.

40. Ben W. Hooper to Warren G. Harding, October 24, 1921, Harding Papers, Library of Congress (microfilm, Herbert Hoover Presidential Library).

41. "Are the Railroads Wasting $1,000,000,000 a Year?" *Literary Digest*, May 7,

1921, 5 –7; "The Public's Representation on the Labor Board," *Railway Age* 70 (1921): 777 – 78.

42. Even after World War I, the railroads recognized the brotherhoods, conceding "There can be no question in the mind of any fair-minded student that the brotherhoods have been of great usefulness." Hines, *War History*, 175 – 80; A. C. Davis, "The Principles Underlying the Present Railway Situation," *Railway Age* 71 (1921): 675.

43. "W. G. McAdoo Defends Railroad Administration," *Railway Age* 72 (1922): 371 –74; "Labor Conditions during Federal Control," *Railway Age* 66 (1919): 181 – 86.

44. "Government Control of Railroad Labor," *Railway Age* 66 (1919): 182.

45. Sakolski, "Practical Tests," 382.

46. Jewell, "The Railway Strike," 204.

47. Harding to Herbert Hoover, July 15, 1921, Commerce Papers, President Harding, Hoover Papers, Herbert Hoover Presidential Library, West Branch, Iowa.

48. Davis, "Principles Underlying the Present Railway Situation," 676.

49. Only A. O. Wharton, the former president of the Railroad Employees Department in the AFL and one of the three employee representatives on the board, voted against terminating the national agreements. U.S. Railroad Labor Board, Decision 119, April 14, 1921, addendum no. 2, 87 – 96, 535 – 37. Wharton stated in Decision 222 (another decision defining work conditions for the Federal Shop Crafts employees) that the board did not take into consideration that some of the national agreements dated from before the war and should therefore not be terminated. See Wolf, *Railroad Labor Board*, 195 – 96.

50. American Federation of Labor, Convention, *Proceedings* 41 (1921): 70.

51. Bert Jewell, president, Railway Employees Department, American Federation of Labor; J. F. Anderson, vice president, International Association of Machinists; Edward Tegtmeyer, vice president, Brotherhood of Blacksmiths, Drop Forgers, and Helpers of America; William Atkinson, assistant president, International Brotherhood of Boilermakers, Iron Shipbuilders, and Helpers of America; J. W. Burns, representing Amalgamated Sheet Metal Workers International Alliance; Edward J. Evans, representing International Brotherhood of Electrical Workers; and Martin F. Ryan, general president, Brotherhood Railway Carmen of America, to Harding, April 7, 1921, Harding Papers, Library of Congress (microfilm, Herbert Hoover Presidential Library).

52. See *Pennsylvania R. Co. v. United States Railroad Labor Board*. See also Dixon, "Functions and Policies," 25.

53. Dixon, "Functions and Policies," 25.

54. Jewell, "The Railway Strike," 202 –7.

55. Supposedly, the national adjustment boards were biased toward organized labor. "Section 301 of the Esch-Cummins Transportation Act," *New Republic*, December 15, 1920, 56. In an annual dinner for railroad executives, John A. Droege further stated that national boards of adjustment presupposed the renegotiation of national agreements. The railroad executives would therefore only meet representatives of the railroad workers in pro forma conferences outside the adjustment boards' jurisdiction just to satisfy the Railroad Labor Board's requirement.

56. Ibid.

57. Dixon, "Functions and Policies," 25.

58. See Wolf, *Railroad Labor Board*, 166 – 67.

59. "Decisions of the Railroad Labor Board, the Pennsylvania Railroad Cases," *Labor Monthly Review* 17 (1923): 122–29.

60. "Informal Memorandum upon the Shopmen's Strike in the Pennsylvania System," n.d., Commerce Papers, Railroads, Strikes; Lawrence G. Brooks to Hoover, July 26, 1922, both in Hoover Papers, Herbert Hoover Presidential Library, West Branch, Iowa. See Hines, *War History*, 175–77.

61. Wolf, *Railroad Labor Board*, 296.

62. Ibid., 301.

63. Ibid.

64. Heiserman, "Labor Policies of the Transportation Act," 30.

65. Wolf, *Railroad Labor Board*, 301.

66. Ibid., 303.

67. Ibid., 302.

68. Hooper to Harding, July 30, 1921, Harding Papers, Library of Congress (microfilm, Herbert Hoover Presidential Library).

69. Quoted from Wolf, *Railroad Labor Board*, 310.

70. Heiserman, "Labor Policies of the Transportation Act," 32.

71. Ibid.

72. The chair of the board, Barton notified Attorney General Daughtery about the request for a delay. R. M. Barton to Daughtery, August 11, 1921; Hooper to Samuel Rhea, August 10, 1921, Harding Papers, Library of Congress (microfilm, Herbert Hoover Presidential Library).

73. R. M. Barton to Daughtery, August 11, 1921, and Hooper to Samuel Rea, August 10, 1921.

74. After the Pennsylvania Railroad executives sent the petition to the board, the System Federation issued its own complaint. N. P. Good, president of the System Federation, purported that the Pennsylvania Railroad coerced the employees into joining a company organization and also violated a rule against setting arbitrary rates of pay. Good issued a strike warning, and he insisted on prompt board action in his complaint. See Wolf, *Railroad Labor Board*, 295–329.

75. Dixon, "Functions and Policies of the Railroad Labor Board," 26.

76. Ibid.

77. *New York Times*, December 10, 1921.

78. Wolf, *Railroad Labor Board*, 307.

79. 287 Fed. 693 (1922); 282 Fed. 701 (1922). See also Dixon, "Functions and Policies of the Railroad Labor Board," 26.

80. "Power of United States Railroad Labor Board to Enforce Awards," *Monthly Labor Review* 15 (1922): 202.

81. Heiserman, "Labor Policies of the Transportation Act," 38.

82. *New York Times*, April 4, 1922.

83. Hunt, "Labor Policies of the Transportation Act," 54.

84. Ibid.

85. Ibid., 684.

86. Ibid.

87. Ibid., 55.

88. *New York Times*, November 21, 1922.

89. *New York Times*, July 22, 1922.

90. Memorandum by Blackborn Esterline, January 16, 1923, Harding Papers, Library of Congress (microfilm, Herbert Hoover Presidential Library).

91. "Informal Memorandum upon the Shopmen's Strike in the Pennsylvania System."

92. *Pennsylvania R. Co. v. United States Railroad Labor Board*; *Pennsylvania R. System and Allied Lines Federation No. 90 v. Pennsylvania R. Co.*, 267 U.S. 203 (1924).

93. *Pennsylvania R. Co. v. United States Railroad Labor Board*, 72.

94. Ibid., 82.

95. Ibid.

96. Ibid., 74.

97. Ibid., 84.

98. Ibid., 83.

99. Ibid., 83.

100. Ibid., 84.

101. Ibid., 85.

102. Ibid.

103. Ibid., 80.

104. *Washington Post*, February 20, 1923, clipping from the AFL Legislative Reference File, AFL Papers, State Historical Society of Wisconsin.

105. *Chas. Wolff Packing Co. v. Court of Industrial Relations of the State of Kansas*, 262 U.S. 522 (1922).

106. Green to C. H. Franck, July 27, 1925, AFL Papers, State Historical Society of Wisconsin.

107. Secretary of Labor Davis and Secretary of Treasury Andrew Mellon had also, at one time, tried to persuade Atterbury to follow the Railroad Labor Board decisions. W. L. McMenimen to E. T. Clark, February 19, 1925; James J. Davis to Coolidge, February 24, 1925; Davis to Harlan F. Stone, February 28, 1925; and E. T. Clark to James J. Davis, February 24, 1925, Coolidge Papers, Library of Congress (microfilm, Herbert Hoover Presidential Library). Davis also submitted the case to Attorney General Harlan F. Stone for review.

108. Wolf, *Railroad Labor Board*, 321.

109. Quoted from Wolf, *The Railroad Labor Board*, 322.

110. *New York Times*, May 16, 1922.

111. *Pennsylvania R. System and Allied Lines Federation No. 90 v. Pennsylvania R. Co.*, 217.

112. American Federation of Labor Information and Publicity Service, press release, February 20, 1923, AFL Papers, State Historical Society of Wisconsin.

113. *Congressional Record*, 69th Cong., 1st sess., 1926, 67, pt. 4:8974.

114. R. M. Barton to Harding, October 21, 1921, Harding Papers, Library of Congress (microfilm, Herbert Hoover Presidential Library).

115. *New York Times*, July 22, 1922, September 12, 1922, November 28, 1922.

116. The wage decreases varied from 6.3 percent for supervisory to 17.5 percent for maintenance of way and unskilled employees. Almost five hundred thousand workers lost the benefit of the wage increase granted in July 1920, one year later. See Wolf, *Railroad Labor Board*, 306; "How the Railroads Propose to Bring About a Reduction in Rates," reprint from the Association of Railway Executives; and Hoover to Harding, July 2, 1921.

117. The railroad brotherhoods and the Switchman's Union suggested meeting with the carriers for a conference to discuss the issue. The carriers declined the offer and prepared for a strike. At the same time, union members of five operating brotherhoods and the telegraphers' union voted to strike. Jewell, "The Railway Strike," 202–7.

118. Lowell Mellett, "Hoover Expected to Untangle Row over Railroads," *Portland Journal*, March 23, 1921; "Hoover to Help Save Railroads," *Seattle Washington Times*, March 11, 1921, Hoover Papers, Herbert Hoover Presidential Library, West Branch Iowa; Hoover to Harding, 2 July 1921. Herbert Hoover, secretary of commerce, let it be known that he was already prepared to undermine the strike by coordinating food and coal stockpiling. Harding to Hoover, October 24, 1921, Harding Papers, Library of Congress (microfilm, Herbert Hoover Presidential Library); "The Railroad Strike," *New Republic*, October 26, 1921, 228. See also "Are Rail Pay and Rates Blockading Good Times?" *Literary Digest*, October 29, 1921, 7. In the media, only the *New Republic* did not denounce the idea of a strike. "The Outcome of the Railway Dispute," *New Republic*, November 9, 1921, 310. Hoover to E. H. Outerbridge, chairman of the Port of New York Authority, October 25, 1921, Commerce Papers, Railroads: Strikes; "Breaking Strikes Not His Purpose, Declares Hoover," *Labor*, December 10, 1921, reprint found in Commerce Papers, *Labor*, Hoover Papers, Herbert Hoover Presidential Library, West Branch, Iowa.

119. See Shepherd, "Federal Railway Labor Policy," 231–32.

120. Hooper to Harding, October 24, 1921, Barton to Harding, October 21, 1921, Harding to Hooper, October 24, 1921, Harding Papers, Library of Congress (microfilm, Herbert Hoover Presidential Library); Willard to Hoover, October 29, 1921, Hoover Papers, Herbert Hoover Presidential Library, West Branch, Iowa; Hooper to Harding, October 29, 1921, Harding Papers, Library of Congress (microfilm, Herbert Hoover Presidential Library).

121. Hooper to Harding, October 29, 1921.

122. "President Gompers in attendance upon the Executive Council meeting discussing the railroad situation and the proposed strike of the Railroad trainmen and efforts put forth by President Gompers to endeavor to avert the strike, if possible." Gompers Statement, February 27, 1920, Conference File, AFL Papers, State Historical Society of Wisconsin. While the board had no official enforcement powers, the Republican administration could seek extra measures like the labor injunction to enforce its decision. Hooper to Harding, October 29, 1921; Harding to Hooper, October 24, 1921.

123. See Wolf, *Railroad Labor Board*, 302–3, 306. By a 6 to 3 majority, with the Labor Board members in dissent, the board granted this second wage decrease *and* suggested heretofore that wages be adjusted on a region-by-region basis. In a series of three decisions, the board reduced the wages of 1,380,000 workers. Most of these workers were part of the nonoperating railroad labor workforce. The operating railroad workers, represented by the four railway brotherhoods, were not affected by the decreases. First, Decision 1028 reduced the maintenance of way workers' wages beginning July 1, 1922. The 580,000 maintenance of way employees suffered wage decreases varying from 2.1 to 15.7 percent. Docket 1300, 3 *Railroad Labor Board* 383—1028. Second, Decision 1036 decreased the wages of 268,000 shop craft workers from 8.9 to 11.8 percent. Docket 1300, 3 *Railroad Labor Board* 423—1036. Third, Decision 1074 decreased the wages of the clerical staff, station forces, and stationary engine and boiler

room employees. Docket 1300, 3 *Railroad Labor Board* 486—1074. The wages of 174,000 apprentices, car cleaners, and helpers were reduced by 12.6 to 17.7 percent. See also "Reduction in Railway Wages," *New Republic*, June 7, 1922, 29; Shepherd, "Federal Railway Labor Policy," 241; "Will They Strike for an 'Economic Impossibility'?," *Railway Age* 72 (1922): 1713–14; "Why a Railroad Strike," *New Republic*, June 21, 1922, 90; and Wolf, *Railroad Labor Board*, 215–20.

124. Hooper to Harding, May 19, 1922, Harding Papers, Library of Congress (microfilm, Herbert Hoover Presidential Library).

125. Cuyler to B. M. Jewell, June 29, 1922; Cuyler to Harding, July 1, 1922 (Cuyler sent a copy of the letter to Jewell to Hoover); printed letter by Julius H. Barnes, president of the Chamber of Commerce, July 13, 1922, Hoover Papers, Herbert Hoover Presidential Library, West Branch, Iowa; "Power and Weakness of the Railway Labor Board," *Literary Digest*, July 15, 1922, 13; W. L. McMenimen to Harding, July 20, 1922, Harding Papers, Library of Congress (microfilm, Herbert Hoover Presidential Library). See also "Shopmen Begin First General Strike on July 1," *Railway Age* 73 (1922): 53–58.

126. "The Farm Bloc: A Peril or a Hope," *Literary Digest*, December 24, 1921, 10, and Hooper, "Strikes," *Saturday Evening Post*, October 14, 1922, 6–7.

127. Carter, "Effect of Federal Control."

128. The Railroad Labor Board handed down the "outlaw resolution" because it was controlled by antiunion members. The two new board members, Hooper and McMenimen, whom Harding appointed in 1921, publicly denounced the railroad unions' actions. Because of his activities during the Shopmen's strike of 1922, the railroad labor unions called McMenimen a "labor Judas . . . who was appointed by President Harding over the protest of organized labor." Quoted from Wolf, *Railroad Labor Board*, 376, from *Labor*, May 19, 1923; Jewell, "The Railway Strike," 202–7; Gompers to Jewell, July 21, 1922, AFL Papers, State Historical Society of Wisconsin. In April 1922, Harding had removed Judge Barton from the board's chairmanship and gave this position to Hooper—the most vocal antiunion member on the board. When the Shopmen walked out on strike, it was Hooper who introduced the "outlaw resolution." And when the board voted on this resolution, only Wharton and Phillips, the labor members, dissented.

129. Cuyler to B. M. Jewell, June 29, 1922, and Cuyler to Harding, July 1, 1922.

130. *New York Times*, July 22, 1922.

131. Ibid.

132. Chief Executives of Brotherhood of Locomotive Engineers, Brotherhood of Locomotive Firemen and Enginemen, Order of Railway Conductors, Brotherhood of Railroad Trainmen, International Switchman's Union of North America, Order of Railroad Telegraphers, United Brotherhood of Maintenance of Way Employees and Railway Shop Laborers, Brotherhood of Railroad Signalmen of American and American Train Dispatchers' Association to Harding, August 12, 1922, Harding Papers, Library of Congress (microfilm, Herbert Hoover Presidential Library).

133. *New York Times*, July 22, 1922.

134. Hooper to Harding, July 11, 1922, July 16, 1922, July 20, 1922, July 25, 1922, Harding Papers, Library of Congress (microfilm, Herbert Hoover Presidential Library).

135. Attorney General Harry D. Daughtery said, "We believe you should ad-

dress both sides to contention at once and not the Board." Daugherty to Harding, 6 August 1922, Harding Papers, Library of Congress (microfilm, Herbert Hoover Presidential Library).

136. "Text of President Harding's Suggestions for Ending Shopmen's Strike and the Reply by the Railway Executives," *Railway Age* 73 (1922): 245–53, and "Reply by Railway Executives to President Harding's Proposals for Railroad Strike Settlement—Seniority Proposal Rejected," *Commercial and Financial Chronicle* 115 (1922): 610–14.

137. See "President Harding's Second Plan," *Railway Age* 73 (1922): 275. See also commentary in the *Commercial and Financial Chronicle* 115 (1922): 720, for the reply of the ARE to the president's second plan; "President Proposes New Plan to Settle Strike," *Railway Age* 73 (1922): 279–85; and "President's Plan Rejected by Shop Crafts," *Railway Age* 73 (1922): 341–44.

138. General Conference Committee of Railroad Labor Unions to Harding, August 3, 1922; Harding to B. M. Jewell, August 7, 1922; Harding to T. DeWitt Cuyler, August 7, 1922; and press clipping of "President's Proposal for Ending Railroad Strike and Executives' Reply Rejecting Them," Hoover Papers, Herbert Hoover Presidential Library, West Branch, Iowa; To President Harding from the Presidents of the International Association of Machinists, the International Brotherhood of Electrical Workers, Brotherhood of Railroad Carmen, Brotherhood of Boilermakers, Iron Ship Builders and Helpers, International Brotherhood of Stationary Firemen and Oilers, International Brotherhood of Blacksmiths, Crop Forgers and Helpers, Railway Employees Department of the AFL, and the Amalgamated Sheet Metal Workers International Alliance, August 11, 1922, Harding Papers, Library of Congress (microfilm, Herbert Hoover Presidential Library).

139. Harding's secretary of commerce, Hoover received a number of letters from railroad executives and business associations to convince the president not to capitulate on the issue of seniority rights. Master Builders Association of Boston to Hoover, July 25, 1922, Rockford Manufacturers' and Shippers' Association, July 28, 1922, Hoover Papers, Herbert Hoover Presidential Library, West Branch, Iowa. The Shopmen declared, "Seniority was not and is not now an issue or a dispute in this strike." See also *New York Times*, July 22, 1922.

140. Harding was aware of the railroad managers' unwillingness to obey the decisions of the Railroad Labor Board in other situations. The *Nation* reported that "ninety-two railroads violated [the board's decisions] in 104 instances prior to July 1 with complete impunity." "Railroad Strike, Defeat or Victory," *Nation*, September 27, 1922, 297; and William H. Johnston, president of the International Association of Machinists, to Harding, July 12, 1922, Harding Papers, Library of Congress (microfilm, Herbert Hoover Presidential Library). Harding to Senator George Wharton Pepper, July 31, 1922; Harding to G. S. McElroy, August 7, 1922; and Fred Underwood, August 4, 8, 1922, Harding Papers, Library of Congress (microfilm, Herbert Hoover Presidential Library). In the last letters, Harding wrote, "The strike situation would be more easy to handle if the railroad managers had accepted the Board's decision with the same fidelity which they now seem to expect at the hands of the employees."

141. "Where Harding Stands," *New Republic*, August 9, 1922, 291–92.

142. While Hoover arranged informal negotiations between the railroad executives and organized labor, Daughtery prepared reports listing the number of illegal incidents that occurred during the strike as evidence that an equity court must interrupt

the strike. Shortly after Hoover's last attempt to secure negotiations had failed, Harding agreed to Daughtery's request for an injunction to restrain the strikers. Hoover met with Gompers. Telephone Conversation Minutes between B. M. Jewell and Gompers, August 29, 1922; Memorandum, August 30, 1922, AFL Papers, State Historical Society of Wisconsin. Daughtery called for federal troops to curb the violence of the strike and to ensure that the mail would be able to travel by rail. Daughtery to Harding, July 29, August 14, 16, 19, 1922, Harding Papers, Library of Congress (microfilm, Herbert Hoover Presidential Library). Daughtery also submitted a state-by-state digest of the strike situation. Daughtery to Harding, July 26, 1922, Harding to Daughtery, July 31, 1922, Harding Papers, Library of Congress (microfilm, Herbert Hoover Presidential Library). See also "The Strike Situation in the East," *Railway Age* 73 (1922): 103–4. See commentaries in the *Railway Age* 73 (1922): 452, 469.

143. "Administration Trying to Prevent Railroad Labor Conflict," *Railway Age* 72 (1922): 196.

144. See Zieger, "From Hostility to Moderation," 28. Daughtery was one of Harding's longest and closest political allies and served as his campaign manager. Daughtery viewed the strike as an extreme assault against the government. "Mr. Daughtery's Injunction," *New Republic*, November 1, 1922, 231; *Commercial and Financial Chronicle* 115 (1922): 1393.

145. "Government by Daughtery," *Nation*, September 13, 1922, 243.

146. Daughtery sent a copy of his closing remarks in the injunction proceeding to Harding, September 2, 1922; Harding congratulated Daughtery in a letter dated September 2, 1922, Harding Papers, Library of Congress (microfilm, Herbert Hoover Presidential Library). See also "U.S. Gets Blanket Injunction against Shopmen," *Railway Age* 73 (1922): 469–70, and "The Attitude of the Government," *Railway Age* 73 (1922): 470–72.

147. "Injunction against the Railroad Shopmen," *Monthly Labor Review* 15 (1922): 176–78, and "Government by Daughtery," 243.

148. "The Failure of Railroad Arbitration," *New Republic*, September 20, 1922, 86–87; Memorandum, September 9, 1922; Gompers to F. W. Prather, September 19, 1922; Conference between Samuel Gompers and Representatives of the Press, September 1, 1922; Gompers to Honorable Anthony J. Griffin, August 25, 1922; Gompers to F. W. Prather, September 19, 1922, AFL Papers, State Historical Society of Wisconsin. A number of labor unions sent letters of objection to President Harding. AFL Legislative Committee, G. B. Evans, J. L. Hall, C. F. McQunicy, to Harding, October 10, 1922, Harding Papers, Library of Congress (microfilm, Herbert Hoover Presidential Library).

149. "The Railroad Strike: Defeat or Victory?" *Nation*, September 27, 1922, 297; "Daugherty's Dud," *Nation*, September 20, 1922, 271–72; and "American Labor and Judge Wilkerson," *New Republic*, October 4, 1922, 409.

150. "Smothering a Strike by Injunction," *Literary Digest*, September 16, 1922, 8.

151. "Legal Battle over 'Daughtery Injunction' Opens," *Railway Age* 73 (1922): 507–9, and "Government's Evidence in Support of Sabotage and Conspiracy Charges against the Striking Shopmen," *Commercial and Financial Chronicle* 115 (1922): 1279–80. The legal counsel for the labor unions, Donald R. Richberg, responded by calling the affidavits "an avalanche of hearsay, mixed with perjury." "Hearings on Injunction Completed," *Railway Age* 73 (1922): 560.

152. "Injunction against Strike Violation Made Permanent," *Railway Age* 75 (1923): 112.

153. Gompers to Peter A. Balir, July 31, 1922; Gompers to J. Cleave Dean, December 1, 1922; Gompers and W. C. Roberts to Bert M. Jewell, July 21, 1922, AFL Papers, State Historical Society of Wisconsin.

154. Jewell and the ARE finally settled the strike with no help from the board. See "S. Davies Warfield Explains How Agreement Was Reached with Shopmen," *Commercial and Financial Chronicle* 115 (1922): 1282–83; "Statement by B. M. Jewell on Partial Settlement of Shopmen's Strike," *Commercial and Financial Chronicle* 115 (1922): 1283; "Chairman Hooper's Statement on Strike Settlement Agreement," *Commercial and Financial Chronicle* 115 (1922): 1283; "Secretary Davis's Statement on Shopmen's Strike Settlement Agreement," *Commercial and Financial Chronicle* 115 (1922): 1283; "Secretary Hoover's Statement on Losses to Country from Strike," *Commercial and Financial Chronicle* 115 (1922): 1283–84; Wolf, *Railroad Labor Board*, 257; and "President's View on Strike," *Railway Age* 73 (1922): 714.

155. See Zieger, "From Hostility to Moderation," 31.

156. "Union Leaders' Concessions Show Strike without Cause," *Railway Age* 73 (1922): 187.

157. Harding to Grable, September 2, 1922, Harding Papers, Library of Congress (microfilm, Herbert Hoover Presidential Library).

158. Hooper to Harding, October 29, 1921.

159. Paul Blancard, "The Pennsylvania's War on Labor," *Nation*, June 25, 1923, 79.

160. *Pennsylvania R. Co. v. United States Railroad Labor Board*, 85.

## Chapter 6

1. *Pennsylvania R. Co. v. United States Railroad Labor Board*, 261 U.S. 72 (1922), and *Pennsylvania R. System and Allied Lines Federation No. 90 v. Pennsylvania R. Co.*, 67 U.S. 203 (1924).

2. See Zakson, "Railway Labor Legislation"; Zieger, "From Hostility to Moderation"; Troy, "Labor Representation on American Railways"; and Zieger, *Republicans and Labor*.

3. See Vadney, *The Wayward Liberal*, 51.

4. See "President Discusses Transportation Problems," *Railway Age* 73 (1922): 1550.

5. Ibid., 1551.

6. April 16, 1926, Calvin C. Coolidge Papers, Library of Congress (microfilm, Herbert Hoover Presidential Library). See also "Hearings on Railway Labor Bill," *Railway Age* 80 (1926): 269; *Congressional Record*, 69th Cong., 1st sess., 1926, 67, pt. 4:4574, 4652–53; and *Congressional Record*, 68th Cong., 1st sess., 65, 1924, pt. 10:10157.

7. Hoover suggested to Coolidge that his adminstration not take responsibility for the Watson–Parker bill to better ensure its passage. See Garrison, "The National Railroad Adjustment Board," 573; "Railroad Peace with Justice," *New Republic*, January 20, 1926, 232.

8. *Congressional Record*, 68th Cong., 1st sess., 1924, 65, pt. 8:7713. Hoover drafted the segments concerning the railroads and the coal industry for Coolidge's inaugural address. Hoover to Coolidge, November 22, 1923, Hoover Papers, Herbert Hoover

Presidential Library, West Branch, Iowa; Secretary to the President, C. B. Slemp to Fred H. Fljozdal, December 31, 1924, Coolidge Papers, Library of Congress (microfilm, Herbert Hoover Presidential Library).

9. "Why Rock the Boat?" *Railway Business Association Bulletin to Members*, November 21, 1923, clipping taken from the Calvin Coolidge Papers, Library of Congress (microfilm, Herbert Hoover Presidential Library).

10. Untitled memorandum in the railroad conferences file, n.d., Hoover Papers, Herbert Hoover Presidential Library, West Branch, Iowa. Hoover also utilized this paragraph of the memorandum for a speech, January 9, 1924, for the Transportation Conference in Washington, D.C.; and "Annual Report of the Secretary of Commerce," 1923, Hoover Papers, Herbert Hoover Presidential Library, West Branch, Iowa.

11. Unsigned memo entitled "Memorandum of Howell-Barkley Bill Progress," February 1–20, 1925; Richberg to D. B. Robertson, January 17, 1924, Richberg Papers, Chicago Historical Society.

12. Although Coolidge took no credit for the Watson-Parker bill, he still kept abreast of the railroad executives' and the labor union leaders' progress in the conferences. The ARE sent Coolidge memorandums to inform him about these conferences. Untitled memorandums, April 24, 26, 1926, and other undated memorandums on microfilm reel 176; Association of Railway Employees to Coolidge, January 8, 1926, Coolidge Papers, Library of Congress (microfilm, Herbert Hoover Presidential Library). Hoover was also informed about the meetings. E. S. Gregg to Hoover, December 11, 1925; Hoover to Everett Sanders, December 12, 1925; E. S. Gregg to Hoover, January 4, 1926, Hoover Papers, Herbert Hoover Presidential Library, West Branch, Iowa.

13. Untitled Commerce Department memorandum, May 21, 1925, Hoover Papers, Herbert Hoover Presidential Library, West Branch, Iowa. See also "Hearings on Railway Labor Bill," 269.

14. As Hoover explained, "The committee of Railway Employees and Railway Presidents have practically settled the form of their proposed legislation, and it seems to me it will be much better if it is introduced into Congress by them—not by the Administration. I believe also that it would be better if we take no part in the question." Hoover to Everett Sanders, December 12, 1925, Hoover Papers, Herbert Hoover Presidential Library, West Branch, Iowa.

15. The president of the Locomotive Firemen and Enginemen, D. B. Robertson, explained, "We had failed to secure the co-operation of the railroad executives." D. B. Robertson to Ralph M. Easley, September 5, 1924, AFL Papers, State Historical Society of Wisconsin.

16. Ibid.

17. *Congressional Record*, 68th Cong., 1st sess., 1924, 65, pt. 8:7713.

18. The Executive Council of the AFL in August 1920 called for a conference between the AFL and other unions to discuss the question of railroad legislation. On April 12, 1921, a committee of representatives from the Railway Employees Department, International Association of Machinists, Brotherhood of Railway Carmen of America, among others, met. April 12, 1921, AFL Papers, State Historical Society of Wisconsin.

19. Quoted from Hicks, *Republican Ascendancy*, 88–89.

20. Murray, *The Harding Era*, 317–19.

21. Ibid.

22. Goldman, *Democratic Party in American Politics*, 93; Tobin, *Organize or Perish*, 141–42; and Hicks, *Republican Ascendancy*, 88–89.

23. The historian Robert K. Murray describes the Democratic Party in the 1920s as "disintegrated" into a "confederation of sectional groups." Murray, *The 103rd Ballot*.

24. Memorandum to President Gompers, 1923, AFL Papers, State Historical Society of Wisconsin.

25. Quoted from unsigned draft memorandum, Easley Ralph M. File, Hoover Papers, Herbert Hoover Presidential Library, West Branch, Iowa. In a memorandum from the chairman of the Railroad Labor Board, Ben W. Hooper, to Calvin Coolidge's secretary Sanders, Hooper emphasized that the president was concerned for the welfare of the public, not just that of organized labor and the railroad executives. Ben W. Hooper to Coolidge's secretary Sanders, Coolidge Papers, Library of Congress (microfilm, Herbert Hoover Presidential Library).

26. American Federation of Labor, *Proceedings* 41 (1921): 70.

27. American Federation of Labor, *Proceedings* 44 (1925): 68. Conferences were held with the AFL, the Railroad Brotherhood, and Senator Howell and Representative Barkley. Conference at the office of Senator Howell, February 25, 1924, Legislative Reference File, AFL Papers, State Historical Society of Wisconsin. At one conference about the legislation, Gompers stated that for the first time in his memory the three groups of railway workers consisting of the operating group, the mechanical group, and the shopmens' group had agreed on a bill affecting all their interests to be introduced in Congress. David E. Lilenthal to Edwin E. Witte, director of Wisconsin Legislative Reference Service, September 11, 1923, Richberg Papers, Chicago Historical Society.

28. Although Richberg and Lilenthal were drafting legislation that would affect only the railroad unions, the AFL also scrutinized their progress, thinking that this legislation might set a precedent for labor legislation affecting all industries. Conference with Donald Richberg, D. B. Robertson, President Locomotive Firemen and Enginemen, E. H. Fitzgerald, President, Brotherhood of Railway Carmen, Samuel Gompers, President of AFL, December 12, 1923, Legislative Reference File, AFL Papers, State Historical Society of Wisconsin. David E. Lilenthal had been Felix Frankfurter's student at Harvard. Richberg took him into his practice upon Frankfurter's suggestion. See Vadney, *The Wayward Liberal*, 53.

29. Conference Minutes, February 7, 1924, Legislative Reference File, AFL Papers, State Historical Society of Wisconsin. Gompers, Morrison, AFL Secretary, Mathew Woll, Vice-President of AFL, Andrew Furuseth, President International Seaman's Union, William H. Johnston, International Association of Machinists, D. B. Robertson, President, Brotherhood of Locomotive Firemen and Enginemen, McGrady, Legislative Committee of AFL, and W. C. Roberts, Legislative Committee of AFL, were present at the conference.

30. *Congressional Record*, 68th Cong., 1st sess., 1924, 65, pt. 8:7880–85.

31. Unsigned "Memorandum of Howell-Barkley Bill Progress," February 1–20, 1925.

32. Murray, *Politics of Normalcy*, 135.

33. See "Hearing on Railway Labor Bill," *Railway Age* 76 (1924): 794. Hoover also called for amendments to the Transportation Act in January 1924 at a Transportation

Congress. See *Congressional Record*, 68th Cong., 1st sess., 1924, 65, pt. 8:7716. Ben W. Hooper, the chair of the Railroad Labor Board, also knew of the president's request for revisions of the board but still rejected the Howell-Barkley bill as "a vicious, partizan [*sic*], socialistic measure." Ben W. Hooper to C. B. Slemp, secretary to the president, May 31, 1924, and Ben W. Hooper to Coolidge, April 17, 1924; Memorandum to Everett Sanders from Hooper, January 3, 1925, Coolidge Papers, Library of Congress (microfilm, Herbert Hoover Presidential Library).

34. Secretary of Labor James J. Davis to Coolidge, December 9, 1925, Coolidge Papers, Library of Congress (microfilm, Herbert Hoover Presidential Library).

35. Secretary of Commerce Hoover began arranging meetings with the railroad executives and organized labor before the Howell-Barkley bill was defeated. Unsigned memorandum entitled "Memorandum of Howell-Barkley Bill Progress," February 1–20, 1925.

36. Hoover had arranged these meetings. Memorandum from Sterns or Butler in the Commerce Department, May 21, 1925, Hoover Papers, Herbert Hoover Presidential Library, West Branch, Iowa. See "Hearings on Railway Labor Bill," 269.

37. Barkley referred to these meetings in the House committee hearings. *Congressional Record*, 69th Cong., 1st sess., 1926, 67, pt. 1:107. Samuel Gompers, William H. Johnston, president of the International Association of Machinists, and Joseph A. Franklin, Brotherhood of Boilermakers, had met with Daniel Willard, president of the Baltimore and Ohio Railroad, in March 1924 concerning labor legislation for the railroads. Gompers to B. M. Jewell, President of the Railways Employee Department, AFL, March 24, 1924, AFL Papers, State Historical Society of Wisconsin; Memorandum for Senator Cummins, December 15, 1924, Hoover Papers, Herbert Hoover Presidential Library, West Branch, Iowa.

38. Howell had the support of the progressive Republican senators Norris, Johnson, Brookhart, and Frank R. Gooding of Idaho and progressive Democratic senators Burton D. Wheeler of Montana, David I. Walsh of Montana, Kenneth McKellar of Tennessee, Henry F. Ashurst of Arizona, Clarence Dill of Ohio, and Key Pittman of Nevada, and the Farmer-Laborites Shipstead and Magnus Johnson of Minnesota. *Congressional Record*, 68th Cong., 2d sess., 1925, 66, pt. 4:3729–30.

39. Ibid. Senators Fess, Watson, Warren, Charles Curtis of Kansas, Frederick Hale of Maine, Walter Edge of New Jersey, David E. Reed of Pennsylvania, Lawrence Phipps of Colorado, George W. Moses of New Hampshire, Bert M. Fernald of Maine, and Reed Smoot of Utah were some of the old guard Republicans voting.

40. In a debate with Glen Plumb concerning the board, Hooper argued that the Railroad Labor Board should not be abandoned but that its decisions should be made enforceable by Congress. See "Hooper and Plumb Discuss Settlement of Labor Problems," *Railway Age* 72 (1921): 318. Association of Employers of Indiana to Coolidge, May 15, 1924, Coolidge Papers, Library of Congress (microfilm, Herbert Hoover Presidential Library).

41. In the Senate hearings for the Howell bill in the Committee for Interstate Commerce, there were no witnesses favoring the bill except the railroad brotherhoods and their counsel, Richberg. "Labor Bill Criticized," *Railway Age* 76 (1924): 1112, and "The Railroads Oppose the Labor Bill," *Railway Age* 76 (1924): 891.

42. "Labor Bill Criticized," 1112.

43. See "U.S. Chamber of Commerce Opposes Howell-Barkley Bill," *Railway Age*

77 (1924): 919; "Effort to Take Labor Bill from Committee," *Railway Age* 76 (1924): 984; and "The Railroad Battle in Congress," *Literary Digest*, May 17, 1924, 14.

44. See "Independent Organizations of Employees Oppose Bill," *Railway Age* 76 (1924): 935, and "Labor Union to Dictation to Congressmen," *Railway Age* 76 (1924): 1126.

45. "Labor Bill Criticized," 1112; Willard to Coolidge, August 30, 1923, Coolidge Papers, Library of Congress (microfilm, Herbert Hoover Presidential Library).

46. Association of Employers of Indiana to Coolidge, May 15, 1924, Coolidge Papers, Library of Congress (microfilm, Herbert Hoover Presidential Library).

47. "U.S. Chamber of Commerce Opposes Howell-Barkley Bill," 919; "Effort to Take Labor Bill from Committee," 984.

48. A memorandum regarding the "section [which] dealt with the matter of management conferring with the employees and the election or selection of their representatives." Conference in the office of Senator Howell, February 25, 1924, Legislative Reference File, AFL Papers, State Historical Society of Wisconsin.

49. Ibid. The American labor movement included this provision because, as it suggested to Senator Howell, perhaps only the railroads with company unions would object to it. D. B. Robertson, president of the Brotherhood of Locomotive Firemen and Enginemen, posited that he "did not think that this would be an object of attack as only about twenty-five percent of the railroads have company unions and in [Robertson's] opinion only the railroads having such unions will object." Robertson and the labor union leaders, however, miscalculated how vehemently the railroad managers would lobby against this protective provision and the entire legislation.

50. "Legislation," *American Federationist* 32 (1925): 256.

51. "Railroad Legislation in Congress," *Railway Age* 78 (1925): 459.

52. Conference, May 22, 1924, Legislative Reference File, AFL Papers, State Historical Society of Wisconsin.

53. "Report of the Legislative Committee," *American Federationist* 31 (1924): 509.

54. Conference in the office of Congressman Alben W. Barkley, February 27, 1924, AFL Papers, State Historical Society of Wisconsin.

55. *Congressional Record*, 68th Cong., 1st sess., 1924, 65, pt. 8:7874–75.

56. "Memorandum to Congressmen," May 1924, Richberg Papers, Chicago Historical Society.

57. Ibid.

58. *Congressional Record*, 68th Cong., 1st sess., 1924, 65, pt. 10:10157. The president of the Brotherhood for Locomotive Firemen and Enginemen, D. B. Robertson, also explained, "On twenty-four roll calls, the majority had voted with the proponents, but through a filibuster, we could not get a vote on the bill." See also "Railroad Legislation in Congress," *Railway Age* 78 (1925): 459; "Howell-Barkley Not Passed in House," *Railway Age* 78 (1925): 195; "Railroad Legislation in Congress," *Railway Age* 76 (1924): 1263; *Congressional Record*, 68th Cong., 2d sess., 1924, 65, pt. 4:3318.

59. "Railroad Legislation in Congress," *Railway Age* 78 (1925): 459.

60. *Congressional Record*, 68th Cong., 1st sess., 1924, 65, pt. 7:6389.

61. *Congressional Record*, 68th Cong., 2d sess., 1924, 65, pt. 4:3318. The bill was only reported out of the Senate because LaFollette rose from his sickbed to vote. After sixteen roll call votes on the Howell bill, Congress adjourned before the bill was sub-

mitted to a vote. "Railroad Legislation in Congress," *Railway Age* 78 (1925): 459; "Legislation," *American Federationist* 32 (1925): 256.

62. Unsigned "Memorandum of Howell-Barkley Bill Progress," February 1–20, 1925.

63. Ibid.

64. Not all the progressive Republicans abandoned the GOP. Senator William E. Borah even went so far as to campaign for "Silent Cal." To woo more progressive Republicans back to the party fold, President Coolidge asked Borah to become his vice presidential running mate. Despite Coolidge's persistence, however, Borah refused. All of Coolidge's efforts show that he did not want to close the door on the progressive factions of Republicans within Congress. See Ashby, *The Spearless Leader*.

65. "Government Regulation of Railroad Labor," November 9, 1923, Hoover Papers, Herbert Hoover Presidential Library, West Branch, Iowa; *Congressional Record*, 69th Cong., 1st sess., 1926, 67, pt. 5:4587, 4654, 4656.

66. There had long been a division of loyalty among the members of the ARE: moderates, taking the side of Daniel Willard, argued for conciliation with some labor unions such as the four railroad brotherhoods; and antilabor union railroad managers, taking the side of William W. Atterbury, contested the value of signing any labor union contracts. The two sides merged, however, when the committee for the Watson-Parker bill was established. Both Willard and Atterbury became members of the subcommittee to write legislation in conference with union officials. Other members of the subcommittee were Hale Holden of Chicago, Burlington and Quincy; P. E. Crowley of New York Central; and C. H. Markham, Illinois Central. The union leaders represented at the conference were W. B. Prenter, Brotherhood of Locomotive Engineers, D. B. Robertson, William Doak, and L. E. Sheppard, president of the Order of Railway Conductors. Coolidge to Daniel Willard, November 12, 1924; Coolidge to Secretary of Labor Davis, December 15, 1925; Davis to Coolidge, December 16, 1925, Coolidge Papers, Library of Congress (microfilm, Herbert Hoover Presidential Library); Hoover to Everett Sanders, December 12, 1925, Hoover Papers, Herbert Hoover Presidential Library, West Branch, Iowa. See also "New Railway Labor Bill," *Railway Age* 80 (1926): 223.

67. By a vote of 52 to 20 the railroads endorsed the bill in the ARE meeting. This number of votes meant that the members maintaining 80 percent of the roads endorsed the Railroad Labor bill. See "ARE Meeting," *Railway Age* 80 (1926): 1201. The conference of railroad labor and executives then presented the bill to President Coolidge in January 1926.

68. See Vadney, *The Wayward Liberal*, 64.

69. *Congressional Record*, 69th Cong., 1st sess., 1926, 67 pt. 8:9207. See "Seventy-Two Senators. . . ." *Railway Age* 80 (1926): 1061, for Richberg's description of the support in the Senate for the Watson-Parker bill.

70. *Congressional Record*, 69th Cong., 1st sess., 1926, 67, pt. 4:4777–78. "Labor Bill Passed By Senate," *Railway Age* 80 (1926): 1323, and "Labor Bill Passed by House," *Railway Age* 76 (1924): 1259.

71. See "ARE Meeting," 1201.

72. *Congressional Record*, 69th Cong., 1st sess., 1926, 67, pt. 8:9050.

73. Ibid., pt. 4:4573.

74. Ibid., pt. 8:8974.

75. Samuel Gompers, "The Poor Old Railroad Board," *American Federationist* 30 (1923): 242.

76. See *Congressional Record*, 69th Cong., 1st sess., 1926, 67, pt. 8:8809, and *Congressional Record*, 69th Cong., 1st sess., 1926, 67, pt. 4:4568, 4573.

77. "Labor Bill to Be Reported," *Railway Age* 80 (1926): 488.

78. "Hearings on Railway Labor Bill," 326. If both chose to arbitrate a dispute, the arbitration awards extended by the Mediation Board would bind the parties legally. And if the Mediation Board failed to resolve a labor dispute and either party refused to arbitrate the dispute, the president would have the authority to form an emergency board. No strikes, lockouts, or contractual changes would be permitted while an emergency board conducted an investigation of the labor dispute, and the railroad executives and the railroad workers would be legally bound not to alter their working conditions for sixty days.

79. Ibid.

80. See Lothian, "The Political Consequences of Labor Law Regimes," 1003-8.

81. See Wolf, *Railroad Labor Board*, 417.

82. Ibid., 418.

83. The general counsel for the Association of Railway Executives, Alfred Thom, purported that the bill was not "theoretically" superior to the Transportation Act but that it was a workable alternative. Thom stated, "We think it more important for this bill to go through as written than to have it amended even as we might desire." "Hearings on Railway Labor Bill," 326. He emphasized that "the theoretical criticisms of the bill be disregarded and that it be considered from the practical standpoint." "Labor Bill to Be Reported," 488.

84. *Congressional Record*, 69th Cong., 1st sess., 1926, 67, pt. 5:4650. Jacobstein pointed out that this situation was a trade-off for organized labor. He claimed that the Railway Labor Act was the first bill to recognize organized labor and that "labor gave up something in return for the recognition it received." Further, "For the first time that I know of the Congress of the United States is establishing in law the fact that organized labor shall be collectively represented in an important labor agreement recognized and sanctioned by an act of Congress."

85. *Congressional Record*, 69th Cong., 1st sess., 1926, 67, pt. 8:8894-95. In distinguishing the Erdman's and Newlands Acts from the Railway Labor Act, Senator Simeon Fess of Ohio pointed out that the latter act provided permanent mediation and arbitration boards.

86. Committee on Interstate and Foreign Commerce, *Railroad Labor Disputes: Hearings for H.R. 7180*, 69th Cong., 1st sess., 1926, 11.

87. *Congressional Record*, 69th Cong., 1st sess., 1926, 67, pt. 8:8894.

88. Ibid. The railroad labor unions supported legislation that, as Senator Fess described, "would write into law the principle that bodies can contract through chosen or selected representatives." Fess further stated that "these different elements in the contract, the management on the one hand and the employees on the other, [could] speak to one another through representatives." Old guard Republican senators, still baffled by the American labor movement's change in position, asked if the railroad labor unions even knew of this court enforcement provision. The old guard senator

David E. Reed of Pennsylvania asked: "Does the Senator suppose that the representatives of labor who are backing the bill realize that it could put them in that position?" To correct any misapprehensions, Watson stated, "I think they are fully aware of the consequences."

89. Ibid. Mr. Newton answered the question by Mr. Carl E. Mapes, a Republican from Michigan, by stating, "The provision in the question is merely a statement of the fundamental law of the land as interpreted by the courts, both in the state and in the Nation. That is all there is in the provision."

90. *Congressional Record*, 69th Cong., 1st sess., 1926, 67, pt. 5:4586.

91. Ibid., pt. 8:8891–93. The progressive senator Wheeler cited *Adair v. United States*, 208 U.S. 161 (1908), and *Coppage v. Kansas*, 236 U.S. 1 (1915), as well as *Adkins v. Children's Hospital*, 261 U.S. 525 (1922). The question of interfering with the contractual rights of employers and employees was brought up during the Senate debate of the Curtis amendment.

92. Richberg to D. B. Robertson, September 15, 1930, Richberg Papers, Chicago Historical Society.

93. Undated memorandum, 1930, Richberg Papers, Chicago Historical Society.

94. *Texas & New Orleans R. Co. v. Brotherhood of Railway & Steamship Clerks*, 281 U.S. 548 (1930). James Clark McReynolds did not hear the case.

95. *Pennsylvania R. Co. v. United States Railroad Labor Board*, 261 U.S. 72 (1922), and *Pennsylvania R. System and Allied Lines Federation No. 90 v. Pennsylvania R. Co.*, 267 U.S. 203 (1924).

96. *Texas & New Orleans R. Co. v. Brotherhood of Railway & Steamship Clerks*, 551.

97. Ibid., 563.

98. Ibid., 565.

99. Ibid., 569–70. The chief justice ruled that the *Adair* and *Coppage* cases were inapplicable to the case at bar.

100. Ibid., 571.

101. *Adair v. United States*, *Kansas v. Coppage*, *Hitchman Coal & Coke Co. v. Mitchell, Individually*, 245 U.S. 225 (1917). See also Cushman, "Doctrinal Synergies and Liberal Dilemmas," 261–65.

102. *Texas & New Orleans R. Co. v. Brotherhood of Railway & Steamship Clerks*, 570.

**Chapter 7**

1. See Witte, *Government in Labor Disputes*; Witte, "New Developments in Labor Injunctions"; Ross, *A Muted Fury*, 172, 186; Forbath, "Shaping of the American Labor Movement," 1151; Ernst, "Yellow-Dog Contract and Liberal Reform," 256; and Petro, "Injunctions and Labor Disputes," 351–53.

2. See Tomlins, *State and the Unions*, 117–18, for a different interpretation of the Norris-LaGuardia Act despite agreement about the formation of the Wagner Act.

3. Most labor law historians have not credited the coalition with the passage or the content of the Norris-LaGuardia Act. Gregory says this anti-injunction legislation belongs to the legislative agenda of economic voluntarism central to politics at the time. As Gregory argues, economic interests, not civil rights, constitutes the basis of the act. See Gregory, *Labor and the Law*, 197.

4. See Tomlins, *State and the Unions*, 102.

5. "Notes," *Columbia Law Review* 37 (1937): 471.

6. See Frankfurter and Landis, *Business of the Supreme Court*.

7. Livermore, *Politics Is Adjourned*, and Murray, *Politics of Normalcy*.

8. Murray, *Politics of Normalcy*.

9. Witte has been associated with industrial pluralism rather than legal realism. When he changes his views about the Clayton Act, he joins the perspective offered by the legal realists. See Ernst, "Common Laborers?," 62–68.

10. *Bedford Cut Stone Co. v. Journeymen Stone Cutters' Association of North America*, 274 U.S. 37 (1927).

11. Gompers to Donald R. Richberg, September 13, 1923, Richberg Papers, Chicago Historical Society. Gompers mentioned Ralston's and Sayre's help and attached memorandums entitled "An Act Concerning the Granting of Injunctions" and "An Act Concerning Labor Organizations." Gompers also contacted Donald R. Richberg, the progressive labor lawyer representing the railroad brotherhoods (who later became one of the authors of the Railway Labor Act of 1926), to "prepare a statement as to the best wording to be used in bills to be presented in Congress to limit the use of the injunction in labor disputes and in defining the legal rights of wage earners in labor disputes."

12. Ibid.

13. Ibid.

14. Edwin E. Witte, "An Act to Define, Regulate, and Limit the Equity Jurisdiction of the Federal Courts," December 22, 1928, Witte Papers, State Historical Society of Wisconsin.

15. Witte reviewed a proposal submitted by the AFL labor leaders on December 22, 1925, called "An Act Defining Combination and Conspiracies in Trade and Labor Disputes and Prohibiting the Issuance of Injunctions Therein," January 12, 1926, Witte Papers, State Historical Society of Wisconsin.

16. Ibid.

17. The Shipstead bill (S.R. 1482) was introduced on December 12, 1927. See Jurgen Kuczynski and Marguerite Steinfield, "Wages in Manufacturing Industries, 1899–1927," *American Federationist* 35 (1928): 834–35; "Injunction before the Senate," *American Federationist* 35 (1928): 145; and Lowitt, *George W. Norris*, 520.

18. See Frankfurter and Greene, "Congressional Power over the Labor Injunction," 386, and Zucker, *George W. Norris*, 104.

19. Memorandum, February 11, 1928, AFL Papers, State Historical Society of Wisconsin; "Injunction Defenders," *Law and Labor* 10 (1928): 51; and "The Labor Injunction Issue in Organized Labor's Own Nutshell," *Law and Labor* 10 (1928): 76.

20. American Federation of Labor, Convention, *Proceedings* 46 (1926): 307–18.

21. Ibid., 312.

22. Link, *Wilson, the New Freedom*, 266.

23. John J. Blaine to Witte, February 13, 1928; Witte to Blaine, November 3, 1928, Witte Papers, State Historical Society of Wisconsin.

24. Memorandum entitled "Does the Thirteenth Amendment to the Constitution Amend the Fifth? Did Man Become Free?" by Andrew Furuseth, n.d., and Joseph O. Carson to Norris, December 23, 1931, Norris Papers, Library of Congress.

25. Frankfurter to Roger N. Baldwin, December 9, 1931, Norris Papers, Library of Congress. See also Sayre, "Labor and the Courts," 683.

26. Throughout the 1920s, Walsh worked more with the progressive Republicans than with members from his own party. In 1924, for instance, he worked for Robert M. LaFollette's presidential campaign.

27. John J. Blaine to Witte, February 13, 1928.

28. Sayre, "Labor and the Courts," 683; and Blaine to Witte, February 13, 1928.

29. *Bedford Cut Stone v. Journeymen Stone Cutters'*; *Duplex v. Deering*, 254 U.S. 443 (1921); *Truax v. Corrigan*, 257 U.S. 312 (1921); and *American Steel Foundries v. Tri-City Central Trades Council*, 257 U.S. 184 (1921).

30. Witte to Blaine, March 6, 1928, and Witte to Blaine, November 3, 1928, July 14, 19, 28, 1928, Witte Papers, State Historical Society of Wisconsin.

31. See Vadney, *The Wayward Liberal*, 85–91.

32. At the time, Witte was the chief Wisconsin legislative reference librarian, Oliphant taught law at Columbia, Frankfurter taught law at Harvard, and Richberg served as counsel for numerous progressive causes in addition to the brotherhoods and the AFL. In drafting legislation, Richberg wrote to Norris that he was representing the public's interest rather than organized labor's interest. From May 1 through May 3, 1928, Sayre, Witte, Frankfurter, Oliphant, and Richberg held a conference to draft this bill. After this initial meeting, they corresponded among themselves to iron out all the problems associated with this legislation. Frankfurter and Oliphant wrote the final draft after receiving all the written criticism from the other members of the committee. Oliphant to Frankfurter, May 21, 1928; Witte to Blaine, May 25, 1928; Witte to Richberg, May 12, 1928; A "Tentative Draft" was written by this committee, May 1, 2, 3, 1928, Witte Papers, State Historical Society of Wisconsin; Oliphant to Norris, December 2, 1929; Richberg to Norris, February 11, 1930, Norris Papers, Library of Congress. See also Ernst, "Yellow-Dog Contract and Liberal Reform," 267–69.

33. Memorandum entitled an "Outline of Explanation of Bill Drafted to Limit and Define the Jurisdiction of the Federal Courts in Labor Cases," n.d., Norris Papers, Library of Congress.

34. Richberg reviewed the primary Supreme Court cases since the passage of the Clayton Act to get a clear picture of injunction law. Richberg to Norris, May 18, 1928, Norris Papers, Library of Congres.

35. Frankfurter to Witte, May 29, 1928; "Suggestions and Criticism of Mr. Francis B. Sayre, with regard to proposed Tentative Draft of Bill Limiting the Use of Injunctions," May 17, 1928, and Witte to Sayre, May 26, 1928, Witte Papers, State Historical Society of Wisconsin.

36. Cushman, "Doctrinal Synergies and Liberal Dilemmas," 269.

37. Frankfurter memorandum, n.d., Frankfurter Papers, Library of Congress (microfilm); the Norris substitute bill echoed a definition of liberty of contract that had appeared in *American Steel Foundries v. Tri-City Central Trades Council.*

38. "Outline of Explanation of Bill Drafted to Limit and Define the Jurisdiction of the Federal Courts in Labor Cases."

39. Quoted from a memorandum entitled "Arguments Supporting the Draft of a Bill Limiting the Power of Courts to Issue Labor Injunctions," January 1931, Witte Papers, State Historical Society of Wisconsin.

40. Frankfurter memorandum, n.d.

41. Ibid.

42. See Christ, "Federal Anti-Injunction Bill," 535–36.

43. Frankfurter and Greene, "Congressional Power over the Labor Injunction," 409.

44. Quoted from "Argument Supporting the Draft of a Bill Limiting the Power of Courts to Issue Labor Injunctions," h.

45. Quoted from "Outline of Explanation of Bill Drafted to Limit and Define the Jurisdiction of the Federal Courts in Labor Cases."

46. "Argument Supporting the Draft of a Bill Limiting the Power of Courts to Issue Labor Injunctions," h.

47. Quoted from "Outline of Explanation of Bill Drafted to Limit and Define the Jurisdiction of the Federal Courts in Labor Cases."

48. Frankfurter memorandum, n.d.

49. Quoted from "Outline of Explanation of Bill Drafted to Limit and Define the Jurisdiction of the Federal Courts in Labor Cases."

50. "Argument Supporting the Draft of a Bill Limiting the Power of Courts to Issue Labor Injunctions," k.

51. Frankfurter memorandum, n.d.

52. Ibid.

53. Ibid.

54. See, e.g., *United Mine Workers of America v. Coronado Coal Co.*, 259 U.S. 344 (1922), and *Coronado Coal Co. v. United Mine Workers of America*, 268 U.S. 295 (1925).

55. Ibid.

56. Sturges, "Unincorporated Association."

57. "Notes," *Columbia Law Review* (1937): 411.

58. "Outline of Explanation of Bill Drafted to Limit and Define the Jurisdiction of the Federal Courts in Labor Cases."

59. "Argument Supporting the Draft of a Bill Limiting the Power of Courts to Issue Labor Injunctions," k.

60. "Notes," *Columbia Law Review* (1937): 471.

61. Senate Subcommittee of the Judiciary, "Defining and Limiting the Jurisdiction of the Courts Sitting in Equity," statement by Norris in the Senate Hearings, April 28, 1930, 72d Cong., 2d sess., 1930, 22, Norris Papers, Library of Congress.

62. The AFL debated about whether or not it should support the Norris substitute bill in American Federation of Labor, Convention, *Proceedings* 49 (1929): 317–52. By November 1929, the AFL sent Norris a comparison of the substitute bill with an indorsed bill proposed by the AFL. Norris to Witte, November 26, 1929, Witte Papers, State Historical Society of Wisconsin. Norris sent this to Witte, Oliphant, and Frankfurter for their criticism.

63. Senate Subcommittee of the Judiciary, "Defining and Limiting the Jurisdiction of the Courts Sitting in Equity," 22.

64. "Federation's Injunction Proposal," *American Federationist* 36 (1929): 1301, and American Federation of Labor, Convention, *Proceedings* 49 (1929): 352.

65. On November 26, 1929, the AFL sent Norris a copy of his bill marked with revisions penned by Richberg. Richberg drafted the AFL revisions in "Memorandum

Concerning Amendments to Anti-Injunction Bill Suggested by the American Federation of Labor," Norris to Witte, March 6, 1930, Witte Papers, State Historical Society of Wisconsin; Frankfurter to Norris, January 28, 1930, Norris Papers, Library of Congress; Frankfurter, Witte, and Oliphant, "Observations on Amendments Proposed in the AFL to the Injunction Bill Drafted by the Sub-Committee of the Senate Committee on the Judiciary," n.d., Norris Papers, Library of Congress; Witte to Frankfurter, December 6, 1929, Witte Papers, State Historical Society of Wisconsin; Frankfurter to Norris, January 28, 1929, Norris Papers, Library of Congress. The AFL was referring to section 8. Norris to Witte, November 26, 1929. After the meeting in New Orleans, Richberg wrote a memorandum entitled "Memorandum Concerning Amendments to Anti-Injunction Bill suggested by the AF of L," with the help of Sayre, Frankfurter, Witte, and Oliphant. Norris to Richberg, March 6, 1930; Richberg to Witte, March 13, 1930, Witte Papers, State Historical Society of Wisconsin; Richberg also sent a memorandum, "Comment upon Briefs filed in opposition to the Sub-Committee Anti-Injunction Bill," May 5, 1930, Norris Papers, Library of Congress.

66. Norris to Witte, November 26, 1929; Norris to Richberg, March 6, 1930; and Witte to Norris, March 13, 1930, Witte Papers, State Historical Society of Wisconsin.

67. Norris to Witte, November 26, 1929.

68. Green gave a speech at the Association of American Law Schools, December 29, 1929, AFL Papers, State Historical Society of Wisconsin.

69. Green to Witte, February 11, 1930, Witte Papers, State Historical Society of Wisconsin.

70. Green to Witte, July 9, 1928; Frankfurter to Oliphant, June 19, 1928; Norris to Witte, June 11, 1928; Witte to Blaine, November 3, 1928, and Frankfurter to Witte, June 15, 1928; Witte to Blaine, November 3, 1928, Witte Papers, State Historical Society of Wisconsin; "Critical Analysis by Special AFL Committee S.1482," box 198; "Proposed Anti-Injunction Legislation" memorandum found in Norris Papers, Library of Congress.

71. For the first time in thirty-six years, the Senate rejected the president's Supreme Court nominee. See Zucker, *George W. Norris*, 104.

72. The National Association for the Advancement of Colored People opposed the racist remarks Parker had made during his 1920 campaign to become governor of North Carolina and therefore opposed his appointment. Parker to Honorable Lee S. Overman, April 24, 1930, Hoover Papers, Herbert Hoover Presidential Library, West Branch, Iowa. See also Fish, "*Red Jacket* Revisited."

73. *International Organization, United Mine Workers of America v. Red Jacket Consolidated Coal and Coke Co.*, 18 Fed. (2d) 839 (1927); Green to Hoover, April 16, 1930, Hoover Papers, Herbert Hoover Presidential Library, West Branch, Iowa.

74. Parker to Senator Lee S. Overman, April 24, 1930, Hoover Papers, Herbert Hoover Presidential Library, West Branch, Iowa.

75. Parker to Overman, April 22, 1930, Hoover Papers, Herbert Hoover Presidential Library, West Branch, Iowa; Frankfurter and Greene, "Congressional Power over the Labor Injunction," 387.

76. "Memorandum on the Opinion of Circuit Judge John J. Parker in *International Organization, United Mine Workers of America v. Red Jacket Consolidated Coal and Coke Co.* 18 Fed. (2d) 839,*" Department of Justice statement on Parker, released April 13,

1930, Hoover Papers, Herbert Hoover Presidential Library, West Branch, Iowa. The Department of Justice also prepared the "Memorandum on Hitchman," in Hoover Papers.

77. Ibid.

78. Edward Berman, "Judge Parker and the Sherman Act," *American Federationist* 37 (1930): 1379–81.

79. See Witte, "Federal Anti-Injunction Act," 655.

80. At this point, the old guard Republicans were quietly encouraging Hoover to withdraw Parker's nomination. Hoover, however, refused. See Lowitt, *George W. Norris*, 439.

81. Untitled memorandum, n.d., Supreme Court Endorsement File, Hoover Papers, Herbert Hoover Presidential Library, West Branch, Iowa. Hoover also declared, "Even more sinister is the reasoned opposition, in both the Hughes and Parker cases, of a group of Senators who base their hostility solely upon the ground that the nominee had not proven himself to be an adherent of certain political theories. . . . The attempt to control the decisions of the Supreme Court by recall, or by a review of decision, by the legislative branch of the government had repeatedly failed. . . . The necessary result, if this group of Senators should succeed, would be to subordinate the Court, not merely to the legislative branch but to the prevailing political views of the Senate alone."

82. Lowitt, *George W. Norris*, 439.

83. See Bonnett, "Yellow-Dog Contract in Its Relation to Public Policy," 315, and "Yellow-Dog Contract," 110.

84. The AFL played an active role in the nomination. See American Federation of Labor, Convention, *Proceedings* 50 (1930): 113. The AFL wrote protests to Hoover. Green to Hoover, April 4, 16, 1930, Hoover Papers, Herbert Hoover Presidential Library, West Branch, Iowa.

85. Charles S. Deneen, Ferderick H. Gillett, and Frederick Steiwer were considered the Hoover administration stalwarts who later lost their seats in Congress or on the Judiciary Committee by the time the Norris-LaGuardia Act passed in 1932. Lowitt, *George W. Norris*, 526.

86. Edward F. McGrady to William Green, June 9, 1930, AFL Papers, State Historical Society of Wisconsin.

87. See Frankfurter and Greene, "Congressional Power over the Labor Injunction," 390.

88. Ibid., 395.

89. Ibid., 397.

90. Memorandum from Edward F. McGrady to William Green, June 9, 1930, in the AFL interest listed the advocates and the opponents of the bill. The minority report was written by Blaine, Walsh, Norris, Borah, Caraway, Ashurst, and Dill.

91. Frankfurter and Greene, "Congressional Power over the Labor Injunction," 389.

92. Senate Judiciary Committee. On June 20, 1930, the Judiciary Committee sent the bill to the attorney general. Memorandum by Edward F. McGrady, May 28, 1930, AFL Papers, State Historical Society of Wisconsin.

93. Ibid.

94. Ibid. Those who were against sending the bill to the attorney general were

Senators Borah, Blaine, Norris, and Ashurst. The senators supporting this move were Deneen, Gillett, Robinson, Waterman, Hastings, Overman, and Stephens. Hebert, Walsh, Caraway, King, and Dill were not present during the vote.

95. Upset that the anti-injunction legislation was again defeated, just before Congress adjourned, the AFL leaders convinced Shipstead to reintroduce his measure. The AFL brought out another anti-injunction bill written by its attorney Winter S. Martin and introduced by Shipstead on the last day of the seventy-first Congress. Witte to Roger N. Baldwin, December 24, 1931; Frankfurter to Roger N. Baldwin, December 9, 1931, Witte Papers, State Historical Society of Wisconsin; and Frankfurter and Greene, "Congressional Power over the Labor Injunction," 388.

96. Warren, *Herbert Hoover and the Great Depression*, 125. When the plot was discovered, however, the old guard had to abandon it.

97. Lowitt, *George W. Norris*, 509. The Democratic progressive Edward P. Costigan of Colorado won his bid for the Senate.

98. Warren, *Herbert Hoover and the Great Depression*, 128.

99. Olson, *Historical Dictionary of the 1920s*, 110.

100. Ibid.

101. Goldman, *The Democratic Party in American Politics*, 92.

102. Lubell, *Future of American Politics*, 45.

103. Ibid.

104. Ibid.

105. Ibid., 48–49.

106. John J. Blaine (Wisconsin), William E. Borah (Idaho), Smith W. Brookhart (Iowa), Arthur Capper (Kansas), James Couzens (Michigan), Bronson Cuttings (New Mexico), Lynn J. Frazier (North Dakota), Robert B. Howell (Nebraska), Hiram Johnson (California), Robert M. LaFollette Jr. (Wisconsin), Charles L. McNary (Oregon), Peter Norbeck (South Dakota), George W. Norris (Nebraska), Gerald P. Nye (North Dakota), and Thomas D. Schall (Minnesota) were the Republican progressive members of the coalition. William E. Ashurst (Arizona), Robert J. Bulkley (Ohio), Marcus Coolidge (Massachusetts), Edward P. Costigan (Colorado), Clarence C. Dill (Washington), Cordell Hull (Tennessee), J. Hamilton Lewis (Illinois), George McGill (Kansas), Mathew M. Neely (West Virginia), Robert F. Wagner (New York), Burton K. Wheeler (Montana), Thomas J. Walsh (Montana), and David I. Walsh (Massachusetts) were the thirteen Democrat progressive members of the coalition. Henrik Shipstead (Minnesota) was a Farmer-Laborite member of the coalition.

107. Anxious to coax the progressive Republicans back into the fold, the old guard leaders in the House, Speaker of the House Nicholas Longworth and Bertrand Snell, the chairman of the Committee of the Rules, respectively, sponsored two progressive demands at the end of the seventy-first session and before the seventy-second session of Congress. First, despite earlier bitter battles with the progressives about the lame-duck session, Speaker Longworth finally allowed a bill about this issue to be released from its House committee pigeonhole. Norris, and other Republican progressives, had long fought to change the beginning of the president's and the vice president's terms to January 15, rather than April. Beginning in January would have eliminated Congress's lame-duck session, which, in effect, created a thirteen-month delay between the congressional elections and the subsequent congressional session. Second, Congressman Snell advised Norris that if he promised to support the Republican administra-

tion and not fight for a special session of the seventy-second Congress, the old guard leadership would back the progressive sponsored Muscle Shoals project. See Lowitt, *George W. Norris*, 515–18.

108. Warren, *Herbert Hoover and the Great Depression*, 122, 128.

109. Ibid.

110. The only Farmer-Laborite from Minnesota and four Wisconsin progressive Republicans voted for George J. Schneider of Wisconsin. See *Congressional Record*, 72d Cong., 1st sess., 1931, 75, pt. 1:439–40.

111. Warren, *Herbert Hoover and the Great Depression*, 292–301.

112. Schwarz, *Interregnum of Despair*, 51.

113. Ibid., 59.

114. Ibid., 64.

115. American Federation of Labor, Convention, *Proceedings* 50 (1930): 324–25.

116. In February 1931, Norris announced that the Senate Judiciary Committee would not introduce the anti-injunction legislation until the next Congress met in 1932. Norris to Richberg, March 6, 1930, and Norris to Roger Baldwin, December 15, 1930, Norris Papers, Library of Congress.

117. Secretary John P. Robertson, November 4, 1932, writing about Norris in the Norris Papers, Library of Congress.

118. See Frankfurter and Greene, "Congressional Power over the Labor Injunction," 385. The *New Republic* stated, "Probably the most important bill now before Congress has nothing to do with the existing depression." See "Anti-Injunction Bill," *New Republic*, March 2, 1932, 55.

119. The AFL noted that the Norris bill was only passed after two years of hard work. See William Green, "Injunction Legislation," *American Federationist* 39 (1932): 18, and William Green, "The Norris Injunction Bill," *American Federationist* 39 (1932): 378.

120. The Committee on Labor Injunctions conducted a poll in December 1931. Twenty-eight senators indicated their support for the Norris bill, six senators favored the general aim of the bill but not the bill, twelve senators opposed the legislation, twenty-seven senators refused to commit themselves, and twenty-three senators sent back no reply to the Committee on Labor Injunctions. Alexander Fleisher to Witte, December 18, 1931, Witte Papers, State Historical Society of Wisconsin.

121. Ibid.

122. *Congressional Record*, 72d Cong., 1st sess., 1932, 75, pt. 5:5019. Witte wrote Senator John J. Blaine, "I have been delighted with the way the anti-injunction bill has gone through Congress. The overwhelming majority proves that the work your sub-committee did getting all of the difficulties ironed out was well done." Witte to John J. Blaine, March 16, 1932, Witte Papers, State Historical Society of Wisconsin.

123. Ibid.

124. *Nation*, March 9, 1932,, 269.

125. Ibid.

126. Lowitt, *George W. Norris*, 314.

127. Witte to Frankfurter, February 23, 1932, Witte Papers, State Historical Society of Wisconsin.

128. Ibid.

129. Beginning in 1924, he introduced anti-injunction legislation in every session of Congress.

130. Lowitt, *George W. Norris*, 524–26. LaGuardia, moreover, was known as a vocal critic of the labor injunction; he condemned President Harding for resorting to this measure during the 1922 shopmen's strike and the coal mine strikes.

131. Norris to Baldwin, 12, December 1931, Norris Papers, Library of Congress, and untitled memorandum, Frankfurter Papers, Library of Congress (microfilm). To avoid any delay that might result from reconciling these minor differences, the House sent its bill to the Senate Judiciary Committee. Norris then requested that the Judiciary Committee unanimously agree to consider the LaGuardia bill. He maintained, "Again one of the things we have to contend with is the clamor for hearings and delays. If we put our bill in such shape that a plausible reason can be given for additional hearings, it means one delay after another, with the object of finally wearing out those who favor the legislation and keeping up the delays until Congress adjourns. This has occurred in the past. It means not only no results, but it means the taking up of time of friends of the measure to an unnecessary extent." If the Senate gave its unanimous consent, Norris could strike out all but the enacting clause in the LaGuardia Act and insert his own legislation.

132. Lowitt, *George W. Norris*, 525.

133. *Congressional Record*, 72d Cong., 1st sess., 1932, 75, pt. 5:5511–12.

134. Witte to Frankfurter, 23 February 1932, and Blaine to Witte, March 2, 1932; Witte to Blaine, February 26, 1932; February 24, 1932, Witte Papers, State Historical Society of Wisconsin.

135. Richberg to Norris, September 27, 1932, Richberg Papers, Chicago Historical Society. See also Vadney, *The Wayward Liberal*, 92.

136. Vadney, *The Wayward Liberal*, 92.

137. Walter H. Newton to Attorney General, March 15, 1932, and Attorney General to Walter H. Newton, March 16, 1932, Hoover Papers, Herbert Hoover Presidential Library, West Branch, Iowa. For campaign information, see Campaign Pamphlet, "Against 'Yellow-Dog Contracts' and 'Government by Injunction,'" William L. Hutcheson, director of Labor Bureau, Republican National Committee, 1928 Campaign File, Hoover Papers, Herbert Hoover Presidential Library, West Branch, Iowa.

138. In 1932, all the Republican progressives but one, Arthur Capper of Kansas, worked to elect Franklin D. Roosevelt, the Democratic governor of New York. Norris himself became the chairman of the National Progressive League, which tried to persuade progressive Republicans to vote for Roosevelt.

139. Zucker, *George W. Norris*, 107.

140. Norris to Wilber Tillotson, November 4, 1932, Norris Papers, Library of Congress, and Newton to Snell, March 8, 1932, Hoover Papers, Herbert Hoover Presidential Library, West Branch, Iowa.

## Chapter 8

1. *Schechter Poultry Corporation v. United States*, 295 U.S. 495 (1935).
2. The Taft-Hartley Labor-Management Relations Act of 1947 and the Landrum-

Griffin Labor-Management Reporting and Disclosure Act of 1959 represent the two most significant pieces of federal legislation that modified American labor policy.

3. See Orren, *Belated Feudalism*, and Hattam, *Labor Visions and State Power*.

4. See Brody, *Workers in Industrial America*; Perlman and Taft, *History of Labor in the United States*; Casebeer, "Holder of the Pen"; and Plotke, "The Wagner Act, Again."

5. See Finegold and Skocpol, "State, Party, and Industry"; Skocpol, "Political Response to Capitalist Crisis"; and Skocpol and Finegold, "State Capacity and Economic Intervention." For insightful criticism of Skocpol's and Finegold's argument, see Cammack, "Review Article."

6. Goldfield, "Worker Insurgency, Radical Organization, and New Deal Labor Legislation," and Goldfield, Skocpol, and Finegold, "Explaining New Deal Labor Policy." See also Goldfield, *Decline of Organized Labor*.

7. Tomlins, Irons, and Bernstein also determine state motivation by exploring what specific forces contributed to the act's construction. Tomlins, for instance, argues that the legislative authors derived the statist ideology underlying the act, which the majority rule principle in the NLRB embodied, from the 1923 *Schelsinger v. Quinto* case, a legal precedent established by Wagner himself. Tomlins, *State and the Unions*, 115. Irons, on the other hand, claims that the legislative authors of the Wagner Act were preoccupied with crafting legislation that would withstand judicial scrutiny of the Supreme Court. Irons, *New Deal Lawyers*. Bernstein, finally, maintains that they used the Railway Labor Act of 1926, which had been upheld by this Court, as a model for the Wagner Act. Bernstein, *New Deal Collective Bargaining Policy*.

8. According to Weber, legal development in Western capitalist societies could not be characterized as simply a conflict between liberty and equality. Freedom to contract, for instance, led to exploitation as well as liberation. Nor did the law merely serve the capitalists, as Marxists proclaimed. Instead, Weber presented an alternative approach to legal theory. What he called legal formalism helped explain how systems of law could be created that operated relatively independently of the needs of markets and capital. Weber, *Economy and Society*, vol. 2. See also Kronman, *Max Weber*; Trubeck, "Max Weber's Tragic Modernism"; Holton and Turner, *Max Weber on Economy and Society*; and Cotterrell, "Legality and Political Legitimacy," for excellent interpretations of Weber's concept of legal formalism.

9. Weber, *Economy and Society*, 2:x.

10. Ibid., 811.

11. See Mason, "Labor Clauses of the Clayton Act," 493; Mink, *Old Labor and New Immigrants*; and Ernst, "The Labor Exemption."

12. Taft to Judge Jeremiah Smith, December 24, 1914, Taft Papers, Library of Congress (microfilm, Herbert Hoover Presidential Library); Mink, *Old Labor and New Immigrants*, 247–78; and Link, *Woodrow Wilson and the Progressive Era*, 55.

13. See Cooper, *Warrior and the Priest*, xii.

14. Samuel Gompers, "The Charter of Industrial Freedom," *American Federationist* 21 (1914): 971–72.

15. See *Duplex v. Deering*, 254 U.S. 443 (1921); *American Steel Foundries v. Tri-City Central Trades Council*, 257 U.S. 184 (1921); and *Bedford Cut Stone Co. v. Journeymen Stone Cutters' Association*, 247 U.S. 37 (1927).

16. Link, *Woodrow Wilson and the Progressive Era*, 61–63, 73–74, 236–37.

17. See Sklar, *Corporate Reconstruction*, 424.

18. See Boemke, "Wilson Administration."

19. See Zucker, *George W. Norris*, x; Sarasohn, *Party of Reform*, 169; and Schlabach, *Edwin E. Witte*, 56.

20. Conner, *National War Labor Board*, vii–viii, and Dubofsky, "Abortive Reform."

21. See Wehle, "War Labor Policies," 329.

22. Ibid.

23. Memorandum entitled a "Chronological Development of 'Collective Bargaining' under Executive and Administration Orders and Decisions of the National Labor Board and the National Labor Relations Board," n.d.; "Statement Concerning Section 7(a) of National Industrial Recovery Act," August 4, 1933, National Recovery Administration (NRA) Public Records, National Archives, Washington D.C.; and Memorandum entitled "Labor Provisions of NIRA," tentative date written on top of October 1933, Richberg Papers, Library of Congress. For an argument that regards section 7(a) as a more integral part of the NIRA, see Gordon, *New Deals*, 206–39.

24. See Taft, *Organized Labor in American History*, 128; Fine, *Automobile under the Blue Eagle*, 32; and Hawley, *New Deal and the Problem of Monopoly*, 22–25.

25. "Analysis of 7(a) of N.I.R.A. Subdivisions 1 and 2 Argument (in absence of estoppel)," NRA Records, National Archives.

26. Fine, *Automobile under the Blue Eagle*, 33–34.

27. See Bernstein, *New Deal Collective Bargaining Policy*, 33–34. The AFL was not pleased with the first version of this employee representation provision: it did not want the NRA to protect the employees' right *not* to join a labor organization. Instead, the union leaders advised that the employers should explicitly be prohibited from compelling an employee to join a "company union." The progressive Democrat Burton K. Wheeler as well as the Republican progressives George W. Norris and Robert M. LaFollette Jr. helped the AFL secure this revision. When the NIRA came to the Senate floor, Norris was instrumental in helping defeat an amendment benefiting company unionism proposed by the southern Democrat Champ Clark of Missouri.

28. Not to ostracize the progressive Republicans and Democrats who supported the Black bill, Roosevelt asked key progressives to help draft this plan. Roosevelt requested that the progressive Republican senator Robert M. LaFollette Jr. and congressman Clyde Kelly in addition to the progressive Democratic senator Robert F. Wagner and congressman Meyer Jacobstein help formulate the NIRA. Working in LaFollette's office, LaFollette, Wagner, and Jacobstein developed a plan that provided public works and industrial loans. See Hawley, *New Deal and the Problem of Monopoly*, 24–25; Fraser, *Labor Will Rule*, 289; and Schwarz, *Interregnum of Despair*, 208–9.

29. See Irons, *New Deal Lawyers*, 203, and Schlesinger, *Coming of the New Deal*, 91–92.

30. See Hawley, *New Deal and the Problem of Monopoly*, 22.

31. See Schlesinger, *Coming of the New Deal*, 91–92, 95.

32. Hawley, *New Deal and the Problem of Monopoly*, and Brand, *Corporatism and the Rule of Law*.

33. Memorandum by Donald R. Richberg and General Hugh S. Johnson, "Statement Concerning Section 7(a) of National Industrial Recovery Act," August 24, 1933, NRA Records, National Archives. See also Brand, *Corporatism and the Rule of Law*, 90–91.

34. This board was not to promote or protect in any sense labor's "rights," unless

the abridgment of their rights was the source of a particular conflict. While organized labor and the members of Roosevelt's administration sympathetic to the labor movement's plight applauded the construction of this board, they were concerned that its sole function was mediatory. William Leiserson, who had been the chairman of the National Mediation Board, became the executive secretary of the National Labor Board, and Milton Handler, an antitrust lawyer, worked as general counsel. See Bernstein, *New Deal Collective Bargaining Policy*, 58, and Bowman, *Public Control of Labor Relations*, 30.

35. Immediately, the AFL began protesting that "labor should have representation on every Code Authority." Witte to Leon C. Marshall, December 11, 1933, Witte Papers, State Historical Society of Wisconsin; memorandum to Hugh S. Johnson, n.d., Green Files, AFL Papers, State Historical Society of Wisconsin; W. C. Roberts to Green, December 19, 1933, Witte Papers, State Historical Society of Wisconsin.

36. *Congressional Record*, 74th Cong., 1st sess., 1935, 79, pt. 7:7568–70. See also Brody, *Workers in Industrial America*, 134–35.

37. A memorandum by W. M. McFarland to Blackwell Smith, assistant counsel for the NRA, November 14, 1933, NRA Records, National Archives; memorandum from W. C. Roberts to Green, December 20, 1933, AFL Papers, State Historical Society of Wisconsin.

38. See Seiler, "Effect of Section 7(a)," 242, and Brand, *Corporatism and the Rule of Law*, 233–35.

39. Thereafter, the NLB's majority rule proviso was referred to as the "Reading Formula." See Tomlins, *State and the Unions*, 113–14; Bowman, *Public Control of Labor Relations*, 30; Brand, *Corporatism and the Rule of Law*, 237; Irons, *New Deal Lawyers*, 206–7; and Gross, *Making of the National Labor Relations Board*, 21–23.

40. Tomlins, *State and the Unions*, 113–14.

41. See Fraser, *Labor Will Rule*, 233–35.

42. Fine, *Automobile under the Blue Eagle*, 191.

43. Memorandum from W. C. Roberts to Green, December 20, 1933; W. C. Roberts to Green, December 19, 1933.

44. See Seiler, "Effect of Section 7(a)," 242.

45. Ibid., 242–43.

46. Irons, *New Deal Lawyers*, 210.

47. Gross, *Making of the National Labor Relations Board*, 27.

48. Ibid., 41–45.

49. Memorandum, "Chronology of Section 7(a)," n.d., NRA Records, National Archives.

50. Memorandum by Blackwell Smith entitled "President's Announcement on Section 7(a) and Settlement of Automobile Strike," March 26, 1934, NRA Records, National Archives.

51. See Seiler, "Effect of Section 7(a)," 242.

52. According to Francis Biddle, Roosevelt had never been "enthusiastic" about the idea of majority rule. See Fine, *Automobile under the Blue Eagle*, 223.

53. Unsigned memorandum from the Petroleum Labor Policy Board to Frances Perkins, April 11, 1934, Leiserson Papers, State Historical Society of Wisconsin.

54. See Skocpol and Finegold, "State Capacity and Economic Intervention," 255–78.

55. Goldfield also challenges the argument made by Skocpol and Finegold about state capacity. Unlike the argument in this book, he argues that the unrest in 1934 convinced the president to construct the NLRB. See Goldfield, "Worker Insurgency," 1257–82, and Goldfield, *Decline of Organized Labor*, 69.

56. Memorandum from Hugh S. Johnson to the AFL, entitled "Order, Industrial Relations Committees, No. X-12," March 30, 1934, AFL Papers, State Historical Society of Wisconsin.

57. Wyzanski, "Review Article," 182–84.

58. Edwin E. Witte to William Green, July 24, 1933, Witte Papers, State Historical Society of Wisconsin. See also Crager, "Company Unions under the National Labor Relations Act," 831, and Alper, "Collective Bargaining, an Interpretation," 417. Alper indicates that on June 16, 1933, the number of company unions had increased to 1,164,294 from 423,945 on February 10, 1934. The number of labor unions had gone from 2.8 million to 4.1 million members.

59. Bernstein, *New Deal Collective Bargaining Policy*, 64–72. See also Fine, *Automobile under the Blue Eagle*, 216–27.

60. Fine, *Automobile under the Blue Eagle*, 216.

61. William M. Leiserson, Milton Handler, William G. Rice Jr., and Benedict Wolf also helped draft the Trade Disputes bill. Leiserson to Wagner, March 8, 1934, Wagner Papers, Georgetown University Archives. See also Bernstein, *New Deal Collective Bargaining Policy*, 63, and Schlesinger, *Coming of the New Deal*, 150.

62. Wagner to John A. Mayer, March 9, 1935, Wagner Papers, Georgetown University Archives.

63. Wagner and Keyserling, however, had not been the first to discuss the Keynesian implications to labor dispute legislation. An unsigned and undated (written in approximately the fall or winter of 1933 or the spring of 1934) memorandum entitled "Six Questions and Answers about Section 7(a)" stated that "increased purchasing power is effected by putting the worker on an equal bargaining level with the employer." NRA Records, National Archives. See Casebeer, "Holder of the Pen," for an argument about how central these implications were for the Trade Disputes bill.

64. See Tomlins, *State and the Unions*, 122.

65. Wagner to William H. Kelley, June 21, 1934, Wagner Papers, Georgetown University Archives.

66. See Tomlins, *State and the Unions*, 119–27.

67. *Congressional Record*, 69th Cong., 1st sess., 1926, 67, pt. 8:8891–93. The progressive senator Wheeler cited *Adair v. United States*, 208 U.S. 161 (1908), and *Coppage v. Kansas*, 236 U.S. 1 (1915), as well as *Adkins v. Children's Hospital*, 261 U.S. 525 (1922). The question of interfering with the contractual rights of employers and employees was brought up during the Senate debate of the Curtis amendment.

68. Undated memorandum, 1930, Richberg Papers, Chicago Historical Society.

69. Sturges, "Unincorporated Associations," 387.

70. Wagner to William H. Kelley, June 21, 1934. The author has underlined the text.

71. Witte explained, "I doubt whether this bill can be passed unless the President sends in a message urging its passage. Senator Wagner told me that he thought he could get the President to do so." Witte to John B. Andrews, March 23, 1934, Witte Papers, State Historical Society of Wisconsin.

72. Richberg wrote a letter to Wagner, indicating his opinion on the Trade Dis-

putes bill, S.R. 2248. Richberg to Wagner, April 24, 1934, Wagner Papers, Georgetown University Archives. See also Irons, *New Deal Lawyers*, 213.

73. Bernstein, *New Deal Collective Bargaining Policy*, 72–74.

74. Ibid., 72.

75. Witte to Senators Robert M. LaFollette Jr. and Robert F. Wagner, June 12, 1934; Witte to William Green, June 8, 1934; Witte to Charles E. Wyzanski Jr., June 12, 1934; Witte to W. G. Rice Jr., June 8, 1934, all in Witte Papers, State Historical Society of Wisconsin. Wagner had solicited the help of Edwin E. Witte. Witte to Sumner H. Slichter, February 8, 1934, Witte Papers, State Historical Society of Wisconsin.

76. Bernstein, *New Deal Collective Bargaining Policy*, 72.

77. Ibid., 74.

78. William Green to Edwin E. Witte, June 19, 1934, Witte Papers, State Historical Society of Wisconsin.

79. The rank and file in the Amalgamated Association of Iron, Steel, and Tin Workers were dissatisfied with this AFL affiliate's response to the formation of company unions in the steel industry. When militant workers threatened a strike, industry and management proposed that a labor board similar in construction to the Auto Labor Board, which implemented plurality rule, be erected. At the last minute the AFL convinced the steel workers not to strike by getting Roosevelt to comply with their request to implement labor-management relations machinery more favorable to the union. See Brand, *Corporatism and the Rule of Law*, 253–54.

80. Drafted by Wyzanski, Public Resolution #44 established a National Labor Relations Board within the Department of Labor to interpret section 7(a) of the NIRA. The secretary of labor would appoint either conciliators, mediators, or arbitrators to resolve labor disputes. See Casebeer, "Drafting Wagner's Act," 94.

81. The minority Senate leader, Charles McNary (Oregon), appointed James J. Davis (Pennsylvania), James Couzens (Michigan), Frederic C. Walcott (Connecticut), P. L. Goldsborough (Maryland), and Frederick Steiwer (Oregon) to draft their suggestions. See Bernstein, *New Deal Collective Bargaining Policy*, 77–78, and Gross, *Making of the National Labor Relations Board*, 69.

82. Senators Walcott and Steiwer had led the opposition against the Norris-LaGuardia Anti-Injunction Act. Edward F. McGrady to William Green, June 9, 1930, AFL Papers, State Historical Society of Wisconsin.

83. Schlesinger, *Coming of the New Deal*, 151; Bernstein, *New Deal Collective Bargaining Policy*, 78; Millis and Brown, *From the Wagner Act to Taft-Hartley*, 24–25.

84. See Bernstein, *New Deal Collective Bargaining Policy*, 84–87. The board had thirty-three noncompliance cases during its lifetime.

85. Henry I. Harriman, president of Chamber of Commerce, to Richberg, December 28, 1934, Richberg Papers, Library of Congress.

86. Memorandum entitled "Legal Remedies against Labor Unions," by Leon Keyserling, n.d., Wagner Papers, Georgetown University Archives.

87. Wagner to Kelley, June 21, 1934.

88. Tomlins, *State and the Unions*, 115–16.

89. Ibid. Tomlins, by contrast, in identifying the *Schlesinger v. Quinto* decision as the source of Wagner's formula, cites him as an isolated advocate of this interpretation of unionization. He argues that the other state and federal courts paid scant attention to the question of union authority.

90. See, e.g., *Schlesinger v. Quinto*, 194 N.Y. Supp. 401 (1922); *Gary v. Central of Georgia R.*, 44 Ga. App. 120, 160 S.E. 716 (1931); *Hall v. St. Louis–San Francisco R.*, 244 Mo. App. 431, 28 S.W. (2d) 687 (1930); *McCoy v. St. Joseph Belt R.*, 77 S.W. (2d) 175, 179 (Mo. App. 1934); *Piercy v. Louisville & N.R.*, 198 Ky. 477, 248 S.W. 1042 (1923); *West v. Baltimore & Ohio R.*, 103 W. Va. 417, 137 S.E. 654 (1927); *Snow Iron Works v. Chadwick*, 227 Mass. 382, 390, 116 N.E., 801, 806 (1917); *Mosshamer v. Wabash R.*, 221 Mich. 407, 408, 191 N.W. 210, 211 (1922); *Boucher v. Godfrey*, 119 Conn. 622, 178 Atl. 655 (1935).

91. *United Mine Workers of America v. Coronado Coal Co.*, 259 U.S. 344 (1922), and *Coronado Coal Co. v. United Mine Workers of America*, 268 U.S. 295 (1925).

92. *Coronado Coal Co. v. United Mine Workers of America*, 304.

93. "Notes," *Columbia Law Review* 38 (1938): 455.

94. Memorandum entitled "Legal Remedies against Labor Unions," by Leon Keyserling, n.d. In this memorandum, Keyserling also addresses the first *Coronado* decision and how Taft had ruled that an unincorporated union could be sued and that this set a dangerous precedent that had not been followed by the state and federal courts.

95. *Texas & New Orleans R. Co. v. Brotherhood of Railway & Steamship Clerks*, 281 U.S. 548 (1930). James Clark McReynolds did not hear the case.

96. Ibid., 571.

97. *Adair v. United States, Kansas v. Coppage, Hitchman Coal & Coke Co. v. Mitchell*, 245 U.S. 225 (1917).

98. Wagner to Kelley, June 12, 1934, Wagner Papers, Georgetown University Archives. In this letter Wagner explained, "The worker is left absolutely free to determine whether he will bargain individually or collectively."

99. Leiserson to Wagner, March 9, 1935, and Leiserson to Franklin D. Roosevelt, November 12, 1938, Leiserson Papers, State Historical Society of Wisconsin; Irons, *New Deal Lawyers*, 215–30; and Tomlins, *State and the Unions*, 134–40.

100. Memorandum entitled "Legal Remedies against Labor Unions," by Leon Keyserling, n.d.

101. Irons, *New Deal Lawyers*, 215–30, and Tomlins, *State and the Unions*, 133–40.

102. Casebeer, "Holder of the Pen," 292.

103. "Memorandum of Conference on Labor Disputes Bill," February 26, 1935, Perkins Papers, Columbia University Rare Book and Manuscript Library.

104. "Memorandum comparing S. 1958, 74th Congress, 1st Session, a bill introduced by Senator Wagner on February 21, 1935 to create a National Labor Relations Board and for other purposes, with the Bill reported by Senator Walsh on May 26, 1934 as a substitute for S.2926, 73rd Congress, also introduced by Senator Wagner," March 11, 1935, Perkins Papers, Columbia University Rare Book and Manuscript Library.

105. Harris, "The Snares of Liberalism?," 167–68; Klare, "Judicial Radicalization," 268–69.

106. William M. Leiserson, chairman of the National Mediation Board, to Wagner, March 9, 1935, Wagner Papers, Georgetown University Archives. In this letter, Leiserson tried to persuade Wagner not to include this provision. Leiserson reiterated this position in a letter to President Franklin D. Roosevelt, November 12, 1938, Leiserson Papers, State Historical Society of Wisconsin.

107. *Texas & New Orleans R. Co. v. Brotherhood of Railway & Steamship Clerks*.

108. Tomlins, *State and the Unions*, 133–37.

109. Ibid. Tomlins takes this position.

110. Memorandum entitled "Legal Remedies against Labor Unions," by Leon Keyserling, n.d.

111. Hearings for the Wagner bill were heard in the Senate Labor Committee hearings from March 11 until April 2, 1935. *Schechter Poultry Corporation v. United States.*

112. Irons, *New Deal Lawyers*, 230.

113. The meeting at the White House was called for May 24, 1935. Three days later, the assistant attorney general drafted a memorandum entitled "S. 1958, Report No. 972, Union Calendar, No. 328 in the House of Representatives," evaluating the Wagner bill. NRA Records, National Archives. See also Irons, *New Deal Lawyers*, 231.

114. Memorandum, "S. 1958, Report No. 972, Union Calendar, No. 328 in the House of Representatives." During subsequent negotiations, Stephens and Richberg argued, first, that the public policy declaration uniting Congress's ability to regulate interstate commerce with labor relations would be considered unconstitutional; second, that the National Labor Relations Board should not be established as an independent agency; and third, that Senator Tydings's amendment should be written into the final Wagner bill. Stephens maintained that employees, in addition to the employers, must have a duty not to interfere with their fellow employees' right to representation.

115. The author underlined the text. Stephens, memorandum entitled "S. 1958, Report No. 972, Union Calendar, no. 328 in the House of Representatives."

116. Untitled memorandum about the formation of the NLRB, Perkins Papers, Columbia University Rare Book and Manuscript Library. Another memorandum, entitled "Detailed List of the Changes which the Secretary of Labor is to suggest to the Committee on Education and Labor in regard to the Wagner Labor Relations Bill," shows that Perkins thought the NLRB should be placed in the Department of Labor.

117. See Feinman, *Twilight of Progressivism*, 93.

118. Felix Frankfurter to President Franklin D. Roosevelt, May 30, 1935, Frankfurter Papers, Library of Congress (microfilm). Frankfurter encouraged the president to sponsor this bill. See also Cushman, "Stream of Legal Consciousness."

119. By May 30, Wagner issued a public statement declaring that the *Schechter* decision did not establish a precedent that would lead the Court to strike down his legislation for industrial relations. Nonetheless, Wagner asked Keyserling, Levy, and Magruder to rewrite a few passages to ensure the constitutionality of the National Labor Relations bill. See Bernstein, *New Deal Collective Bargaining Policy*, 120–22, and Irons, *New Deal Lawyers*, 231.

120. Bernstein, *New Deal Collective Bargaining Policy*, 124; Bowman, *Public Control of Labor Relations*, 55; and *Congressional Record*, 74th Cong., 1st sess., 1935, 79, pt. 9:9676–9711, 9715–31.

## Conclusion

1. See Eisenach, "Reconstituting the Study of American Political Thought," 169–70, for an explanation of what he calls the populist-progressive genre of American political thought that captures this spirit in that it "stress[es] the apocalyptic struggles to achieve democracy of the past and to reaffirm in the reader a commitment to extend the struggles in the future."

2. See Feldman, "Interpretation of Max Weber's Theory of Laws," 208.

3. Skocpol, *Protecting Soldiers and Mothers*.

4. Dubofsky also captures the ambiguity of state intervention. He notes that the first studies that take the state into account focus on its repressive capacity. See Dubofsky, *The State and Labor in Modern America*, xvii. Tomlins, *State and the Unions*, drew upon Klare, "Judicial Deradicalization," and Stone, "Post-War Paradigm."

5. *United Mine Workers of America v. Coronado Coal Co.*, 259 U.S. 344 (1922). See also *Coronado Coal Co. v. United Mine Workers of America*, 268 U.S. 295 (1925).

6. *Pennsylvania R. Co. v. United States Railroad Labor Board*, 261 U.S. 72 (1922), and *Texas & New Orleans R. Co. v. Brotherhood of Railway & Steamship Clerks*, 281 U.S. 548 (1930).

7. See Plotke, "The Wagner Act, Again," 143.

8. Lichtenstein, "From Corporatism to Collective Bargaining," 123.

9. *Congressional Record*, 80th Cong., 1st sess., 1947, 93, pt. 4:5010.

10. See Rogers, "Divide and Conquer."

11. Tobriner, "Taft-Hartley Act after Three Years," 1215–16.

12. See O'Brien, "Taking the Conservative State Seriously."

# BIBLIOGRAPHY

**Archival Sources**

*Chicago, Illinois*
Chicago Historical Society
  Donald R. Richberg Papers

*Louisville, Kentucky*
University of Louisville Archives
  Louis D. Brandeis Papers (microfilm, University of Wisconsin, Madison)

*Madison, Wisconsin*
State Historical Society of Wisconsin
  AFL Papers
  John J. Esch Papers
  William Leiserson Papers
  Edwin E. Witte Papers

*New York, New York*
Columbia University Rare Book and Manuscript Library
  Frances Perkins Papers
New York Public Library
  Fiorello LaGuardia Papers

*Philadelphia, Pennsylvania*
Historical Society of Pennsylvania
  William B. Wilson Papers

*Washington, D.C.*
Georgetown University Archives
  Robert F. Wagner Papers
Library of Congress, Manuscript Division
  Calvin C. Coolidge Papers (microfilm, Herbert Hoover Presidential Library,
    West Branch, Iowa)
  James J. Davis Papers
  Felix Frankfurter Papers (microfilm)

Warren G. Harding Papers (microfilm, Herbert Hoover Presidential Library,
    West Branch, Iowa)
Charles Evans Hughes Papers
William G. McAdoo Papers
George W. Norris Papers
Donald R. Richberg Papers
Harold Stephens Papers
William Howard Taft Papers (microfilm, Herbert Hoover Presidential Library,
    West Branch, Iowa)
National Archives
National Recovery Administration Public Records
Private Collection
Leon D. Keyserling Papers

*West Branch, Iowa*
Herbert Hoover Presidential Library
Herbert Hoover Papers


## Selected Published Sources

Adler, Edward A. "Labor, Capital, and Business at Common Law." *Harvard Law Review* 29 (1916): 241–76.
"An Advance in Labor Legislation—the Anti-Injunction Act." *Georgetown Law Journal* 21 (1933): 344–51.
Agger, Caroline E. "Equitable Relief and Damages at Law." *Marquette Law Review* 8 (1934): 256–58.
Albertsworth, E. F. "The Federal Supreme Court and Industrial Development." *American Bar Association Journal* 16 (1930): 317–22.
———. "Industrial Law—Constitutionality of Bill Making Unenforceable Contracts Not to Join Labor Unions and Employers' Associations." *Illinois Law Review* 25 (1923): 307–15.
Alper, Carl. "Collective Bargaining, an Interpretation." *St. John's Law Review* 8 (1934): 416–29.
Ames, J. B. "Mutuality in Specific Performance." *Columbia Law Review* 3 (1903): 1–12.
Anderson, Grant T. "Collective Bargaining Agreements." *Oregon Law Review* 15 (1936): 229–53.
Andersen, Kristi. *The Creation of a Democratic Majority, 1928–1936.* Chicago: University of Chicago Press, 1979.
Andrews, John B. "The President's Conference on Unemployment—Success or Failure." *American Law and Labor Review* 11 (1921): 307–10.
———. "Progress of American Labor Legislation." *American Law and Labor Review* 13 (1923): 119–23.
Arnesen, Eric. "'Like Banquo's Ghost, It Will Not Down': The Race Question and the American Railroad Brotherhoods, 1880–1920," *American Historical Review* 99 (1994): 1601–33.

Ashby, Leroy. *The Spearless Leader: Senator Borah and the Progessive Movement in the 1920s.* Urbana: University of Illinois Press, 1972.

Asher, Lester. "Labor Law—Collective Labor Agreement Violated by Employer—Action for Damages by Non-Member of Union." *Illinois Law Review* 26 (1932): 922–25.

Atkins, Willard E., and Reed Kitchen. "Some Problems in the Legal Status of Unionism." *North Carolina Law Review* 2 (1924): 160–68.

Auerbach, Jerold S. "The LaFollette Committee: Labor and Civil Liberties in the New Deal." *Journal of American History* 51 (1964): 437–56.

Baer, Denise L., and David A. Bositis. *Elite Cadres and Party Coalitions, Representing the Public in Party Politics.* New York: Greenwood Press, 1988.

Baker, Leonard. *Brandeis and Frankfurter.* New York: Harper & Row, 1984.

Baker, Newton D. "Labor Relations and the Law." *American Bar Association Journal* 8 (1922): 731–36.

Ballantine, Arthur A. "Railway Strikes and the Constitution." *Columbia Law Review* 17 (1917): 502–22.

Barenburg, Mark. "The Political Economy of the Wagner Act: Power, Symbol, and Workplace Cooperation." *Harvard Law Review* 106 (1993): 1381–1496.

Barnard, Harry. *Independent Man: The Life of Senator James Couzens.* New York: Charles Scribner's Sons, 1958.

Barnett, George E. "American Trade Unionism and the Standardization of Wages during the War." *Journal of Political Economy* 27 (1919): 670–93.

———. "The Present Position of American Trade Unionism." *American Economic Review* 12 (1922): 44–79.

Bender, Thomas. "Wholes and Parts: The Need for Synthesis in American History." *Journal of American History* 73 (1986): 120–36.

Berk, Gerald. "Constituting Corporations and Markets: Railroads in Gilded Age Politics." *Studies in American Political Development* 4 (1990): 130–68.

Berman, Edward. *Labor and the Sherman Act.* New York: Harper & Brothers, 1930.

———. *Labor Disputes and the President of the United States.* Studies in History, Economics, and Public Law, 111, no. 2. New York: Longmans, Green & Co., 1924.

Bernhardt, Joshua. *The Division of Conciliation.* Institute for Government Research, Service Monographs, no. 2. Baltimore: Johns Hopkins Press, 1923.

———. *The Interstate Commerce Commission.* Institute for Government Research, Service Monographs, no. 18. Baltimore: Johns Hopkins Press, 1923.

———. *The Railroad Labor Board.* Institute for Government Research, Service Monographs, no. 19. Baltimore: Johns Hopkins Press, 1923.

Bernstein, Irving. *The Caring Society.* Boston: Houghton Mifflin, 1985.

———. *The Lean Years: A History of the American Worker, 1920–1933.* Boston: Houghton Mifflin, 1960.

———. *The New Deal Collective Bargaining Policy.* Berkeley: University of California Press, 1950.

———. "The Railway Labor Act." *Academy of American Political Science Proceedings* 22 (1946): 51–63.

Bickel, Alexander M. *The Unpublished Opinions of Mr. Justice Brandeis: The Supreme Court at Work.* Cambridge: Harvard University Press, Belknap Press, 1957.

Bing, Alexander M. "The Coal and Rail Strikes." *American Labor Legislation Review* 12 (1922): 150–54.

———. *War Time Strikes and Their Adjustment.* New York: E. P. Dutton & Co., 1921.

———. "The Work of the Wage Adjustment Board." *Journal of Political Economy* 27 (1919): 421–56.

Blankenhorn, Heber. *The Strike for Union.* New York: H. W. Wilson Co., 1924.

Block, Fred. "The Ruling Class Does Not Rule." *Socialist Revolution* 7 (1977): 6–28.

Blum, John Morton. *The Progressive Presidents.* New York: W. W. Norton, 1980.

———. *The Republican Roosevelt.* Cambridge: Harvard University Press, 1954.

Boemke, Manfred Franz. "The Wilson Administration, Organized Labor, and the Colorado Coal Strike, 1913–1914." Ph.D. diss., Princeton University, 1983.

Boinville, Barbara R. de, ed. *Origins and Development of Congress.* Washington, D.C.: Congressional Quarterly Press, 1976.

Bonnett, Clarence E. *History of Employers' Associations in the United States.* New York: Vintage Press, 1956.

———. "The Origin of the Labor Injunction." *Southern California Law Review* 5 (1931): 105–25.

———. "The Yellow Dog Contract in Its Relation to Public Policy." *Tulane Law Review* 7 (1933): 315–40.

———. "The Yellow Dog Contract in Its Relation to Public Policy." *Tulane Law Review* 7 (1933): 557–79.

Bowles, Samuel, and Herbert Gintis. "The Crisis of Liberal Democratic Capitalism: The Case of the U.S." *Politics and Society* 11 (1982): 51–93.

Bowman, D. O. *Public Control of Labor Relations: A Study of the National Labor Relations Board.* New York: Macmillan, 1942.

"Boycott on Materials." *Harvard Law Review* 31 (1918): 482–85.

Brady, David W. "A Reevaluation of Realignments in American Politics: Evidence from the House of Representatives." *American Political Science Review* 79 (1985): 32–49.

Brand, Donald R. *Corporatism and the Rule of Law: A Study of the National Recovery Administration.* Ithaca, N.Y.: Cornell University Press, 1988.

Brandes, Stuart D. *American Welfare Capitalism, 1880–1940.* Chicago: Chicago University Press, 1970.

Braunthal, Gerard. *Socialist Labor and Politics in Weimar Germany: The General Federation of German Trade Unions.* Hamden, Conn.: Archon Books, 1978.

Brecher, Jeremy. *Strike!.* Boston: South End Press, 1972.

Breckinridge, S. P. "Two Decisions Relating to Organized Labor." *Journal of Political Economy* 13 (1905): 593–97.

Bridges, Amy. *A City in the Republic: Antebellum New York and the Origins of Machine Politics.* New York: Cambridge University Press, 1984.

Brody, David. *Steelworkers in America: The Non-Union Era.* New York: Harper & Row, 1960.

———. *Workers in Industrial America: Essays on the Twentieth Century Struggle.* New York: Oxford University Press, 1980.

Broesamle, John J. "The Democrats from Bryan to Wilson." In *The Progressive Era,* edited by Lewis L. Gould, 83–113. Syracuse, N.Y.: Syracuse University Press, 1974.

Brown, W. Jethro. "Law, Industry, and Post-War Adjustments." *Harvard Law Review* 35 (1922): 223–44.

Bruere, Robert W. "Can We Eliminate Labor Unrest?" *Annals of American Academy of Political and Social Science* 81 (1919): 95–100.

Buenker, John D. *Urban Liberalism and Progressive Reform.* New York: Charles Scribner's Sons, 1973.

Buenker, John D., John C. Burnham, and Robert M. Crunden. *Progressivism.* Cambridge: Schenkman Publishing Co., 1977.

Burch, Philip H. "The National Association of Manufacturers as an Interest Group." *Politics and Society* 4 (1973): 97–130.

Burdick, Francis M. "Injunction in Labor Disputes." *North American Review* 188 (1908): 271–84.

Burner, David. "John H. Clarke." In *The Justices of the United States Supreme Court, 1789–1969: Their Lives and Major Opinions,* edited by Leon Friedman and Fred L. Israel, 2077–87. New York: Chelsea House, 1969.

———. *The Politics of Provincialism: The Democratic Party in Transition, 1918–1932.* New York: Alfred A. Knopf, 1968.

Burnham, James. *The Machiavellians.* New York: John Day Co., 1943.

Burnham, Walter Dean. "Party Systems and the Political Process." In *The American Party Systems: Stages of Political Development,* edited by Walter Dean Burnham and William Nisbet Chambers, 277–307. New York: Oxford University Press, 1975.

Burton, David H. *Oliver Wendall Holmes, Jr.* Boston: Twayne, 1980.

Caldwell, R. J. "Collective Bargaining—the Democracy of Industry." *Proceedings of the Academy of Political Science* 8 (1919): 79–84.

Cammack, Paul. "Review Article: Bringing the State Back In?" *British Journal of Political Science* 19 (1989): 261–90.

Capper, Arthur. "Industrial Peace." *Annals of American Academy of Political and Social Science* 90 (1920): 165–71.

Carlton, Frank Tracy. *The History and Problems of Organized Labor.* Boston: D. C. Heath & Co., 1920.

Carmen, Ernest C. "The Outlook from the Present Legal Status of Employer and Employees in Industrial Disputes." *Minnesota Law Review* 6 (1922): 533–59.

Carnoy, Martin. *The State and Political Theory.* Princeton: Princeton University Press, 1984.

Carter, W. S. "The Adamson Law: The Employees' Viewpoint." *Proceedings of the Academy of Political Science* 7 (1917): 170–78.

———. "Effect of Federal Control on Railway Labor." *Proceedings of the Academy of Political Science* 8 (1919): 198–210.

———. "The Objections of Organized Labor to Compulsory Arbitration." *Proceedings of the Academy of Political Science* 7 (1917): 36–43.

Casebeer, Kenneth M. "Drafting Wagner's Act: Leon Keyserling and the Precommittee Drafts of the Labor Disputes Act and the National Labor Relations Act." *Industrial Relations Law Journal* 11 (1989): 73–131.

———. "Holder of the Pen: An Interview with Leon Keyserling on Drafting the Wagner Act." *University of Miami Law Review* 42 (1987): 285–363.

Chafee, Zechariah, Jr. "The Internal Affairs of Associations Not for Profit." *Harvard Law Review* 43 (1930): 993–1029.

Chamberlain, J. P. "The Federal Anti-Injunction Act." *American Bar Association Journal* 18 (1932): 477–79.

———. "The Legislature and Labor Injunctions." *American Bar Association Journal* 11 (1925): 815–17.

Chandler, Alfred D., Jr. *The Visible Hand: The Managerial Revolution in American Business.* Cambridge: Harvard University Press, 1977.

Chase, John Dennis. "John R. Commons and the Democratic State." *Journal of Economic Issues* 20 (1986): 759–81.

Chiu, Chang-Wei. *The Speaker of the House of Representatives since 1896.* New York: Columbia University Press, 1928.

Christ, Jay Finley. "The Federal Anti-Injunction Bill." *Illinois Law Review* 16 (1932): 516–39.

———. "Is the Norris Act Constitutional?" *Virginia Law Review* 19 (1932): 51–59.

Christenson, C. Lawrence. "Legally Enforceable Interests in American Labor Union Working Agreements." *Indiana Law Journal* 9 (1933): 69–108.

"Civil Liability of Members of Unincorporated Labor Unions." *Harvard Law Review* 42 (1929): 550–54.

Clarkson, John T. "The Industrial Court Bill." *Iowa Law Bulletin* 6 (1921): 153–64.

Clubb, J. M., W. H. Flanigan, and Nancy H. Zingale. *Partisan Realignment: Voters, Parties, and Government in American History.* Beverly Hills, Calif.: Sage, 1980.

Cochrane, Cornelius. "Injunction Legislation Pending in Congress." *American Labor Legislation Review* 18 (1928): 318–19.

———. "Labor's Campaign against 'Yellow-Dog' Contracts Makes Notable Gains." *American Labor Legislation Review* 17 (1927): 142–45.

———. "Public Opinion Plays Judicial Approval of 'Yellow-Dog' Contracts." *American Labor Legislation Review* 20 (1930): 181–84.

———. "Why Organized Labor Is Fighting 'Yellow-Dog' Contracts." *American Labor Legislation Review* 15 (1925): 227–34.

———. "'Yellow-Dog' Abolished in Wisconsin." *American Labor Legislation Review* 19 (1929): 315–16.

Cohen, Julius Henry. "A League to Enforce Industrial Peace." *Proceedings of the Academy of Political Science* 7 (1917): 108–43.

Colburn, David R., and George E. Pozzetta, eds. *Reform and Reformers in the Progressive Era.* Westport, Conn.: Greenwood Press, 1983.

Colby, Bainbridge. "The Adamson Law: The Public Viewpoint." *Proceedings of the Academy of Political Science* 7 (1917): 185–88.

Cole, Newton. "The Civil Suability, at Law, of Labor Unions." *Fordham Law Review* 8 (1939): 29–44.

Coleman, John R. "The Compulsive Pressures of Democracy in Unionism." In *Labor and Trade Unionism,* edited by Walter Galenson and Seymour Martin Lipset, 207–15. New York: John Wiley & Sons, 1960.

"Collective Labor Agreements." *Columbia Law Review* 31 (1931): 1156–69.

Commons, John R. *Institutional Economics: Its Place in Political Economy*. Madison: University of Wisconsin Press, 1934.

————. "Karl Marx and Samuel Gompers." *Political Science Quarterly* 41 (1924): 281–86.

————. "Law and Economics." *Yale Law Journal* 34 (1925): 375.

Commons, John R., and John B. Andrews. *Principles of Labor Legislation*. New York: Harper & Brothers, 1936.

Commons, John R., David J. Saposs, Helen L. Sumner, E. B. Mittleman, H. E. Hoagland, John B. Andrews, and Selig Perlman, eds. *History of Labor in the United States*. 4 vols. New York: Macmillan, 1936.

*Congressional Quarterly Book of Elections*. Washington, D.C.: Congressional Quarterly Press, 1989.

Conner, Valerie Jean. *The National War Labor Board, Stability, Social Justice, and the Voluntary State in World War One*. Chapel Hill: University of North Carolina Press, 1983.

"Constitutionality of Proposed Labor Injunction Legislation." *Iowa Law Review* 17 (1931): 110–13.

"Constitutional Validity of the Kansas Industrial Court Act." *Michigan Law Review* 20 (1922): 893–97.

"Contract to Employ Only Union Labor Held Invalid." *Central Law Journal* 99 (1926): 239–41.

Cook, Walter Wheeler. "Agency by Estoppel." *Columbia Law Review* 5 (1905): 36–47.

————. *Cases and Other Authorities on Equity: Selected from Decisions of English and American Courts*. St. Paul, Minn.: West, 1925.

————. "The Present Status of the 'Lack of Mutuality' Rule." *Yale Law Journal* 36 (1927): 897–911.

————. "Privileges of Labor Unions in the Struggle for Life." *Yale Law Journal* 27 (1918): 779–801.

Coolidge, Calvin. *The Autobiography*. New York: Cosmopolitan Book Corp., 1929.

Cooper, J., and David W. Brady. "Institutional Context and Leadership Style: The House from Cannon to Rayburn." *American Political Science Review* 74 (1980): 411–25.

Cooper, John Milton, Jr. *The Warrior and the Priest: Woodrow Wilson and Theodore Roosevelt*. Cambridge: Harvard University Press, Belknap Press, 1983.

Corbin, Arthur L. "Contracts for the Benefit of Third Persons." *Yale Law Journal* 27 (1918): 1008–29.

————. "Does a Pre-existing Duty Defeat Consideration?: Recent Noteworthy Decisions." *Yale Law Journal* 27 (1918): 362–81.

"The Coronado Case." *Illinois Law Quarterly* 5 (1923): 126–30.

"The Coronado Coal Case." *Yale Law Journal* 32 (1922): 59–65.

Cotterrell, Roger. "Legality and Political Legitimacy in the Sociology of Max Weber." In *Legality, Ideology, and the State*, edited by David Sugerman, 69–93. London: Academic Press, 1981.

Covington, J. Harry. "The Preservation of Industrial Peace." *Annals of American Academy of Political and Social Science* 90 (1920): 159–64.

Cox, Archibald. "The Legal Nature of Collective Bargaining Agreements." *Michigan Law Review* 57 (1958): 1–36.

Cox, James M. *Journey through My Years*. New York: Simon & Schuster, 1946.

Crager, Burton. "Company Unions under the National Labor Relations Act." *Michigan Law Review* 40 (1942): 831–55.

Croly, Herbert David. *The Promise of American Life*. Edited by Arthur Schlesinger Jr. Cambridge: Harvard University Press, Belknap Press, 1965.

Cronin, James E. *Labour and Society in Britain, 1918–1979*. New York: Schocken Books, 1984.

Cuff, Robert D. *The War Industries Board: Business-Government Relations during World War One*. Baltimore: Johns Hopkins University Press, 1973.

Cunningham, Richard. "The Railroads under Government Operation I." *Quarterly Journal of Economics* 35 (1921): 288–340.

———. "The Railroads under Government Operation II." *Quarterly Journal of Economics* 36 (1921): 30–71.

Cushman, Barry. "Doctrinal Synergies and Liberal Dilemmas: The Case of the Yellow-Dog Contract." *Supreme Court Review* 7 (1992): 235–93.

———. "A Stream of Legal Consciousness: The Current of Commerce Doctrine from *Swift* to *Jones & Laughlin*." *Fordham Law Review* 61 (1992): 105–60.

Dahl, Robert. *A Preface to Democratic Theory*. Chicago: University of Chicago Press, 1956.

Darling, Charles R. "The Adair Case." *American Law Review* 42 (1908): 884–90.

Davis, Allen F. "Welfare, Reform, and World War I." *American Quarterly* 19 (1967): 516–17.

Davis, Colin J. "The 1922 Railroad Shopmen's Strike in the Southeast: A Study of Success and Failure." In *Organized Labor in the Twentieth-Century South*, edited by Robert H. Zieger, 113–34. Knoxville: University of Tennessee Press, 1989.

Davis, James C. "Liquidation of Federal Railroad Control." *American Bar Association Journal* 8 (1922): 327–30.

Davis, James J. "Government Counselors and Efforts to Promote Cooperation." *Proceedings of the Academy of Political Science* 9 (1922): 121–29.

Dean, John S. "The Fundamental Unsoundness of the Kansas Industrial Court of Law." *American Bar Association Journal* 7 (1921): 333–36.

Degler, Carl. "American Political Parties and the Rise of the City." In *Political Parties in American History, 1890–Present*, vol. 3, edited by Paul L. Murphy, 949–68. New York: G. P. Putnam's Sons, 1974.

———. "The Nineteenth Century." In *Theory and Practice in American Politics*, edited by William H. Nelson, 25–42. Chicago: University of Chicago Press, 1964.

Dewey, John. "The Historic Background of Corporate Legal Personality." *Yale Law Journal* 25 (1926): 655–73.

DeWitt, Benjamin Parke. *The Progressive Movement*. New York: Macmillan, 1915.

Dickinson, J. M. "Chief Justice W. H. Taft." *American Bar Association Journal* 7 (1921): 331.

"Discussion of Governmental Mediation and Arbitration." *Proceedings of the Academy of Political Science* 7 (1917): 31–35.

"Discussion of Trade Union and Compulsory Arbitration." *Proceedings of the Academy of Political Science* 7 (1917): 81–87.

"Discussion of Trade Union and Mediation and Conciliation." *Proceedings of the Academy of Political Science* 7 (1917): 162–64.

Dixon, Frank H. "Functions and Policies of the Railroad Labor Board." *Proceedings of the Academy of Political Science* 10 (1922): 19–28.

Doak, William N. "Labor Policies of the Transportation Act from the Point of View of Railroad Employees." *Proceedings of the Academy of Political Science* 10 (1922): 39–48.

Dodd, Edwin Merrick. *American Business Corporations until 1860*. Cambridge: Harvard University Press, 1954.

———. "Dogma and Practice in the Law of Associations." *Harvard Law Review* 42 (1929): 977–1014.

Donovan, Paul. "Legislation Affecting Labor Injunctions." *American Bar Association Journal* 16 (1930): 561–63.

Douglas, Paul H. "Shop Committees: Substitute for, or Supplement to, Trade Unions?" *Journal of Political Economy* 29 (1921): 89–107.

Downs, Anthony. *An Economic Theory of Democracy*. New York: Harper & Row, 1957.

Drury, Horace B. "The Causes and Antidote for Industrial Unrest." *Journal of Political Economy* 28 (1920): 219–39.

Dubofsky, Melvyn. "Abortive Reform: The Wilson Administration and Organized Labor, 1913–1920." In *Work, Community, and Power: The Experience of Labor in Europe and America, 1900–1920*, edited by James E. Cronin and Carman Sirianni, 197–220. Philadelphia: Temple University Press, 1983.

———. *Industrialism and the American Worker, 1865–1920*. Arlington Heights, Ill.: Harlan Davidson, 1985.

———. *The State and Labor in Modern America*. Chapel Hill: University of North Carolina Press, 1994.

"Due Process and the Employment Contract." *Harvard Law Review* 44 (1931): 1287–91.

Duguit, Leon. "Collective Acts as Distinguished from 'Contracts.'" *Yale Law Journal* 27 (1917–18): 753–68.

Dunn, Robert W. *The Americanization of Labor*. New York: International Publishers, 1927.

Duverger, Maurice. *Political Parties*. New York: John Wiley & Sons, 1954.

Eagles, Charles W. *Democracy Delayed: Congressional Reapportionment and Urban-Rural Conflict in the 1920s*. Athens: University of Georgia Press, 1990.

Edwards, David V. *The American Political Experience*. Englewood Cliffs, N.J.: Prentice-Hall, 1985.

Eggert, Gerald. *Railroad Labor Disputes: The Beginnings of Federal Strike Policy*. Ann Arbor: University of Michigan, 1967.

Eisenach, Eldon J. *The Lost Promise of Progressivism*. Lawrence: University of Kansas Press, 1994.

———. "Reconstituting the Study of American Political Thought in a Regime-Change Perspective." *Studies in American Political Development* 4 (1990): 169–230.

Ekirch, Arthur A., Jr. *Progressivism in America: A Study of the Era from Theodore Roosevelt to Woodrow Wilson*. New York: New Viewpoints, 1974.

Eldersveld, Samuel. *Political Parties: A Behavioral Analysis*. Chicago: Rand, 1964.

Ellerd, Harvey G. "Our Experiences with Employee Representation." *Proceedings of the Academy of Political Science* 13 (1928): 110–19.

Ernst, Daniel R. "Common Laborers? Industrial Pluralists, Legal Realists, and the Law of Industrial Disputes, 1915–1943." *Law and History Review* 11 (1993): 62–68.

———. "Free Labor, the Consumer Interest, and the Law of Industrial Disputes, 1885–1900." *American Journal of Legal History* 36 (1992): 19–35.

———. "The Labor Exemption, 1908–1914." *Iowa Law Review* 74 (1989): 1151–74.

———. *Lawyers against Labor: From Individual Rights to Corporate Liberalism.* Urbana: University of Illinois, 1995.

———. "The Yellow-Dog Contract and Liberal Reform, 1917–1932." *Labor History* 30 (1989): 251–74.

Ewing, Cortez A. M. *Congressional Elections, 1896–1944.* Norman: University of Oklahoma Press, 1947.

Farmer, James. "A Boom Business in Busting Unions." *Business and Society Review* 31 (1979): 55–58.

Feinman, Ronald L. *Twilight of Progressivism: The Western Republican Senators and the New Deal.* Baltimore: John Hopkins University Press, 1981.

Feldman, Gerald D. *Army, Industry, and Labor in Germany, 1914–1918.* Princeton: Princeton University Press, 1966.

Feldman, Stephen M. "An Interpretation of Max Weber's Theory of Laws: Metaphysics, Economics, and the Iron Cage of Constitutional Law." *Law and Social Inquiry* (1991): 205–34.

Feller, David E. "A General Theory of the Collective Bargaining Agreement." *California Law Review* 61 (1973): 663–856.

Ferguson, Thomas. "From Normalcy to New Deal: Industrial Structure, Party Competition, and American Public Policy in the Great Depression." *International Organization* 38 (1984): 41–49.

"A Few of the Fundamentals of the Kansas Industrial Court Act." *American Bar Association Journal* 7 (1921): 265–70.

Filene, Peter G. "An Obituary for 'The Progressive Movement.'" *American Quarterly* 22 (1970): 20–34.

Fine, Sidney. *The Automobile under the Blue Eagle: Labor, Management, and the Automobile Manufacturing Code.* Ann Arbor: University of Michigan Press, 1963.

———. *Laissez-Faire and the General Welfare State: A Study of Conflict in American Thought.* Ann Arbor: University of Michigan Press, 1956.

Finegold, Kenneth, and Theda Skocpol. "State, Party, and Industry: From Business Recovery to the Wagner Act in America's New Deal." In *Statemaking and Social Movements,* edited by Charles Bright and Susan Harding, 159–92. Ann Arbor: University of Michigan Press, 1984.

Fink, Leon. *In Search of the Working Class: Essays in American Labor History and Political Culture.* Urbana: University of Illinois, 1994.

———. "Labor, Liberty, and the Law: Trade Unionism and the Problem of the American Constitutional Order." *Journal of American History* 74 (1987): 904–25.

————. *Workingmen's Democracy: The Knights of Labor and American Politics.* Urbana: University of Illinois Press, 1983.

Fish, Peter Graham. "*Red Jacket* Revisited: The Case That Unraveled John J. Parker's Supreme Court Appointment." *Law and History Review* 5 (1987): 51–104.

Fitch, John A. *The Causes of Industrial Unrest.* New York: Harper & Brothers, 1924.

————. "Government Coercion in Labor Disputes." *Annals of American Academy of Political and Social Science* 90 (1920): 74–82.

————. "Newer Interpretations of the Sherman Act." *American Labor Legislation Review* 18 (1928): 289.

————. "The Open and the Closed Shop." *American Review* 1 (1923): 138–48.

————. "The Public and the Labor Struggle." *American Labor and Legislation Review* 13 (1923): 190–94.

Fitzpatrick, Ellen. *Endless Crusade: Women Social Scientists and Progressive Reform.* New York: Oxford University Press, 1990.

Foner, Eric. "Why Is There No Socialism in the United States?" *History Workshop* 17 (1984): 57–80.

Forbath, William E. "Courts, Constitutions, and Labor Politics in England and America: A Study of the Constitutive Power of Law." *Law and Social Inquiry* 16 (1991): 1–34.

————. *Law and the Shaping of the American Labor Movement.* Cambridge: Harvard University Press, 1991.

————. "The Shaping of the American Labor Movement." *Harvard Law Review* 102 (1989): 1109–1256.

Foster, William Z. *The Great Steel Strike and Its Lessons.* New York: B. W. Huebsch, 1920.

Frankfurter, Felix. "Legislation Affecting Labor Injunctions." *Yale Law Journal* 38 (1929): 879–935.

————. "A Note on Advisory Opinions." *Harvard Law Review* 37 (1924): 1002–9.

Frankfurter, Felix, and Nathan Greene. "Congressional Power over the Labor Injunction." *Columbia Law Review* 31 (1931): 385–415.

————. *The Labor Injunction.* New York: Macmillan, 1930.

Frankfurter, Felix, and James M. Landis. *The Business of the Supreme Court: A Study in the Federal Judicial System.* New York: Macmillan, 1927.

Fraser, Steven. *Labor Will Rule: Sidney Hillman and the Rise of American Labor.* New York: Free Press, 1991.

Frayne, Hugh. "Good Will and Cooperation in Industry from the Worker's Point of View." *Proceedings of the Academy of Political Science* 9 (1922): 115–20.

Freeman, Joshua. "Delivering the Goods: Industrial Unionism during World War II." In *The Labor History Reader*, edited by Daniel J. Leab, 383–406. Urbana: University of Illinois Press, 1985.

Freeman, Richard B., and James L. Medoff. *What Do Unions Do?* New York: Basic Books, 1984.

Freund, Paul. "Oliver Wendell Holmes." In *The Justices of the United States Supreme Court, 1789–1969: Their Lives and Major Opinions*, edited by Leon Friedman and Fred L. Israel, 1755–62. New York: Chelsea House, 1969.

Frey, John P. "The Double Standard in Applying the Sherman Act." *American Labor Legislation Review* 18 (1928): 302–8.

Fuess, Claude Moore. *Calvin Coolidge: The Man from Vermont*. Boston: Little, Brown, 1940.

———. *Joseph B. Eastman: Servant of the People*. New York: Columbia University Press, 1952.

Fulmer, William E. "When Employees Want to Bust Their Unions." *Harvard Business Review* 56 (1978): 163–70.

Furner, Mary O. "Knowing Capitalism: Public Investigation and the Labor Question in the Long Progressive Era." In *The State and Economic Knowledge: The American and British Experiences*, edited by Mary O. Furner and Barry Supple, 241–86. New York: Cambridge University Press, 1990.

Gable, Richard W. "Birth of an Employers' Association." *Harvard Business Review* 33 (1959): 535–45.

Galambos, Louis. "The Emerging Organizational Synthesis in Modern American History." *Business History Review* 44 (1970): 279–90.

———. "Technology, Political Economy, and Professionalization: Central Themes of the Organizational Synthesis." *Business History Review* 57 (1983): 471–93.

Garraty, John A. *Henry Cabot Lodge*. New York: Alfred A. Knopf, 1953.

Garrison, Lloyd. "Labor Relations in the Railroad Industry." *Proceedings of the Academy of Political Science* 17 (1937): 27–37.

———. "The National Railroad Adjustment Board: A Unique Administrative Agency." *Yale Law Journal* 46 (1937): 567–98.

Geldart, W. L. "Legal Personality." *Law Quarterly Review* 27 (1911): 90–108.

George, Alexander L., and Juliette L. George. *Woodrow Wilson and Colonel House*. New York: Dover Publications, 1956.

Gerber, Larry G. "Corporatism in Comparative Perspective: The Impact of the First World War on American and British Labor Relations." *Business History Review* 62 (1988): 93–127.

Gienapp, William E. *The Origins of the Republican Party, 1852–1856*. New York: Oxford University Press, 1987.

Gilfond, Duff. *The Rise of Saint Calvin*. New York: Vanguard Press, 1932.

Gillman, Howard. *The Constitution Besieged: The Rise and Demise of Lochner Era Police Powers Jurisprudence*. Durham, N.C.: Duke University Press, 1993.

Gitelman, H. M. "Adolph Strasser and the Origins of Pure and Simple Unionism." *Labor History* 6 (1965): 71–83.

———. "Management's Crisis of Confidence and the Origin of the National Industrial Conference Board, 1914–1916." *Labor History* 58 (1984): 153–77.

———. "Perspectives on American Industrial Violence." *Business History Review* 47 (1973): 1–23.

Glad, Paul W. "Progressives and the Business Culture of the 1920's." *Journal of American History* 53 (1966): 75–89.

Glushien, Morris. "Equity: Specific Performance of Collective Bargaining Contract at the Suit of a Trade Agreement." *Cornell Law Quarterly* 16 (1930): 96–102.

Goldfield, Michael. *The Decline of Organized Labor in the U.S.* Chicago: University of Chicago Press, 1987.

————. "Worker Insurgency, Radical Organization, and New Deal Labor Legislation." *American Political Science Review* 83 (1989): 1257–84.

Goldfield, Michael, Theda Skocpol, and Kenneth Finegold. "Explaining New Deal Labor Policy." *American Political Science Review* 84 (1990): 1297–1315.

Goldman, Ralph M. *The Democratic Party in American Politics*. New York: Macmillan, 1966.

Goldstein, Justin. *Political Repression in Modern America*. New York: Schenkman Publishing Co., 1983.

Gompers, Samuel. "Attitude of Labor towards Governmental Regulation of Industry." *Annals of American Academy of Political and Social Science* 32 (1908): 75–81.

————. *Labor and the Employer*. New York: E. P. Dutton & Co., 1920.

————. "Labor Standards after the War." *Annals of American Academy of Political and Social Science* 81 (1919): 182–87.

————. *Seventy Years of Life and Labor*. New York: E. P. Dutton & Co., 1925.

Gordon, Colin. *New Deals: Business, Labor, and Politics in America, 1920–1935*. New York: Cambridge University Press, 1994.

Gordon, Robert. "Critical Legal Histories." *Stanford Law Review* 36 (1984): 57–126.

Grant, James. *Bernard M. Baruch: The Adventures of a Wall Street Legend*. New York: Simon & Schuster, 1983.

Green, James R. *The World of the Worker*. New York: Hill and Wang, 1980.

Greenbaum, Fred. *Fighting Progressive: A Biography of Edward P. Costigan*. Washington, D.C.: Public Affairs Press, 1971.

————. *Robert Marion LaFollette*. Boston: Twayne, 1975.

Greenstone, J. David. *Labor in American Politics*. Chicago: Chicago University Press, 1977.

Gregg, Gerald B. "The National War Labor Board." *Harvard Law Review* 33 (1919): 39–63.

Gregory, Charles O. *Labor and the Law*. New York: W. W. Norton, 1946.

Gross, James A. *The Making of the National Labor Relations Board*. Albany: University of New York Press, 1974.

Gutman, Herbert. *Work, Culture, and Society in Industrializing America*. New York: Vintage Press, 1977.

Hager, Mark M. "Bodies Politic: The Progressive History of Organizational 'Real Entity' Theory." *University of Pittsburgh Law Review* 50 (1989): 575–654.

Hall, Kermit L. *The Magic Mirror: Law in American History*. New York: Oxford University Press, 1989.

Hall, Stuart. "The Toad in the Garden: Thatcherism among the Theorists." In *Marxism and the Interpretation of Culture*, edited by Cary Nelson and Lawrence Grossberg, 35–74. Urbana: University of Illinois Press, 1988.

Halstead, Murat. *The Life of Theodore Roosevelt*. New York: Saalfield Publishing Co., 1902.

Hamilton, Milo Fowler. "Individual Rights Arising from Collective Labor Contracts." *Missouri Law Review* 3 (1928): 252–69.

Hansen, Alvin H. "Cycles of Strikes." *American Economic Review* 11 (1921): 616–21.

————. "The Economics of Unionism." *Journal of Political Economy* 30 (1922): 518–30.

Hanson, Charles, Sheila Jackson, and Douglas Miller. *The Closed Shop: A Comparative Study in Public Policy and Trade Union Security in Britain, the U.S.A., and West Germany*. New York: St. Martin's Press, 1982.

Harrington, Elbert W. "Political Ideas of Albert B. Cummins." *Iowa Journal of History and Politics* 39 (1941): 339–86.

Harris, Howell. "The Snares of Liberalism? Politicians, Bureaucrats, and the Shaping of Federal Labour Relations Policy in the United States, ca. 1915–1947." In *Shop Floor Bargaining and the State: Historical and Comparative Perspectives*, edited by Steven Tolliday and Jonathon Zeitlin, 148–91. New York: Cambridge University Press, 1985.

Harris, Seymour. *Saving American Capitalism: A Liberal Economic Program*. New York: Alfred A. Knopf, 1948.

Hartz, Louis. *The Liberal Tradition in America*. New York: Harcourt, Brace and Co., 1955.

Hattam, Victoria C. "Economic Visions and Political Strategies: American Labor and the State, 1865–1896." *Studies in American Political Development* 4 (1990): 82–129.

———. "Institutions and Political Change: Working-Class Formation in England and the United States." *Politics and Society* 20 (1992): 133–66.

———. *Labor Visions and State Power: The Origins of Business Unionism in the United States*. Princeton: Princeton University Press, 1993.

Hawley, Ellis. "The Discovery and Study of a 'Corporate Liberalism.'" *Business History Review* 52 (1978): 309–20.

———. "Herbert Hoover, the Commerce Secretariat, and the Vision of an Associative State." *Journal of American History* 61 (1974): 116–40.

———. *The New Deal and the Problem of Monopoly*. Princeton: Princeton University Press, 1966.

Hays, Samuel P. "The Organizational Society." In *Building the Organizational Society: Essays on Associational Activities in Modern America*, edited by Jerry Israel, 1–15. New York: Free Press, 1972.

———. *The Response to Industrialism, 1885–1914*. Chicago: University of Chicago Press, 1957.

Heald, Morell. "Management's Responsibility to Society: The Growth of an Idea." *Business History Review* 31 (1957): 375–84.

Heineman, Robert A. *Authority and the Liberal Tradition*. Durham: North Carolina Academic Press, 1984.

Heiserman, C. B. "Labor Policies of the Transportation Act from the Point of View of Railway Management." *Proceedings of Academy of Political Science* 10 (1922): 29–38.

Hennessy, M. E. *Calvin Coolidge*. New York: G. P. Putnam's Sons, 1924.

Hentz, George F. L. "A Forward Step in Labor Regulation." *St. John's Law Review* 12 (1933): 316–21.

Hicks, John W. *Republican Ascendancy*. New York: Harper Torchbooks, 1960.

Himmelberg, Robert F. "Business, Anti-Trust Policy, and the Industrial Board of the Department of Commerce, 1919." *Business History Review* 42 (1968): 1–23.

———. *The Origins of the National Recovery Administration: Business, Government, and the Trade Association Issue, 1921–1933*. New York: Fordham University Press, 1976.

Hines, Walter D. "The New Basis of Rate-Making." *Proceedings of Academy of Political Science* 10 (1922): 87–93.
——. *War History of American Railroads.* New Haven: Yale University Press, 1928.
Hoffman, Charles. "The Depression of the Nineties." *Journal of Economic History* 16 (1956): 137–64.
Hofstadter, Richard. *The Age of Reform: From Bryan to F.D.R.* New York: Alfred A. Knopf, 1955.
Holmes, Oliver Wendell, Jr. "Privilege, Malice, and Intent." *Harvard Law Review* 8 (1894): 1–14.
Holt, James. *Congressional Insurgents and the Party System, 1909–1916.* Cambridge: Harvard University Press, 1967.
Holton, Robert J., and Bryan S. Turner. *Max Weber on Economy and Society.* London: Routledge Press, 1989.
Hooper, Ben W. "Labor, Railroads, and the Public." *American Bar Association Journal* 9 (1923): 15–18.
——. *The Unwanted Boy: The Autobiography of Governor Ben W. Hooper.* Knoxville: University of Tennessee Press, 1963.
Hoover, Hebert Clark. "A Challenge to Our Moral and Economic System." *American Labor Legislation Review* 11 (1921): 302–3.
——. *The Memoirs of Herbert Hoover: The Cabinet and the Presidency.* Vol. 2. New York: Macmillan, 1952.
——. "The Problem of the Reorganization of the Federal Government." *Proceedings of Academy of Political Science* 9 (1922): 120–22.
Horowitz, Ruth. *Political Ideologies of Organized Labor: The New Deal Era.* New Brunswick, N.J.: Transaction Books, 1978.
Horwitz, Martin J. *The Transformation of American Law, 1780–1860.* Camridge: Cambridge University Press, 1977.
——. *The Transformation of American Law, 1870–1960: The Crisis of Legal Orthodoxy.* Oxford: Oxford University Press, 1992.
Hovenkamp, Herbert. "Labor Conspiracies in American Law, 1880–1930." *Texas Law Review* 66 (1988): 919–65.
Howard, Sidney. *The Labor Spy.* New York: Republic Publishing Co., 1924.
Hoxie, Richard Franklin. "President Gompers and the Labor Vote." *Journal of Political Economy* 16 (1908): 693–700.
——. "The Trade Union Point of View." *Journal of Political Economy* 15 (1907): 345–63.
——. *Trade Unions in the United States.* New York: D. Appleton & Co., 1920.
Huggins, William L. "Just What Has the Supreme Court Done to the Kansas Industrial Act? Why Did It Do It?" *American Bar Association Journal* 11 (1925): 363–67.
Hunt, Alan. "The Ideology of Law: Advances and Problems in Recent Applications of the Concept of Ideology to the Analysis of Law." *Law and Society Review* 19 (1985): 11–37.
Hunt, Henry T. "Labor Policies of the Transportation Act from the Standpoint of the Public Group." *Proceedings of Academy of Political Science* 10 (1922): 49–59.
——. "Make the Laws More Explicit." *American Labor Legislation Review* 18 (1928): 309–11.

Hurvitz, Haggai. "The Meaning of Industrial Conflict in Some Ideologies of the Early 1920s: The AFL, Organized Employers, and Herbert Hoover." Ph.D. diss., Columbia University, 1971.

"Inducing Breach of Agreement by Employees Not to Join a Labor Union." *Michigan Law Review* 16 (1918): 250–57.

"Inducing Breach of Contract in Labor Disputes." *Columbia Law Review* 24 (1924): 184–92.

"Injunction—Inducing Employers to Join Union in Violation of Contract of Employment." *Columbia Law Review* 22 (1922): 78–79.

"Injunctions—Acts Restrained: Breach of Contract—Enforcement of Closed Shop Agreements." *Harvard Law Review* 43 (1930): 1158–59.

"Injunctions—Labor Unions—Enforcement of Employer's Agreements." *Columbia Law Review* 30 (1930): 410–11.

"Injunctions in Labor Disputes." *Harvard Law Review* 31 (1918): 648–49.

Irons, Peter. *The New Deal Lawyers.* Princeton: Princeton University Press, 1982.

Jacobs, Clyde E. *Law Writers and the Courts: The Influence of Thomas M. Cooley, Christopher G. Tiedman, and John F. Dillon upon American Constitutional Law.* Berkeley: University of California Press, 1954.

Jacoby, Sanford M. *Employing Bureaucracy.* Ithaca, N.Y.: Cornell University Press, 1985.

Jaenicke, Douglas W. "The Jacksonian Integration of Parties into the Constitutional System." *Political Science Quarterly* 101 (Centennial Year, 1886–1986): 85–107.

Jewell, B. M. "The Railway Strikes: Strikers' Viewpoint." *Current History* 17 (1922): 202–7.

Johnson, Donald Bruce, comp. *National Party Platforms.* Vol. 1. Urbana: University of Illinois Press, 1956.

Johnson, Emory R. "The Problem of Railroad Control." *Political Science Quarterly* 36 (1921): 353–75.

Jones, Dallas L. "The Enigma of the Clayton Act." *Industrial and Labor Relations Review* 10 (1957): 201–21.

———. "The Wilson Administration and Organized Labor, 1912–1919," Ph.D. diss., Princeton University, 1954.

"Judicial Action in Labor Disputes." *American Bar Association Journal* 6 (1920): 19–20.

Kalman, Laura. *Legal Realism at Yale.* Chapel Hill: University of North Carolina, 1986.

Katz, Nathan. "Equity: Injunction: Legality of Peaceful Picketing." *Cornell Law Quarterly* 12 (1927): 226–29.

Kaufmann, Jacob J. *Collective Bargaining in the Railroad Industry.* New York: Columbia University, King's Crown Press, 1954.

Keane, John. "The Legacy of Political Economy: Thinking with and against Claus Offe." *Canadian Journal of Political and Social Theory* 2 (1978): 49–91.

Keir, Malcolm. "Post-war Causes of Labor Unrest." *Annals of American Academy of Political and Social Science* 81 (1919): 101–9.

Kendall, Henry P. "Post-war Standards for Industrial Relations." *Annals of American Academy of Political and Social Science* 81 (1919): 163–66.

Kennedy, Walter B. "Law and the Railroad Labor Problem." *Yale Law Journal* 32 (1923): 553–74.

Kens, Paul. "The Source of a Myth: Police Powers of the States and Laissez-Faire Constitutionalism, 1900–1937." *American Journal of Legal History* 35 (1991): 70–98.

Kerr, K. Austin. *American Railroad Politics, 1914–1920: Rates, Wages, and Efficiency.* Pittsburgh: University of Pittsburgh Press, 1968.

———. "Decision for Federal Control: Wilson, McAdoo, and the Railroads, 1917." *Journal of American History* 54 (1967): 550–60.

Klare, Karl E. "Judicial Deradicalization of the Wagner Act and the Origins of Modern Legal Consciousness, 1937–1941." *Minnesota Law Review* 62 (1978): 265–339.

Kolko, Gabriel. "The Premises of Business Revisionism." *Business History Review* 33 (1959): 330–44.

———. *Railroads and Regulations, 1877–1916.* Princeton: Princeton University Press, 1965.

Kopold, Sylvia. *Rebellion in Labor Unions.* New York: Bond & Liverright, 1924.

Krasner, Stephen. *Defending the National Interest: Raw Materials Investments and U.S. Foreign Policy.* Princeton: Princeton University Press, 1978.

Kronman, Anthony T. *Max Weber.* Stanford: Stanford University Press, 1983.

Kutler, Stanley Ira. "The Judicial Philosophy of Chief Justice Taft and Organized Labor, 1921–1930." Ph.D. diss., Ohio State University, 1960.

———. "Labor, the Clayton Act, and the Supreme Court." *Labor History* 3 (1982): 19–38.

"Labor Injunctions—Federal Statute Defining and Limiting the Jurisdiction of Courts Sitting in Equity." *Michigan Law Review* 30 (1932): 1257–70.

"Labor Law—Employer-Union Contracts—Burden of Proof." *Yale Law Journal* 37 (1928): 526–27.

"Labor Law—Employment Contracts—Interest Protected." *Yale Law Journal* 33 (1924): 440–41.

"Labor Law—Freedom of Speech—Injunction against Interference with 'Yellow-Dog' Contract." *Yale Law Journal* 41 (1932): 923–24.

"Labor Law—Injury—Illegality." *Texas Law Review* 11 (1932): 131–33.

"Labor Law—Peaceful Picketing to Induce a Breach of Contract for a Term with a Rival Union." *Columbia Law Review* 32 (1932): 1248–49.

"Labor Laws and Decisions." *American Labor Legislation Review* 9 (1919): 231–35.

Ladd, Everett Carl. *American Political Parties, Social Change, and Political Response.* New York: W. W. Norton, 1970.

Landes, William M., and Richard A. Posner. "The Positive Economic Theory of Tort Law." *Georgia Law Review* 15 (1981): 871–77.

Landis, James. "Crucial Issues in Administrative Law." *Harvard Law Review* 53 (1940): 1077–1102.

Lash, Joseph P. *Dealers and Dreamers: A New Look at the New Deal.* New York: Doubleday, 1988.

Laski, Harold J. "British Labor Reconstruction Proposals and the American Labor Attitude." *Proceedings of Academy of Political Science* 8 (1919): 193–97.

————. "The Personality of Associations." *Harvard Law Review* 29 (1916): 404–26.

Laslett, John H. M., and Seymour Martin Lipset, eds. *Failure of a Dream?* Berkeley: University of California Press, 1974.

Lathem, Edward Connery. *Your Son, Calvin Coolidge.* Montpelier: Vermont Historical Society, 1968.

Laughlin, J. Laurence. "The Unions versus Higher Wages." *Journal of Political Economy* 14 (1906): 142.

Laurent, Francis W. "Labor Law—Responsible in Tort of Voluntary Unincorporated Associations—Developments since the *Coronado* Case." *Wisconsin Law Review* 12 (1937): 523–30.

Lay, George C. "The Coronado Coal Case and Its Consequences." *Iowa Law Review* 8 (1923): 162–76.

Lecht, Leonard. *Experience under Railway Labor Legislation.* New York: Columbia University Press, 1955.

"Legal Consequences Flowing from Trade Agreements." *Columbia Law Review* 24 (1924): 409–15.

"Legal History of Trade Unions." *Virginia Law Review* 6 (1919): 47–53.

"The Legality of Combinations of Employers for the Purpose of Uniform Dealing with Labor." *Columbia Law Review* 26 (1926): 344–48.

"Legislative Power to Restrict Freedom of Labor Contracts." *Michigan Law Review* 13 (1915): 497–501.

Lehmbruch, Gerard, and Phillippe C. Schmitter. "Introduction: Neo-corporatism in Comparative Perspective." In *Patterns of Corporatist Policymaking.* Beverley Hills: Sage Press, 1992.

Leiserson, William M. "Employee Representatives—A Warning to Both Employers and Unions." *Proceedings of Academy of Political Science* 13 (1928): 96–109.

————. "Theories of Labor Relations." *American Review* 2 (1926): 6–15.

Les Benedict, Michael. "Laissez-Faire and Liberty: A Re-evaluation of the Meaning of Laissez-Faire Constitutionalism." *Law and History Review* 3 (1985): 293–331.

*Letters of Louis D. Brandeis, Elder Statesman, 1921–1941.* Vol. 5. Edited by Melvyn Dubofsky and David W. Levy. New York: State University of New York Press, 1978.

Leuchtenburg, William E. *The Perils of Prosperity, 1914–1932.* Chicago: University of Chicago Press, 1958.

————. "The Pertinence of Political History: Reflections on the Significance of the State in America." *Journal of American History* 73 (1986): 585–600.

Leupp, Francis E. *The Man Roosevelt.* New York: D. Appleton & Co., 1904.

Lichtenstein, Nelson. "From Corporatism to Collective Bargaining: Organized Labor and the Eclipse of Social Democracy in the Postwar Era." In *The Rise and Fall of the New Deal Order, 1930–1980,* edited by Steve Fraser and Gary Gerstle, 122–52. Princeton: Princeton University Press, 1989.

Lichtenstein, Nelson. *Labor's War at Home: The CIO in World War II.* New York: Cambridge University Press, 1982.

Lichtman, Allan J. *Prejudice and the Old Politics: The Presidential Election of 1928.* Chapel Hill: University of North Carolina Press, 1979.

Link, Arthur S. "What Happened to the Progressive Movement in the 1920's?"
   *American Historical Review* 64 (1959): 833–51.

———. *Wilson: The New Freedom*. Princeton: Princeton University Press, 1956.

———. *Woodrow Wilson and the Progressive Era, 1910–1917*. New York: Harper &
   Row, 1954.

Lipset, Seymour Martin. "Radicalism or Reformism: The Sources of Working-Class
   Politics." *American Political Science Review* 77 (1983): 1–19.

Livermore, Seward W. *Politics Is Adjourned: Woodrow Wilson and the War Congress,
   1916–1918*. Middletown, Conn.: Wesleyan University Press, 1966.

Llewellyn, Karl. "The Effect of Legal Institutions upon Economics." *American
   Economic Review* 15 (1925): 665–83.

Locke, John. *Political Writings*. Edited with an Introduction by David Wootton.
   New York: Mentor Books, 1993.

Lothian, Tamara. "The Political Consequences of Labor Law Regimes: The Contractualist and Corporatist Models Compared." *Cardozo Law Review* 7 (1986):
   1001–71.

Lowitt, Richard. *George W. Norris: The Persistence of a Progressive, 1913–1933*.
   Urbana: University of Illinois Press, 1971.

Lubell, Samuel. *The Future of American Politics*. New York: Harper & Row, 1951.

Lubove, Roy. *The Struggle for Social Security, 1900–1935*. Pittsburgh: University of
   Pittsburgh Press, 1986.

McCabe, David A. "Federal Intervention in Labor Disputes under the Erdman,
   Newlands, and Adamson Acts." *Proceedings of Academy of Political Science* 7
   (1917): 94–107.

McCormick, Richard L. *The Party Period and Public Policy: American Politics from
   the Age of Jackson to the Progressive Era*. New York: Oxford University Press,
   1985.

———. "Progressivism: A Contemporary Reassessment." In *The Party Period and
   Public Policy: American Politics from the Age of Jackson to the Progressive Era*,
   263–88. New York: Oxford University Press, 1985.

McCraw, Thomas K. *Prophets of Regulation*. Cambridge: Harvard University Press,
   Belknap Press, 1984.

———. *Regulation in Perspective: Historical Essays*. Cambridge: Harvard University
   Press, 1981.

McDonagh, Eileen Lorenzi. "Representative Democracy and State-Building in the
   Progressive Era: The Impact of Grassroots Opinion on House Roll Call Voting
   Sixty-third to Sixty-sixth Congresses, 1913–1921." *American Political Science
   Review* 86 (1992): 938–50.

MacDonald, Donald. "The Constitutionality of Wisconsin's Statute Invalidating
   'Yellow Dog' Contracts." *Wisconsin Law Review* 6 (1931): 86–100.

McKenna, Marian C. *Borah*. Ann Arbor: University of Michigan Press, 1961.

MacVeagh, Rogers. *The Transportation Act, 1920: Its Sources, History, and Text,
   Together with Its Amendments of the Interstate Commerce Act*. New York: Henry
   Holt & Co., 1923.

Macy, V. Everett. "Seven Points for Reconstruction Labor Policy." *Annals of American Academy of Political and Social Science* 81 (1919): 80–86.

Magill, Katherine B., and Roswell F. Magill. "The Suability of Labor Unions."
   *North Carolina Law Review* 1 (1922): 81–87.
Magruder, Calvert. "A Half Century of Legal Influence upon the Development of
   Collective Bargaining." *Harvard Law Review* 50 (1937): 1071–1117.
Mann, Arthur. *LaGuardia: A Fighter against His Times, 1882–1933*. Chicago: Uni-
   versity of Chicago Press, 1959.
———. *LaGuardia Comes to Power, 1933*. Chicago: University of Chicago Press,
   1965.
———, ed. *The Progressive Era: Liberal Renaissance or Liberal Failure?* New York:
   Holt, Rinehart and Winston, 1963.
March, John G., and Johan P. Olsen. "The New Institutionalism: Organizational
   Factors in Political Life." *American Political Science Review* 78 (1984): 734–49.
Margulies, Herbert F. *Senator Lenroot of Wisconsin: A Political Biography, 1900–
   1929*. Columbia: University of Missouri Press, 1977.
Markovits, Andrei S. *The Politics of West German Trade Unions: Strategies of Class
   and Interest Representation in Growth and Crisis*. New York: Camrbidge University
   Press, 1986.
Martin, George. *Madam Secretary, Frances Perkins*. Boston: Houghton Mifflin, 1976.
Mason, Alpheus T. *Brandeis: A Free Man's Life*. New York: Viking Press, 1946.
———. "The Labor Clauses of the Clayton Act." *American Political Science Review*
   18 (1924): 489–512.
———. "Louis D. Brandeis." In *The Justices of the United States Supreme Court,
   1789–1969: Their Lives and Major Opinions*, edited by Leon Friedman and
   Fred L. Israel, 2043–59. New York: Chelsea House, 1969.
———. *Organized Labor and the Law; with Special Reference to Sherman and Clayton
   Acts*. Durham, N.C.: Duke University Press, 1925.
———. "Organized Labor as Party Plaintiff in Injunction Cases." *Columbia Law
   Review* 30 (1930): 466–87.
———. "William Howard Taft." In *The Justices of the United States Supreme Court,
   1789–1969: Their Lives and Major Opinions*, edited by Leon Friedman and
   Fred. L. Israel, 2103–21. New York: Chelsea House, 1969.
Mayer, George H. *The Republican Party, 1854–1966*. New York: Oxford University
   Press, 1967.
Meeker, Royal. "Employees' Representation in Management of Industry." *American
   Economic Review* 10 (1920): 89–102.
———. "Industrial Democracy." *Annals of American Academy of Political and Social
   Science* 90 (1920): 18–21.
Merritt, Walter Gordon. "The Sherman Act: A Bulwark of Freedom." *American
   Labor Legislation Review* 18 (1928): 291–301.
Metre, T. W. Van. "Railroad Regulation under the Transportation Act." *Annals of
   American Academy of Political and Social Science* 110 (1922): 3–12.
Michels, Robert. *Political Parties*. New York: Free Press, 1966.
Millis, Harry A., and Emily Clark Brown. *From the Wagner Act to Taft-Hartley*.
   Chicago: Chicago University Press, 1950.
Mink, Gwendolyn. *Old Labor and the New Immigrants in American Political Develop-
   ment: Union, Party, and State, 1875–1920*. Ithaca, N.Y.: Cornell University
   Press, 1986.

Mitchell, Wesley C. "Commons on Institutional Economics." *American Economic Review* 25 (1935): 635–52.

Mittelman, Edward B. "Opposition to Amalgamation and Politics at Portland: Bias for American Federation of Labor." *Journal of Political Economy* 32 (1924): 86–100.

Montgomery, David. *Citizen Worker: The Experience of Workers in the United States with Democracy and the Free Market during the Nineteenth Century*. New York: Cambridge University Press, 1993.

———. *The Fall of the House of Labor: The Workplace, the State, and American Labor Activism, 1865–1925*. New York: Cambridge University Press, 1987.

———. *Workers' Control in America*. New York: Cambridge University Press, 1979.

Moore, R. Laurence. "Directions of Thought in Progressive America." In *The Progressive Era*, edited by Lewis L. Gould, 35–54. Syracuse, N.Y.: Syracuse University Press, 1974.

Morawetz, Victor. "The Railway Problem, I." *North American Review* 209 (1919): 330–44.

Morgan, George T. "No Compromise—No Recognition: John Henry Kirby, the Southern Lumber Operators' Association, and Unionism in the Piney Woods, 1906–1916." *Labor History* 10 (1969): 193–204.

Mowry, George E. "The California Progressive and His Rationale: A Study in Middle Class Politics." *Mississippi Valley Historical Review* 36 (1949): 241–50.

———. *The California Progressives*. Berkeley: University of California Press, 1951.

Murray, Robert K. *The Harding Era* Minneapolis: University of Minnesota Press, 1969.

———. *The 103rd Ballot*. New York: Harper & Row, 1976.

———. *The Politics of Normalcy: Governmental Theory and Practice in the Harding-Coolidge Era*. New York: W. W. Norton, 1973.

———. "Public Opinion, Labor, and a Clayton Act." *Historian* 21 (1959): 255–70.

———. *Red Scare: A Study in National Hysteria, 1919–1920*. New York: McGraw-Hill Book Co., 1964.

Nagel, Charles. *Speeches and Writings: 1900–1928*. Edited by Otto Heller. New York: G. P. Putnam's Sons, 1931.

*National Party Platforms*. Vol 1. Compiled by Donald Bruce Johnson. Urbana: University of Illinois Press, 1956.

Nelson, Daniel. "Scientific Management, Systematic Management, and Labor, 1880–1915." *Business History Review* 48 (1974): 479–500.

Nelson, Daniel, and Stuart Campbell. "Taylorism versus Welfare Work in American Industry: H. L. Gantt and the Bancrofts." *Business History Review* 46 (1972): 1–16.

Nelson, Milton N. *Open Price Association*. Urbana: University of Illinois Press, 1922.

"A New Approach to Labor Problems." *Yale Law Journal* 37 (1927): 249–54.

"The New Labor Laws: Legislation of 1924." *American Labor Legislation Review* 14 (1924): 259–327.

Noble, David F. *America by Design, Science Technology, and the Rise of Corporate Capitalism*. New York: Alfred A. Knopf, 1977.

———. *The Progressive Mind, 1890–1917*. Chicago: Rand McNally & Co., 1973.

Norris, George W. "Injunctions in Labor Disputes." *Marquette Law Review* 16
    (1932): 157–67.
"The Norris–LaGuardia Act: Cases Involving or Growing Out." *Harvard Law
    Review* 50 (1937): 1295–1303.
Norton, Thomas J. "Further Light on Pending Anti-injunction Measure." *American
    Bar Association Journal* 17 (1931): 59–62.
November, Julius. "The 'Yellow-Dog' Contract." *St. John's Law Review* 6 (1932):
    428–31.
Nye, Russel B. *Midwestern Progressive Politics*. East Lansing: Michigan State Univer-
    sity Press, 1959.
Obenauer, Marie L. "Who Are the Coal Mine Workers?" *North American Review*
    219, no. 822 (1924): 609–15.
O'Brien, Ruth. "'Business Unionism' versus 'Responsible Unionism': Common Law
    Confusion, the American State, and the Formation of Pre–New Deal Labor Pol-
    icy." *Law and Social Inquiry* 18 (1993): 255–98.
———. "Taking the Conservative State Seriously: Statebuilding and Restrictive
    Labor Practices in Postwar America." *Labor Studies Journal* 21 (Winter 1997):
    33–63.
Offe, Claus. "Advanced Capitalism and the Welfare State." *Politics and Society* 3
    (1972): 479–88.
Ohl, John Kennedy. *Hugh S. Johnson and the New Deal*. De Kalb: Northern Illinois
    University Press, 1985.
O'Leary, Kevin C. "Herbert Croly and Progressive Democracy." *Polity* 26 (1994):
    533–52.
Oliphant, Herman. "A Return to Stare Decisis." *American Bar Association Journal* 14
    (1928): 71–76.
Olson, James S. *Historical Dictionary of the 1920s: From World War I to the New Deal,
    1919–1933*. New York: Greenwood Press, 1988.
Orren, Karen. *Belated Feudalism: Labor, the Law, and Liberal Development in the
    United States*. New York: Cambridge University Press, 1991.
Palmer, Gill. *British Industrial Relations*. London: George Allen & Unwin, 1983.
Parkinson, Thomas I. "Constitutional Aspects of Compulsory Arbitration." *Proceed-
    ings of Academy Political Science* 7 (1917): 44–80.
Parks, J. Lewis. "Equitable Relief in Contracts Involving Personal Services." *Univer-
    sity of Pennsylvania Law Review* 66 (1918): 251–66.
Patterson, James T. *Congressional Conservatism and the New Deal: The Growth of the
    Conservative in Coalition Congress, 1933–1939*. Lexington: University of Ken-
    tucky Press, 1967.
"Peaceful Picketing in New York, 1912–1926." *Yale Law Journal* 36 (1927):
    557–66.
Pelling, Henry. *American Labor*. Chicago: Chicago University Press, 1960.
Perlman, Selig. *A History of Trade Unionism in the United States*. New York: Augus-
    tus M. Kelley, 1950.
Perlman, Selig, and Philip Taft. *History of Labor in the United States, 1896–1932*.
    New York: Macmillan, 1935.
Petro, Sylvester. "Injunctions and Labor Disputes: 1880–1932." *Wake Forest Law
    Review* 14 (1978): 351–53.

Piven, Frances Fox. "The Decline of Labor Parties: An Overview." In *Labor Parties in Post-industrial Societies*, edited by Frances Fox Piven, 1–19. New York: Oxford University Press, 1992.

Plotke, David. "The Wagner Act, Again: Politics and Labor, 1935–1937." *Studies in American Political Development* 2 (1987): 105–56.

Plumb, Glenn E. "Should Labor Participate in Management?" *Annals of American Academy of Political and Social Science* 86 (1919): 222–26.

Polk, Charles M. "Are Agreements Which Provide for Employment of Union Labor Exclusively Invalid as Contrary to Public Policy?" *Central Law Journal* 74 (1920): 67–69.

Pollock, Sir Frederick, and Frederic William Maitland. *The History of English Law, before the Time of Edward I*. Washington, D.C.: Lawyers' Literary Club, 1959.

Portender, A. J. "Reconstruction: A Survey and a Forecast." *Annals of American Academy of Political and Social Science* 82 (1919): 111–23.

Porter, Mary Cornelia. "That Commerce Shall be Free: A New Look at the Old Laissez-Faire Court." *Supreme Court Review* (1976): 135–59.

Pound, Roscoe. "The End of Law As Developed in Legal Rules and Doctrines." *Harvard Law Review* 27 (1914): 195–234.

———. "Liberty of Contract." *Yale Law Journal* 18 (1909): 454–87.

Powell, Thomas Reed. "Protecting Property and Liberty, 1922–1924." *Political Science Quarterly* 40 (1925): 404–37.

———. "The Supreme Court's Control over the Issue of Injunction in Labor Disputes." *Proceedings of Academy of Political Science* 13 (1928): 37–77.

Prescott, William B. "The Services of Labor Unions in the Settlement of Industrial Disputes." *Annals of American Academy of Political and Social Science* 27 (1906): 521–30.

"Present Day Labor Litigation." *Yale Law Journal* 30 (1921): 618–23.

"The Present Status of Collective Labor Agreement." *Harvard Law Review* 51 (1938): 520–33.

"President Hoover Addresses Association." *American Bar Association Journal* 18 (1932): 701–3.

"President Says Twelve Hour Day Must Go." *American Labor Legislation Review* 13 (1923): 85.

Preston, William, Jr.. *Aliens and Dissenters: Federal Suppression of Radicals, 1903–1933*. 2d ed. Urbana: University of Illinois Press, 1994.

Priest, George L. "The Invention of Enterprise Liability: A Critical History of the Intellectual Foundations of Modern Tort Law." *Journal of Legal Studies* 14 (1985): 461–528.

"Primary Secondary and Tertiary Boycotts in Labor-Disputes." *Columbia Law Review* 23 (1923): 579–82.

"Prior Illegal Acts as a Ground for Blanket Injunctions against Picketing." *Harvard Law Review* 44 (1931): 971–75.

"Privilege of a Labor Union to Induce a Breach of Contract." *Yale Law Journal* 32 (1922): 171–78.

"The Privilege of a Labor Union to Persuade Employees to Terminate Their Employment in Order to Join the Union." *Columbia Law Review* 18 (1918): 252–55.

"The Privilege of Labor Union Officials to Induce a Breach of Contract." *University of Pennsylvania Law Review* 71, no. 2 (1923): 138–41.

"Problems of Social Unrest, IV: The Future of Labor Unionism." *Central Law Journal* 89 (1919): 405–7.

Purves, Alexander. "Harmonizing Labor and Capital by Means of Industrial Participation." *Annals of American Academy of Political and Social Science* 20 (1902): 61–77.

Quigg, Murray T. "Function of the Law in Relation to Disputes between Employers and Employees." *American Bar Association Journal* 9 (1923): 795–801.

Rayback, Joseph G. *A History of American Labor*. New York: Macmillan, 1966.

*Report of the Investigators to the Commission of the Inquiry, the Interchurch World Movement*. Public Opinion and the Steel Strike, Supplementary. New York: Harcourt, Brace & Co., 1921.

"Responsibility of Labor Unions for Acts of Members." *Columbia Law Review* 38 (1938): 454–73.

Rice, William Gorham. "Collective Labor Agreements in American Law." *Harvard Law Review* 44 (1931): 572–608.

Richberg, Donald R. *Government and Business Tomorrow*. New York: Harper & Brothers, 1943.

———. *Labor Union Monopoly: A Clear and Present Danger*. Chicago: H. Regency Co., 1957.

———. "A National Labor Policy." *Proceedings of Academy of Political Science* 22 (1926): 86–93.

"Right of a Labor Union to Induce Its Members to Compel an Employer to Unionize His Business." *Central Law Journal* (1918): 39–40.

"Right of Labor Union to Prescribe Minimum Number of Employees in a Business of Enterprise." *Central Law Journal* 86 (1918): 239–40.

"Right of Members of Labor Union to Sue on Union's Contract with Employer." *Virginia Law Review* 18 (1931): 182–85.

Ripley, Randall B. *Congress: Process and Policy*. New York: W. W. Norton, 1975.

———. "Functions of the Party Leaders." In *The Congressional System: Notes and Readings*, edited by Leroy N. Rieselbach. Belmont, Calif.: Wadsworth Publishing, 1970.

———. *Majority Party Leadership in Congress*. Boston: Little, Brown, 1969.

"Rival Unions: A Test of the Liberal Approach to Labor Problems." *Harvard Law Review* 46 (1932): 125–34.

Robertson, James Oliver. *No Third Choice: Progressives in Republican Politics, 1916–1921*. New York: Garland Publishing, 1983.

Rogers, Joel. "Divide and Conquer: The Legal Foundations of Postwar U.S. Labor Policy." Ph.D. diss., Princeton University, 1984.

Rogin, Michael. "Voluntarism: The Political Functions of an Anti-political Doctrine." *Industrial and Labor Relations Review* 15 (1962): 521–35.

Roosevelt, Theodore. *An Autobiography*. New York: Macmillan, 1919.

Ross, Dorothy. *Origins of American Social Science*. New York: Cambridge University Press, 1990.

Ross, William G. *A Muted Fury: Populists, Progressives, and Labor Unions Confront the Courts, 1890–1937*. Princeton: Princeton University Press, 1994.

Rowntree, B. Seebohm. "The Way to Industrial Peace: From an English Employee's Point of View." *Proceedings of Academy of Political Science* 9 (1922): 98–114.

Royce, Alexander B. "Labor, the Federal Anti-trust Laws, and the Supreme Court." *New York University Law Review* 5 (1928): 19–28.

Rumble, Wilfried E. *American Legal Realism: Skepticism, Reform, and the Judicial Process.* Ithaca, N.Y.: Cornell University Press, 1968.

Rutherford, Malcolm. "J. R. Commons's Institutional Economics." *Journal of Economic Issues* 17 (1983): 721–44.

Ryan, John A. "Americanization in Industry." *Annals of American Academy of Political and Social Science* 90 (1920): 126–30.

Sakolski, A. M. "Practical Tests of the Transportation Act." *Political Science Quarterly* 36 (1919): 376–90.

Salvatore, Nick. *Eugene V. Debs: Citizen and Socialist.* Urbana: University of Illinois Press, 1982.

Saposs, David. J., and Elizabeth T. Bliss. *Anti-labor Activities.* New York: League for Industrial Democracy, 1938.

Sarasohn, David. *The Party of Reform: Democrats in the Progressive Era.* Jackson: University of Mississippi Press, 1989.

Sargent, Noel. "Public Contracts and Union Labor." *Central Law Journal* 97 (1924): 295–98.

Sayre, Francis Bowen. "Inducing Breach of Contract." *Harvard Law Review* 36 (April 1923): 663–703.

———. "Labor and the Courts." *Yale Law Journal* 39 (1920): 682–705.

Schlabach, Theron F. *Edwin E. Witte: Cautious Reformer.* Madison: State Historical Society of Wisconsin, 1969.

Schlegel, John Henry. *American Legal Realism and Empirical Social Science.* Chapel Hill: University of North Carolina Press, 1995.

Schlesinger, Arthur M., Jr. *The Coming of the New Deal.* Boston: Houghton Mifflin, 1959.

———. *The Crisis of the Old Order, 1919–1933.* Boston: Houghton Mifflin, 1957.

———. *The Politics of Upheaval.* Boston: Houghton Mifflin, 1960.

Schlesinger, Joseph A. "The New American Political Party." *American Political Science Review* 79 (1985): 1153–69.

Schriftgiesser, Karl. *This Was Normalcy.* Boston: Little, Brown, 1948.

Schumpeter, Joseph. *Capitalism, Socialism, and Democracy.* New York: Harper & Brothers, 1942.

Schwab, Charles M. "Capital and Labor." *Annals of American Academy of Political and Social Science* 81 (January 1919): 157–162.

Schwarz, Jordon A. *The Interregnum of Despair: Hoover, Congress, and the Depression.* Urbana: University of Illinois Press, 1970.

Seager, Henry R. "Company Unions vs. Trade Unions." *American Economic Review* 13 (1923): 1–13.

———. "Railroad Labor and the Labor Problem." *Proceedings of Academy of Political Science* 10 (1922): 15–18.

———. "Trade Unionism and Employee Representation Plans." *Proceedings of Academy of Political Science* 13 (1928): 93–95.

Seiler, J. Martin. "The Effect of Section 7a of the National Industrial Recovery."
    *New York Law Quarterly Review* 11 (1933): 237–51.
*Selections from the Correspondence of Theodore Roosevelt and Henry Cabot Lodge,*
    *1884–1918.* Vol. 1. New York: Charles Scribner's Sons, 1925.
Shafer, Byron E., ed. *Is America Different?: A New Look at American Exceptionalism.*
    New York: Oxford University Press, 1991.
Shapiro, Stanley. "The Great War and Reform: Liberals and Labor, 1917–1919."
    *Labor History* 12 (1971): 323–44.
Sharfman, I. L. *The Interstate Commerce Commission: A Study in Administrative Law*
    *and Procedure.* New York: Commonwealth Fund, 1931.
———. "The Sherman Act a Necessary Evil?" *American Labor Legislation Review*
    18 (1928): 312–14.
Shepherd, Allen Laverne. "Federal Railway Labor Policy, 1913–1926." Ph.D. diss.,
    University of Nebraska, 1971.
Shulman, Harry. "Reason Contract and Law in Labor Relations." *Harvard Law*
    *Review* 68 (1955): 999–1024.
Sigmund, Elwin Wilber. "Federal Laws Concerning Railroad Labor Disputes: A
    Legislative and Legal History, 1877–1934." Ph.D. diss., University of Illinois,
    1961.
Simpson, Sidney Post. "Constitutional Rights and the Industrial Struggle." *West*
    *Virginia Law Quarterly* 30 (1924): 125–51.
Sinclair, Barbara. *Congressional Realignments, 1925–1978.* Austin: University of
    Texas, 1982.
———. "Party Realignment and the Transformation of the Political Agenda: The
    House of Representatives, 1925–1938." *American Political Science Review* 71
    (1977): 940–53.
Skaggs, Julian C., and Richard L. Ehrlich. "Profits, Paternalism, and Rebellion: A
    Case Study in Industrial Strife." *Business History Review* 54 (1980): 155–74.
Sklar, Martin J. *The Corporate Reconstruction of American Capitalism, 1890–1916:*
    *The Market, the Law, and Politics.* New York: Cambridge University Press, 1988.
Skocpol, Theda. "Bringing the State Back In: Strategies of Analysis in Current Re-
    search." In *Bringing the State Back In*, edited by P. Evans, D. Rueschemeyer, and
    Theda Skocpol, 3–33. New York: Cambridge University Press, 1985.
———. "Political Response to Capitalism Crisis: Neo-Marxist Theories of the State
    and the Case of the New Deal." *Politics and Society* 10 (1981): 155–210.
———. *Protecting Soldiers and Mothers: The Political Origins of Social Policy in the*
    *United States.* Cambridge: Harvard University Press, 1992.
Skocpol, Theda, and Kenneth Finegold. "State Capacity and Economic Intervention
    in the Early New Deal." *Political Science Quarterly* 97 (1982): 255–78.
Skowronek, Stephen. *Building a New American State: The Expansion of National*
    *Administrative Capacities, 1877–1920.* New York: Cambridge University Press,
    1982.
Slichter, Sumner. "Current Labor Policies of American Industries." *Quarterly Jour-*
    *nal of Economics* 43 (1929): 393–435.
Slichter, Sumner. "The Management of Labor." *Journal of Political Economy* 27
    (1919): 813–39.

Slomp, Hans. *Labor Relations in Europe: A History of Issues and Developments.* New York: Greenwood Press, 1990.

Smith, A. Beverly. "The 'Mutual Government' of 'Joint Commission' Plan of Preventing Industrial Conflicts." *Annals of American Academy of Political and Social Science* 24 (1906): 531–39.

Smith, John F. "Organized Labor and Government in the Wilson Era, 1913–1921: Some Conclusions." *Labor History* 3 (1962): 265–81.

Smith, Richard Norton. *An Uncommon Man the Triumph of Herbert Hoover.* New York: Simon & Schuster, 1984.

Smith, Steven F., and Christopher J. Deering. *Committees in Congress.* Washington, D.C.: Congressional Quarterly Press, 1984.

Sofchalk, Donald G. "The Chicago Memorial Day Incident: An Episode of Mass Action." *Labor History* 6 (1965): 3–43.

Sombart, Werner. "American Capitalism's Economic Rewards." In *Failure of a Dream?* Edited by John H. M. Laslett and Seymour Martin Lipset. Berkeley: University of California Press, 1974.

———. *Why Is There No Socialism in the United States?* New York: M. E. Sharpe, 1976.

"Statutory Attempts to Eliminate the 'Yellow Dog' Contract." *University of Pennsylvania Law Review* 71 (1932): 68–76.

Steever, Miller D. "The Control of Labor through Union Discipline." *Cornell Law Quarterly* 16 (1931): 212–26.

Steigerwalt, Albert K. "The N.A.M. and the Congressional Investigations of 1913." *Business History Review* 34 (1960): 335–44.

Stephan, Alfred. *The State and Society: Peru in Comparative Perspective.* Princeton: Princeton University Press, 1978.

Stern, Horace. "A New Legal Problem in the Relations of Capital and Labor." *University of Pennsylvania Law Review* 74 (1926): 523–51.

Sternau, H. G. "The Railroad Strike Injunction." *American Labor Legislation Review* 12 (1922): 157–62.

Stone, Harlan Fiske. "Fifty Years' Work of the United States Supreme Court." *American Bar Association Journal* 14 (1928): 428–36.

———. "The 'Mutuality' Rule in New York." *Columbia Law Review* 16 (1916): 443–64.

Stone, Katherine Van Wezel. "Labor Relations on the Airlines: The Railway Labor Act in the Era of Deregulation." *Stanford Law Review* 42 (1990): 1485–92.

———. "The Post-war Paradigm in American Labor Law." *Yale Law Review* 90 (1981): 1509–80.

Stoney, Moorfield. "The Right to Strike." *Yale Law Journal* 32 (1922): 99–108.

Straus, Oscar S. "Arbitration of Labor Disputes Affecting Public Service Corporations." *Proceedings of Academy of Political Science* 7 (1917): 165–69.

———. "Results Accomplished by the Industrial Department of the National Civic Federation." *Annals of American Academy of Political and Social Science* 20 (1902): 37–42.

Streeck, Wolfgang. "Organizational Consequences of Neo-corporatist Co-peration in West German Labour Unions." In *Patterns of Corporatist Policy-Making,* edited by Gerhard Lehmbruch and Philippe C. Schmitter, 35–36. Beverly Hills, Calif.: Sage, 1982.

"Strikes and Boycotts." *Harvard Law Review* 34 (1921): 880–88.

Stromquist, Shelton. *A Generation of Boomers: The Pattern of Railroad Labor Conflict in Nineteenth-Century America*. Urbana: University of Illinois Press, 1987.

Strum, Philippa. *Louis D. Brandeis: Justice for the People*. Cambridge: Harvard University Press, 1984.

Sturges, Wesley A. "Unincorporated Association as Parties to Actions." *Yale Law Journal* 33 (1924): 383–405.

Sullivan, William F. "Constitutional Law: Statutory Limitation of Injunctions in Labor Disputes." *Cornell Law Quarterly* 17 (1932): 666–74.

Sundquist, James L. *Dynamics of the Party System*. Washington, D.C.: Brookings Institution, 1973.

"Supreme Court Bench and Bar Honor Memory of Taft and Sanford." *American Bar Association Journal* 17 (1931): 423–29.

"Supreme Court Refuses Appeal from the Injunction Protecting the West Virginia Mines." *Law and Labor* 9 (1927): 299.

"The Supreme Court's Attitude toward Liberty of Contract and Freedom of Speech." *Yale Law Journal* 41 (1931): 262–71.

Swensen, Rhinehart John. *The Administrative Process: A Study of the Growth, Nature, and Control of Administrative Action*. New York: Ronald Press Co., 1952.

Taft, Philip. *The American Federation of Labor from the Death of Gompers to the Merger*. New York: Harper & Brothers, 1959.

———. *Organized Labor in American History*. New York: Harper & Row, 1964.

Taft, William H. *The Anti-trust Act and the Supreme Court*. New York: Harper & Row, 1914.

———. "The Possible and Needed Reforms in Administration of Justice in Federal Courts." *American Bar Association Journal* 8 (1922): 601–7.

Taylor, Albion Guilford. "Labor Policies of the National Association of Manufacturers." *University of Illinois Studies in the Social Sciences* 15 (1927): 1–184.

Tead, Ordway. "Company Unions and Labor Unions: A Functional View." *American Review* 3 (1925): 29–35.

Tedlow, Richard S. "The National Association of Manufacturers and Public Relations during the New Deal." *Business History Review* 50 (1976): 25–45.

Thayer, Ezra Ripley. "Liability without Fault." *Harvard Law Review* 29 (1916): 801–15.

Thelen, David P. *Robert M. LaFollette and the Insurgent Spirit*. Boston: Little, Brown, 1976.

"Theories of Enforcement of Collective Labor Agreements." *Yale Law Journal* 41 (1932): 1221–26.

Thompson, E. P. *The Making of the English Working Class*. New York: Vintage Books, 1966.

Tipple, John. "The Anatomy of Prejudice." *Business History Review* 33 (1959): 510–23.

Tobin, Eugene M. *Organize or Perish: America's Independent Progressives, 1913–1933*. New York: Greenwood Press, 1986.

Tobriner, Mathew O. "The Taft-Hartley Act after Three Years." *Labor Law Journal* 1 (1950): 1215–16.

Tolman, Edgar Bronson. "Review of Recent Supreme Court Decisions." *American Bar Association Journal* 7 (1921): 157–59.

Tomlins, Christopher L. *Law, Labor, and Ideology in the Early American Republic.* New York: Cambridge University Press, 1993.

———. *The State and the Unions: Labor Relations, Law, and the Organized Labor Movement in America, 1880–1960.* New York: Cambridge University Press, 1985.

Trachtenberg, Alan. *The Incorporation of America: Culture and Society in the Gilded Age.* New York: Hill and Wang, 1982.

"Trade Unions: Persuading Employe[e]s in Non-union Shop to Join Union." *Cornell Law Quarterly* 3 (1918): 317–19.

"Trade Unions—Closed Shop Agreement—Liability for Procuring Discharge or Preventing Employment." *Yale Law Journal* 28 (1919): 611.

Troy, Leo. "Labor Representation on American Railways." *Labor History* 2 (1961): 295–322.

Trubek, David M. "Max Weber's Tragic Modernism and the Study of Law in Society." *Law and Society Review* 20 (1986): 573–98.

———. "Reconstructing Max Weber's Sociology of Law." *Stanford Law Review* 37 (1985): 919–35.

Trumbell, Frank. "The Adamson Law: The Employers' Viewpoint." *Proceedings of Academy of Political Science* 7 (1917): 179–84.

Tufts, James H. "The Legal and Social Philosophy of Mr. Justice Holmes." *American Bar Association Journal* 7 (1921): 359–63.

Twining, William. *Karl Llewellyn and the Realist Movement.* London: Willmer Brothers, 1973.

Twiss, Benjamin R. *Lawyers and the Constitution: How Laissez Faire Came to the Supreme Court.* Princeton: Princeton University Press, 1942.

Unger, Roberto Mangabeira. *The Critical Legal Studies Movement.* Cambridge: Harvard University Press, 1983.

———. *Knowledge and Politics.* New York: Free Press, 1975.

"Union Labor and the Courts." *Central Law Journal* 89 (1919): 75–77.

Urofsky, Melvin I. "Myth and Reality: The Supreme Court and Protective Legislation in the Progressive Era." *Yearbook of the Supreme Court in Historical Society* (1983): 53–72.

"Use of the Injunction by the Employee against the Employer and Third Parties." *Dakota Law Review* 2 (1929): 454–57.

Vadney, Thomas E. *The Wayward Liberal: A Political Biography of Donald Richberg.* Lexington: University of Kentucky Press, 1970.

Vale, Vivian. "American Laborer's Political Freedom: A British View." *Political Studies* 13 (1965): 281–99.

Vance, William Reynolds. "The Kansas Court of Industrial Relations with Its Background." *Yale Law Journal* 30 (1921): 456–77.

*A Verbatum [sic] Report of the Discussion on the Political Programme at the Denver Convention of the American Federation of Labor, December 14, 15, 1894.* New York: Freytag Press, 1895.

Vogel, David. "The Power of Business in America: A Re-appraisal." *British Journal of Political Science* 13 (1983): 19–43.

Vorse, Mary Heaton. *Men and Steel*. London: Labour Publishing Co., 1922.

Voss, Kim. *The Making of American Exceptionalism: The Knights of Labor and Class Formation in the Nineteenth Century*. Ithaca, N.Y.: Cornell University Press, 1993.

Vreeland, H. H. "Some Guiding Priniciples in the Adjustment of the Relations between Employer and Employee." *Annals of American Academy of Political and Social Science* 27 (1906): 507–9.

Wakstein, Allen M. "The National Association of Manufacturers and Labor Relations in the 1920s." *Labor History* 10 (1969): 163–76.

———. "The Origins of the Open Shop Movement, 1919–1920." *Journal of American History* 51 (1964): 460–75.

Warren, Charles. *The Supreme Court in United States History*. Vol. 3. Boston: Little, Brown, 1923.

Warren, Harris Gaylord. *Herbert Hoover and the Great Depression*. New York: Oxford University Press, 1959.

Weber, Max. *Economy and Society: An Outline of Interpretive Sociology*. Vol. 2. Berkeley: University of California Press, 1978.

Wehle, Louis B. "War Labor Policies and Their Outcome in Peace." *Quarterly Journal of Economics* 33 (1919): 321–43.

Weiler, Paul. "Striking a New Balance: Freedom of Contract and the Prospects for Union Representation." *Harvard Law Review* 98 (1984): 351–420.

Weinstein, James. *The Corporate Ideal in the Liberal State: 1900–1918*. Boston: Beacon Press, 1968.

Weir, Margaret, Anna Shola Orloff, and Theda Skocpol. Introductory essay to *The Politics of Social Policy in the United States*, edited by Margaret Weir, Anna Shola Orloff, and Theda Skocpol, 3–27. Princeton: Princeton University Press, 1989.

Wickersham, George W. "Industrial Stability and the President's Second Industrial Conference." *Annals of American Academy of Political and Social Science* 90 (1920): 131–37.

Wiebe, Robert H. *Businessmen and Reform: A Study of the Progressive Movement*. Chicago: Quadrangle Paperbacks, 1962.

———. *The Search for Order, 1877–1920*. New York: Hill and Wang, 1967.

Wiecek, William M. *Liberty under Law: The Supreme Court in American Life*. Baltimore: Johns Hopkins University Press, 1988.

Wilensky, Norman M. *Conservatives in the Progressive Era: The Taft Republicans of 1912*. Gainesville: University of Florida Press, 1965.

Wilentz, Sean. *Chantz Democracy, New York City, and the Rise of the American Working Class, 1788–1850*. New York: Oxford University Press, 1984.

Willard, Daniel. "The Railroads on a Sound Basis." *Worker's World* 42 (1921): 137.

———. "Transportation Act of 1920." *Proceedings of Academy of Political Science* 10 (1922): 77–86.

Williams, T. Yeoman. "Injunction and Labor Disputes." *Proceedings of Academy of Political Science* 13 (1928): 78–83.

Wilson, Edward. "The Organization of an Open Shop under the Midvale Plan." *Annals of American Academy of Political and Social Science* 85 (1919): 214–19.

Windmuller, John P. *Labor Relations in the Netherlands.* Ithaca, N.Y.: Cornell University Press, 1969.

Witmer, T. Richard. "Collective Labor Agreements in the Courts." *Yale Law Journal* 48 (1938): 195–239.

Witte, Edwin E. "Administration and Legislation." *University of Chicago Law Review* 1 (1934): 572–77.

———. "The Federal Anti-injunction Act." *Minnesota Law Review* 16 (1932): 638-58.

———. *The Government in Labor Disputes.* New York: Arno and the New York Times, 1932.

———. "New Developments in Labor Injunctions." *American Labor Legislation Review* 19 (1929): 308–13.

———. "Results of Injunctions in Labor Disputes." *American Labor Legislation Review* 22 (1922): 197–202.

———. "The Value of Injunctions in Labor Disputes." *Journal of Political Economy* 32 (1924): 335–56.

———. "'Yellow Dog' Contracts." *Wisconsin Law Review* 6 (1930): 21–33.

Wolf, Harry D. *The Railroad Labor Board.* Chicago: University of Chicago Press, 1927.

Wooley, Charles M. "The Labor Aspect of Reconstruction." *Annals of American Academy of Political and Social Science* 82 (1919): 91–100.

"Workmen's Compensation Act: Related Purpose Doctrine." *Minnesota Law Review* 15 (1931): 257–58.

Wright, Carroll D. "Consolidated Labor." *North American Review* 174 (1902): 42–45.

Wrigley, Chris. *Lloyd George and the Challenge of Labour: The Post-war Coalition, 1918–1922.* New York: St. Martin's Press, 1990.

Wyzanski, Charles E., Jr. "Review Article of Public Control of Labor Relations." *Yale Law Journal* 52 (1942–43): 182–84.

Yellen, Sam. *American Labor Struggles.* New York: Harcourt, Brace & Co., 1936.

"The Yellow-Dog Contract." *Marquette Law Review* 15 (1931): 110–15.

"The 'Yellow-Dog' Device as a Bar to the Union Organizer." *Harvard Law Review* 41 (1928): 770–75.

Zakson, Laurence Scott. "Railway Labor Legislation, 1888 to 1930: A Legal History of Congressional Railway Labor Relations Policy." *Rutgers Law Journal* 20 (1989): 317–391.

Zieger, Robert H. *American Workers, American Unions, 1920–1985.* Baltimore: Johns Hopkins University Press, 1986.

———. "From Antagonism to Accord: Railroad Labor Policy in the 1920s." *Labor History* 9 (1968): 23–38.

———. "From Hostility to Moderation: Railroad Labor Policy in the 1920s." *Labor History* 9 (1961): 23–38.

———. "Herbert Hoover, the Wage-Earner, and the 'New Economic System,' 1919–1929." *Business History Review* 51 (1977): 161–89.

———. *Republicans and Labor, 1919–1929.* Lexington: University of Kentucky Press, 1969.

Zucker, Norman L. *George W. Norris: Gentle Knight of American Democracy.* Urbana: University of Illinois Press, 1966.

## Proceedings and Periodicals

American Federation of Labor Convention, *Proceedings* (annual)
*American Federationist*
*American Industries*
*Atlantic Monthly*
*Commercial and Financial Chronicle*
*Congressional Record*
*Current History*
*Iron Age*
*Labor*
*Labor and Law*
*Literary Digest*
*Monthly Labor Review*
*Nation*
*New Republic*
*New York Times*
*Railway Age*

# INDEX